The Novel and the Sea

translation
TRANSNATION

SERIES EDITOR **EMILY APTER**

The Novel and the Sea

Margaret Cohen

PRINCETON UNIVERSITY PRESS

PRINCETON AND OXFORD

Published by Princeton University Press,
41 William Street, Princeton, New Jersey 08540
In the United Kingdom: Princeton University Press,
6 Oxford Street, Woodstock, Oxfordshire OX20 1TW

Library of Congress Cataloging-in-Publication Data

Cohen, Margaret, 1958–
    The novel and the sea / Margaret Cohen.
        p. cm. — (Translation/transnation)
    Includes bibliographical references and index.
    ISBN 978-0-691-14065-0 (hardcover : alk. paper)
1. Sea stories, English—History and criticism. 2. Adventure stories,
English—History and criticism. 3. Naval art and science in literature.
4. Seafaring life in literature. 5. Sailors in literature. I. Title.
    PR830.S4C65 2010
    823.009'32162—dc22
                                            2010021709

British Library Cataloging-in-Publication Data is available

This book has been composed in Sabon

Printed on acid-free paper ∞

press.princeton.edu

Printed in the United States of America

10 9 8 7 6 5 4 3 2 1

Contents

Illustrations

Acknowledgments

> For the bringing of which into this homely and rough-hewn
> shape, which here thou seest, what restless nights, what painful
> days, what heat, what cold I have endured; how many long
> and chargeable journeys I have travelled; how many famous
> libraries I have searched into.
>
> —Richard Hakluyt, Preface to the
> *Principal Navigations, Voyages, Traffiques,*
> *and Discoveries of the English Nation*

WHEN RICHARD HAKLUYT INTRODUCED his *Principal Navigations* to his readers in 1598, he compared his own forays into libraries to the path-breaking travels of the adventurers who were his subject of study. Though consulting research materials is infinitely easier in our era of passenger jets and the Internet, writing a scholarly book remains an arduous process. This book's journey began over ten years ago, during a year's fellowship at the New York University (NYU) International Center for Advanced Studies, 1999–2000, under the aegis of Thomas Bender. Dialogue around that year's Sawyer Seminar lecture series, "Cities, Modernism, and the Problem of National Culture," opened my horizons to the study of literature and culture beyond the nation state. While at NYU, I pursued these questions with Carolyn Dever and Nancy Ruttenburg, who were then my colleagues there, and with my students in seminars on the novel and maritime modernity, notably, Bregtje Hartendorf-Wallach and Mariano Siskind. I am grateful to Emily Apter for her insights into transnational literature and culture in memorable conversations that have played out across a range of professional venues.

As I started to present my ideas on the novel and the work of the sea, my perspective was honed in a series of conferences in the early 2000s. These included a conference on global cities organized by Thomas Bender and Alev Cinar in Antalya, Turkey, in May 2001; a conference on "The City and the Sea" in London in October 2001; the Nineteenth-Century French Studies Colloquia in Madison, Wisconsin, in 2001 and in Tucson, Arizona, in 2003; the Joseph Conrad Society Conference in London/Greenwich in 2002; the inaugural meeting of the Société des Dix-Neuviémistes organized by Timothy Unwin and Nigel Harkness in London in September 2002; and the History of the Maritime Book Conference at Princeton University, New Jersey, organized by Jonathan Lamb in October 2002.

In 2002–2003, the National Endowment of the Humanities and the John Carter Brown Library's Alexander O. Vietor Memorial Fellowship in early maritime history gave me the opportunity to work in the John Carter Brown Library. During this year, Director Norman Fiering, together with John Hattendorf, were completing a book and an exhibition on print culture genres of the global age of sail. I learned much from this project, as well as from my co-fellows, about the early modern global world. I thank in particular Sunil Agnani for his insights about practical reason.

In 2004–2005, I received a fellowship from the Stanford Humanities Center to start writing up my research, and I appreciate the support of the dean of the Humanities at the time, Keith Baker. John Bender, then director of the Humanities Center, also extended his warm support. While I directed Stanford's Center for the Study of the Novel (CSN) in 2004–2007, I had an opportunity to explore issues defining the project in dialogue with CSN guests and audiences. Notable, in particular, were the conferences on the "Maritime in Modernity" and "Adventure," as well as book conversations with Jonathan Lamb, Pascale Casanova, and Jody Greene. Following my directorship at CSN, Stanford University enabled me to complete my book with a year's research leave in 2007–2008. I am grateful to the Stanford Humanities and Science deans for this opportunity, and also to Russell Berman, the chair of Comparative Literature, for enabling me to clear the decks and finish. I thank Roland Greene and the research unit of the Division of Literature, Culture, and Languages at Stanford for funding the book's images.

Across my research and writing, some masters of the craft (to paraphrase Conrad) have provided ongoing guidance and inspiration. My thanks to Franco Moretti exceed any summary, but some keywords would be genres, geographies, and a polestar, unwavering and luminous, to be relied on for orientation. Sharon Marcus has been a bracing and generous interlocutor, and my ability to frame the project owes a great deal to her feedback on manuscript drafts from the beginning of the process to its end. Anne Higonnet is another beacon, both as regards conversation on aesthetic processes in modernity and for her patience in working through questions of audience and framing. My thanks go to Vanessa Schwartz, fellow adventure lover and connoisseur of Verne, for dialogue on transnational modernity, adventure, and mobility studies—in two visits to the University of Southern California (USC) in 2002 and 2006, as well as in conversations up and down the coast of California. Though the Writing and Surfing group convened infrequently, I thank them for sharing their expertise on early modern and postcolonial questions. My conversations with Paul Young about the sublime have been illuminating.

It is a pleasure to work again with Princeton University Press. My editor, Hanne Winarsky, has made the review and publication process smooth-going. I also thank her for her keen observations on the manuscript. I am grateful for the perspicacious and detailed suggestions of my anonymous readers from Princeton University Press. Jennifer Liese was an attentive reader at a difficult stage of the composition process, and I appreciate her insights bringing out the argument of the manuscript. I appreciate the clarity and care of Jennifer Harris, my copy editor, as well as her comprehension for the time-consuming nature of the review process. I have learned a great deal from Nikolai Slivka, who has provided outstanding research support, drawing my attention to numerous relevant contexts, as well as making useful and provocative suggestions

Family and friends know that the process of writing this book has been a long haul. Daniel Klotz provided support and encouragement when the project was starting out, along with an introduction to Patrick O'Brian. Leslie Camhi knows how to put it all into perspective and what to do on a day off. Barbara Fried has sustained me through dark hours and shared some bright mornings, too. Reuben Ruiz inducted me into the brethren of the California Coast. I am grateful to my parents, Bernard and Phoebe Cohen, who have modeled the honor of labor across my life. This book owes a debt to my grandmother, Mary Frieman, and her confidence in me. She passed away last year, and I regret that she did not get to see the book's publication, even if it is not the swashbuckling novel about Lafitte that we dreamed of writing together. To my children, Samuel and Maxwell Klotz: Thank you for everyday fun and for adventures, discoveries, and wonder.

NOTES ON THE TEXT

An initial version of chapter 4 first appeared under the title "Traveling Genres," for a special issue of *New Literary History* on "Theorizing Genres II," 34, no. 3 (2003): 481–99. I recapitulate the section on Conrad's maritime modernism in chapter 5 in an article titled "Narratology in the Archive of Literature," *Representations* 108 (fall 2009): 51–75. Methodological issues raised as I wrote the book are summarized in "Literary Studies on the Terraqueous Globe," *PMLA*, vol. 125, no. 3, May 2010.

All translations, unless otherwise indicated, are mine.

Margaret Cohen
Stanford, January 2010

The Novel and the Sea

Fenimore Cooper's expert pilot John Paul Jones in *The Pilot* (1824) and the dashing pirate of *The Red Rover* (1827); the agile harpooners on Herman Melville's *Pequod*; and the hardworking captains and seamen of novels written at the turn of the twentieth century by Joseph Conrad. Odysseus's descendants include action heroes in popular fiction by Captain Frederick Marryat, Eugène Sue, Robert Louis Stevenson, Jules Verne, C. S. Forester, and Patrick O'Brian, among many others.

If Odysseus applied his practical resourcefulness in an enchanted cosmos, his descendants use their practical skills to survive amidst the risks and dangers of a world "abandoned by God."[3] I take this phrase from the argument about the cultural significance of the modern novel made by Georg Lukács whose *The Theory of the Novel* (1920), set the terms for novel studies as we know them today. While the epics of antiquity portrayed heroes at one with their society and the cosmos, Lukács pronounced the novel to express the "transcendental homelessness" of modern consciousness in a disenchanted world, where heroes, sundered from nature and community, set off in quest of interiority, psychology and "essence."[4] For Lukács, Odysseus was within the epic tradition; however, Theodor Adorno and Max Horkheimer noted how Odysseus suffered from the homesickness of the moderns, when they took Odysseus as the harbinger of Enlightenment rationality. Diagnosing Odysseus as the proto-modern individual, they made the telos of his journey "attaining self-realization only in self-consciousness." They also placed Odysseus at the threshold of the modern novel in his abstraction from the physical world and nature, calling him "*homo œconomicus*, for whom all reasonable things are alike: hence the Odyssey is already a *Robinsonade*."[5]

But there is nothing interiorized or abstract about the agency of Odysseus the seafarer who survives storms, shipwrecks, and other saltwater dangers, and the same can be said of his modern descendants, from Robinson Crusoe to John Paul Jones, Jack Aubrey, and beyond. In celebrating the practical skills of oceangoing adventurers, sea fiction explores an aspect of modern consciousness as constitutive as transcendental homelessness and abstraction. This aspect is a capacity: a distinctively modern form of practical reason, which is the philosophical term for the intelligence distinguishing people who excel in the arts of action. Practical reason is an embodied intelligence, drawing on the diverse aspects of our humanity. Rationality is one of its tools, but so are the senses, intuitions, feelings, and the body. The arenas for practical reason are specific shifting situations, often harboring unruly forces that can be negotiated but not controlled. As a situation-specific capacity, practical reason has historically taken many different forms. There are both continuities and differences in the competences needed by doctors, parents, teachers, politicians, coquettes, and generals, as well as mariners who contend with

the might of the sea. While for Lukács and the Frankfurt School thinkers, the disenchanted cosmos is steeped in melancholy if not despair, in
sea adventure novels, disenchantment, though painful, yields opportunity. Unmoored from divine authority as well as assistance, the heroes of
sea fiction perform their capacity to negotiate the edges of an unknown,
expanding, chaotic, violent, and occasionally beautiful sublunary realm
relying on human agency alone.

The protagonists in sea adventure fiction battle life-threatening storms,
reefs, deadly calms, scurvy, shipwreck, barren coasts, sharks, whales, mutinies, warring navies, natives, cannibals, and pirates—in short, they have
adventures, as many such novels emphasized with the wording of their
titles. To understand the celebration of practical reason in sea fiction, it
is necessary to take seriously adventure forms. In Lukács's *Theory of the
Novel*, as in many subsequent influential accounts, "the Novel" implies
some version of the novel of manners (novel of education, historical novel,
domestic novel, etc.), while adventure fiction has been devalued as mere
popular fiction. One notable exception to this trend is Mikhail Bakhtin's
theory of adventure.[6] In an essay included in *The Dialogic Imagination*,
Bakhtin argued that adventure fiction subjects its protagonists to dangers to test and thereby affirm their identity—an identity that expresses
a culture's constitutive values. Prominent among the values tested across
the history of adventure forms are different forms of practical reason,
including the *metis* of Odysseus, the *virtu* of the knight in medieval romance, and the popular cunning of the early modern *picaro*.[7] The secular
resourcefulness of Crusoe and his brethren is one more value that the
adventure pattern vindicates through trial.

Across the lineage of sea adventure novels, novelists modeled the heroism of their fictional protagonists after the historical seamen of Western
modernity. The figure of the mariner was imbued with a gritty glamour
during four centuries, stretching from the navigations of Vasco da Gama
and Columbus to the race across frozen seas for the poles at the turn of
the twentieth century. This span was defined by two distinct but inter-
related histories: the working age of global sail and the era of global
exploration. The mariner's glamour was inseparable from the promi-
nence of the oceans across this span as one of modernity's most dynamic,
productive frontiers. A century before *Robinson Crusoe*, philosopher Sir
Francis Bacon cited the nautical compass enabling cross-ocean travel
as one of three technologies, along with gunpowder and the printing
press, that had changed "the whole face and state of things throughout
the world," more influential than any "empire . . . sect . . . [or] star."[8]
Bacon was not overstating the impact of saltwater transport networks
that functioned as the circuitry of global capitalism and European imperialism. Ships transported information, along with people and goods,

and remained the most efficient means of global communications until the invention of the telegraph. The oceans of the globe were also a frontier of science and technology. The immense wealth and power at stake in maritime transport led governments and companies to pour resources into exploration, ship technology, navigation, and other research and development.

The profitable work of global ocean transport was a dangerous and difficult enterprise. The oceans are wild spaces, ruled by great forces beyond human control. Wooden sailing ships were sophisticated but imperfect technologies that progressed through "yielding to the weather and humouring the sea."[9] For much of the era of global sail, technologies of navigation were sophisticated yet imperfect as well. Until 1759, for example, no instrument existed with the ability to calculate accurately longitude at sea, and hence to let sailors know where they were in the course of a traverse; a lack that also impeded accurately charting the world. Adding to the dangers of global seafaring were the facts that scurvy was not understood for the first three hundred years of global navigation and that the high seas were in large measure a zone beyond the reach of law. Might made right, and the only freedom was the "freedom of the seas," an amoral freedom of movement without regard for the purpose of such travel.

Amidst such hostile conditions, the "perfect" or "compleat mariner," as he was called, achieved iconic status for his ability to navigate a path safely through the marine element of "flux, danger, and destruction," to cite Hegel from this chapter's epigraph. The perfect mariner exhibited this demeanor in the ordinary work of global ocean transport and achieved international celebrity for path-breaking explorations, yielding a cultural narrative that Jonathan Lamb has called "the romance of navigation."[10] Romance is an enduring literary mode plumbing an enchanted world. In literary history, it has been the name given to many premodern adventure forms, where protagonists test their practical reason against supernatural powers. The romance of navigation, in contrast, was a thoroughly secular romance of men at work; a romance of human practice.[11]

The Novel and the Sea begins by reconstructing the contours of the mariner's heroism across the global age of sail. This heroism would fascinate novelists and comprised the figure's cultural mystique. Though the mariner's capacity once would have been common knowledge, it has been largely forgotten today, more than a century after the demise of "the wooden world." Throughout my study, I shall follow Joseph Conrad, master mariner as well as master novelist, in calling this capacity "craft." To reconstruct the mariner's capacity in a chapter titled "The Mariner's Craft," I use a nonfictional corpus of writing spanning the working era of sail that detailed the practices of seamanship and that played an influential role in work at sea. This corpus is also essential to understanding how novelists, starting with Defoe, transferred craft from contemporary history and cultural mythology into fiction.

Global ocean travel took off with the printing press, and print culture was an important element in its success. Since overseas voyages occurred in a remote space, their vital information and events were known only to their participants and depended on writing to be passed on. The first writings of the maritime corpus took the form of manuscripts, often based on oral report. Relations of historical navigations began appearing in print as early as 1523, when *De Moluccis Insulis*, the first account of Magellan's circumnavigation of the globe (1519–1522), was published. By the seventeenth century, the maritime corpus included accounts of notable voyages by mariners from across the oceangoing nations of Europe, as well as accounts of shipwreck, dating to the mid-sixteenth century anonymous Portuguese *Account of the very remarkable loss of the Great Galleon S. João*. Other genres in the flourishing maritime corpus were practical manuals of seamanship, pilot's guides, and sea atlases, and by the eighteenth century, sensationalized pirate biographies, a form that soared to European celebrity with *The Buccaneers of America* by the Huguenot Alexandre Exquemelin, first published in Dutch in 1678.[12] By the middle decades of the eighteenth century and into the nineteenth century, the maritime bookshelf also included genres illuminating other aspects of the sailor's experience beyond purely professional capacity; such as accounts that justified behaviors in mutinies, like the accounts arising from the wreck of the *Wager* (1741) in the squadron of Lord Anson during his circumnavigation; narratives by black seamen like Olaudah Equiano, showing the horrors of the Middle Passage and black sailors' struggles for freedom; and narratives recounting the hard life of the ordinary sailor before the mast, to echo the classic *Two Years Before the Mast* (1840) by Richard Henry Dana Jr., who tasted life at sea for two years following his graduation from Harvard.

Across its different forms, the maritime corpus depicted the exploits and techniques of work—the profitable and difficult work of sailing and navigation.[13] The primary audience for most of its texts was hence initially professional. Along with seamen, these professionals included politicians and government officials, as well as scientists, engineers, entrepreneurs, and merchants. But the maritime book also quickly appealed to armchair sailors. Some readers looked to the news of the sea to be up-to-date on the modernity of their present. Yet others savored historical explorers, castaways, and buccaneers for entertainment. Nonfictional narratives were the most popular form with armchair sailors, but pleasure readers also possessed books of sea charts and treatises on seamanship; indeed, some of these books were published in large formats, with

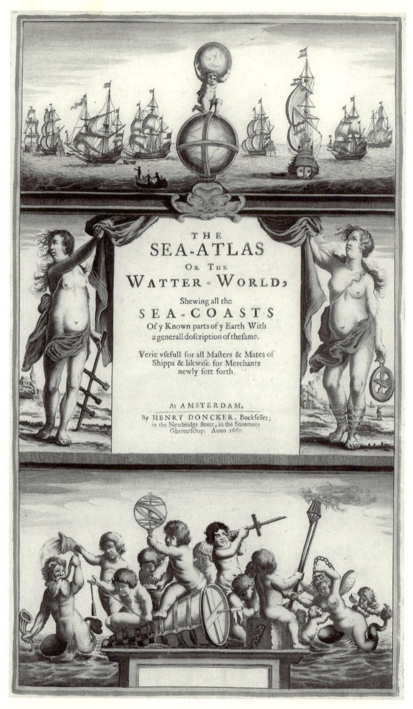

Figure I.1. The lavish frontispiece to this first edition of Doncker's *Sea-Atlas*, more suitable for a merchant's study than a working ship, presents the terraqueous globe as a theater to admire the power of maritime modernity. Henry Doncker, *The Sea Atlas Or The Watter-World, Shewing all the Sea-Coasts of y Known parts of y Earth* (Amsterdam: Henry Doncker, 1660). Courtesy of the John Carter Brown Library at Brown University.

lavish ornamentation more appropriate for a luxurious study than the ship's deck (figure I.1).[14]

We are used to drawing a distinction between practical and entertainment literature. But in the case of the maritime book, the very same literature that served a practical function for professionals also entertained general audiences. This overlap gave a technical and practical cast to the culture's romance with the mariner's heroism.

In England, at the time of Defoe, the maritime corpus was thriving. Publishers of practical nautical literature like Richard Mount counted scores of volumes in their lists, and nonfictional overseas voyage literature outstripped even devotional literature in its popularity.[15] In chapter 2, "Remarkable Occurrences at Sea and in the Novel," I explain how Defoe devised a new poetics of adventure in *The Life and Strange Surprising Adventures of Robinson Crusoe of York, Mariner*, in competition with the success of the maritime book. The key to Defoe's invention was his appropriation of a kind of episode that figured prominently in best-selling nonfictional sea voyage literature. This episode was what was called "the remarkable occurrence," which made its way into sea voyage narratives from the written protocols of work at sea.

Historians of science have shown how the use of "remarkable" in the early modern era was part of the transformation from a theological to a secular worldview, designating phenomena that fall outside recognized explanations but that are not subsumable to sacred wonder. But "remarkable" had another, technical use in the ship's log, which is a form of written narrative essential to work of the sea. In the ship's log, "the remarkable occurrence" was a category where mariners recounted any unusual events of the voyage, and in particular extraordinary dangers and the measures they took to survive. When mariner-authors consolidated accounts of their travels, writing for a mixed audience of professionals and general readers, these episodes of danger took pride of place. The account of remedies for unexpected dangers served the welfare of navigation, potentially of use to voyagers who might navigate the same waters. Such "remarkable occurrences" were also the most thrilling parts of sea voyages and valued by readers seeking entertainment. Captain Cook subtitled the journal of his voyage that he penned for posterity, "Remarkable occurrences on board His Majestys Bark Endeavour."

Even as Defoe modeled Crusoe's strange and surprising adventures on the remarkable occurrences in sea voyage literature, he wrought some significant formal changes. Defoe was critical of such narratives, along with their seamen authors, for a diffuse organization and for their understated enumeration of dangers. Defoe, in contrast, dramatized the search for a solution as part of the action, including mistakes as well as the successful expedient. In addition, while sea voyage authors set down events as they had occurred in the chronology of a voyage, Defoe tightened up this organization. Dangers and remedies were yoked in cause-and-effect fashion, and problems were immediately followed by solutions, which became new problems in their turn. Finally, Defoe unified problems and solutions according to a single action or concern—how to make a raft, how to hunt goats, what to do about the cannibals, etc.

The result was a well-oiled narrative chain of problem-solving. With this innovation, Defoe devised a plot mechanism where the reader could exercise her ingenuity as well. While Crusoe struggled for survival with the full might of his embodied craft, the reader enjoyed the cerebral, low-risk pleasures of applying and manipulating information, drawn both from within the novel and without. Information thus enjoys a prestigious role in sea adventure fiction, stimulating the reader's creativity. The creative act of reading in sea fiction solicits a pragmatic use of the imagination, as the reader searches for expedients that do not violate the laws of nature, that could be performed, and that could plausibly work. This plausibility of performance contrasts with a plausibility of mimesis, which measures events and characters according to their historical and social verisimilitude.[16]

Across the next two centuries, Defoe's adventure poetics became a popular, adaptable "traveling genre." *The Novel and the Sea* proceeds to describe sea fiction's travels, focusing on the traditions of the United Kingdom and France, and adding the United States, because of American authors' formative contribution in the nineteenth century. These three nations were where the poetics of sea adventure fiction was first forged and where the form flourished, before it spread to other traditions later in the nineteenth century.[17] Even as sea fiction was first practiced in these three nations, however, it was popular with readers across a transatlantic literary field.

The first stop in the travels of Defoe's pattern is the proliferation in the 1720s–1740s of novels I call the *maritime picaresque*. These novels were penned by Defoe as well as William Rufus Chetwood, Alain René Le Sage, the Abbé Prévost, and Tobias Smollett. As I describe at the end of chapter 2, the maritime picaresque portrays the adventures of roving protagonists buffeted around the globe. In their varied adventurers, writers tested the contours and flexibility of craft. Craft became the province of heroes identified with different social groups—aristocratic or democratic, female as well as male, collective rather than individual, engineers as well as mariners—and was put in the service of motives ranging from pillage and profit to humanitarian reform.

As sea fiction traveled, it had a complex, sometimes surprising relation to contemporary developments at sea. The maritime picaresque was, for example, dormant in the era of Pacific exploration, when nonfictional accounts of the pioneering voyages of Anson, Bougainville, Cook, and La Pérouse captivated international audiences. Was the market for maritime books so saturated with nonfiction that there was no demand for novels? I speculate on this and other reasons for the discrepancy between the prestige of global ocean travel in this era and the absence of sea adventure fiction in an abbreviated chapter 3, "Sea Adventure Fiction, 1748–1824?"

At other moments, maritime history catalyzes generic innovation. As I explain in chapter 4, "Sea Fiction in the Nineteenth Century: Patriots, Pirates, and Supermen," James Fenimore Cooper forges a new kind of sea fiction, what contemporaries would call the "sea novel," with *The Pilot* of 1824. Cooper penned this work in competition with Walter Scott, seeking to draft a kind of historical novel suited to the postcolonial American nation. If Cooper used sea adventure literature as the framework for his enterprise, the choice was shaped not only from his own experience at sea, but also by the American "maritime nationalism" of the era. Cooper celebrates American prowess on the seas as the United States aspired to overtake Great Britain's global saltwater empire. At the same time, Cooper's sea fiction continues to depict the mariner's craft as an ethos beyond conventional ethics and one that knows no national borders (viz the Scottish John Paul Jones, crafty mariner of *The Pilot*, who serves the American Revolution but ends up, in history, as Cooper's final pages make clear, an admiral to an absolute ruler, Catherine the Great). Juggling nationalist and internationalist imperatives, Cooper scales sea fiction to the U.S. sense of its destiny as "a nation among nations," to quote Thomas Bender's resonant phrase.

The specific impact of maritime history on the novel continues when Cooper's sea novel achieves international success and catalyzes what I call a "traveling genre," turning back across the Atlantic to be taken up by writers in Europe. Cooper's innovative poetics is indeed, I believe, the first new kind of novel invented outside of Western Europe that returns to alter decisively practices in the literary regions where the modern form first appeared. His sea novel is introduced into France by Eugène Sue, with the explicit goal of revitalizing French naval prestige, in shambles following France's maritime defeats in the Napoleonic wars. While the challenge to rebuild the navy proves too great for sea fiction to accomplish, Sue's project has unintended consequences that benefit French fiction. Instead of translating the crafty mariner to France, Sue takes craft to the drawing rooms of French society, and in the process invents supermen above the law, who will inspire Honoré de Balzac's Vautrin and Alexandre Dumas's Count of Monte Cristo, aka the seaman Edmond Dantès.

One transformation in maritime labor and technology decisive for the fortunes of sea fiction in the later nineteenth century is the routinization of the work of the sea. This routinization is an ongoing process that occurred across centuries and that accelerated after John Harrison perfected the marine chronometer permitting the calculation of longitude at sea in 1759. Navigation became more accurate, followed by the conquest of scurvy, and throughout, mariners continued to fill in information completing the charts of all the world's oceans. With the supersession of sail by steam in the mid-nineteenth century, routinization was accomplished. In the words of Conrad, "your modern ship which is a steamship makes her passages on other principles than yielding to the weather and humouring the sea. She receives smashing blows, but she advances; it is a slogging fight, and not a scientific campaign."[18]

After the routinization of seafaring, craft was on the wane, as was the mariner's cultural prestige. With the demise of craft as well as its mythology, the sea novel could no longer glorify the work of navigating modernity's dynamic frontiers. At the same time, the poetics of sea fiction was in splendid working order. This study's fifth and concluding chapter, "Sea Fiction beyond the Seas," discusses how innovative novelists transported the adventures of craft to other historical and imaginary frontiers of the later nineteenth century, including the frontiers of speculation and art. Herman Melville, Victor Hugo, and Joseph Conrad, among others, disrupted sea fiction's poetics to create a maritime modernism challenging the writer and reader to the difficult work of navigating the foggy, uncharted seas of language and thought. Jules Verne, in contrast, left sea fiction's poetics of problem-solving intact. He transported sea fiction's patterns to frontiers as of yet unachieved by science and technology, and invented an influential form of science adventure fiction. Detective fiction and spy fiction are two other forms of the novel that flourish at the turn of the twentieth century, using sea fiction's adventures in problem-solving to explore the expanding frontier of information. Sea fiction is visibly morphing into spy fiction in Conrad's *The Secret Agent* (1907) and Erskine Childers's *The Riddle of the Sands* (1903).

Even as the sea adventure novel transforms into other genres, sea fiction remains alive into our present. *The Novel and the Sea* concludes with an afterword, "Jack Aubrey, Jack Sparrow, and the Whole Sick Crew," sketching sea fiction's continuing legacy. While the ethos of craft continues to appeal into the twenty-first century, its significance is now nostalgic. Rather than modeling the capacity needed to practice modernity's emerging frontiers, sea fiction yearns for embodied, multidimensional human agency in an increasingly abstract and specialized world, dominated by vast forces of society and technology beyond the individual's comprehension and control, which are the man-made equivalents to the world's oceans. With this last nostalgic turn of craft, path-breaking Odysseus becomes exiled Odysseus longing to return home.

As I have reconstructed the history of sea adventure fiction over centuries, I have observed a decisive cultural shift in how European culture imagines the ocean. I tell the story of this shift in a more interdisciplinary "interlude" set between chapters 3 and 4. This shift is a process I call "The Sublimation of the Sea," occurring across the eighteenth century in visual arts and literature, as well as aesthetic theory. In this process, ships and sailors were progressively erased from imaginative depictions of the sea, as Enlightenment aesthetics cordoned off instrumental reason and work from the noninstrumental realms of the arts. The sublimation of the seas culminated in the empty seas of the Romantic sublime. Cleared of historical mariners, the sea was then open to imaginative repopulation by poets, novelists, and artists. In literature, its imaginary denizens included archaic figures, like Samuel Taylor Coleridge's Ancient Mariner or the the demonic, one-eyed, Mephistophelean pilot Schriften of *The Phantom Ship* (1838–1839) by Captain Frederick Marryat, a retelling of the legend of the Flying Dutchman. Among the diverse and fanciful cast of nineteenth-century sea adventure novels, one even finds female epitomes of the crafty mariner, like Fanny Campbell, heroine of Lieutenant Murray Ballou's *Fanny Campbell, or The Female Pirate Captain* (1844).

Novel scholars will recognize that sea adventure fiction does not correspond to our dominant accounts of the rise of the novel, though it belongs to the same era, and is, indeed, practiced by a number of familiar authors (Defoe, Prévost, Smollett, etc.). Sea adventure depicts action rather than psychology, its organization is episodic, and it measures plausibility by performance rather than mimesis. The heroism of skilled work substitutes for education and love, and sea fiction gives pride of place to communities of laboring men, bonded in the struggle for survival, rather than communities of private sociability, strongly associated with women, shaped by passion, virtue, and taste. (Robinson Crusoe is the exception making the rule when Defoe imbues a single individual with skills and capacities elsewhere distributed throughout the ship's crew, including in Defoe's own *Life, Adventures & Piracies of the Famous Captain Singleton*.) If virtue appears in sea fiction, it is as an afterthought; motives of characters range from survival, power, money, or knowledge, to the sheer thrill of the new. Rather than civic or liberal freedom, the ruling freedom in sea fiction is the amoral freedom of movement corresponding to the juridical notion of the "freedom of the seas." Wild terraqueous environments "beyond the line" replace salons, city streets, and country taverns, and when sea adventure novels unify the nation as an imagined community, it is always with an eye on the horizon of the globe. Rather than a centripetal pull inward toward the metropolis and closure, a centrifugal movement outward to the edges of the known world and beyond, as well as plots that conclude with the promise of a "farther account" of "some very surprising Incidents in some new Adventures."[19]

The Novel and the Sea focuses on a single adventure lineage. However, in putting sea adventure fiction back on the map of the novel, I hope to encourage critics to reexamine the cultural significance of adventure forms more generally. The case of sea fiction suggests, specifically, that this examination could resolve a conundrum challenging novel scholars. The conundrum involves the novel's seeming lack of interest in work. Work is a consuming aspect of our daily lives, yet it occupies disproportionately little space in the genre of the novel, if critical accounts are to be believed. [20] In *Resisting Representation*, Elaine Scarry speculates that work, such a constant in human life, is "a deeply difficult subject to represent. The major source of this difficulty is that work . . . has no identifiable beginning or end. . . . It is the essential nature of work to be perpetual, repetitive, habitual."[21]

But sea adventure fiction is an exception to such neglect. Work does appear in the guise of craft, a capacity that Conrad called "the honour of labour."[22] If the novel has seemed to have so little to do with work, it may reflect less the absence of work in the novel than that novel scholars do not attend to novels where work appears. The forms that showcase work are not the novels of manners that trace character growth and development, but adventure forms like maritime fiction, where work can be dramatized and distilled into an ethos, giving it transcendence beyond the bare struggle for subsistence. That sea adventure novels glorified work was evident to Hugo in his comments framing his own contribution to the genre. Drafting his preface for a novel tellingly titled *Les Travailleurs de la mer* [Workers of the Sea], Hugo declared that "work could be epic."[23] As he described his aim in the final draft, his epic of labor portrayed humans wrestling with "the *ananke* [fatality] of things," "nature," and the material world, "obstacles . . . under the form of the elements," comprising the struggle for subsistence: "it is necessary for him to live, hence the plow and the ship."[24]

The mariner's craft is only one kind of practical reason displayed in the long lineage of adventure narrative. Across its varied genres, there are other versions of heroic performance in dangerous zones, often at the edges of existing knowledge and society. Though these performances of practical reason are not salaried work in the modern sense of the term, they nonetheless heroize different kinds of skills necessary to win food, clothing, and shelter. I have mentioned the *metis* of Odysseus, the *virtu* of the knight, and the popular cunning of the *picaro* on what Giancarlo Maiorino calls "the margins" of his society, which is another application of practical reason to survive.[25] So too is the cunning of rogues, con men and women, and outlaws in the eighteenth-century urban picaresque,

practiced by Defoe, Le Sage, Prévost, and Smollett, who were also novelists of sea adventure.

The lovely serving girl who is the heroine of Samuel Richardson's
Pamela (1740) betters her situation financially using feminine wiles, fi-
nesse and social tact. Would *Pamela*, too, then, be a form of adventure
novel? While sea fiction performs the masculine heroism of craft at the
edge zones of the globe, eighteenth-century domestic novels like *Pamela*
and Fanny Burney's *Evelina* (1778) test their heroines' mastery of a kind
of feminine practical reason that permits them to negotiate the edges
of class society. The analogy with sea adventure fiction may well apply
to the domestic novel's narrative poetics, as well as its ennoblement of
feminine labor. If the remarkable occurrence from the mariner's log is the
basis for Defoe's poetics of craft, the poetics of domestic fiction similarly
builds on nonfictional textual genres of middle-class women's work. Indeed, critics have already explored how such feminine workaday genres
as the letter, the diary, and the household account fed into the form of the
domestic novel, from the time Richardson started off composing a letter-
writing manual and ended up with *Pamela* instead.[26]

The novel of social climbing is another subset of the novel of manners
that may well prove to be about work when read through the lens of adventure. These novels, too, test a protagonist's capacity for survival at the
margins—which, as in domestic novels, are the margins of class society.
Protagonists of these novels are often aristocrats, or pose as such, and
hence belong to a class that, like middle-class women, is not supposed
to work. But the impoverished Rastignac in Restoration Paris uses his
micropolitical skills of social manipulation to survive. So too does William Makepeace Thackeray's female adventurer, Becky Sharp in Victorian
England, pursuing self-advancement through a deft, remorseless application of the techniques mastered by the perfect young lady.

The Novel and the Sea invites novel critics to revise the dominant narrative about the rise of the novel in a second way, along with making a
place in its pantheon for adventure fiction. This revision involves the need
to move beyond our long-standing prejudice that those processes and
events defining the modern novel occur on land. In his lyrical opening
to *The Theory of the Novel*, Lukács set the tone for novel studies' indif-
ference to the maritime world. "Happy are those ages . . . whose paths
are illuminated by the light of the stars," Lukács declared, contrasting
the ancients to the modern period when "Kant's starry firmament now
shines only in the dark night of pure cognition . . . [and] no longer lights
any solitary wanderer's path."[27] Lukács's lyricism notwithstanding, his
figure makes no sense. Odysseus may have steered by the stars, but it was
only with the development of scientific navigation that mariners used the
heavens to find their way across the entire globe.

Following in Lukács's wake, novel critics across the twentieth century treated even those novels with oceangoing themes as allegories of processes back on land. *The Life and Strange Surprising Adventures of Robinson Crusoe of York, Mariner* is read as the memoirs of a capitalist *homo economicus*, or of a colonialist; the sailors on the *Pequod* in Melville's *Moby-Dick* offer an image of factory labor; and Conrad's "The Secret Sharer" becomes the portrait of a narcissist ripe for a Freudian case study, rather than representing a novice captain using his practical skills to master the fears that accompany his first command.[28] This disregard for global ocean travel, even when a novel portrays nautical subject matter, is so spectacular, it might be called hydrophasia. Such hydrophasia is part of a more pervasive twentieth-century attitude that the photographer and theorist Allan Sekula has called "forgetting the sea."[29] We have seen Bacon single out the compass as a world historical event in 1620, and two centuries later, Hegel treated cross-ocean travel as the theater of global capitalism. By the time of Lukács, for all his respect for Hegel, the modernity of seafaring had been obscured, and *The Theory of the Novel* projected celestial navigation into the mists of antiquity.

As we begin the twenty-first century, however, such hydrophasia is starting to ebb. Walter Benjamin famously observed that historiography is a constellation that the present makes with the past; put another way, the present is able to seize upon aspects of the past that are in some way resonant with its own urgent concerns. Our ability to perceive the importance of the maritime frontier may be an example of such a constellation between an earlier era of intensive globalization and our own. Today, reporting on the front page of U.S. newspapers and websites concerns pirates off the coast of Somalia and on the South China seas, the need to enhance our Navy to protect against global terrorism by sea, the problem of freedom of movement and the threat of piracy on the high seas of the Internet, as well as the uncontrollable forces of terraqueous nature unleashed in global warming. Such topics are just a few aspects of our current era of globalization that hearken back to the global age of sail.

In the university, too, scholars are rediscovering the importance of oceanic regions and transport for social and economic history, of course, but also for understanding culture, aesthetics, and epistemology. Within literary studies, postcolonial or transnational paradigms paved the way for a new interest in maritime transport, sociability, and culture. Initially, these paradigms passed over the sea as a dead zone between histories that unfolded on land. But in the first decade of the twenty-first century, saltwater networks heave into view.[30] My literary history of sea adventure fiction, too, invites novel critics *to leave the land and to embark*.

CHAPTER 1

The Mariner's Craft

> Though prudence, intrepidity, and perseverance united, are not
> exempted from the blows of adverse fortune; yet in a long series
> of transactions, they usually rise superior to its power . . .
> —Richard Walter, *A Voyage Round the World In the*
> *Years MDCCXL, I, II, III, IV. By George Anson, Esq.*[1]

> *If* Earth *and* Water *make one* Globe, *then he*
> *Must like a* Stranger *to his* Country be,
> *That's ignorant in* Navigation . . .
> —John Gadbury, preface to Samuel Sturmy,
> *The Mariner's Magazine*[2]

TODAY, when the Global Positioning System (GPS) enables a vessel to determine precise location via satellites and microwave signals at the touch
of a finger, it is easy to forget how dangerous seafaring was throughout
the working age of sail. Imagine: Columbus crossing the Atlantic on ships
measuring no more than a hundred feet long, constrained in his course to
keep his square sails before the wind, without the ability to fix his position on the earth—a fundamental uncertainty of navigation that would
persist for centuries. To manage such perils, mariners developed elaborate
professional practices, which they shared, compared, and refined. These
practices included specific skills, and they included a characteristic set
of demeanors. Taken together, these skills and demeanors comprise the
mariner's excellence in action that Conrad called "craft."

The ethos of craft, a practical necessity for oceangoing survival, became a cultural myth. The compleat or perfect mariner, as he was called
in the literature, was an icon of effective practice and human ingenuity,
able to beat brutal high-risk conditions against all odds, while pushing
knowledge to the frontier and beyond. In his epic narrating Vasco da
Gama's navigation to India, *The Lusíads* (1572), the poet Luís Vaz de
Camões celebrated the mariner's skill in action as a new kind of romance
befitting modernity: a romance of practice. When Camões depicted da
Gama taunting those he had vanquished with the epic hero's pride, da
Gama's objects of scorn were the heroes of antiquity and their creators,
constrained by the marvels of fable in contrast to his own extraordinary

deeds of fact. "Do you imagine that Aeneas and subtle / Ulysses ever ventured so far?" "For all the poetry / Written about them, did they say a fraction / Of what I know through strategy and action? . . . My own tale in its naked purity / Outdoes all boasting and hyperbole."[3] The notion that the great deeds of the high seas were a modern romance of fact was still circulating three centuries later. Lord Anson, who provides this chapter's epigraph, circumnavigated the globe in 1740–1744 and was known for his cool command on the high seas. The Victorian historian Thomas Carlyle called the account of Anson's *Voyage Round the World*, scribed by Anson's chaplain, Richard Walter, a "real Poem in its kind, or Romance all Fact."[4]

Craft's romance of fact was distinguished by this capacity's simultaneous practical importance and mythic allure. Craft remained an ideal of maritime labor, even as the ethos was exported beyond maritime contexts and transformed into an icon of powerful human agency. Now, of course, the practice of seamen did not always measure up to craft's ideal. Lord Anson's expedition is a case in point. The vessel under his command was the only one of the six ships in his squadron that returned home in a voyage that was otherwise a debacle, beset by bad weather, scurvy, shipwrecks, and mutiny. Carlyle noted that Anson's celebrated persona "sheds some tincture of heroic beauty over that otherwise altogether hideous puddle of mismanagement, platitude, disaster."[5] But the shortcomings of specific voyages do not change craft's practical value. Indeed, the disasters on voyages like Anson's show the terrible consequences where craft was wanting.

The capacity of craft is the ethos performed and celebrated by sea adventure fiction. Though it would have been familiar for readers during the rise of the novel that coincided with the global age of sail, it has been forgotten today. As a prelude to my discussion of novels, this first chapter reconstructs the contours of craft. To effect this reconstruction, I utilize the maritime print corpus that grew up together with print culture and that flourished across the global age of sail. Authors of sea adventure fiction from Defoe forward were familiar with the maritime book. They scattered references to it throughout their writings, and in some cases, they themselves contributed to its different genres—whether it was Defoe, who most likely penned or at least co-authored *A General History of the Pyrates* under the pseudonym of Captain Johnson; Smollett and Prévost, who put together anthologies of notable historical voyages; or Captain Marryat, contributing a treatise that proposed a system using flags in signal codes.[6] An exuberant homage to the many genres of the maritime book is Melville's prologue on cetology in *Moby-Dick*. Despite the casual tone, the Sub-Sub librarian's "random allusions" grubbed in "the long Vaticans and street-stalls of the earth" in fact offer a "bird's eye view" of the major genres of the maritime book, amidst encyclopedic citations on the work of whaling from the Bible to the popular fiction of Melville's present.[7]

In my account of craft, I focus on the character traits of those who excel in work at sea. The personality of craft was more accessible to a general audience than the specific kinds of expertise that also comprised craft, including navigation, seamanship, maritime warfare, and managing ships and supplies. Craft's human face took center stage when novelists transferred craft from the deck to the printed page. At the same time, its demeanors are the aspects of craft that are least conceptualized in the practical literature of the sea. Practical treatises straightforwardly describe maneuvers and recommend techniques, but the human agency that performs them must be read between the lines.

The mariner's agency is, in contrast, more visible in historical narratives, where the recipes of practical literature come to life contending with specific challenges. I have thus unfolded my archaeology of craft using a single anecdote that is arguably the most famous remarkable deed in the annals of navigation. This deed was Captain Cook's salvage of the HMS *Endeavour* from the Great Barrier Reef. He discovered this natural wonder by running aground on it in a nearly fatal accident on his first voyage. I frame this anecdote with evidence from practical texts and sea voyage literature spanning several centuries. There was significant continuity in craft across the age of sail, even as its techniques were decisively modified by inventions such as the marine chronometer.[8] Such continuity emphasizes the difference between the periodizations we are used to from the land and the epochs demarcating the history of work at sea.

As I formed a picture of the mariner's professional character using historical voyages and practical manuals, I was guided by two remarkable works on seamanship. The *Traitté de la marine et du devoir d'un bon marinier* [Treatise on Seamanship and on the Duty of a Good Seaman] (1632) was appended by the navigator Samuel de Champlain to his multivolume account of his voyages of exploration in Eastern Canada. It adheres to the Renaissance genre of treatises in the practical arts, where the competences of a calling or profession were written as a character study, a genre epitomized by Machiavelli's *The Prince* (1532). I also draw on Conrad's *The Mirror of the Sea* (1906), which eulogized craft at its sunset.[9]

In focusing on Cook's deed, the question arises of what source to cite. There are a number of accounts of Cook's first voyage, by members of the expedition and by professional writers. The most widely circulated, translated, and reprinted version was the official account commissioned by the British Admiralty, published in 1773. Narrated in the persona of Cook, it was in fact penned by the professional writer, John Hawkesworth, using the ship's log and all the journals kept by members of the expedition. Hawkesworth's *An Account of a Voyage round the World, in the years MDCCLXVIII, MDCCLXIX, MDCCLXX, and MDCCLXXI by Lieutenant James Cook, Commander of his Majesty's Bark the Endeavour,* is the version of Cook's exploits familiar to readers until the twentieth century. It was "[r]eprinted again and again in one form or another [and] . . . became a sort of classic unacknowledged by the historians of literature . . . a classic not of English prose but of English adventure."[10]

But Hawkesworth's was not the only narrative published at the time. Sir Joseph Banks, Cook's chief scientist, wrote an account of the first voyage, as did Sydney Parkinson, its artist. So did Cook himself, though the account was not published in his lifetime. Indeed, though Hawkesworth's was the official account published by the admiralty, Cook was not asked to approve it before it appeared, nor did he like it when he later read it.[11] Cook did not give reasons, but contemporaries censured this professional writer for his ignorance about the sea. Hawkesworth evinces his own literary preferences by using rhetorical ornaments and emotional amplification that have no bearing on his practical subject matter. Such beautification is at the antipodes from mariners' professional way of recording: informational, blunt "plain style."[12]

Hawkesworth's version, though influential, is thus not the best to limn the features of craft. In describing Cook's salvage of the *Endeavour,* I instead quote from the narrative penned by Cook himself. Cook's narrative has some overlap with Hawkesworth's, since Hawkesworth draws heavily from Cook's log in his own account. However, Cook's journal drafted with a public in view revises his rough journal substantially. Though "Cook is not a conscious artist," the revised journal was, as the twentieth-century editor of Cook's complete journals, J. C. Beaglehole comments, "carefully done indeed. It is . . . the product of a great deal of writing, drafting, and re-drafting, summarizing and expanding, with afterthoughts both of addition and deletion."[13] This journal is the record of events, but it is also Cook's own effort to fix his legacy. It affords the compelling view of a premier mariner during the global age of sail detailing his craft to claim his place in the pantheon of masters.

PRUDENCE (MONDAY, JUNE 11, 1770, 6 PM)

Captain James Cook almost perished on his first voyage to the South Pacific (1768–1771), when he discovered the Great Barrier Reef that he would subsequently put on European charts of the world. He came upon this natural wonder by accident, in the early evening of June 11. Sighting "two low woody Islands," he became concerned about running aground and decided to spend the night in deep water. Sailing out to sea, he attained a safe depth of 21 fathoms. But this uncharted terrain defied his experience. As Cook described the event in his journal:

> My intention was to stretch off all night as well to avoid the dangers we saw ahead as to see if any Islands lay in the offing . . . having the advantage of a fine breeze of wind and a clear moonlight night. In standing off from 6 untill near 9 oClock we deepen'd our water from 14 to 21 fathom when all at once we fell into 12, 10, and 8 fathom. At this time I had every body at their stations to put about and come too an anchor but in this I was not so fortunate. . . . before the Man at the lead could heave another cast the Ship Struck and stuck fast. Emmediatly upon this we took in all our sails hoisted out the boats and sounded round the Ship, and found that we had got upon the SE edge of a reef of Coral rocks. . . .[14]

Cook's experience in other waters had taught him to be on guard for reefs close to land, but not so far out to sea. As the depth quickly diminished, Cook called his sailors to their stations to drop anchor, but to no avail. The *Endeavour*'s captain and crew found themselves stranded on an offshore reef, with a badly damaged ship, on dangerous, uncharted, indeed hitherto unimaginable terrain.

Cook wrecked his ship on the Great Barrier Reef adhering to the exemplary quality of prudence that would also serve him so well across his career. Carefully saving his explorations for daylight, he instead stumbled on an unexpected danger with no correspondence to his previous experience of coastal navigation. In Cook's age, as in the early modern era, prudence did not just designate caution and an aversion to risk, as it does today. It also designated foresight, care for detail, and nuanced attention to the specificity of the situation. Indeed, prudence still retained its flavor from the Renaissance era, as a synonym for practical reason.

Across different areas of endeavor, the qualities of prudence were laid out in treatises on the arts of action. Champlain emphasized the importance for the mariner of prudence amidst other capacities in his 1632 *Traitté de la marine et du devoir d'un bon marinier*. The stranding of the *Endeavour* recalled the warning of Champlain that the good mariner "must be apprehensive of finding himself in ordinary dangers," for these foreseeable dangers are a waste of energy and resources, and could weaken the chances of contending with dangers that were unforeseen.[15] These ordinary dangers, Champlain went on to spell out, might include "when you run before a wind in shore, [or] doggedly try to double a cape, or pursue a dangerous course by night among sandbanks, shoals, reefs, islands, rocks, or ice."[16] Champlain cautioned that the good mariner should be "wary and hold back rather than run too many risks . . . in th[e] . . . fog or in the dark no one is a pilot."[17] Cook did hold back, but prudence is shaped by experience, and Cook's past experience failed before a feature of the ocean's physical geography hitherto unknown to European navigators.

In Renaissance treatises, prudence was an elite value, intrinsic to the arts of command. Like Machiavelli's prince and Castiglione's courtier, Champlain's perfect mariner, too, was an elite commander, ornamented with the graces of the *honnête homme*, the seventeenth-century nobleman of honor. Champlain exhorted the perfect mariner to be "pleasant and affable in conversation," even as he was absolute in his authority.[18] But men of exceptional talent could use their mastery of craft to rise up through the punishing hierarchies of shipboard life. Cook was the son of a farm laborer. He got his start sailing coal ships in the North Sea and worked his way up the ranks in the British Navy for thirteen years before receiving command of the *Endeavour* in 1768. Captain William Dampier, who circumnavigated the globe three times at the end of the seventeenth century, was another man of modest origins who rose to a position of authority through his exceptional capacity.[19] Both Cook and Dampier excelled at all the aspects of craft: not just the care and foresight of prudence, but also the ability to call on other demeanors and skills when prudence was exceeded by extraordinary events.

Sea Legs (Night of June 11, 1770)

Putting out the longboat and getting anchors ready, Cook himself took a turn around the ship to sound the depths and survey the situation. This personal involvement might seem surprising on the part of a commander. Because of the grave danger of the moment, Cook did not delegate the work to a crewmember, as he might in a more routine situation. He wrote:

> As soon as the long boat was out we struck yards and Topm^{ts} and carried out the stream Anchor upon the starboard bow, got the Costing anchor and cable into the boat and were going to carry it out the same way; but upon my sounding the second time round the Ship I found the most water a stern and therefore had this anchor carried out upon the Starboard quarter and hove upon it a very great strean which was to no purpose the Ship being quite fast . . . (139)

Later, in seeking a path out of a particularly treacherous section of the Great Barrier Reef, Cook emphasized again his physical engagement as part of his duty as a commander: "I went my self and buoy'd the Channel" (142).

Cook's bodily participation demonstrates the importance of physical strength and agility in the mariner's craft. Champlain took care to spell out this embodied aspect of the seafarer's duties. He instructed his perfect mariner to "always sleep in his clothes, so as to be promptly on hand for accidents,"[20] and to not "allow himself to be overcome by wine; for when a captain or a seaman is a drunkard it is not very safe to entrust him with command or control, on account of the mischances that may result while he is sleeping like a pig . . ."[21] Most thoroughly, the perfect mariner "should be robust and alert [*dispos*], with good sea legs [*le pied marin*] . . . so that whatever happen he may be able to remain on deck, and in a strong voice give everybody orders what to do. Sometimes he must not be above lending a hand to the work himself, in order to make the sailors more prompt in their attention . . ."[22] The imperative to be ready [*dispos*] encompasses both physical preparedness and attitude. In depending on the body working together with the mind, craft disrupts traditional philosophical hierarchies, which separate what are framed as the admirable pursuits of the mind from the devalued body.

PROTOCOL (NIGHT OF JUNE 11–MORNING OF JUNE 12, 1770)

When the *Endeavour* ran onto the reef, Cook followed the standard protocols for stranding in work at sea. He rounded the ship to take soundings, getting information on the shallows. He then proceeded to try to lighten the ship by throwing overboard anything dispensable:

> [W]e went to work to lighten her as fast as possible which seem'd to be the only means we had left to get her off as we went a Shore about the top of high-water. We not only started water but throw'd over board our guns Iron and stone ballast Casks, Hoops staves oyle Jars, decay'd stores &c[a], many of these last articles lay in the way at coming at heavyer. All this time the Ship made little or no water. (139)

In this crisis, Cook executed maneuvers promptly, yet also methodically, both essential features of protocol in the work of the sea. Extraordinary measures might be required to contend with a hitherto unimaginable obstacle, but not until ordinary best practices had failed.

REMARKABLE OCCURRENCES (NOON, JUNE 12, 1770)

Though his ship was on the verge of sinking, Cook took care to measure and note latitude, along with recording his expedients: "At Noon she lay

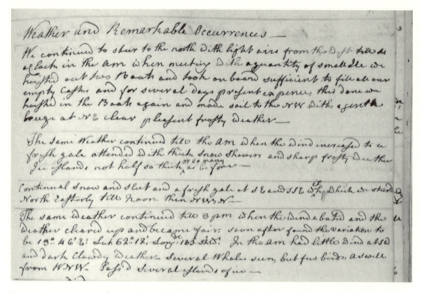

Figure 1.1. A page from the logbook of the HMS *Endeavour*, showing the category of the remarkable occurence, a convention of this written technology that was essential to the work of the sea. Extract from the *Log-Book of Lieutenant James Cook, in the "Endeavour."* Courtesy of the British Library, London.

with 3 or 4 Strakes heel to Starboard. Latitude Observed 15°45' South" (139). In doing so, Cook adhered to another kind of nautical protocol: the written technology of the ship's log (figure 1.1). James Atkinson urged that such record-keeping must be "punctual" in *Epitome of the Art of Navigation; or a Short, Easy and Methodical Way to become a Compleat Navigator*, a book first printed in 1686 that was continuously reprinted into the era of Cook. In the 1744 edition, we read "Know that a *Journal*, or Sea-Reckoning, is a punctual writing down every Day (in a Book fit for that Purpose) the Course, Distance, Difference of Latitude, and Departure the Ship hath made, what Latitude and Longitude she is in; and also the Wind, Weather, with all Accidents, and Occurrences that happen."[23] The concise, conventional layout of the ship's log, with its columns for various categories of information, remained relatively constant across national cultures and history and offers a good snapshot of protocol—the detailed, punctual adherence to procedure so important in the craft of the sea.

The ship's log not only helped mariners keep track of positions and events in the course of a traverse, it also served future mariners, and the "common welfare of Navigation."[24] When Sanson Le Cordier described "everything" that "should be found in the journals of the best pilots," he emphasized "the dangers that they [mariners] have run, the remedies they found; if a mast broke, a sail carried off; if someone in the crew passed away, whether by natural or violent death."[25] It was particularly important to note the position of "whatever rock, bank or reef that was not marked on the Charts of Hydrographers or the Navy, where the most experienced Pilots, like the least able, might suffer a fatal shipwreck."[26] When James Cook recorded the latitude where he was stranded, he was collecting valuable information for subsequent navigators concerning the location of a danger.

This care to record dangerous conditions dates to the first printed account of global exploration. The narrative of the voyage of Magellan (1519–1522), composed by Antonio Pigafetta, is replete with "strange and uncommon" dangers and the mariners' response. Sailing down the coast of Africa, for example, the expedition met with "sixty days of rain," "a thing very strange and uncommon, in the opinion of the old people and those who had sailed there several times before"—but thanks to Pigafetta's account, that mariners could henceforth anticipate.[27] The common welfare served by such documentation extended from mariners to all whose livelihood was connected to the oceangoing world, from merchants and government officials to "the good of the Republic."[28]

The diverse categories of the ship's log—which included compass bearings, winds, courses, depth, longitude and latitude—became the warp and the woof of nonfictional maritime travel narratives. One established log category in particular entered the title of the first work of modern shipwreck literature: the *Account of the very remarkable loss of the Great Galleon S. João*, the Portuguese narrative of a 1552 shipwreck that was to inspire *The Lusíads* by Camões.[29] This category was the "remarkable" occurrence; "everything that occurred in short worthy of remark," was Le Cordier's term.[30] Pigafetta's "strange and uncommon" are synonyms for the remarkable occurrence; so are "surprising" and "extraordinary." The remarkable occurrence would become a prominent feature of maritime narratives, useful for mariners and enjoyed by those who read overseas voyage literature for entertainment. Cook, too, evoked this term in the subtitle of his journal of his first voyage: *Remarkable occurrences on board His Majestys Bark Endeavour*.

Historians of science have tracked the use of the adjective "remarkable" in the early modern era as a way to designate sacred wonders on their way to becoming the object of scientific curiosity. In this usage, remarkable is at the threshold between an enchanted and a secular worldview.[31] But "remarkable" had another meaning in the mariner's journal, where it designated unusual events in a voyage, with an emphasis on dangers, obstacles, or challenges. Such accounts of dangers were inseparable from the expedients taken by craft. When readers of overseas travel literature opened a book whose title included "accident," "occurrence," and "remarkable," or synonyms, such as "extraordinary," "strange," "dangerous," "uncommon," and "surprising," they could be sure they would read of great perils and risks, but also find narratives of extraordinary deeds.[32]

ENDEAVOR (EVENING OF JUNE 11–AFTERNOON OF JUNE 12, 1770)

Despite Cook's care, the situation was too grave to be alleviated by ordinary measures. When lightening the ship's load did not succeed, Cook called on patience, another essential quality of craft. Profiting from good weather but unfamiliar with tidal patterns in these "far distant parts," Cook sat through one tidal cycle, then another, since tidal swings differ and the evening high tide might be fuller (168). He writes:

> At a 11 oClock in the AM being high-water as we thought we try'd to heave her off without success, she not being a float by a foot or more notwithstanding by this time we had thrown over board 40 or 50 Tun weight; as this was not found sufficient we continued to Lighten her by every method we could think off.... Fortunatly we had little wind fine weather and a smooth Sea all these 24 hours which in the PM gave us an oppertunity to carry out the two bower Anchors ... Got blocks and tackles upon the Cables brought the falls in abaft and hove taught. (139)

Even as Cook waits, he is attentive to prudence and protocol. He prepares the anchors, blocks, and tackles for the moment when he will try to work the ship off the reef.

In surviving a shipwreck, the ability to wait, amid danger and physical distress, was essential. In *The Strange and Dangerous Voyage of Captaine Thomas James* (1633), we read of James and his crew exploring the Arctic waters of Canada in search of a Northwest Passage becoming progressively locked in ice in early fall. Trapped with no path to the open sea, they wintered for eight months on a desolate bank of what is now called James Bay, battling cold, hunger, polar bears, scurvy, and solitude. At the other end of the history of polar exploration, Ernest Shackleton's failed bid to reach the South Pole almost four hundred years later (1914–1917) was beset by a similarly grim waiting period. In *South*, Shackleton paints a vivid portrait of floating with his crew on an ice floe (aptly named "Patience Camp") for three and a half months, until they got close enough to a whaling station to have a hope of sailing to it.

The name of Cook's ship, *Endeavour*, speaks to the patience, determination, and persistence of the mariner. In Champlain's words, the consummate mariner was "inured to hardships and toil."[33] Mariners exercised endeavor even in the face of setbacks and failures—indeed setbacks and failures were when endeavor was critical to survival. In James's ill-fated voyage, the verb "endeavor" runs through his description of the persistent but fruitless efforts to find a path through the encroaching ice as the winter closed in: "The seventh and eight dayes, we indeavoured to double about *Cape Farewell*; being still pestered with much Ice."[34] "We indeavoured to gaine the North shoare; kept our selves within a league of the shoare of the *Island of Resolution*, where we had some cleere water to saile thorow."[35] Even if unsuccessful, endeavor permits the crafty mariner to court an opportunity when his luck may take a more favorable turn.

RESOLUTION (TUESDAY, JUNE 12, 1770, 9 PM)

On the evening of June 12, Cook's patience was rewarded with a fuller high tide. But as the ship started to float, the water surged into a gash cut through the hull. Faced with the likelihood that the *Endeavour* would be swamped, Cook resolved to "resk all and heave her off," in a dangerous, but potentially life-saving maneuver:

> At 9 oClock the Ship righted and the leak gaind upon the Pumps considerably. This was an alarming and I may say terrible circumstance and threatend immidiate destruction to us as soon as the Ship was afloat. However I resolved to resk all and heave her off in case it was practical and accordingly turnd as many hands to the Capstan & windlass as could be spared from the Pumps and about 20' past 10 oClock the Ship floated and we hove her off into deep water having at this time 3 feet 9 Inches water in the hold. (139–40)

Rather than disaster, Cook's maneuver is indeed "practical": the tide carried the stranded *Endeavour* off the reef back into the ocean. Though he now had to contend with a foundering ship, at least it was in deep water, the mariner's ally.

Cook was a master at seizing the critical moment in an unfolding situation, choosing opportunity over prudence and turning hazard into salvation. In Greek antiquity, this dangerous moment of opportunity was personified as Chairos, son of Chronos, the god of time. To recognize and take advantage of *chairos* takes experience, character, knowledge, and a kind of tact or feel. Cook's word for the attitude of the commander who seizes opportunity is "resolution," the name given to one of his ships on his second expedition. This term for the bold, opportune maneuver recurs throughout the maritime corpus during the global age of sail.

Champlain characterized this calculated boldness as "manly courage," inciting the mariner to "a steady voice," and "cheery resolution [*resolution gaye*]."[36] This last adjective picks up on a secondary attribute of resolution: optimism. When Joseph Banks, Cook's chief naturalist, described the stranding of the *Endeavour* in his journal, he noted the "cheerful" attitude of the crew in the face of danger: "All this time the Seamen workd with surprizing chearfullness and alacrity; no grumbling or growling was to be heard throughout the ship, no not even an oath (tho the ship in general was as well furnishd with them as most in his majesties service)."[37] Cook also noted the energy and vigor of all on board in the face of desperate circumstances.

For Champlain, as for Cook, optimism was strategic rather than existential. The commander's confident attitude could "dispel fear from even the most cowardly bosoms," and thus helped effect a favorable outcome: "for when they find themselves in a hazardous situation, every one looks to the man who is thought to have experience; for if he is seen to blanch and give his orders in a trembling and uncertain voice, all the others lose courage, and it is often seen that ships are lost in situations from which they might have got clear away if the men had seen their captain undaunted and determined, giving his orders boldly and with authority."[38]

The demeanor of optimism in such a dire situation was an aspect of craft that utilized deceit. This deceit draws attention to craft's instrumentality, turning even people into tools to procure a successful outcome. Resolution notably made use of deception in desperate situations. Strategic optimism was one way to keep up morale; another was to withhold knowledge. In *The Strange and Dangerous Voyage of Captaine Thomas James* (1633), James recounts how he selected sailors who had no prior knowledge of the dangerous terrain they were engaging high in the Arctic Circle in order to intensify his crew's dependence on him, nor did he acquaint them with what they could expect.[39] Cook employed a more benign deception in forcing his crew to eat "sour krout," which he believed would ward off scurvy. "The Sour Krout the Men at first would not eate untill I put in pratice a Method I never once knew to fail with seamen, and this was to have some of it dress'd every Day for the Cabbin Table, and permitted all the Officers without exception to make use of it and left it to the option of the Men either to take as much as they pleased or none atall; but this practice was not continued above a week before I found it necessary to put every one on board to an Allowance" (38).

The amoral, instrumentalizing exercise of craft, so visible in dangerous navigations, is on a spectrum that ends with the deeds of notorious pirates. The resolution of pirates took them beyond bounds not of previously navigated terrain but of morality, and they evinced resolution not just in bold navigations but in their criminal and cruel pursuits. Even as the law cast the pirate as an enemy of the entire human race, a romance of piracy was launched by *The Buccaneers of America*, by Alexandre Exquemelin, first published in 1678. These bloodthirsty pirates of the Caribbean commanded readers' admiration for their willingness to transgress morals, law, and even taboo to achieve their aims, viz Exquemelin's tableau of François l'Olonnais ripping out the heart of one of his prisoners and biting into it in order to terrify their fellows and extract information about the surroundings. At least one etymology connects the pirate's resolution to the project of Enlightenment. The Greek *peira*, "trial," gives us both pirate and empirical, connecting the pirate's willingness to risk all in trying his fortune on the high seas to experimental inquiry pushing at the edge of scientific knowledge through trial and error.

The quality of resolution is important for all those who work in zones of risk and great unpredictability. Daniel Defoe pondered the difficulty differentiating between bold gestures and dumb luck in the risky, uncertain practice of speculation when he gave advice to budding capitalists, writing at the time the London Stock Market first took off. In his 1697 *An Essay upon Projects*—the term of his time for financial speculation and other schemes to strike it rich—Defoe included the following verses on men who were deemed pirates or heroes depending on the outcome of their resolute actions in risky ventures: "*Sir* Francis Drake *the* Spanish Plate-fleet Won, / He had been a Pyrate if he had got none / Sir* Walter Rawleigh *strove, but miss'd the Plate, / And therefore Di'd a Traytor to the State.*"[40] James Cook had his own version of these sentiments when he reflected on the dilemmas attending his exploration of unknown coasts in the journal of his first voyage. If an explorer turns back out of prudence, Cook reflects, "he is than charged with *Timorousness* and want of Perseverance"; however, "if on the other hand he boldly incounters all the dangers and obstacles he meets and is unfortunate enough not to succeed he is than charged with *Temerity* and want of conduct" (168).

The countenance of resolution meets our gaze in portraits of Cook from his time, whether in his formal likeness by the society painter Nathaniel Dance (figure 1.2) or shown dressed more casually as he would appear in the course of a voyage, in the portrait by William Hodges (figure 1.3), the artist who accompanied his second expedition.

Likewise, Defoe's contemporary, the navigator William Dampier, confronts the viewer with the countenance of resolution in his portrait by Thomas Murray, *Captain William Dampier: Pirate and Hydrographer* (figure 1.4). Cook and Dampier have in common the determined chin, the hard-nosed profile, and the firm mouth. Their gazes are cold, keen, and penetrating. Other aspects of craft are intimated in these portraits as well. The captains' foreheads are lit by the light of noon, the hour at which mariners punctually measure the sun's angle to ascertain their latitude.

Figure 1.2. In this portrait, Captain Cook exhibits the countenance of craft, with his capable hand on a chart of the Southern Ocean, one of the contributions to knowledge of his dangerous navigations. *James Cook*, by Nathaniel Dance (1775–1776, oil on canvas). Courtesy of the National Maritime Museum, London.

They have circles under their eyes, indicating that they sleep little, ever on the alert for danger. In the Dance portrait, Cook puts his capable hand on a chart, signaling dominion like a King, only he claims an empire of knowledge that he has earned through work. He points to one of his own path-breaking charts of unknown waters, like that of Endeavour Straits

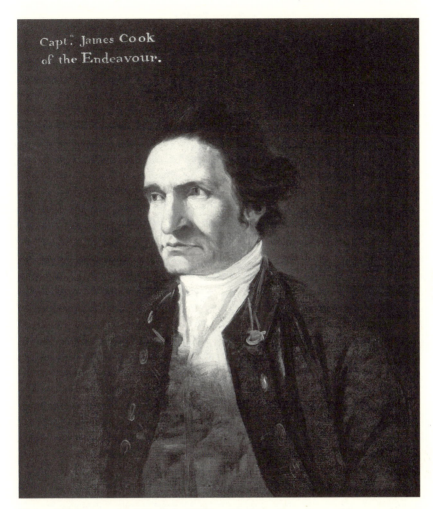

Capt.ⁿ James Cook
of the Endeavour.

Figure 1.3. A portrait of Cook by William Hodges, the artist, on his second expedition. Here Cook's dress is more casual than in the portrait by Dance (figure 1.2), but his keen gaze and resolute mouth are unwavering. *Captain James Cook*, by William Hodges (1775–1776, oil on canvas). Courtesy of the National Maritime Museum, London.

(figure 1.5). Dampier too recalls his own contribution to knowledge, holding his *New Voyage Round the World* (1697) that would be valued by professionals of the maritime world for its "careful and thorough data on places, winds and currents," and by "scientists and geographers" for its "graphic descriptions of plants and animals," as well as by creative writers and general readers for Dampier's "adventurous life," and the account's "wealth of exotic knowledge of all kinds."[41]

Figure 1.4. Pilot, privateer, pirate, and hydrographer William Dampier. Dampier gazes at us with the keen countenance of the perfect mariner, holding a copy of his *New Voyage Round the World*, valued for its professional accuracy and popular with general readers for its remarkable adventures and vivid details. *Captain William Dampier: Pirate and Hydrographer*, by Thomas Murray (1697–1698, oil on canvas). Courtesy of the National Portrait Gallery, London.

JURY-RIGGING (TUESDAY, JUNE 12, 1770, 10:20 PM–NIGHT OF
    WEDNESDAY, JUNE 13, 1770)

Once Cook succeeded in moving the *Endeavour* off the reef, the leak increased drastically. Searching for an expedient to keep the ship afloat, he recalled a technique called "fothering," by which a sail, slathered with

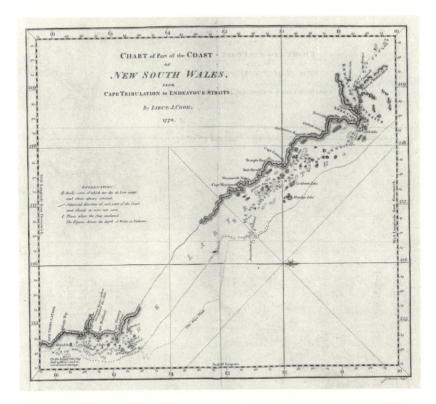

Figure 1.5. Cook's chart of the coast where his expedition almost perished. It offers detailed information, in contrast to the more panoramic chart in his portrait by Nathaniel Dance (figure 1.2). "Endeavour Straits, Cook's chart," from John Hawkesworth, *An Account of the Voyages Undertaken by the Order of his Present Majesty for Making Discoveries in the Southern Hemisphere, And successively performed by Commodore Byron, Captain Wallis, Captain Carteret, and Captain Cook, in the Dolphin, the Swallow, and the Endeavour* (London: W. Strahan and T. Cadell, 1773, vol. 3, before p. 589). Courtesy of the John Carter Brown Library at Brown University.

oakum (tarred rope fiber), as well as wool, and dung, is slung around the ship's hull and slid back and forth until the sticky mixture is sucked up into the holes. Here is how he describes the maneuver:

> some hands employ'd sewing ockam wool &cᵃ into a lower Studding sail to fother the Ship. . . . The manner this is done is thus, we Mix ockam & wool together (but ockam alone would do) and chop it up small and than stick it loosly by handfulls all over the sail and throw over it sheeps dung or other filth. Horse dung for this purpose is the

best. The sail thus prepared is hauld under the Ships bottom by ropes and if the place of the leak is uncertain it must be hauld from one part of her bottom to a nother untill the place is found where it takes effect; while the sail is under the Ship the ockam &cᵃ is washed off and part of it carried along with the water into the leak and in part stops up the hole. (140–42)

Cook's decision to fother at this moment was ingenious and situation-specific. Such creative improvisation on the shifting terrain of practice is an essential component of craft. In fothering, Cook had the combination of knowledge and ingenuity to shift the sail from its position aloft, where it served as a source of energy, to underwater, where it helped to patch a gash. The maritime term for such creative improvisation is "jury-rigging": "a temporary makeshift to bring a disabled vessel back to harbour . . . jury rig is the contrivance of masts and sails to get a ship under way after she has been disabled."[42]

Jury-rigging does not discriminate about the sources of its expedients. In extreme challenges, mariners found expedients beyond the bounds not only of norms but even taboos, drawing the creative mariner toward the transgressions of the pirate. In the story of Major Gibbons that opened James Janeway's Puritan collection of shipwreck narratives, *Legacy to his Friends: Containing Twenty Seven Famous Instances of Gods Providences in and about Sea Dangers and Deliverances* (1674), the threat of cannibalism was miraculously averted by God's providence. When the *Nottingham Galley* shipwrecked off the coast of New Hampshire en route from London to Boston in 1710, in contrast, the members of its company turned to cannibalism in the course of a month-long ordeal that stimulated a series of narratives as early as 1711.[43] Two cases of survival cannibalism the most publicized with stay-at-home audiences at the beginning of the nineteenth century were the wreck of the frigate *Méduse* (1816), which was the subject of the painter Théodore Géricault's *Raft of the Medusa*, and the disaster of the whaleship *Essex* (1821), which Nathaniel Philbrick recently resurrected with his 2001 *In the Heart of the Sea*. The mariner's willingness to use any expedient to survive remarkable dangers helps explain the interest of consummate jury-riggers in creative improvisation they witnessed among indigenous peoples encountered on the far side of the globe. William Dampier filled *A New Voyage Round the World* with descriptions of native ingenuity. Hierarchies of technologies and knowledge fall away as Dampier described, for example, how he and his buccaneer fellows learned from the Moskito Indians how to hunt the manatees whose skins the buccaneers used for canoe oarlocks.[44]

Noting creative technological application wherever it appeared was a way to add to the mariner's storehouse of experience. The more examples, the greater would be the repertoire at a mariner's disposal in a crisis demanding innovative solutions. Detailing the specific gestures characterizing jury-rigging is part of how to teach this creative ability to contend with the unforeseen. Feats such as Cook's salvage of the *Endeavour* from the Great Barrier Reef made the accounts of his voyage indispensable reading for subsequent mariners who cultivated not just the specific techniques of craft, but also the ability to act decisively in unknown situations.

When Cook details the steps of fothering, he slips from the retrospective narration of what happened to the present tense used to give instructions in practical manuals: "the manner this is done is thus" (141). There is one aspect of his gesture, however, that he does not include in such instructions. This is the thought process of the jury-rigging sensibility that decided upon the right expedient. How to teach the creativity of improvisation is a challenge in the case of craft, as in other arts of action, much more difficult to impart than specific competences.

Joseph Conrad was interested in the difficulty of teaching the situation-specific creativity of craft and drew attention to its importance in his fiction. His Lord Jim learns "a little trigonometry and how to cross top-gallant yards" in his education "on a 'training ship for officers of the mercantile marine.'"[45] But when confronted with unexpected circumstances, Jim cannot come up with an effective response. As a lad in training, Jim fails to go to the rescue of a drowning comrade, deficient at once in creative improvisation and at seizing the moment (*chairos*), which are two aspects of craft that often go together. Jim also does not come up with the expedient that would alleviate the distress of the *Patna* in the disaster that leads to his trial. In the tale *Typhoon*, Conrad gives us the stupid, steadfast Captain MacWhirr, who inexplicably decides to sail through rather than around a terrible storm. Unable to devise any plan beyond staying the course, MacWhirr retreats from the gales to his chartroom and comically peruses a chapter on storms in a practical treatise, losing himself "amongst advancing semi-circles, left- and right-hand quadrants, the curves of the tracks, the probable bearing of the centre, the shifts of wind and the readings of barometer." Thoroughly baffled, a victim rather than beneficiary of his instruction, MacWhirr becomes "contemptuously angry with such a lot of words, and with so much advice, all head-work and supposition, without a glimmer of certitude."[46] MacWhirr lacks imagination, Conrad tells us repeatedly, a faculty that is not usually deemed a hallmark of practice, but that is essential to the creative improvisations of craft amidst uncertainty, in a pragmatic form of the imagination that I describe in the section on "reckoning" later in this chapter.

Across the adventure of the sea, vanguard navigators have compelled admiration for exercising the jury-rigging sensibility amidst extraordinary dangers. At the same time, a more mundane kind of improvisation was also required in the ordinary business of seafaring, viz the routine cache of "jury-masts" carried for replacements on long ocean voyages.

COLLECTIVITY (WEDNESDAY, JUNE 13, 1770)

When Cook detailed "fothering" in his journal, he mentioned "some hands" who carried it out. He is initially reticent about whose idea fothering was in the first place. We assume Cook's own, but Sir Joseph Banks, Cook's head scientist, credited the novel idea to "[o]ne of our midshipmen," who "now proposd an expedient which no one else in the ship had seen practisd, tho all had heard of it by the name of fothering a ship."[47] At the end of Cook's journal, the Captain, too, gives Mr. Munkhouse his due:

> Mr Munkhouse one of my Midshipmen was once in a Merchant ship which sprung a leak and made 48 inches water per hour but by this means was brought home from Virginia to London with only her proper crew, to him I gave the deriction of this who exicuted it very much to my satisfaction. (142)

Does Cook's initial failure to credit Mr. Munkhouse tarnish his reputation? To assume this would be to adhere to an idea of individuality at odds with the collective nature of work at sea. A distinctive aspect of craft is collectivity, what Conrad calls the "bond of the sea." As I have been describing the salvage of the *Endeavour* from the reef, I have been attributing it to Cook; however, the ship's survival depended on the collaboration of captain and crew. No individual could work an oceangoing sailing ship on his own.

Craft's version of collectivity was rigidly hierarchical, and each seaman was allocated duties to fulfill. Hierarchy was particularly intense in navies, and could be comparatively more lax in merchant vessels, but even there, it played an important role. Rigidly defined relations of authority were essential for the prompt execution of maneuvers, critical at all times, and above all in moments of danger. In addition, authoritarian hierarchies helped maintain order amidst the extraordinarily stressful conditions of a long voyage. Another function of craft's hierarchical collectivity was to clarify the responsibilities of different members of the expedition for its outcome. Cook took credit for fothering, as he took credit for the *Endeavour*'s salvage. In his journal, he also devotes space to justifying his decisions, for he would be held responsible for the errors as well as successes of his expedition.

The most effective qualification enforcing rank in the maritime hierarchy was capacity and experience in the practice of the craft. Dissension arose when craft's hierarchy of experience was trumped by land-based ranks of birth and privilege. Disasters could ensue, like the shipwreck of the French frigate *Méduse* in 1816, captained by the Vicomte du Chaumareys, appointed for his royalist politics and rank, but who had not spent time at sea for over twenty years. A disrespect for collectivity is a complaint brought against young gentleman sent to sea for a stint to perfect their education. Struggles with unruly aristocratic midshipmen, for example, run throughout the voyage account of George Vancouver, explorer of the Pacific Northwest.[48] Vancouver himself had served the function of midshipman with Cook, aboard the *Resolution* during Cook's second voyage, and had learned to knuckle down to collectivity as he worked his way through the ranks.

When Champlain summed up the importance of collective wisdom, he emphasized how much was also passed down in an oral culture:

> The wise and cautious mariner ought not to trust too fully to his own judgment, when the pressing need is to take some important step or to deviate from a dangerous course. Let him take counsel with those whom he recognizes as the most sagacious, and particularly with old navigators who have had most experience of disasters at sea and have escaped from dangers and perils ... for it is not often that one head holds everything, and, as the saying is, experience is better than knowledge [*l'experiēce passe science*].[49]

To summarize this paragraph Champlain offered in the margin the maxim, "Not trust in his own judgment alone."[50] This counsel could be oral; but written accounts entered into the wisdom to be taken on board as well. Though narratives of path-breaking navigations entertained broader audiences, they were providing state-of-the-art information for the benefit of collectivity that subsequent navigators would absorb and test. Throughout his journal, Cook compares his observations to those of previous navigators from the preceding two centuries, from the voyage account of the sixteenth-century Portuguese explorer Quirós published at the beginning of the seventeenth century and Abel Tasman's journals of his navigation in the 1640s to Dampier's *A New Voyage Round the World* from 1697 and accounts of Lord Anson's more recent circumnavigation in 1740–1744.

The collectivity of craft shaped practical literature on seafaring as well, evident even in its notion of authorship. The most influential practical treatises were published, revised, and republished, often with extensive emendations, as printers called on either the author or new generations of experts to transform the work in keeping with advances in knowledge and technologies. These innovations were often not credited to specific authors. The 1699 reprint of John Smith's *Sea Grammar* (1627) now sold as a *Sea-Man's Grammar and Dictionary*, specifies on its title page "Now much Amplified and Enlarged, with a variety of Experiments, since his Time, made by several Experienced Navigators and Gunners." I quoted Atkinson's *Epitome of the Art of Navigation*, originally published in 1686, from a 1744 version updated by William Mountaine. Nathaniel Colson's *Mariner's New Kalendar* went through seventy-five editions from 1676 to 1785, and Thomas Haselden's *Seaman's Daily Assistant* went through thirty editions between 1757 and 1803.[51] In other words, publication criteria emphasized collectivity over originality.

In the institutions of literature of the time more generally, the standards of originality were emerging that we hold central to publication today. When Defoe was alive, for example, Grub Street in London was a synonym for hack literature, where imitation was conceived as a defect— as the absence of originality and lack of inspiration. In the professional usage of language that was part of seamanship, in contrast, originality was irrelevant—what mattered were veracity, precision, and legibility. Indeed, originality could even be harmful. In written documents, particularly describing unknown coasts and waters, conventional and recognizable terminology was an advantage. When officers uttered commands across a ship's deck amidst howling winds, the more familiar terms were, the more easily they could be recognized.

Practical treatises on the language of seamanship hence sought to fix words and phrases, stabilizing the maritime lexicon, rather than to invent new usages. How-to manuals reproduced entire passages in the name of consistent collective knowledge. Compare across the seventeenth century the nearly identical phrases that open similar descriptions of how to maneuver a ship in "a hollow grown sea," starting with an edition of Charles Saltonstall's *The Navigator* published in 1636: "The Sea is much growne, we make foule weather, looke our Gunnes be all fast, it is better Spooming."[52] Here is Samuel Sturmy's description from *The Mariner's Magazine* of 1669: "A very hollow grown Sea. We make foul Weather, look the Guns be all fast, come hand the Mizen. The Ship lies very broad off; it is better Spooning before the Sea, than trying or hulling."[53] Here are Daniel Newhouse's instructions, in an edition from 1708: "We make foul Weather, look the Guns be all fast, come hand the Mizen: the Ship lies very broad off, it is better spooning before the Sea, than trying or hulling."[54] *The Mariner's Jewel, Or A Pocket Companion for the Ingenious*, which I consulted in the editions of 1700 and 1703, also includes the language of the previous two quotes.[55]

This role of collectivity in maritime authorship extends to Cook's first voyage as well. As I mentioned at the start of this chapter, the British Admiralty commissioned the professional writer Hawkesworth to draft the official account of its events, collecting all the journals kept by the individuals who had participated. When Cook revised his log himself with an eye toward publication, he was staking a claim to the value of his authorship as an individual. At the same time, Cook justified his account in the name of accuracy that would serve the craft. Of an episode in Hawkesworth's narrative, Cook remarked "How those things came to be thus misrepresented I can not say, as they came not from me . . ."[56] In his own narrative, Cook specifies that he has, in contrast, "with undisguised truth and without gloss inserted the whole transactions of the Voyage and made such remarks and have given such discription of things as I thought was necessary in the best manner I was Capable off."[57] This ambition to tell the truth accurately is in continuity with standards used to justify reprinting practical treatises. Thus, the publisher Richard Mount explained in a note addressed "To the Mariners of Great–Britain," prefacing the third edition of Daniel Newhouse's *Whole Art of Navigation* that he prevailed upon Newhouse "to make such Additions, as might render this Treatise every way Compleat."[58]

COMPLEAT KNOWLEDGE (FRIDAY, JUNE 29, 1770)

By late June, Cook managed to bring the *Endeavour* safely to land. While repairing the ship, Cook pursued the scientific mission of his expedition, recording a variety of observations—from flora and fauna to the movements of the heavens. He wrote in his journal:

> Lieutenant Gore having been 4 or 5 Miles in the Country . . . saw the foot steps of Men and likewise those of 3 or 4 sorts of wild beasts but saw neither man nor beast . . . we found some Wild Yamms or Coccos growing in the swampy grounds . . . the tops we found made good greens and eat exceeding well when boild but the roots were so Acrid that few besides my self could eat them. This night Mr Green and I observed an Emersion of Jupiter first Satellite which happen'd at 2^h 58'53" in the AM, the same Emersion happend at Greenwich according to calculation on the 30th at 5^{h}17'43" in the PM; the difference is 14^{h}18'50" equal to 214°42'30" of Longitude which this place is west of Greenwich, and its Latitude is 15° 26' South. (147–48)

To observe the passage of satellites across the face of Jupiter was one important scientific task that had been laid at Cook's charge. There were many others. In his voyage to the South Pacific, Cook had been instructed by the Royal Society to observe the transit of Venus across the face of the sun in order to help them determine the size of the solar system. The Royal Society further specified that Cook should "explore diligently the coasts he might discover; 'carefully observing the true situation thereof both in Latitude and Longitude, the Variation of the Needle, bearings of head Lands, Height, direction and Course of the Tides and Currents, Depths and Soundings of the Sea, Shoals, Rocks &ca and also surveying and making Charts, and taking Views of such Bays, Harbours and Parts of the Coast as may be useful to Navigation.'"[59]

This directive is quoted by J. C. Beaglehole, who stressed that, while carrying out scientific studies, Cook was not a scientist. In Beaglehole's words, Cook "was a connoisseur of the instruments he used, but he could not make a Bird quadrant, a Ramsden sextant, a Dollond reflecting telescope . . . [however] [h]e could use instruments, when he got them, with a skill and an accuracy that few other men could match."[60] Beaglehole's reflection speaks to the mastery of craft over a diverse skill set ranging from strength to calculation, encompassing, among many competences, local knowledge, naval strategy, and managing the ship.

Cook's voyage was an extraordinary voyage of scientific discovery. But throughout the more ordinary work on the high seas as well, craft's "compleat" knowledge encompassed diverse, heterogeneous skills. Practical authors understood these skills as spanning the conventional philosophical divide between higher forms of knowledge that were "theorick"—pure—and applied knowledge, the "practick," to cite the seventeenth-century mariner, Charles Saltonstall. In his introduction to *The Navigator* (1636), a practical treatise on seamanship, Saltonstall explains that it presents theoretical knowledge about astronomy and mathematics—and practical knowledge about how to manufacture instruments for navigation, and use them, as well as about how to build a ship. In Saltonstall's words:

> [T]he Theorick will fully informe you of the composition of the *Spheare* in generall, and in particular of the Figure, Number, and Motions made in the Heavens . . . the Theoricke will also informe you how the Elements are disposed, with their quantities, and situations, especially in the composition of the Earth, and Waters . . . The Practick part is properly placed upon the making and using of divers instruments, as Crosse-staves, Back-staves, Nocturnals, Planispheares, instruments for the Moone and Tydes [as well as] . . . the unparaleld Fabrick of a gallant Ship.[61]

Though theory and practice required different kinds of skills, and though in the work of the sea the areas of expertise were distributed among different members of the crew, the ideal of the compleat mariner was the capacity to have at one's disposal the full arsenal of competences, both theoretical and practical, to contend with the marine element of "flux, danger and destruction" (figure 1.6).

A synonym for the "compleat" mariner was the "perfect" mariner. At the root of "perfect" is the Latin verb for acting, *facere*, an etymology

Figure 1.6. The frontispiece to *The Mariner's Mirrour*, the first work to compile sea charts and sailing directions. The illustration features images of the "Theorick" and the "Practick," placing astronomers who chart the heavens over mariners surrounded by different kinds of tools of measurement (cross staff, quadrant, astrolabe, compass, calipers, sounding line, and hourglass) essential for the practice of navigation.

Title page, from Lucas Waghenaer, *The Mariners Mirrour: wherin may playnly be seen the courses, heights, distances, depths, soundings, flouds and ebs, risings of lands, rocks, sands and shoalds, with the marks for th'entrings of the Harbouroughs, Havens and Ports of the greatest part of Europe: their seueral traficks and commodities: Together w.[th] the Rules and instrume[n]ts of Navigation*, trans. Anthony Ashley (London: John Charlewood, 1588). Courtesy of the National Maritime Museum, London.

also visible in the French *parfait*, rooted in the verb *faire*, "to make or do." Champlain employed this qualification in the full title he gave to his treatise on the qualities required of the "bon et parfaict navigateur." The ideal of the mariner, in other words, was realized in action; the notion of complete or perfect was not a synonym for systematic knowledge or artistic refinement but rather for the accomplished deed. The range of techniques covered in the quest for excellence in action were laid out again and again in practical treatises, encompassing the theory and technologies of navigation along with shipbuilding, gunnery, personnel management, and caring for the ship and supplies. At times, the bold, resolute mariner, imbued with "manly courage," sounds domestic, almost like a housewife. Champlain instructed that it was important to be a good and economical manager [*bon œconome*] and to keep everything on board clean and ordered, "after the fashion of the Flemings."[62]

In the practical literature, the mariner's compleat knowledge was often conveyed in different graphic genres: charts, views of important harbors, how-to diagrams, and tables of celestial movements and tides. Different kinds of knowledge were sometimes integrated even within a single diagram. Nathaniel Colson's "Table of the Soundings coming into the Channel, respecting the Bearings and Distances from *Silly, Ushant, the Lizard, etc.* With the various sorts of Ground" correlated knowledge about latitude, depth, and distance with what would be found at the ocean's bottom: "shells and sand like points of Needles," "red and black sand with glistering shells," "hakes teeth and shells like oatmeal husks," "great stones like beans and peas," etc. (figure 1.7).[63] The variegated texture of such minute particles was part of how mariners gauged when the shore approached, and thus of the greatest interest, for ships wreck far more easily in the shallows than the open sea. In these assorted grains of sand, we find a microcosm of the detailed, divergent, textured quality of compleat knowledge, which extended from the local details of coastal bottoms to movement of the distant planets in the heavens.

This notion of the mariner's craft as compleat, whole, or perfect knowledge persisted throughout the seventeenth and eighteenth centuries. The representation of compleat knowledge remained constant from the seventeenth-century treatises of Saltonstall and Daniel Newhouse to a 1751 *Mariner's Guide*, by Thomas Crosby, whose full title speaks for itself:

Mariner's Guide: Being A Compleat Treatise Of Navigation Both in Theory and Practice. Containing Every Thing Necessary in that most useful Art, from the first Setting Out, to the Completion, of A Perfect Seaman. With Practical Examples, wrought at Large; and nothing

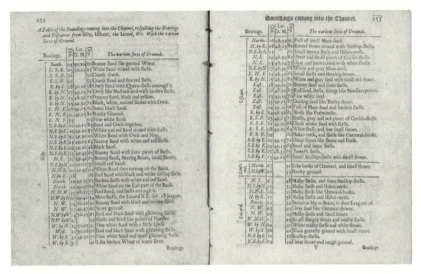

Figure 1.7. Note the textured, local, and variegated nature of the knowledge found in this table of soundings by Nathaniel Colson, where different kinds of sand are correlated with different bearings and depths in the English Channel. "Table of soundings," in Nathaniel Colson, *The Mariner's New Kalendar* (London: Richard Mount, 1693, pp. 154–55). Courtesy of the John Carter Brown Library at Brown University.

therein Speculative or Superfluous. Together with all the Tables Necessary and Useful for the Mariner's Practice. The Whole Comprised in so Plain and Easy a Manner, that Persons of a mean Understanding may Comprehend what is contained therein.[64]

"Compleat," "theory and practice," "necessary," "useful," "perfect," "practical," "nothing speculative or superfluous," "plain," and "easy" are all terms that recur throughout expositions of craft. They indicate the importance in seamanship of the values of efficiency, practicality, and economy. In the work of the sea, it was imperative that "no waste be made," to cite the "Ordinances for the intended voyage to Cathay" by Sebastian Cabot concerning provisions, from Richard Hakluyt's *Principal Navigations* of 1589.[65] The need for economy when it came to stocking the ship, as in its management, reflected the fact that the ship was a closed environment, forced to be largely self-sufficient over a long voyage. The importance of conservation of resources more generally responded to the harsh nature of the marine environment and the fatiguing demands of its practice.

PLAIN STYLE (TUESDAY, AUGUST 7, 1770)

As repairs to the *Endeavour* wound up, Cook and his officers scanned the coast, seeking a passage to the open sea, but discovering shoals and surf as far as they could see. In his journal, Cook notes all the conditions of the scene:

> Strong gales at SE, SEBS & SSE with clowdy weather. At Low-water in the PM I and several of the officers kept a lookout at the Mast head to see for a passage between the Shoals, but we could see nothing but breakers all the way from the South round by the East as far as NW, extending out to sea as far as we could see, it did not appear to be one continued shoal but several laying detach'd from each other, on the Eastermost that we could see the Sea broke very high which made me judge it to be the outermost, for on many of those within, the sea did not break high attall. (158)

In recounting how he estimated the contours of the reef from the height of distant breakers, as in detailing crises, Cook employed "plain style," a convention of mariners' journals over four centuries. Plain style was the language of work at sea, and here, as in other aspects of work at sea, efficiency and economy were paramount. The observations recorded in the ship's log and carried over into retrospective voyage narratives, conveyed the maximum of accurate, precise information with the minimum effort and space. In the preceding excerpt from Cook's journal, a day's worth of "clowdy weather" and shifting winds are concisely shorthanded in a sentence fragment. Cook's blunt, terse descriptions, his careless spelling and syntax, and his use of technical maritime terms without explanation all are characteristic of the mariner's plain style. Le Cordier framed precision as a mariner's duty, giving it an ethical cast: "It is the pilot's duty & he is even ordered by Navy directives to make an accurate and specific observation . . ."[66]

The same concision of plain written style extended to the spoken terminology of the sea. No sailor could work effectively on a ship until he had learned the precise names for each line, sail, and part of the ship, which the captain would use as he commanded maneuvers. Numerous manuals explained these tools of language, and the term technology itself was first coined to praise one such manual, the previously mentioned *A Sea Grammar* (1627), by John Smith, the first governor of Virginia. Among the prefatory endorsements, *A Sea Grammar* includes a sonnet by Wye Saltonstall emphasizing the importance of language as a tool of work on the ship: "Each Science termes of Art hath wherewithal / To expresse themselves, called *technologicall.*"[67] In the margins, Saltonstall has included a gloss, explaining: "*Technologicall*, a Greeke word compounded of two Greeke words, τεχνή-λο-γὸς signifies words of Art."

Plain style is just that: words of art, with art used in the sense of métier, craft, a specialized field of practical knowledge. The qualities we appreciate in literary language were not only useless but could also be potentially harmful in the maritime application of both spoken and written language as a tool of efficient performance. In the spoken use of language at sea, ornamentation, substitutions, figures of speech, puns, or humor could delay understanding in time-critical contexts. These graces of literary style had other dangers as well. Written narratives recounted information gathered in contexts completely unknown to their audiences, who could not draw on their knowledge from beyond the text to clarify a meaning. What might be entertaining ambiguity for the pleasure reader would have fatal consequences for professionals, when the mariner went to use the information offered in previous sea voyage narratives as the basis of his own navigation.

Plain style is the term given to the mariner's way of writing in English. Its traits are similarly palpable in maritime narratives written in other European languages, as far back as Pigafetta. This continuity across national context and centuries reminds us that the mariner's plain style was a tool, shaped by the demands of work. Pigafetta's English translator and editor, R. A. Skelton, writes that Pigafetta's prose "has no elegance of construction or rhythm; it bursts from him in a succession of rather breathless short sentences. His vocabulary is homely, without sophistication or scholarship."[68] "Champlain writes with an extremely natural style, with no rhetoric, one word driving the next," declares one of his editors, Robert Marteau.[69]

Critics of the novel have most often associated plain style in eighteenth-century English fiction with the new spirit of scientific observation pioneered by Sir Francis Bacon and the Royal Society.[70] However, the Royal Society took plain style from the world of work, where it served efficient performance. Thomas Sprat explicitly made the connection between plain style and work in his *History of the Royal Society* (1667). Ilse Vickers cites a passage where Sprat comments on the "close, naked, natural way of speaking; positive expressions; clear senses; a native easiness: bringing all things as near the Mathematical plainness, as they can: and preferring the language of Artizans, Countrymen, and Merchants, before that, of Wits, or Scholars."[71]

By the late seventeenth century, the mariner's plain style signified the ethos of craft, when it was used in nonfictional travel narratives. In the guise of apologizing for his plain style, Dampier vaunted his achievements as a mariner: "As to my Stile, it cannot be expected, that a Seaman should affect Politeness . . . yet I think I should be little sollicitous about it, in a work of this Nature. . . . I am perswaded, that if what I say be intelligible, it matters not greatly in what words it is express'd."[72] With this seeming apology, Dampier at the same time implied that his work more than made up for its absence of literary qualities with extraordinary adventures and rich contribution to what Dampier called "that general Magazine, of the knowledge of Foreign Parts . . ."[73] When Cook apologized for his lack of literary style at the beginning of his journal three-quarters of a century later, he implied that plain style arose from something far more important for the mariner than literary niceties—immense experience at sea. "I have neither natural or acquired abilities for writing," Cook explained to his reader, after having been "constantly at sea from my youth."[74] In the introduction to *The Voyage of François Leguat* (1708), Leguat characterized plain style as provoking mockery from the "Critical Reader," quoting as example a passage from a travel narrative by the Abbot of Choisy, whose English title is the *Voyage to Siam*: "*We cast [a]nchor. We made ready to sail. . . . Robin is dead. We said mass. We vomited.*"[75] But this barbarism had its own anti-ornamental eloquence, focusing attention on just the facts with a concision we readers today more often associate with journalistic and informational writing of our present. By the beginning of the eighteenth century, when plain style was transferred from the accounts given by mariners into narratives of seafaring adventures, plain style evoked an atmosphere of craft even before any deeds had been performed. This effect of authenticity would be utilized by Defoe and other sea adventure novelists.

As Dampier's *New Voyage* illustrates, there was a contrast in plain style between the precision of the observations and their disorganized presentation. In the ship's log, the frame of the 24-hour day used for each entry held together events and details without regard to their logical relation. When these logs were turned into retrospective voyage narratives, however, the 24-hour frame fell away. With the absence of other literary qualities, narratives in plain style lacked devices to organize the events of narrative, such as biography; unity of action; emotional tone; the notion that an episode should have a beginning, a middle, and an end; or a poetics of suspense. The result was, as in *A New Voyage*, dense paragraphs held together by chronology, teeming with disparate kinds of information. Thus, rounding Cape Horn, Dampier gives bearings, the visual aspects of the islands there, the course, the winds, and common wisdom about the smoke and fire to be seen at Tierra del Fuego:

The 7th Day at Noon being off the East-end of *States-Island,* I had a good Observation of the Sun, and found my self in Lat. 54 d. 52 m. South.

At the East-end of *States-Island* are three small Islands, or rather Rocks, pretty high, and white with the Dung of Fowls. Wherefore having observed the Sun, we haled up South, designing to pass round to the Southward of Cape *Horne*, which is the Southermost land of *Terra del Fuego.* The Winds hung in the Western quarter betwixt the N.W. and the West, so that we could not get much to the Westward, and we never saw *Terra del Fuego* after that Evening that we made the Streights *Le Mair.* I have heard that there have been Smoaks and Fires on *Terra del Fuego,* not on the tops of Hills, but in Plains and Valleys, seen by those who have sailed thro' the Streights of *Magellan*; supposed to be made by the Natives.[76]

Sea voyage narratives like Dampier's were the best-selling literature of the era. For today's readers, in contrast, habituated to narratives that convey information organized by suspense and psychology, the information overload can be fatiguing. It also takes some work to process the extraordinary details and occurrences that plain style crowds into its eventful paragraphs.

PROVIDENCE (THURSDAY, AUGUST 16, 1770)

Craft courts luck and opportunity, yet there are moments when craft runs out of expedients. At those moments, even mariners of the Enlightenment such as Cook appealed to a higher power. On August 16, the *Endeavour,* now heading back out to sea, was threatened once again with crashing on this reef that stretched on seemingly without end. Reduced to a stratagem that Cook represents as desperate—pitting the assistance of his small boats to struggle against the current—Cook also calls on Providence—one of the very few times in his sober, secular account that he invokes the divine:

> A little after 4 oClock the roaring of the Surf was plainly heard and at day break the vast foaming breakers were too plainly to be seen not a Mile from us towards which we found the Ship was carried by the waves surprisingly fast. We had at this time not an air of wind and the depth of water was unfathomable so that there was not a possibility of Anchoring, in this distressed situation we had nothing but Providence and the small Assistance our boats could give us to trust to; the Pinnace was under a repair and could not immidiately be hoisted out, the Yawl was put into the water and the Long-boat hoisted out and both sent ahead to tow which together with the help of our sweeps abaft got the Ships head round to the northward which seem'd to be the only way to keep her off the reef . . . (166)

With this effort and the help of a fickle though "friendly" breeze, Cook manages to stave off immediate shipwreck, and the *Endeavour* finds a small opening in the reef and seeks to pass through (167).[77]

But when the breeze once again fails, the ship drifts toward the "jaws of distruction" (167). All seems lost, when "to our surprise we found the Tide of Ebb gushing out like a Mill stream," a condition that Cook and crew take advantage of to maneuver to deeper water. Cook commemorated this lucky escape by naming the opening occasioning the gushing tide "Providential Channel." His nod to the divine here contrasts with the secular tone of the names given to other coastal features on his charts, whether they commemorate the life found there ("Society Islands," "Botany Bay"); physical features ("Bay of Inlets"); the experiences of the expedition ("Poverty Bay," "Cape Tribulation"); or European patrons and notables back home ("Forbes Island," after the Admiral John Forbes, etc.).

From the beginning of global ocean travel, craft revealed the power of human agency to thread a path through the great forces of nature, challenging a divine view of human fate. But this challenge at first was expressed only hesitantly, in the interstices of religious values. The stated goal of the *Account of the very remarkable loss of the Great Galleon S. João*, a shipwreck in 1552 that was to inspire *The Lusíads* (1572), is to "make men very much fear God's punishments and become good Christians, and bring the fear of God before their eyes so His commandments will not be broken."[78] The narrative's protagonist, Captain Manuel de Sousa, turns into a martyr along with his crew, children, and wife, when they are taken prisoner by the inhabitants of the East African coast, who torture and then murder them. In his resigned and stoic death, Sousa solicits the responses of readers typical of exemplary biographies: Christian compassion (*compassio*) and admiration (*admiratio*) inciting readers to imitate his model.

Other members of the *S. João*'s company, in contrast, including the narrator himself, react to dangers with a rather different comportment: in quest of survival rather than a good Christian death. This struggle for survival is evident from the time the ship first ran into trouble around the Cape of Good Hope, when, the narrator tells us, she met with shifting winds and "[h]eavy seas from west and east [that] swamped the galleon with so much water that with each roll she seemed to be on her way to the bottom." Even when the wind calmed after three days, "[t]he sea was still so heavy and the ship labored so much that it lost three pintles from the rudder, that is, the part of it on which the entire perdition or salvation of a ship depends."[79] These dangers belong to the category of the remarkable occurrence in a ship's log, and as we have seen, they are a prelude to the mariner springing into action. With a broken rudder, the expedition tries to head for shore; however, this effort at remedy provokes a new danger. When the storm breaks out again, the ship cannot steer properly: "the ship refused the helm, which caused it to heel and run toward leeward," and "[t]he savage wind tore the mainsail off the main yard." New danger, new remedy: "seeing themselves without sails, the crew resorted to the foresail when the ship began to heave and labor," and so on in the struggle to navigate through the savage elements. The episode concludes with a practical moral for other mariners. "A wave broke the rotten rudder in two and carried away half of it, leaving the pintles in the sternpost gudgeons. This just shows how much the rudder and sails need to be cared for because of the many trials awaiting ships on this route."[80]

Despite the ambition of the narrative set forth at the beginning—to make men fear God's punishment—concerns for the soul are eclipsed in such paragraphs by the depiction of extraordinary dangers and remedies taken by the human capacity of craft. The Christian martyr and the crafty mariner are never brought into explicit relation, and at times, indeed, the narrative jarringly veers from one value to another. Thus, the acount applies a religious vocabulary to the work of the sea. The mariners were concerned with "perdition or salvation," of the ship, though these are terms one might rather associate with the state of human souls. In one jarring moment, salvation and concerns for survival were yoked within a single sentence: "the captain ordered everyone to turn over their weapons even though their salvation resided in them, apart from God."[81] Fittingly, the narrative had two distinct outcomes. While the commander was martyred, the ship's pilot and several members of the crew survived and returned to Europe to tell their tale.

Was the agency of the mariner purely instrumental, or did it serve a higher cause? The jerky seesaw between survival and salvation in the *Account of the very remarkable loss of the Great Galleon S. João* was characteristic of the early modern era throughout European oceangoing cultures. Take, for example, Champlain's treatise on the duties of the mariner from 1632. Its opening sentences spell out the mariner's duties as service to King and to Cross. As the treatise unfolds, however, "duty," and "good" are used in an amoral, instrumental way. The French word *devoir* ("duty"), in particular, lent itself to Champlain's conflation of the effective and the good. From his title, Champlain used the word to qualify what the mariner "should know and do" to be effective. Sometimes, Champlain explicitly rendered the effective action as a confirmation of God's providence. For instance, he noted the deficiencies in mariners' ability to calculate longitude during their voyage (more about that in the section on "reckoning" later in this chapter) and qualified the other "means supplied to men of avoiding in most voyages the risks which pertain to longitudes" spelled out in his *Treatise* as "the providence of God."[82] The notion that God's providence guided the mariner's ability to navigate safely is also found in *The Sea-man's Practice*, in which Richard Norwood framed the compass as divinely inspired:

Amongst all the Mysteries which God hath of late years discovered to the World for the furtherance of *Navigation*, there is none more necessary, nor yet more admirable than the property of the *Needle* touching with the Load-stone, whereby in the vast Ocean, where all the Landmarks fail, yea even in the darkest nights and closest weather, when neither Sun nor Stars are to be seen, the Mariner (as it were by a Messenger sent from Heaven) is taught which way to direct his Ship; yea, as it were accompanied with a Guide towards his desired Port.[83]

The ambiguous partnership of human agency and faith was tested in extreme situations. From the depths of the Arctic winter of 1631–1632, Captain Thomas James broke with plain style to offer "ragged and teared Rhimes" that question the compass and more broadly the mariner's creed of human enterprise:

> We have with confidence relyde upon
> A rustie wyre, toucht with a little Stone,
> Imcompast round with paper, and alasse
> To house it harmeless, nothing but a glasse,
> And thought to shun a thousand dangers, by
> The blind directions of this senseless flye.
> When the fierce winds shatter'd blacke nights asunder,
> Whose pitchie clouds, spitting forth fire and thunder,
> Hath shooke the earth, and made the Ocean roare;
> And runne to hide it, in the broken shoare:
> Now thou must Steere *by faith*; a better guide
> 'Twill bring these safe to heaven against the tyde
> Of Satans malice. Now let quiet gales
> Of Saving grace, inspire thy zealous sayles.[84]

But James soon retreated from such resignation, and rallied his sailors, reminding them that they inhabit a universe of human agency and technology: "[T]here is nothing too hard for couragious minds: which hitherto you have showne, and I doubt not will still doe, to the uttermost."[85] James ultimately saved his expedition through the compleat skills of craft, including patience, protocol, and resolution, crowned by a brilliant stroke of jury-rigging. As the ice first encroached in October 1631, James sunk his ship in shallow water, where it would winter, protected from the violent movement of the ice that would thwart numerous polar expeditions, including Shackleton's three centuries later at the other end of the globe. Safely out of the way of the ice, James's ship survived the winter under water. When the Arctic ice finally thawed in the late spring of 1632, James planted peas that sprouted and cured the surviving crew of scurvy. With energy restored, they raised the ship out of the water, dried it out, and made it seaworthy. They set sail in July, returning to Bristol on October 22, 1632, a year and a half after setting out.[86]

Seventeenth-century Calvinist writers of shipwreck narratives offered one transitional solution to accommodating survival to salvation on the way to the mariner's completely secular agency, when they recouped the feats of craft as evidence for Providence. James Janeway filled the pages of *Legacy to his Friends: Containing Twenty Seven Famous Instances of Gods Providences in and about Sea Dangers and Deliverances* (1674) with narratives of survival at sea manifesting the different facets of craft, from endeavor to jury-rigging. Janeway recounted, for example, the story of an Englishman, shipwrecked off the coast of Scotland, whose only companion disappeared along with the knife they were using to prepare food. The Englishman then improvised: "I was forced to get out of my Hut a great Nail, which I made a shift to sharpen upon the Rock, that it served me for a Knife . . ."[87] With this knife, he took a little "sea-dog" (seal) fat, stuck it in a crevice, and used it as bait to attract seabirds, which provided his subsistence. Such anecdotes served a theological and moral purpose: revealing that God helped those who helped themselves. Sometimes, Providence furnishes the expedients that procure survival. When Dutch mariners cast away in the Arctic Circle found the driftwood that would help them fight off bears, Janeway framed it as divinely provided: "[B]y a good Providence, the Tide had thrown up a good quantity of Timber, they not knowing from whence it came, it proved a great advantage to them during their abode . . ."[88] At other time, Providence inspires creative improvisation. This is the case of "one *Samuel Snytal*," an apprentice on a ship whose Captain is washed overboard. Syntal already knows something of "the Art of Navigation, and his Master being gone," is helped by God to improve his skill to the point that "by Gods blessing, he carried the ship safe home . . ."[89]

THE EDGE (THURSDAY, AUGUST 16, 1770)

In Cook's entry for the day that the *Endeavour* is snatched by Providence from "the very jaws of distruction," Cook breaks with his conventional plain style (167). His journal contains a few sentences, which depict the reef with an unusual sense of spectacle, vividly portraying one among the many extreme spaces of the globe—including reefs, unknown coasts, great capes, and the remote polar regions—that have appeared throughout this chapter:

> All the dangers we had escaped were little in comparison of being thrown upon this Reef where the Ship must be dashed to peices in a

Moment. A Reef such as is here spoke of is scarcely known in Europe, it is a wall of Coral Rock rising all most perpendicular out of the unfathomable Ocean, always overflown at high-water generally 7 or 8 feet and dry in places at low-water; the large waves of the vast Ocean meeting with so sudden a resistance make a most terrible surf breaking mountains high especially as in our case when the general trade wind blowes directly upon it. (166)

Such spaces at the edge of experience and even imagination are the theater for the consummate display of craft. They exceed the known technologies with which they are accessed, just as they threaten to exceed the mariner's craft that made them practicable in the first place. In their extreme danger, they have a problematic relation to prudence. Spaces on the edge demand the most attentive prudence. At the same time, these navigations themselves are hardly a prudent undertaking. Cook pondered this tension in his journals. We have seen Cook note that if he failed in his expedition, he would be "charged with *Temerity* and want of conduct" (168). At the same time, he justified the imprudence of his risky navigations as serving knowledge: "I have ingaged more among the Islands and shoals upon this coast than may be thought with prudence I ought to have done with a single Ship and every other thing considered, but if I had not we should not have been able to give any better account of the one half of it than if we had never seen it . . ." (168). If his risky undertaking is successful, it will enable future expeditions to navigate these waters with prudence. It yields knowledge that will transform spaces like the Great Barrier Reef from the unknown into well-marked obstacles on the world's charts that can then be navigated in more routine fashion.

Such dangerous spaces at the edge of dynamic knowledge are transformed by the Western practice of exploration according to a distinctive dynamic of innovation. Once such spaces are visited with regularity, explorers gather information that serves the welfare of navigation. Though the spaces remain dangerous, their conditions come to be understood, and they are no longer radically uncertain; at the same time, in accordance with the value placed on innovation and expansion, they lose their allure and the edges of dynamic knowledge migrate elsewhere.

The last maritime edges of the globe were the polar oceans. In the same decades that the poles were reached, the edges of geographical knowledge migrated to air and, later in the twentieth century, to space and, arguably, to virtual reality. When Tom Wolfe described "the right stuff," that is the test pilot's version of the mariner's craft in the era of developing space travel, he too found it conceptualized as a space at the edge: "pushing the outside of the envelope," as it was called in test pilot lingo. NASA self-consciously allied space exploration with an earlier era of maritime

69–HC–1012

Figure 1.8. When the oceans of the globe are mapped, the frontiers migrate elsewhere. Nonetheless, the age of sail still evokes the heroism of vanguard navigations in new arenas of exploration. *Apollo XII* mission seal. Author's collection.

globalization in its logo for *Apollo XII* (figure 1.8). While the spacecraft *Yankee Clipper* was named after the pinnacle of American sailing technology, its lunar module, *Intrepid*, was baptized in keeping with the maritime tradition of naming ships after the ethos of craft, viz Cook's *Endeavour*, or the *Resolution*, *Adventure*, and *Discovery* of Cook's subsequent voyages. Carrying astronauts to the surface of the moon, the *Intrepid* takes to the solar system Cook's boast during his second voyage: "I whose ambition leads me not only farther than any other man has been before me, but as far as I think it possible for man to go . . ." (331). In antiquity, such a boast would have been hubris. In modernity, it is the defiant resolution of craft on the way to its own supersession.

While long-term hopes of profit also drove the exploration of these spaces at the Edge of knowledge and beyond, short-term yields were often unproductive if not destructive. It was, moreover, not always easy to distinguish between the positive and negative yields of such explorations. Some explorations brought back negative knowledge that was useful, like Cook discovering no evidence that would support the existence of a Great Southern Continent when he ventured into southern polar waters. Cook mentions a powerful pleasure attending even unproductive discovery: "Was it not for the pleasure which naturly results to a Man from being the first discoverer, even was it nothing more than sands and Shoals, this service would be insuportable especialy in far distant parts, like this, short of Provisions and almost every other necessary" (168). Though Cook declined to be more specific, there are values of modernity evinced by this keen but unproductive pleasure that cannot be subsumed to ideologies of conquest or perfectability: a value placed on sheer curiosity, as well as a fascination with adventure, attended by the allure of danger and destruction.

For Charles Baudelaire, modernity's fascination with such spaces at the Edge was a fascination with the new that was inseparable from a fascination with death. Baudelaire made this point in "The Voyage," the poem that concluded his lyric cycle on modern life, *Les Fleurs du mal* (1857). Across "The Voyage," Baudelaire tests and discards different justifications for travel, before revealing in the poem's final lines exploration's ultimate quest: "Oh Death, old captain, the time has come! Let's weigh anchor! / We are bored with this land, Oh Death! Let's set sail! / If the sky and sea are black as ink, / Our hearts that you know are filled with rays! / Pour out your poison to comfort us! / We want, burning with its fire, / To plunge to the depths of the abyss, Hell or Heaven, what does it matter? / To the depths of the Unknown to find something *new*!"[90]

The deadly Northwest Passage is one example of a space at the Edge that never offered any commercial or political return. Or rather, the commercial return was in popular narratives, like the account by James—provided survivors returned to tell their tales. In his *Strange and Dangerous Voyage*, James warned that his words could hardly give an account of the extremity of his suffering, which defied not only the writing but perhaps also the reading: "Such miseries as these, we indured amongst these shoalds and broken grounds: or rather more desperate then I have related: (very unpleasant perchance to be read) . . ."[91] Unpleasant perhaps, but the popularity of his and similar "strange and dangerous" adventures with readers across centuries, testifies to the curiosity of his readers, too, in narratives, which portrayed the potentially life-threatening pleasures of an unknown navigation.

RECKONING (THURSDAY, AUGUST 23, 1770)

To emphasize modernity's romance with dangerous adventure is not, of course, to downplay the obvious scientific and colonial aims of Cook's expedition. Science met British colonial ambition in Cook's charge to draw up charts of these unknown waters. Cook explains different measures he took to produce a chart that would be as accurate as possible, given the conditions of his work.

> I beleive it will be found to contain as few errors as most Sea Charts which have not under gone a thorough correction, the Latitude and Longitude of all or most of the principal head lands, Bays &cᵃ may be relied on, for we seldom faild of geting an Observation every day to correct our Latitude by, and the observation for Settleing the Longitude were no less numberous and made as often as the Sun and Moon came in play, so that it was impossible for any material error to creep into our reckoning in the intermidiate times. (173)

One fundamental problem for Cook was how to discern his longitude accurately while at sea. From the beginning of global ocean travel, sailors determined their latitude by measuring the angle of heavenly bodies relative to the horizon. As the author of *The Illustrated Longitude*, Dava Sobel, explains, "Any sailor worth his salt can gauge his latitude . . . by the length of the day, or by the height of the sun or known guide stars above the horizon." In contrast, the measurement of "longitude meridians . . . is tempered by time. To learn one's longitude at sea, one needs to know what time it is aboard ship and also the time at the home port or another place of known longitude—at that very same moment." This presented a problem, as "[p]recise knowledge of the hour in two different places at once . . . was utterly unattainable up to and including the era of pendulum clocks."[92] The problem of gauging longitude at sea was perceived as so important to the welfare of Britain that the British Parliament offered a £20,000 prize for its discovery in 1714, a huge sum at the time. While the solution was expected to come from astronomy, it was eventually achieved with the invention of a chronometer accurate enough to keep true time over a long voyage, perfected by the engineer John Harrison in 1759. On Cook's second voyage, one of his duties was to test this new tool, which would delight him with its accuracy.

In Sobel's account, navigators before Harrison's chronometer relied on faith, superstition, and luck to get to where they wanted to go. In fact, however, they supplemented the deficiency in technology with nuanced, though partial, techniques of what was called "reckoning," calling on different kinds of knowledge ranging from mathematics to common sense. Familiarity with such diverse techniques was essential, and their details were advertised as a selling point in practical literature in the seventeenth and eighteenth centuries. When Champlain summarized his treatise on the title page of his *Voyages de la Nouvelle France*, he emphasized that it included "the skills and qualifications required of a good and perfect Navigator to know the different kinds of reckoning that are found in Navigation. The Indices and signs that God's Providence put in the Seas to help Mariners rectify their route, without which they would fall into great dangers."[93] In addition to describing useful mathematical and astronomical measurements, Champlain explained the importance of observing weather, tides, and currents, the sand hauled up from the bottom, plants, and animals. When a mariner in the Northwest Atlantic spotted seabirds called murres, he knew he was approaching the Great Banks, where they flocked. Common sense, too, came into play. For instance, the mariner should always "overestimate rather than underestimate the distance traversed," so as not to approach land unprepared.[94]

Measurements and observations were recorded in the ship's log, then cross-checked before the navigator came up with a best guess about position and pricked it on the marine chart.[95] This process of reckoning often yielded results that were surprisingly accurate. Champlain termed the human faculty at issue in the craft of reckoning *fantaisie*, by which he meant something quite different from the Romantic notion of the imagination as an escape from everyday reality. Rather, Champlain described a pragmatic imagination that negotiated uncertainty to approach the real, resting on calculation, but also integrating experience and a kind of tact. The English word "conjecture," used by Champlain's English translator, was frequently associated with this exercise of the pragmatic imagination in science, and it is found in maritime contexts as well. In his use of the word *estime*, reckoning, Champlain underscored that it was a finely tuned art developed to contend with the absence of some basic information: "But if the navigator were certain of his course he would not have to take a reckoning, but would specify rather the exact spot where the vessel is when he would wish to prick his chart."[96]

With Harrison's chronometer, the safety of navigation radically improved. And yet, uncertainty still remained, along with the fine art of reckoning. Well into the nineteenth century, not every captain could afford a chronometer, and even when its use became widespread, celestial navigation was still an artisanal enterprise, attended by grave consequences in the event of human error. The anthropologist Edwin Hutchins anatomizes the laborious process of locating a ship even in the early 1990s, before GPS. Essential to this process were diverse kinds of information to confirm bearings, even while such navigation was radically more precise than navigation in the era of global sail, not only before but also after the invention of the marine chronometer. Hutchins cites a Navy protocol instructing the navigation officer to obtain position fixes from a number of different sources: visual bearings, radar ranges, radar bearings, fathometer, and so on.[97] As he puts it, "[t]he tools of navigation share with one another a rich network of mutual computational and representational dependencies."[98] But with the widespread use of GPS, Hutchins predicted, this interdependent network would fade from importance. And indeed, although in 2002, an authoritative practical treatise charges the mariner not to "rely solely on electronic systems . . . [which] are always subject to failure" and "never [to] forget that the safety of his ship and crew may depend on skills that differ little from those practiced generations ago," this counsel simultaneously attests to the demise of navigational skills that once would have been indispensable.[99] The finely tuned art of navigation so admirable in craft, that is to say, flourishes in conditions of lack, compensating for deficiencies in knowledge.

Conrad noted the pathos of this dynamic in *The Mirror of the Sea*: "[T]he special call of an art which has passed away is never reproduced. It is as utterly gone out of the world as the song of a destroyed wild bird."[100] Conrad's eulogy for craft in *The Mirror of the Sea* diagnoses a fundamental self-negating dynamic in the modern pursuit of the new. For the pragmatic mariner of the future, as Conrad recognized, craft's heroism was ancient history. "In his own time a man is always very modern," Conrad observed. "The seamen of three hundred years hence will . . . glance at the photogravures of our nearly defunct sailing-ships with a cold, inquisitive, and indifferent eye."[101]

PRACTICAL REASON (SEVENTH CENTURY BC–AD 2010)

When the Frankfurt School philosophers Theodor Adorno and Max Horkheimer characterized Enlightenment as the project of domination ("What men want to learn from nature is how to use it in order wholly to dominate it and other men"), they named Odysseus as the harbinger of Enlightenment reason.[102] Among the triumphs of Odyssean reason, they distinguished his encounter with the Sirens. Here is the Siren episode in its translation by George Chapman, published in 1614 from "the heart of a maritime culture," as Jonathan Raban observes[103]:

> . . . Up then flew
> My friends to worke; strooke sail, together drew,
> And under hatches stow'd them: sat, and plied
> Their polisht oares; and did in curls divide
> The white-head waters. My part then came on;
> A mighty waxen Cake, I set upon;

Chopt it in fragments, with my sword; and wrought
With strong hand, every peece, till all were soft.
The great powre of the Sunne, in such a beame
As then flew burning from his Diademe,
To liquefaction helpt us. Orderlie,
I stopt their [the crew's] eares; and they, as faire did ply
My feete, and hands with cords; and to the Mast
With other halsers, made me soundly fast.[104]

In the view of Adorno and Horkheimer, this episode shows Odysseus
wreaking the disenchantment of myth using bourgeois abstraction. In pitting his human cunning against the Sirens' supernatural wiles, Odysseus
disregards the Sirens' mythical specificity, and makes all forces fungible,
equalizing humans and the gods. In the words of Adorno and Horkheimer
cited in the introduction, "The wily solitary is already *homo œconomicus*,
for whom all reasonable things are alike, hence the Odyssey is already
a *Robinsonade*."[105] Further anticipating bourgeois reason is Odysseus's
reliance on a Cartesian division of labor to effect his plan. Odysseus is
immobilized, lashed to the mast, to consume the Siren's seductive song,
while the deaf crew do the hard, physical work of propelling the ship.
To use Hegel's terms for this division of labor that would be taken up by
Marxian thinkers, Odysseus assumes the stance of the lord, leaving the
manipulation of the material world to his stupefied bondsmen.

Adorno and Horkheimer's diagnosis of Enlightenment reason's ability
to wreak disaster is indisputable. At the same time, Enlightenment reason
is not a monolithic, monophonic episteme. As regards Odysseus, specifically, their diagnosis does not do justice to aspects of Odyssean cunning
that anticipate the craft of the modern mariner, as well as other kinds of
excellence in action, which are as much a part of Enlightenment reason
as bourgeois abstraction.[106] There are multiple aspects of Odysseus's passage by the island of the Sirens that fall out of Adorno and Horkheimer's
reductive account. First of all, in this episode, Odysseus is not a wily
solitary, but rather a commander distributing tasks in an exceptionally
dangerous navigation, in keeping with craft's hierarchical collectivity and
respecting protocol: "Orderlie I stopt their eares."[107] Odysseus's intelligence is physical; he shows himself "robust and alert [*dispos*], with good
sea legs, inured to hardship and toil."[108] In the Siren episode, Homer depicts his palpable physical might in chopping a large cake of wax. His
embodiment is also palpable when Homer emphasizes how strongly his
men bind his body with cables, and how he strains against them.

Odysseus furthermore differs from his portrait by Adorno and Horkheimer in how he devises a path through seemingly impassable waters. He
does so through creative jury-rigging and technological improvisation,

not by language or logic-chopping: finding the escape clause in a contract is Adorno and Horkheimer's legalistic phrase for Odysseus's trick with the Cyclops. When Odysseus has himself lashed to the mast with the ship's cables ("halsers"), he ingeniously refunctions shipboard technology, similar to Cook's fothering. When Odysseus softens the wax with the sun, he presses into his service the great and potentially destructive forces of nature, like Cook exploiting the shifting tides. Such creative, situation-specific remedies devised by Odysseus the mariner are far from the "leveling domination of abstraction" that "makes everything in nature repeatable," just as they are not identical with a paradigm of work offered by "industry (for which abstraction ordains repetition)."[109] The Edge zone of the Sirens' island is unique, and it takes some imagination to conceive of another situation where earplugs and hawsers used as physical restraints are the key to survival.

Finally, in taking on the navigation of the Sirens' island, Odysseus is more open-endedly curious, rather than avid for knowledge that can be monetized and pressed into bourgeois relations of exchange. For Odysseus, the navigation of the Sirens' island turns out to yield the opportunity to hear the Sirens' song of everything that has happened in the world. This navigation also affords knowledge of the contours of an unknown coast, though Odysseus, in this point similar to Captain Cook, did not conceptualize the pleasure that naturally results from being the first discoverer, even were it of nothing more than sands and shoals.

Adorno and Horkheimer's failure to grasp Odysseus's distinctively saltwater skills may reflect the twentieth-century "hydrophasia" identified in the introduction. Marxian thinkers, indeed, evince this hydrophasia dating back to the nineteenth century, as Allan Sekula observes, from the time Frederick Engels began *The Condition of the Working Class in England* by inviting his readers to turn their eyes from the majestic sailing ships on the Thames connoting British imperial grandeur to the hovels and poverty of the London slums.[110] Certainly, Adorno and Horkheimer's account of Odysseus evinces their high philosophical prejudices. For all their distaste for Enlightenment, Adorno and Horkheimer perpetuate a key feature of Cartesian models of knowledge: the privilege accorded the mind over the body, attended by the denigration of embodiment, applied knowledge, and practical reason. To view Odysseus as a harbinger of bourgeois *ratio*, Adorno and Horkheimer must turn a blind eye to those aspects of Odysseus's intelligence that are not abstract. They then take him to task for an abstraction that in fact marks the limits of their own perspective.

The Odyssey does not tell us what happened to the Sirens after Odysseus heard their song, Adorno and Horkheimer note, suggesting that in tragedy, these mythic forces would shrivel up and disappear, for their era had come to an end. When James Cook and his expedition came upon the Great Barrier Reef, they would survive its dangers and then locate it on European charts of the world. This achievement had plural yields. Even as Cook's navigation made the ocean safer for global transport, such transport is part of a history of technological advancement, with benefits but also destruction, such as environmental pollution. At the turn of the twenty-first century, this pollution threatens to destroy the existence of the Great Barrier Reef itself, as global warming is in the process of devastating the world's coral.

The craft of the mariner is one strand in the entangled, multivalent formation we call modern reason. Craft manifested an admirable, at times incredible, ability to navigate situations of great danger and risk with limited resources. With concerns of safety and knowledge paramount, craft eschewed ideology in favor of pragmatism, and indeed, the writings of Dampier, Cook, and their colleagues on unfamiliar indigenous peoples were at moments remarkably sober and nonjudgmental. At the same time, the mariner utilized craft in service of profit and conquest; the world of the ship was violent; and as we shall see in sea adventure fiction, the heroism of the mariner was pressed into ideological and cultural work for nationalism and capitalism back on land. To add yet another twist, even as the mariner served domination, craft called on capacities with the potential to open lines of escape. These capacities include the power of embodied reason, creative improvisation, and the honor of labor.

To tease apart the different strands of modern reason should be an aim of cultural analysis, both in order to do justice to the complexity of historical practice and to enrich our repertoire of creative action. Under the shadow of the Holocaust and the atom bomb, Adorno and Horkheimer vindicated the intransigence of theory that kept thought alive at a conjuncture when the passage from ideals to their realization had disappeared. More modest than the intransigence of theory, craft models another posture that might yield safety in the jaws of destruction. Flexible and pragmatic, this adaptive capacity is ready to utilize any expedient that fits the situation, be it patient waiting, following prior wisdom, bold gestures, or creative jury-rigging with sheep dung, oakum, and canvas.

CHAPTER 2

Remarkable Occurrences at Sea and in the Novel

> With the discovery of gunpowder the individual passion of
> battle was lost. The romantic impulse towards a casual kind
> of bravery passed into other adventures . . . the exploration of
> the earth, or the discovery of the passage to the East Indies.
> America was discovered, its treasures and people—nature,
> man himself; navigation was the higher romance of commerce.
> The present world was again present to man as worthy of the
> interests of mind; thinking mind was again capable of action.
> —G.W.F. Hegel, "Modern Philosophy, Introduction,"
> in *Lectures on the History of Philosophy*[1]

DANIEL DEFOE, who helped invent the modern novel, was a writer
deeply familiar with the maritime book. Defoe counted forty-nine volumes of overseas travel literature in his personal library and across his
career penned works inspired by a number of saltwater genres.[2] Narrow escapes both on land and sea figured in his version of the account
of God's Providence amidst disasters: *The Storm: Or, a Collection of
the most Remarkable Casualties and Disasters which happen'd in the
Late Dreadful Tempest both by Sea and Land* (1704)—recalling Calvinist shipwreck narratives like James Janeway's *Legacy to his Friend*
(1674).[3] Defoe wrote an imaginary voyage narrative in 1725 that simply
appropriated the title of Dampier's celebrated nonfictional *A New Voyage Round the World*, though Defoe then offered a variation when he
continued *By a Course never sailed before*. Scholars believe that Defoe
coauthored and very possibly was the sole author of *A General History
of the Pyrates* (1724), a popular and enduring collection of pirates' biographies inspired by Alexandre Exquemelin's best-selling *The Buccaneers
of America*, using the pen name of Captain Johnson. And Defoe echoed
the title of the famous book of global sea charts by John Seller, the *Atlas
Maritimus* (1672), as well as the collection of world maps in the *Atlas
Geographus* by his contemporary, the preeminent marine cartographer
Hermann Moll. Defoe's publication was entitled the *Atlas Maritimus
& Commercialis* (1728), and it offered a defense of English imperial
expansion.

Defoe's association of his writing with the maritime print corpus was a bid for popularity and prestige. He allied himself with the best-selling practices of his time seeking to earn literary celebrity, a well-recognized behavior of authors that the sociologist Pierre Bourdieu has theorized in *The Rules of Art*. Defoe was to win most acclaim, of course, for his invention of a new poetics of adventure out of the mariner's craft in *The Life and Strange Surprising Adventures of Robinson Crusoe of York, Mariner* (1719). Defoe's invention quickly inspired other writers, and the sub-genre of sea adventure fiction that I call the maritime picaresque spread in the 1720s to 1740s, practiced by such well-known writers as Alain René Le Sage, the Abbé Prévost, and Tobias Smollett.

In this chapter, I trace how Defoe wrought his new poetics of adventure from the mariner's ethos of craft and its representation in the maritime book. Defoe's *Robinson Crusoe* has long been valued as the forerunner of modern realism, with its detailed interest in describing the empirical world and its emerging focus on psychology in the admittedly rather simplified protagonist. The view from the ship's deck, in contrast, yields a vision of the novel's fiction-making not as the re-presentation of reality, but rather as the reality of that representation—and that reality is the performance of skilled labor. Across Robinson Crusoe's travails, we see Defoe's mariner hero solving problems by exhibiting the admirable, heterogeneous capacities of the compleat mariner. At the same time, Defoe's poetics offers readers an entertaining way to shadow the protagonist's deeds, inviting them to exercise a playful version of the pragmatic imagination: the armchair sailor's conjecture (*fantaisie*).

CRUSOE OF YORK, MARINER

Robinson Crusoe is a tale of a mariner's epic survival relying on the empowered agency of craft. Crusoe has raw ambition but lacks the competence and the demeanor of a seaman. As he describes himself, he is an unskilled young man with the "[i]nclination" to run away to sea, impelled by "rambling Thoughts" and "the wild and indigested Notion of raising my Fortune."[4] But rather than fortune, Crusoe's first hapless forays bring him "Misfortune" until Crusoe apprentices himself to the collectivity of craft, embodied in an "honest" sea captain who makes his living trading with West Africa (13, 14). The sea captain shows Crusoe how to realize a profit from a voyage to Guinea and gives him an education that sounds like the cut–and–pasted title of a contemporary practical manual, consisting of: "a competent Knowledge of the Mathematicks and the Rules of Navigation . . . how to keep an Account of the Ship's Course, take an Observation; and in short . . . some things that were needful to be understood by a Sailor" (14). At the point in the novel when Crusoe refuses his father's advice to stick to the comforts of "the middle state" (5) and life at home, Crusoe lays the blame on his rash and imprudent nature. However, Crusoe's apprenticeship with the sea captain reveals that Crusoe is able to heed advice when it suits his design to profit from high-risk overseas speculation, and this education makes him "in a word . . . a Sailor and a Merchant" (14).

Armed with the Captain's education, Crusoe strikes out on his own to profit from the African trade following the Captain's death. On his first voyage, he is taken prisoner, and sold into slavery in Sallee. The events of Crusoe's captivity and subsequent escape show him transformed from apprentice to master of the craft. During his two long years in captivity, Crusoe evinces the mariner's consummate prudence and patience, meditating on "nothing but my Escape; and what Method I might take to effect it, but found no Way that had the least Probability in it: Nothing presented to make the Supposition of it rational . . . so that for two Years, tho' I often pleased my self with the Imagination, yet I never had the least encouraging Prospect of putting it in Practice" (16). The enslaved Crusoe's patience is finally rewarded when his master outfits a small boat. Sensing a moment of opportunity, *chairos*, Crusoe exhibits the bold willingness to risk all: "resolution." At this critical moment, he springs into action with his "sea legs," hijacks the boat, and navigates his way to freedom along the African coast.

Having been tested in the Atlantic crucible, Crusoe is then ready for a trial yet more extreme: lonely shipwreck on an Edge zone of the modern world, furnished only with the materials he can salvage from the wreck. In his ability to use these materials to jury-rig a comfortable existence, as well as finally to escape, he exercises the mariner's craft to accomplish an extraordinary, epic deed. To achieve success, Crusoe calls on craft's compleat competences, such as a knowledge of geography, arms, shipbuilding, and carpentry. He also exercises craft's human traits, notably prudence, patience, protocol, embodiment, resolution, jury-rigging, and the pragmatic imagination.

To frame Crusoe as a crafty mariner is to give a rather different description of this compelling character than as a model of *homo economicus*: the essence of what makes us human defined as the search to maximize well-being through "[r]ational scrutiny of one's own economic interest."[5] Marx first formulated this view in *Capital*, and its most extensive and influential account for literary criticism was by Ian Watt, who explained Crusoe as "the dynamic tendency of capitalism itself." This dynamism is "Crusoe's 'original sin,'" which precipitates his island purgatory.[6] As Watt reads the novel, the island exile transforms Crusoe from a sinning prodigal into a hardworking, calculating entrepreneur. Watt reads the novel's version of capitalism in the footsteps of Max Weber as well, casting Crusoe's transformation as a secularized, economic version of Bunyan's narrative of redemption in *The Pilgrim's Progress*. As a result of Crusoe's reform, *homo economicus* is rewarded for his efforts with a kingdom produced from the state of nature. As Watt wrote, "Defoe sets back the economic clock, and takes his hero to a primitive environment, where labor can be presented as varied and inspiring, and where . . . there is an absolute equivalence between individual effort and individual reward."[7]

Given the influence of this view of Crusoe as *homo economicus*, it is worth underscoring aspects of Crusoe's story that take on more coherence within a maritime frame. For critics who view the island as a myth of the genesis of capitalism from a state of nature, the toolbox and other goods salvaged from the wreck trouble the moral, and show the novel's ideological sleight of hand.[8] However, from Magellan's expedition as portrayed by Pigafetta to Cook and Shackleton, mariners used limited but well-adapted European technology epitomized by Crusoe's toolbox to survive the sometimes harsh, desolate, and unimaginable conditions of the maritime frontier. Crusoe's island is a laboratory of limits rather than origins: it figures the Edge zones of expanding modernity.[9]

In addition, though *Robinson Crusoe* may seem to convince us of the profit from Crusoe's rational, moderate island economy, this economy is not the source of his reward of wealth at the novel's end. Rather, Crusoe survives on the island thanks to the mariner's craft, which leads to his rescue as well. Fabulous profit comes only when he finally returns home, gets his hands on the goods and accounts of his plantations in the Brasils that have prospered in his absence, and almost dies from "the sudden Surprize of Joy" (205).

What Crusoe does with his fortune at the novel's end is yet another problem with the account of Crusoe as a repentant *homo economicus*. Upon rescue and return to England, Crusoe announces plans to settle down, but then abiding fascination with risk and danger prevail. He tells us, "my Wife dying, and my Nephew coming Home with good Success from a Voyage to *Spain*, my Inclination to go Abroad, and his Importunity prevailed and engag'd me to go in his Ship, as a private Trader to the *East Indies*" (219). Some influential readings have tried to explain this inveterate "rambling" disposition as archaic: Crusoe's longing for the time of Drake or Frobisher, though when the novel was published "[t]he times were too prosaic in England . . . for the bourgeoisie to make anything of Defoe/Robinson's drive toward adventure."[10] In contrast, Defoe offers a fable of "materially productive labor" and its potential to gratify the common Englishman.[11] However, in point of fact, in 1719, the Western adventure of global seafaring was at its height. This was at the dawn of the exploration of the Pacific, which would unfold across the eighteenth century. The myth of a great Southern continent at the bottom of the globe still persisted, and the ability to calculate exact position at sea over the course of a traverse was still unknown. The sea was moreover a frontier of war and capitalism, as well as of contemporary literature. When *Robinson Crusoe* was published, Defoe was competing with the best-selling overseas travel literature depicting pioneering navigations of his present, some by the mariners themselves, such as *A New Voyage Round the World* by William Dampier (1697), Edward Cooke's *A Voyage to the South Seas* (1712), and Woodes Rogers's *A Cruising Voyage Round the World* (1712). Defoe's contemporary, the Third Earl of Shaftesbury, was referring to the success of such adventures *of their own times* when he called overseas voyage narratives "in our present days, what *Books of Chivalry* were, in those of our Forefathers."[12]

HOW TO SUCCEED IN SPECULATION: SAILOR AND MERCHANT

The ideological work of *Robinson Crusoe*, for critics who read it as a fable of *homo economicus*, is to vindicate the power of bourgeois *ratio*, exorcising the risk intrinsic to capitalist profit by banishing it to an early moment in capitalist exploitation. If we reframe Crusoe as a crafty navigator, rather than *homo economicus*, the novel continues to grapple with the problem of capitalism's split personality but solves the dangers of high-risk speculation in a different way. Risk is no longer a stage on the way to a more rational, moderate form of capitalist behavior modeled by the reformed sinner. Rather, high-risk activities are endemic to the capitalist pursuit of profit, and the problem becomes how to undertake them with the best chance of success. The craft of the mariner exemplifies the human comportment to be followed that gives profoundly uncertain undertakings with a great chance of failure the best possibility for a positive outcome. As Crusoe—transformed by the honest sea captain into "a Sailor and a Merchant"—well knows, the ethos of craft contains traits translatable from navigators to speculators (14). Crusoe's plantations in the Brasils prosper because before leaving to go on his ill-fated slave-trading voyage, he arranges his affairs with the mariner's "Caution" and "Prudence" (31).

How to succeed in high-risk speculation was a problem that preoccupied Defoe from the first work of his career as a writer, which spanned the take-off of the London stock market. (*Robinson Crusoe* was, indeed, published just one year before the South Sea Bubble of 1720.)[13] This work was *An Essay upon Projects* (1697) that contoured the exuberant, in some cases extravagant, speculations distinctive to Defoe's era. As *An Essay upon Projects* analyzed a notion then on everyone's lips, the project was an innovative, in some cases purely fantastic, plan to generate surplus value from emerging technologies and expanding global markets. Though projects were dangerous and many lost money, projectors "do really every day produce new Contrivances, Engines, and Projects to get Money, never before thought of."[14] Given the projecting spirit's potential for profit, Defoe was intrigued by how to harness its unruly energy.

Perhaps it was possible to differentiate between successful and fantastical projects, Defoe speculated, from the time they first were conceived. Defoe's essay explored the distinction between "Invention upon honest foundations, and to fair purposes" and "Innumerable Conceptions which dye in the bringing forth, and (like Abortions of the Brain) only come into the Air, and dissolve." Such chimeras were conceived by a "meer Projector," a man "driven by his own desperate Fortune to such a Streight that he must be deliver'd by a Miracle, or Starve; and when he has beat his Brains for some such Miracle in vain, he finds no remedy but to paint up some Bauble or other, *as Players make Puppets talk big*, to show like a strange thing, and then cry it up for a New Invention, gets a Patent for it, divides it into Shares, and *they must be Sold*."[15]

But at the same time, Defoe was fascinated by a project that succeeded against all odds: "there is a kind of Honesty a Man owes to himself and to his Family that prohibits him throwing away his Estate in impracticable, improbable Adventures; but still some hit even of the most unlikely." Defoe was referring here to "Sir *William Phips*, who brought home a Cargo of Silver of near 200,000 *l. sterling*, in Pieces of Eight, fished up out of the open Sea remote from any shore, from an old *Spanish* ship which had been sunk above Forty Years." Phips's speculation was "a mere Project, a Lottery of a Hundred thousand to One odds; a hazard which, if it had failed, everybody would have been ashamed to have owned themselves concerned in; a Voyage that would have been as much ridiculed as Don Quixote's *Adventure upon the Windmill*." As Defoe represented Phips's projecting, it differed from fiction only because of its outcome: "but it had Success, and who reflects upon the Project?"[16]

Though Defoe does not make this point in *An Essay upon Projects*, Phips in fact succeeded because he prosecuted his enterprise with craft. Phips's familiarity with the marine environment reached back to his childhood: one of 26 children in Kennebec, Maine, Phips started his career as a shipbuilder, and then became a sea captain before coming to London and taking up projecting in the 1680s. (Phips was to end up as governor of Massachusetts.) In his treasure hunt, Phips went after specific sunken ships, and to find them, he consulted those who had served aboard them or been involved in their wreck. Thus, the chief patron in his successful expedition was Sir John Narbrough, a preeminent overseas explorer, who was an admiral by the 1680s when Phips took up his search. "According to the Spanish ambassador in England . . . Narbrough's interest [in prospecting for sunken treasure] stemmed from the period in the 1650s when he had served in the Caribbean," and Narbrough had gained information from a pilot of a Spanish galleon wrecked in the 1640s.[17] Phips may further have obtained valuable information about the possible location of the galleon from the Caribbean pirate Captain Bartholomew Sharp (who figures in *The Buccaneers of America* as well as in Dampier's *New Voyage Round the World*).[18]

The feat of Phips is posed as a conundrum in *An Essay upon Projects*, though there are a number of moments when *An Essay upon Projects* connects mariners and maritime inventions to success in high-risk projecting.[19] In *Robinson Crusoe*, in contrast, Defoe answers the riddle. In evaluating a project's practicability, do not consider the risks of the project itself, but rather the character of the projector. The project undertaken by the projector with the demeanor of craft offers the best chance of success. This moral helps explain why the faults ascribed to Crusoe when he first sets out to seek his fortune are those of what *An Essay upon Projects* calls a "meer Projector": a wild speculator who depends for the outcome of his designs on chance. Indeed, when Crusoe's father objects to his son's plans to go to sea, he qualifies his son with one of Defoe's synonyms for the "meer Projector" in *An Essay upon Projects*: "men of desperate Fortunes" (4–5).

Five years after *Robinson Crusoe*, Defoe was to return to craft as a model for how to prosecute high-risk endeavor in his *Complete English Tradesman* (1725), a practical manual for business people. There, Defoe repeatedly used the sea as a figure for the risks of trade, as, for example, when he cautioned creditors to exercise similar "prudence" in extending credit as that exercised in an "adventure by sea." Defoe also admonished the merchant always to be on his guard against "assurance and overconfidence of his knowledge," no matter how great his experience, citing a recent shipwreck where the mariner's characteristic prudence had been lacking on the part of an "old experienc'd pilot": the "fatal disaster in which Sir *Cloudesly Shovel*, and so many hundred brave fellows, lost their lives in a moment upon the Rocks of *Scilly*," a familiar shoal right off the English coast, after returning from a naval victory over the French in 1707. "He that is above informing himself when he is in danger, is above pity when he miscarries," Defoe concluded.[20]

Defoe participated in the discourse of his age when he invoked the mariner's comportment as a model for financial speculations. This association dates at least as far back as Richard Hakluyt's *Principal Navigations, Voyages, and Traffiques of the English Nation* to cite the title of the second edition (1598) that joined the career of mariner and global merchant in its accounts of bold and canny travelers who have "adventured their persons, ships, and goods."[21] The alliance between mariner and entrepreneur was occasioned by the historical overlap of the two activities—the oceans of the globe were a frontier of capitalist speculation—along with their resemblances. This powerful symbiotic alliance persisted across the global age of sail. In 1821, Hegel yoked "the [watery] element of flux, danger, and destruction" with "the passion for gain," when he called the ocean the "natural element for industry, animating its outward movement."[22] Long after craft disappeared, the icons of maritime modernity would return to figure practices at the frontier of capitalist risk. During the 1990s, entrepreneurs and advertisers called on images of tall ships, names of explorers, and the rhetoric of navigation to market the virtual seas of the Internet, along with the expanding universe of mutual funds that emerged as online information and trading democratized access to the stock market.

From Remarkable Occurrence into Adventure Novel

In *Robinson Crusoe*, the mariner tames the projecting spirit to the point of mooring the notion of adventure itself to the written protocols of craft. At the time Defoe wrote, Nerlich observes that adventure had a volatile significance, as at no other moment in its history. Across Crusoe's narrative, this rambling protagonist tries on its different meanings. When Crusoe first identifies himself as a "young Adventurer," he is using the word to designate dangerous undertakings whose outcome depends on chance (7). This kind of adventure characterizes the chimerical imaginings of a "meer Projector." Once Crusoe has been made by the honest sea captain into sailor and merchant, Crusoe's adventures become calculated overseas speculations: he makes a "small Adventure," taking from London about "40 *l.* in . . . Toys and Trifles," which Crusoe then sells for a profit on the gold coast of West Africa. Following the Captain's advice, his speculation bears fruit, and he returns with "5.9 *Ounces* of Gold Dust for my Adventure, which yielded me in *London* at my Return, almost 300 *l.*" (14).

When Crusoe returns after his North African captivity, in contrast, adventure becomes "a full Account of all my Adventures, my Slavery, Escape, and how I had met with the *Portugal* Captain at Sea" (28). Once Crusoe becomes a perfect mariner, adventure is transformed from high-risk speculation to an account of his voyages penned after the fact. And adventure will retain this sense of the mariner's written retrospective narrative of his travels until the novel's end.

As Crusoe's final use of "adventure" would suggest, Defoe does indeed model his mariner hero's adventures on mariners' historical accounts of their travels so popular with a general readership of the time. More specifically, Defoe is interested in one aspect of these accounts: the remarkable occurrences offering a danger and the remedy taken by the crafty mariner. As I mentioned in the previous chapter, these remarkable occurrences derived from a category in the mariner's logbook format, figuring prominently in mariners' accounts and also beloved by armchair sailors. Remarkable occurrences of dangers and remedies are the stuff of Crusoe's "adventures" as well, viz his characterization of his adventure narrative as incorporating "my Slavery"—danger—and "Escape"—the remedy.[23]

When Defoe offered his view of travel accounts by mariner-authors in the preface to his *New Voyage Round the World, By a Course never sailed before* (1725), he singled out their remarkable occurrences as the fit subject matter for a good tale, including "Landings, their Diversions, the Accidents which happen'd to them, or to others, by their Means. The Stories of their Engagement, when they have had any Scuffle either with Natives or *European* Enemies . . . the Storms and Difficulties at Sea or on Shore."[24] Once we understand Defoe's interest in deriving an exciting adventure narrative from remarkable occurrences, we can hear this category resonating even in "the strange" and "surprising" of *Robinson Crusoe*'s full title.[25] In mariners' accounts of the early modern era, "strange" and "surprising" are synonyms for remarkable dangers.[26]

At the same time, *Robinson Crusoe* works a more extensive transformation on mariner-authors' modes of narration; a transformation that remediates a defect Defoe would point out six years later in the preface to his *New Voyage Round the World, By a Course never sailed before*. There, Defoe objected that despite the extraordinary and compelling content of remarkable occurrences, mariner-authors squandered the dramatic interest of their plots. The reason for this disappointment, in Defoe's diagnosis, was that mariner-authors did not narrate these episodes in satisfying fashion, presenting their occurrences "superficially and by Halves."[27] With this dissatisfaction, Defoe refers to the fact that the remarkable occurrences in mariners' narratives were communicated in a fashion that was understated and compressed. The compression was in keeping with the economy of plain style and served the professional audience for such narratives; what this audience valued in the remarkable occurrence was the nature of the danger and how to contend with it. Another aspect of their construction perhaps contributing to Defoe's dissatisfaction may have been the convention of the "mixt relation," to echo the term used by Dampier, when he apologized for his "mixt Relation of places and Actions."[28] Mariners' accounts were characterized by the uncategorized enumeration of anything noteworthy presented in the order in which it was encountered during the voyage.

Could one give a "full Relation" of remarkable occurrences, Defoe mused, it would produce an "Account of . . . [a] voyage, differing from all that I had ever seen before, in the nature of the Observations, as well as the manner of relating them; And this perfectly new in its Form."[29] In penning the phrase "full Relation," did Defoe echo, whether by design or chance, Crusoe's "*full Account* of all my Adventures, my Slavery, Escape, and how I had met with the *Portugal* Captain at Sea" (28; my emphasis)? In any case, Defoe had already accomplished in *Robinson Crusoe*'s new poetics of adventure just the improvements he called for six years later in *A New Voyage Round the World, By a Course never siled before*.

Several aesthetic modifications were key for how Defoe amplified the remarkable occurrences of nonfictional maritime texts. First of all, Defoe focused each episode around a single deed, substituting for the mixt relation the neoclassical unity of action. In addition, Defoe amplified in each remarkable occurrence the danger, but even more, the process by which a remedy was found, spinning out the steps of Crusoe's problem-solving. The effect of this amplification is to emphasize the difficulties of the process and enable the reader to savor the mastery of the character who can overcome them. It also dilates the duration of a narration to give the reader time to process just how extraordinary are the remarkable occurrences and their solutions. Such time for processing is lacking in mariners' narratives, and this makes them, as I mentioned in the previous chapter, more exciting to reread than to read.

With these aesthetic innovations (unity of action and adventures of problem-solution), Defoe attenuates the professional function of both the mixt relation and the compressed description of the remarkable danger. The mixt relation derives from the mariners' working journals at the basis of their retrospective histories. Within a 24-hour entry, the mariner would note diverse kinds of information: episode weather, conditions, remarkable occurrences, and any detail that might be useful or that simply transgressed habitual expectation. (This last usage of "remarkable" is the one discussed by historians of early modern science.) These details might not serve the episode or the expedition, but they could inform future mariners who would use the narrative in their own travels.

The kinds of information offered in the remarkable occurrence, too, served the collectivity of craft. For mariners, what was paramount was how a danger came about and how it was solved, as this information could help other voyagers who would use such accounts to navigate in their wake. The mistakes and thought processes en route to a remedy spun out by Crusoe mattered for historical mariners only if they could warn of actions to avoid. In his preface to *A New Voyage Round the World* Defoe, in contrast, specifically dismissed the interest for most readers of details to the craft. There, he takes to task mariner-authors for filling their accounts with "Directions for Sailors coming that way, the Bearing of the Land, the Depth of the Channels, Entrances, and Barrs, at the several Ports,

Anchorage in the Bays, and Creeks, and the like Things, useful indeed for Seamen going thither again, *and how few are they?* but not at all to the Purpose when we come expecting to find the History of the Voyage."[30]

Not shy about the importance of his innovation, Defoe himself gives us a lesson within the text of *Robinson Crusoe* for how he has transformed his sources in the maritime book. This lesson occurs when Crusoe narrates the same adventure twice, in a retrospective first-person narrative and in a fragment of a journal, which, he tells us, he abandoned when he then ran out of pen and ink. Since this journal duplicates information, it has presented a critical puzzle. Ian Watt, J. Paul Hunter, and John Richetti, among others, have connected Crusoe's journals to Protestant spiritual autobiographies, and Crusoe's way of taking account of his soul has also been linked to merchants' techniques of bookkeeping.[31] Michael McKeon explains the journal as "not unlike that of Cervantes's narrative vertigo," indicating Crusoe's "subjective volatility" and "the way in which things as usual have come to be suspended on the island."[32] However, from the viewpoint of the maritime corpus, the journal pastiched in *Robinson Crusoe* resembles mariners' use of the journal format in their retrospective narratives of their accomplishments, and notably the journal form used by Defoe's best-selling contemporary, William Dampier.

To see how closely Defoe adheres to the journal convention, consider this brief entry from April 1681 in Dampier's *New Voyage Round the World*:

> We lay here all the Day, and scrubb'd our new Bark, that if ever we should be chased we might the better escape: we fill'd our Water, and in the Evening went from thence, having the Wind at S.W. a brisk gale.
>
> The 25th Day we had much Wind and Rain, and we lost the Canoa that had been cut and was joined together; we would have kept all our Canoas to carry us up the River, the Bark not being so convenient.
>
> The 27th Day we went from thence with a moderate gale of Wind at S.W. In the Afternoon we had excessive Showers of Rain.
>
> The 28th Day was very wet all the Morning; betwixt 10 and 11 it cleared up, and we saw two great Ships about a League and the half to Westward of us, we being then two Leagues from the shore, and about 10 Leagues to the Southward of point *Garrachina*. These Ships had been cruising between *Gorgonia* and the Gulf 6 Months; but whether our Prisoners did know it I cannot tell. (12–13)

Now compare it to Robinson Crusoe's fictional journal from the end of December 1659:

> *Dec.* 28, 29, 30. Great Heats and no Breeze; so that there was no Stirring abroad, except in the Evening for Food; this Time I spent in putting all my Things in Order within Doors.

January 1. Very hot still, but I went abroad early and late with my Gun, and lay still in the Middle of the Day; this Evening going farther into the Valleys which lay towards the Center of the Island, I found there was plenty of Goats, tho' exceeding shy and hard to come at, however I resolv'd to try if I could not bring my Dog to hunt them down.

Jan. 2. Accordingly, the next Day, I went out with my Dog, and set him upon the Goats; but I was mistaken, for they all fac'd about upon the Dog, and he knew his Danger too well, for he would not come near them. (56)

Both passages register conditions, activities, and challenges, as well as remedies. Both Crusoe and Dampier use what might be called a *near past* tense, oriented to the 24-hour period of the daily journal entry. Both employ the mariner's workmanlike "plain style," retaining technical details but toning them down for a more general public.

Crusoe is here starting to describe his struggle to hunt goats in order to solve his problem of how to feed himself on his island. When this struggle moves from the journal to Crusoe's retrospective first-person narrative, Defoe groups actions related to goat-hunting together, as the unity of action supersedes the mixt relation:

I presently discover'd that there were Goats in the Island, which was a great Satisfaction to me; but then it was attended with this Misfortune to me, *viz.* That they were so shy, so subtile, and so swift of Foot, that it was the difficultest thing in the World to come at them: But I was not discourag'd at this, not doubting but I might now and then shoot one, as it soon happen'd, for after I had found their Haunts a little, I laid wait in this Manner for them: I observ'd if they saw me in the Valleys, tho' they were upon the Rocks, they would run away as in a terrible Fright; but if they were feeding in the Valleys, and I was upon the Rocks, they took no Notice of me, from whence I concluded, that by the Position of their Opticks, their Sight was so directed downward, that they did not readily see Objects that were above them; so afterward I took this Method, I always clim'd the Rocks first to get above them, and then had frequently a fair Mark. (46)

Problems and efforts to solve them follow each other in a consequent series of actions according to a logic of cause and effect, where each detail is part of either the problem or the solution, sometimes both. The danger is that of starving; the solution: exploration of the island and discovery of the goats. The discovery of the goats in turn presents another problem: they are swift and scare easily, so they are difficult to catch. Solution: observation of the goats and their habits, followed by the realization that because of the way their eyes are positioned, it is possible to hunt them from above. As the narrative proceeds, this method in turn leads to a new problem: that it takes a great deal of effort to hunt the goats. Solution: Crusoe shoots a goat with a kid, he takes the kid home and tries to tame it. The kid does not thrive, and Crusoe shoots it; however, once the possibility of domestication has been raised, Crusoe will eventually go about trying to realize it. Through such tightly sequenced narrative, Defoe keeps the reader's attention unswervingly focused on the excellence in action of his mariner hero.

In this episodic structure forged from the mariner's remarkable occurrence, Defoe is revamping the poetics of adventure. Trial by danger had been the basis of adventure fiction from its beginnings in classical romance. But there is nothing like Defoe's linear, logical plot of problem-solving. Defoe applies this formula within a single episode, exemplified by the goats, as well as across the chain of episodes that form the entire narrative. In Mikhail Bakhtin's seminal taxonomy of adventure fiction, Bakhtin qualified adventure fiction as moving through an "empty time," which was an effect of the haphazard, sometimes disconnected or disordered quality of adventure found in classical romance. In *Robinson Crusoe*'s adventures, in contrast, the time is full—full of problems, efforts, and the performance of craft, which fills up a desolate island with the comforts of civilization.

One thing Defoe has learned from prior adventure fiction is, however, to draft the character of Crusoe as a heroic protagonist. Such singularity enhances the power of Crusoe's capacity, though it contrasts with the collective agency of craft. The mariner, as I have suggested, exercised his agency as part of a skilled community defined by the bonds of work. This collective agency is implicit in the organization of information to serve future mariners, and it is explicit in Dampier's collective narrative voice: "we lay here all the Day, and scrubb'd our new Bark," "we had much Wind and Rain, and we lost the Canoa," "we went from thence with a moderate gale of Wind at S.W.," etc. In Crusoe's case, in contrast, the deeds procuring survival are all his own. With this implementation of a unique hero, Defoe not only focuses attention on the power of Crusoe's agency. He also discovers a character who has the contours of a psychological individual, available for reader identification, although Crusoe is a flat character compared to the eccentric, psychologically rounded characters that we associate with modern subjectivity, like the unique protagonist of Jean-Jacques Rousseau's *Confessions*.[33] There is an ideological yield to Defoe's reduction: isolating the mariner and distilling craft to the heroic deeds of an individual, Defoe gives a liberal countenance of individual capacity to the collectivity of the sea.

Defoe's adventure formula will prove influential for maritime adventure fiction, as for adventure fiction more generally. Jean-Yves Tadié, focusing primarily on nineteenth-century adventure fiction, is describing the pattern that Defoe invents from maritime practices of narration when Tadié writes that "in the organization of the adventure novel, in fact, no question is without an answer, no problem is without a solution, no expectation is without an event . . . and reciprocally, no answer is without a new question, no solution without a problem, no events without expectation, until the close of the narrative."[34]

Performability

Discussing the persuasions of realist fiction, the critic Roland Barthes proposed the influential notion of a "reality effect." With this term, Barthes captured how the realist fiction epitomized by the novels of Balzac and Flaubert persuaded readers as to the reality of the events narrated through an excess of details from the historical context being described. These details were useless as regards the plot, playing no obvious role in moving the narrative forward. Instead, they served what Barthes called the reality effect, reassuring the reader that the narrative was indeed anchored in a reality outside the text.

Defoe's adventure formula of problem-solving, in contrast, takes on life for the reader through a reality effect of another kind; one whose persuasions derive from the structure of the episode rather than the rhetoric of description. As Defoe plays out Crusoe's series of problems and their solutions, adhering to common-sense notions of the natural world, he shows the reader how Crusoe's achievements are operable: how she could effect such deeds, were she in Crusoe's place. To differentiate this kind of persuasion from the reality effect as the term is usually used by novel critics, I call it the "performability effect." The performability effect of *Robinson Crusoe* occurs at the level of the individual episodes, and it also applies to Crusoe's entire deed of survival on a desert island. This survival might from a distance appear implausible, yet when Defoe breaks his struggle down into a series of concrete challenges, each one part of the chain of Crusoe's story, we come to understand how Crusoe's success is achieved.

I choose the term "performability" to remind readers that the context for Defoe's adventure structure comes from the work of the sea, where performance signified the successful accomplishment of a deed, as it does, indeed, in a number of arenas of practical action.[35] In recent cultural and literary studies, the notion of the performative has been used to designate the power of representation and simulation to have practical effects, in a body of theory inspired by the philosopher J. L. Austin's *How to Do Things with Words*. Performativity in this body of thought is language, which, when spoken, accomplishes a deed. Crucial for this accomplishment is the fact that the right words are pronounced in the appropriate context attended by the appropriate protocol. For a couple to be married, which is a change of legal status, a person vested with the appropriate authority must speak precise words in a specific context. When the context is absent or the appropriate protocol is not followed, the performance does not occur.

Austin's insight that context and protocol matter is helpful in laying out the workings of Defoe's performability effect. There are matters of context and protocol that need to be respected for the effect of performability generated by Defoe's narrative to occur. To convince the reader that Crusoe is problem-solving in deed and to vindicate his craft, both problems and solutions need to respect some secular expectations befitting craft's romance of practice. These expectations include (1) that the deeds and environment adhere to basic principles of biology and physics, (2) that the deeds can be performed in Crusoe's specific environment, and (3) that the deeds, as well as their communication, use a logic of cause and effect. Today, such criteria are self-evident, but they would not have been self-evident in the enchanted world of prior romance adventure.

Austin stresses that the criterion for assessing performative language concerns effectiveness rather than referentiality. One asks of a performative utterance whether it works or not—"felicitous" rather than "unfelicitous" in Austin's terms—not whether the statements are true or false. The same is true of Defoe's performability effect. What matters for the reader is whether the details of Crusoe's problem-solving follow each other in a logical sequence and could occur in the sublunary world— whether they are operable, in short. Austin's contrast between the criterion of operability and the criterion of truth helps underscore how Defoe's episodes persuade us of their vitality using a different standard of truth than those commonly viewed as important in fiction around the turn of the eighteenth century. Performability is not verisimilitude, a notion that refers to expectations about what could happen based on the norms of the community outside the text (beyond the basic principles of the physical world and the logic of cause and effect). Nor does performability, however, conform to what McKeon identifies as the naively empirical standard of authenticity often claimed by early modern authors of overseas travel accounts, even at their most extravagant—the ability of an eyewitness to vouch for the fact that the events represented occurred. Certainly, Defoe is to some extent invoking the criterion of authenticity in having Crusoe narrate his adventures with the mariner's plain style. By Defoe's time, as a result of nonfictional overseas travel narratives, the diction of plain style is associated with craft, and its use implies the presence of the ethos before the narrative of remarkable occurrences shows craft in action. At the same time, the promise of craft would be meaningless if it were not subsequently performed. As a standard of verisimilitude anchored in effects internal to the narration appealing to the judgment of the reader, performability is on the way to the notions of probability that would come to define fiction in the later eighteenth century.[36]

The yield of performability is the outcome of the adventure, and this resolved adventure will become the starting point for the next. Defoe's poetics of performability hence plays a role in the forward-looking orientation of adventure fiction. This orientation to the future, embedded in the etymology of the notion of "adventure" itself, has been noted by critics dating at least back to Jacques Rivière, who in 1913 defined the essential poetics of an adventure lineage epitomized by "the novels of Daniel de Foe." In the words of Rivière, "the past never explains the present, rather the present explains the past."[37] The movement into the future of Defoe's maritime adventure pattern may help explain why his novel has been hospitable to sequels, both by Defoe and by subsequent writers—as is adventure fiction more generally.[38] Such an orientation toward the future contrasts with the retrospective gaze of historical fiction representing deeds that might have occurred.

Jonathan Swift was one of the first authors to recognize the power of the performability effect, which he expressed by parodying its success. When Swift needed to transport his reader from the known world to an invented land in *Gulliver's Travels*, he called on a mariner's performance in extreme conditions to make his leap of the imagination operable. In Captain Gulliver's second voyage to Brobdignag, notably, Swift effected the transport through a violent storm: a remarkable danger that would have been organized as a series of problems and solutions if Swift's Captain Gulliver were to follow the lead of Crusoe. Swift, however, slyly takes the performability effect back to its maritime inspiration.

To describe Captain Gulliver's navigation of such dangers, Swift imports wholesale into his novel the protocol for handling a ship in a storm from practical manuals of seamanship found as early as the 1630s, cited in the previous chapter. In Swift's novel, the import begins with the section: "Finding it was like to overblow, we took in our Sprit-sail, and stood by to hand the Fore-sail; but making foul Weather, we look'd the guns were all fast, and handed the Missen. The Ship lay very broad off, so we thought it better spooning before the Sea than trying or hulling," etc.[39] If we return to the practical literature on the sea, it turns out that Swift has collaged together directions in practical manuals of seamanship of the preceding hundred years. These directions come from the paragraph on the maneuvers to take when a storm is about to break, such as the paragraph on what to do in "A growne Sea" (Saltonstall) or "A very hollow grown Sea" (Sturmy).[40] Burdened by overly precise technical language, the storm sequence reverts from Crusoe's performable adventures appealing to a general reader to an inert and specialized protocol.

PERFORMING DESCRIPTION: DAMPIER'S SEA LIONS AND CRUSOE'S GOATS

In the maritime manuals parodied by Swift, descriptions of how to handle the ship in different weather imparted the technical knowledge of the sea by showing it in use. In this practice, maritime manuals transgress a contrast that narratologists have made apropos of nineteenth-century realist fiction between description and narration. While narration is characterized by an active, forward movement, description, in contrast, is static; Roland Barthes put it wittily, when he characterized description as the part of the novel that readers like to skip. Maritime manuals' descriptions through action correspond, in contrast, to an alternative mode of description identified by Philippe Hamon. This mode is what Hamon terms "narration-description," which is when, as Hamon puts it, "the simultaneous givens of the real or the elements accumulated from a nomenclatural travel, take place on the text's stage, with movement of characters."[41]

For Hamon, one use for narration-description is to naturalize technical language, both humanizing and dramatizing it, by incorporating this language—and by implication the tools and practices described—into a character's actions. And certainly, Defoe's descriptions bring technical materials and their uses to life. But they do something more: techniques and tools come to enrich and even generate the twists and turns of the plot, when animated by the performability effect. As Defoe presses information on the island environment into adventures of performance, he simultaneously manufactures the challenges and solutions that constitute Crusoe's struggle for survival. The description of the goats becomes part of Crusoe's struggle to find food. Their swiftness is a detail that becomes a challenge for the hunter. The position of their "opticks" is animated as a clue in the search for how to approach these wily creatures, and so on. To put this in terms of the novel's communication of craft as an ethos: such narration-description utilizes information on the unfamiliar marine environment as a way to enrich the performance of craft, displaying craft's heterogeneous capacities and emphasizing its power.

The technique of performing description is one more practice that Defoe appropriates but also amplifies from the historical sea voyage narratives of mariner-authors. In mariners' historical accounts, performing description is part of the remarkable occurrence. As mariners recount dangers and how they are resolved, they convey information about both the environment and the different facets of craft. Thus, Cook's account of how he is stranded discussed in the previous chapter describes the Great Barrier Reef, as it almost destroys his ship, or thus, Cook initiates his readers into the unfamiliar expedient of fothering as the vessel is foundering. Another use of performing description by mariner-authors was to give anthropological details. Dampier, notably, is fascinated by the pragmatic creativity of indigenous peoples and will often describe them at work in performing descriptions.

At the same time, *Robinson Crusoe* amplifies the use of such description well beyond anything found in the maritime book, applying it to animate almost all the adventures undergone by his mariner hero. Defoe's enhanced version of what Hamon calls narration-description will be so influential in the subsequent history of adventure fiction that it deserves a name of its own. Given its emergence from the work of the sea and its role in the performability effect, I will call it "performing description." Performing description is a distinctive feature of maritime adventure fiction, that is taken up by modern adventure fiction more generally, helping to drive the action forward even as it brings to life a novel's imaginary world. Rivière was, I think, identifying performing description when he noted the incessant "work" of adventure fiction: "the perfect realization of a novel [of adventure] is its perfect activity . . . no place for dreams or immobile settings; all elements are at work."[42] Emphasizing the incorporation of all information in the dynamic narrative thread, Rivière described the adventure novel as one of "those machines, in which nothing sleeps, and which, as soon as they are operating, seem made of countless functions, rather than of materials."[43]

With this extension of performing description to subtend the structure of his adventure episodes, Defoe reaps dramatic reward as well from another reservoir of information found in the maritime book, besides its narratives of remarkable occurrences. This information comprises the rich but disorganized observations mariners made about unfamiliar waters, coasts, animals, lands, and peoples, with the aim of adding to the "general Magazine of the knowledge of Foreign parts," in Dampier's words from his own *A New Voyage Round the World* cited in chapter 1. In mariner-authors' narratives, these details are presented as they are encountered in the course of a voyage, but they have no function within the action of the voyage itself. They are fascinating and thought-provoking, both for governments and entrepreneurs thinking about profiting from foreign lands, as well as for armchair sailors seeking entertainment. At the same time, the details are narratively inert, since they are not part of the action of the voyage.

To illustrate these static descriptions, consider the portrait of sea lions offered by Dampier. In Dampier's *New Voyage*, the sea lion comes up after Dampier has circumnavigated Cape Horn and come into the Pacific Ocean, passing by the Juan Fernando island that is one historical model for Crusoe's island. Dampier then expounds on the acquatic wildlife in the area, distinguishing seals from sea lions. Of the sea lion, Dampier writes: "The *Sea-Lion* is a large Creature about 12 or 14 Foot long," whose "lean Flesh is black, and of a coarse Grain; yet indifferent good Food." "Where 3 or 4, or more of them come ashore together, they huddle one on another like Swine, and grunt like them, making a hideous Noise. They eat Fish, which I believe is their common Food" (70). Dampier's static presentation of fascinating information observed in foreign parts conforms to the rhetorical figure known as the "blazon," a description of different body parts and features of an object. This rhetorical figure is best known through the description of the woman's body in love poems reaching back to the Song of Songs in the Bible. Only Dampier's version of the blazon is utilitarian: rather than the beauty of the woman's form and face, he describes how to recognize and potentially to utilize the unfamiliar flora and fauna encountered on the far side of the world.

Had Defoe run Dampier's utilitarian blazon of the sea lions through his technique of performing description, we can imagine Crusoe startled by their grunts when he hunts them or navigates by them in his canoe, or remarking on their flesh in trying to eat them. The opportunity to reap dramatic yield from all the fascinating information found in mariners' narratives is yet another way Defoe's adventure poetics fulfills his goal stated at the beginning of his *New Voyage Round the World, By a Course never sailed before* of offering a "full relation" of all the interesting incidents that mariner-authors rather present "superficially and by halves."

Defoe applies performing description to reap dramatic yield from the mariner's utilitarian blazons not just to flora and fauna but also to indigenous peoples. Here is how Dampier details the Native Americans encountered on the Corn Islands, adding to the general magazine of anthropological knowledge: "They are a People of mean Stature, yet strong Limbs; they are of a dark Copper-colour, black Hair, full round Faces, small black Eyes, their Eyebrows hanging over their Eyes, low Foreheads, short thick Noses, not high, but flattish; full Lips, and short Chins" (31). For Crusoe, the description of the indigenous dwellers encountered in remote lands becomes either part of the challenge or part of the solution, sometimes both. Crusoe first takes an interest in Friday when he sees that Friday cannot swim and hence cannot escape his pursuers. Friday's weakness gives Crusoe an idea for a solution to one of Crusoe's long-standing problems: "now was my Time to get me a Servant, and perhaps a Companion, or Assistant" (146). Then follows the rescue of Friday from the cannibals and Friday's gratitude. When Friday's physical aspect is subsequently described, even these details become part of Defoe's adventure sequence of challenge followed by problem-solving. In the case of Friday, his physical features reveal Friday's suitability to serve Crusoe as well as to cheer up his solitude: "He was a comely handsome Fellow, perfectly well made; with straight strong Limbs, not too large," and so on (148).

Imaginary Solutions to Real Problems

One tenet of Marxist explanations for the cultural power of novels is that they offer imaginary solutions to intractable problems at the level of real social relations. Though Marxist literary critics never make the link between this view of novel and the adventure poetics of Defoe, they are describing what is in fact one of the great cultural opportunities opened by Defoe's structure of adventure as problem-solving—an opportunity, moreover, that Crusoe takes advantage of in his more spiritual moments. This is the opportunity to use adventures in problem-solving to address other more abstract matters than practical struggles for survival. In *Robinson Crusoe*, specifically, Defoe applies his adventure formula to the great philosophical problems of the early modern era, such as the status of belief in an increasingly secular age or the relativity of cultural values.

A good example of this process is Defoe's approach to the problem of how Christian values make sense of the Other. Indigenous cannibal tribes were a recurring subject in overseas travel literature. As Montaigne's famous essay on cannibals illustrates, their existence offered the occasion to ponder whether Christian values were absolute or relative. Cannibals play the same role in *Robinson Crusoe*. However, they play this role not as an open-ended question but rather as an immediate threat to Crusoe's existence, from his discovery of the footprint on the sand.[44] In commenting on how to generate the ship's position through coordinating different kinds of measurements in navigation, Edwin Hutchins cites Herbert Simon's definition that "solving a problem simply means representing it so as to make the solution transparent."[45] In Crusoe's discovery of the cannibals, we see a process of transformative representation: cannibals are transformed from a philosophical problem to a practical problem, and their challenge then can be problem-solved by the pragmatic imagination.

Faced with what he perceives as a threat to his survival, Crusoe's first approach to the problem of the cannibals is how they are to be killed. As in his escape from Sallee, he ponders a range of stratagems, looking for one that might be practicable. "Night and Day," Crusoe tells us, "I could think of nothing but how I might destroy some of these Monsters in their cruel bloody Entertainment, and if possible, save the Victim they should bring hither to destroy. It would take up a larger Volume than this whole Work is intended to be, to set down all the Contrivances I hatch'd, or rather brooded upon in my Thought" (122). In these ratiocinations, particularly as regards the cannibals' further victims, the practical problem starts to turn philosophical, and this transformation is amplified as Crusoe's reflections proceed. However, Crusoe needs to come up with a solution and cannot afford the open-ended speculations of Montaigne, secure in his gracious chateau in France. At the end of lengthy meditations, then, philosophical questions are collapsed into practical problems. Through such conflation, Crusoe comes up with a practical solution that he offers simultaneously as a philosophical answer: "Upon the whole I concluded, That neither in Principle or in Policy, I ought one way or other to concern my self in this Affair." "Religion joyn'd in with this Prudential, and I was convinc'd now many Ways, that I was perfectly out of my Duty, when I was laying all my bloody Schemes for the Destruction of innocent Creatures, I mean innocent as to me" (125).[46]

Defoe applies a similar process of collapsing philosophical questions into Crusoe's practical problems and then having Crusoe come up with a practical solution, which he offers simultaneously as a philosophical answer when Crusoe confronts the question of how to understand his own capacity to act in relation to Providence. We have seen this question run throughout mariners' records of survival in extreme conditions. Crusoe's practical turn here is first to articulate this relation as a question and then to apply the same problem-solving approach to the relation of agency to Providence that he applies to all his other challenges.[47] The question is posed apropos of a practical yet seemingly miraculous occurrence: when Crusoe discovers some stalks of European barley sprouting on his desert island off the coast of the New World. Crusoe observes, "It is impossible to express the Astonishment and Confusion of my thoughts on this Occasion." Where did the ears of corn come from? Crusoe first speculates that the stalks are a miracle of Providence. Then, remembering some chicken feed he had left over in his pocket, he explains his survival as a natural accident.[48] Once Crusoe has posed the relation between Providence and agency as a problem, the problem can be solved. "I ought to have been as thankful for so strange and unforseen Providence, as if it had been miraculous; for it was really the Work of Providence . . . that 10 or 12 Grains of Corn should remain unspoil'd . . . as also, that I should throw it out in that particular Place" (58).

THE CUNNING READER

Narratologists have suggested that novels compel readers by presenting information that is in some way incomplete. Wolfgang Iser calls the missing information "gaps" in his *Implied Reader: Patterns of Communication in*

Prose Fiction from Bunyan to Beckett. Iser wrote that these gaps are the "very points at which the reader can enter into the text, forming his own connections and conceptions and so creating the configurative meaning of what he is reading."[49] In Iser's account, the function of these gaps is ethical. When novels withhold value judgments about characters and actions, they challenge the reader to sort through conflicting information and come to her own conclusions. In Iser's view, this protocol of reading through gaps revises the kind of reading solicited by prior literature on the lives of individuals used to teach morality in both classical and Christian contexts. Whereas biographies of great people and saints' lives offer examples for the reader to admire and to imitate, novels, in contrast, encourage people to process complex, ambiguous information and draw independent conclusions. Novels thereby offer a nuanced and emancipatory initiation into ethics; and their conflicting signals also make for more entertaining reading. In this way, novels encourage readers to understand morality in action, to reprise Denis Diderot's characterization of the novel form itself.[50]

In Iser's *Act of Reading*, he writes that this kind of reading is "cybernetic in nature."[51] The mathematician Norbert Wiener coined the term "cybernetics" in 1948, after the Greek word for steersman, *kubernetes*. Wiener chose this term because he understood the steersman's activities to be a foundational paradigm for feedback systems, at the basis of the new science of communication and control that Wiener envisaged. Iser views the process of novel reading, too, as a traffic in information, involving "a feedback of effects and information throughout a sequence of changing situational frames; smaller units progressively merge into bigger ones."[52]

Iser's notion that novels invite readers to participate in their action through withholding information helps explain the reader's involvement solicited by *Robinson Crusoe*, though Defoe is a notable absence in Iser's chronology of the English novel. Defoe's reader enters into the text through shadowing Crusoe's application of craft to invent solutions to immediate danger with his impoverished resources. Consider an emblematic moment when Crusoe successfully combines jury-rigging and conjecture, using his pragmatic imagination to devise an expedient. It comes early on in Crusoe's shipwreck, from an episode when he is forced to act as steersman, appropriately enough, but in the absence of sail, rudder, or oar. This moment occurs as he salvages goods from the wreck, which he must find a way to transport to shore. Lacking a means of power, Crusoe perceives a current creating an "indraft" off the coast. He utilizes this current to near his craft to the shore, and, drawing on his knowledge of the sea, also conjectures that the current indicates "some Creek or River . . . which I might make use of as a Port." His conjecture is valid:

"As I imagin'd," he continues, "so it was, there appear'd before me a little opening of the Land, and I found a strong Current of the Tide set into it, so I guided my Raft as well as I could to keep in the Middle of the Stream" (39). "As I imagin'd . . . so it was"—this statement describes the successful application of the pragmatic imagination in conjecture.

The armchair reader cannot share the embodied mastery of craft, nor its technical expertise. But the skills of mariner and reader meet in the organization of partial information by the pragmatic imagination to come up with a best guess about outcome. The reader's ability to shadow Crusoe's struggles by combing through information, both from within the text and from her general store of knowledge, in search of solutions to Crusoe's problems, enhances her engagement with the text. When she finds the solution to a problem on her own, she simulates in thought the mariner's performance, and her participation reinforces *Robinson Crusoe*'s performability effect.

I call such an armchair reader simulating the protagonist's travails and participating in a search for solutions at the level of information organization the "cunning reader." Cunning because "to cun" is the term of art for the activity of steering a ship: the activity that is at the basis of cybernetics, which Iser invokes to describe how novel readers organize and manage information to generate meaning. Cunning also has an archaic early modern usage, which points to the shared activities of steersman and reader. In its archaic usage, cunning was a maritime unit of measurement "equivalent to the distance at which the shore could first be seen from the offing when making landfall." As the cunning reader intimates the form of a problem out of a wealth of information, the goal heaves into view, and it is then a question of how to reach it.[53] Defoe's cunning reader is making practical judgments, not the ethical determinations educating the novel reader, according to Iser. If Iser skips from Bunyan to Richardson in his genealogy of the novel, it is perhaps because there is no clear ethical yield from the reader's involvement in Crusoe's struggle for survival. As the reader makes conjectures involving practical matters, she, too, joins craft's collectivity beyond good and evil.

CUNNING READING: DIVERTING AND USEFUL

For Crusoe, the exercise of the pragmatic imagination, along with the other aspects of craft, procures survival. For the cunning reader of his adventure, the yield is pleasures taken from information, in keeping with Defoe's ambition, announced in the preface to the *New Voyage,* to turn mariners' narratives into something uniquely "diverting" and "useful."[54] Problem-solving along with Defoe's protagonist, the cunning reader garners a diverting introduction into the useful skills and demeanors of craft, as *Robinson Crusoe* is a mariner's manual lite. The reader also gathers information about the world beyond the line that is craft's theater. Thus, the twentieth-century author of the *Swallows and Amazons* series, Arthur Ransome, recommended *Robinson Crusoe* to children "who had enjoyed" his books: It is "'a very important book for those of you who want to know what to do on a desert island. It is also good about shipwrecks and voyages.'"[55]

Defoe devises a particularly effective way to entertain by sharing technical factoids when he poses problems that admit of a general solution at the level of common sense, even as the specific solution is specialized to craft. For examples of this process, we can return to the moment when Crusoe first discovers salvageable goods in the shipwreck. Pondering how to reclaim them, Crusoe starts to break the problem down into its practicable steps. First: "Now I wanted nothing but a Boat," however, "[i]t was in vain to sit still and wish for what was not to be had, and this Extremity rouz'd my Application" (37). The reader who simulates his deeds may well infer that the wreck would provide some kind of material. This is correct. However, she must be knowledgeable in the ways of the sea to identify the solution as a cache of jury-masts and yards habitually kept in reserve on board in lengthy navigations.[56]

Having devised this raft, Crusoe must then figure out how to guide his raft to shore, "having neither Sail, Oar, or Rudder," a particular challenge because the raft is heavily laden (38). That Crusoe might use the environment is a common-sense answer; that an "Indraft of the Water," signals "some Creek or River . . . which I might make use of as a Port to get to Land with my Cargo" is part of the mariner's knowledge of hydrography (39). The upshot of such double answers—at the level of common sense and craft—is to appeal to both specialized and general readers; as well as to enliven technical details that are arid for someone who does not know their context.[57] It is a matter of writerly tact to put solutions within the reader's reach and thus cultivate the reader's sense of agency—too close is boring, too far is frustrating. Defoe further enhances the reader's agency when he varies the problems and includes challenges confronting Crusoe that can be solved purely at the level of common sense.

Robinson Crusoe reinforces the general reader's simulation of craft when Crusoe's adventures give her the chance to use what she has learned. When Crusoe subsequently circumnavigates his island, he is almost killed by "a strong, and indeed, a most furious Current," running around it (101). What is its source? In contrast to the problem of getting the raft ashore, Defoe defers the answer to this question, even as he has Crusoe experience a number of unpleasant brushes with the current that remind the reader of the need for its explanation.

The reader can come up with an answer from the time the current is first mentioned, if she combines what she has learned about the effect of inland bodies of water on coastal currents with a detail from the novel's title page. There, she is told that Crusoe's island is situated "near the Mouth of the Great River of Oroonoque." The reader's ability to reach outside the plot for information underscores that she is engaged in organizing different information than the protagonist; that the challenges confronting her and Crusoe are not the same. Crusoe must wait for the explanation for the current until Friday opens up the scale of his geography beyond the island. Then he realizes that the current is "occasion'd by the great Draft and Reflex of the mighty River *Oroonoko*; in the Mouth or the Gulph of which River, as I found afterwards, our Island lay; and this Land which I perceiv'd to the W. and N.W. was the great Island *Trinidad*" (155).

Most of the information organized by the cunning reader is conveyed through verbal narrative. But this information is also imparted in illustrations that accompany the text, delineating the unknown territory in different genres that offer different kinds of details. When first published, *Robinson Crusoe* was illustrated with a view of Crusoe on the coast (figure 2.1). Its sequels added first an obliquely angled bird's-eye view of the island (figure 2.2) and then a bihemispherical map of Crusoe's travels that Defoe solicited from Herman Moll, the premier marine cartographer of his time, who had indeed made the maps for Dampier's *New Voyage* (figure 2.3).[58] This use of graphic genres to convey different kinds of information is one that unites Defoe's poetics of performability with the mariner sharing information on new waters, and coasts. As Dampier's illustrations supplementing his *New Voyage* exemplify, this information includes representations of what to expect in different genres: maps tracing the voyage routes, elevations of the visual aspect of coastlines approached from the water, charts with compass observations and soundings, and sketches of unknown peoples, objects, flora, and fauna.

With these diverse but partial views of the unknown, mariners' narratives amplify a principle fundamental to navigation in an era before GPS. In situations where there is potentially dangerous uncertainty due to missing information, different kinds of partial measurements and representations are gathered and compared, used to fill in each other's blanks and prepare a best guess amidst uncertainty. As Edwin Hutchins puts it in his anatomy of navigation: "The ship's situation is represented and re-represented [across media] until the answer to the navigator's question is transparent."[59] But while mariners compared different kinds of representation across media, applying the pragmatic imagination to achieve a usable sense of orientation amidst the oceans and coasts of the

Figure 2.1. Crusoe on an Edge of dynamic modernity. Though Crusoe looks quaint in his homemade goatskin outfit, his barren shore was in his time more like outer space or the Internet today than an idyllic state of nature, and the tall ship in the background pitching on the waves, however picturesque, was state-of-the-art technology. His well-molded calves illustrate what I have called "sea legs," the mariner's capable embodiment. Frontispiece to the first edition of Daniel Defoe's *The Life and Strange Surprising Adventures of Robinson Crusoe of York, Mariner*, engraved by John Clark and John Pine (London: W. Taylor, 1719). Courtesy of the John Carter Brown Library at Brown University.

Figure 2.2. A bird's-eye topographical map of Crusoe's island, also including information about its flora and fauna, as well as about its visitors and their crafts that figured in a sequel to *The Life and Strange Surprising Adventures of Robinson Crusoe of York, Mariner*, titled *The Serious Reflections During the Life and Surprising Adventures of Robinson Crusoe* (1720). The map exemplifies one early modern genre for depicting an unknown or barely known territory. In maritime practice, unfamiliar coasts and islands were represented in a number of different visual genres, which complemented each other and which were complemented by verbal descriptions and measurements as well. All these different kinds of representation were compared and coordinated by subsequent voyagers, helping them to orient themselves amidst great uncertainty. Frontispiece to *The Serious Reflections During the Life and Surprising Adventures of Robinson Crusoe* (London: W. Taylor, 1720). Courtesy of the Newberry Library, Chicago.

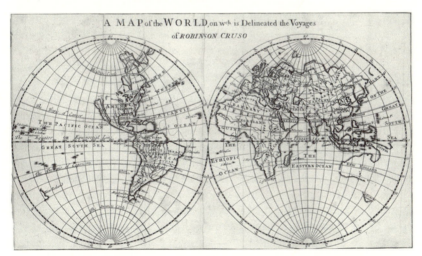

Figure 2.3. The bihemispherical map tracing the route of pioneering navigators, in particular circumnavigators, was another early modern genre that helped depict the unknown spaces of the globe. In including such a map in his sequel to *Robinson Crusoe*, Defoe is also invoking, specifically, the world map that prefaces *A New Voyage Round the World* by William Dampier, a book that he sought to outdo. *The Farther Adventures of Robinson Crusoe*, bihemispherical map by Herman Moll (London: W. Taylor, 1719). Courtesy of the John Carter Brown Library at Brown University.

physical world, the armchair sailor's process is qualitatively different. In her comparison of partial information, she is not forming a picture of an external reality but rather performing the existence of an imaginary world.

With his adventure poetics stimulating the reader to simulate craft through adventures in problem-solving information, Defoe had hit upon an invention that would prove remarkably influential across the history of modern adventure fiction. Not only would *Robinson Crusoe*'s adventures in information be taken up by maritime adventure fiction, across its history, but authors also quickly realized that such games could be transferred to other areas of skilled labor and specialized knowledge—a transfer that yielded other adventure subgenres. Following *Robinson Crusoe*, Defoe was the first to translate such adventures back to the dangerous spaces of the metropolis, such as the criminal underworld. The ups and downs of characters like Moll Flanders, prostitute, thief, speculator, and con woman, or her male counterpart, Colonel Jack, are built on the tricks of the trade. And as the reader simulates her deeds, she is initiated into the techniques of these trades, viz her intiation along with Moll into how to steal a watch under the tutelage of Moll's "governess," or her discovery through Jack's keen observations, even as a boy, of the "careless Way of Men putting their Pocket-books into a Coat Pocket, which is so easily div'd into."[60]

Readers of modern adventure fiction across its history would continue to enjoy the entertaining introduction its poetics offered into different specialized bodies of knowledge as they shadowed its problem-solving protagonists. The importance of specialized bodies of knowledge in two subgenres of adventure fiction that are popular into our present, detective fiction and spy fiction, are cases in point. As Sherlock Holmes solves case after case, Conan Doyle challenges the reader to adventures in problem-solving drawing on chemistry, botany, biology, physiognomy, the history of technology, and ethnography, among other areas of expertise. While Tom Clancy's novels construct problems and solutions mobilizing the details of Cold War bureaucracy, espionage practices, and military technologies, Tony Hillerman's detective novels immerse the reader in Native American cultures of the Four Corners area, tracing the way in which members of these tribes at once belong to contemporary U.S. culture and inhabit their own distinctive world of social practices and religious beliefs. With the novels of Patrick O'Brian, we come full circle, and the adventures of Aubrey and Maturin share with today's readers the specialized techniques of craft, resurrected from the shadows of history.

Beyond diverting the reader with factoids, *Robinson Crusoe*'s poetics of problem-solving has another, less informational yield for the cunning reader. This is to solicit her to flex her pragmatic creativity as she combs through information for the expedients that would procure Crusoe's survival. One aspect of *Robinson Crusoe*'s challenges that stimulate flexibility, for example, involves the need to shift scales to find solutions, including different scales within the novel as well as in her cultural literacy more broadly. Flexibility is also at stake in the need to pick out solutions from episodes where the clues are proferred hidden in a range of different ways. To return to the episode with the raft, some clues offer solutions explicitly, like the current for the raft; clues to other solutions are hidden but inferable. Sometimes the inference is straightforward, like the possibility of extra wood on the shipwreck, but sometimes it involves specialized details that the reader would have little chance of knowing, like the position of goats' opticks in their heads. An eye to the big picture is important when the solution is deferred across episodes, and to big pictures of different kinds. Information about the island's location in explaining the furious current is already on the title page, situating it off the Oroonoque River, and the likely location of the island can also be surmised by reading details on the ship's location in the storm leading to Crusoe's shipwreck. The solution to the mystery of the footprints, in contrast, entails recognizing a scenario found in overseas voyage narratives reaching back to the sixteenth century.

In suggesting that the cunning reader hones her skills at ingenious thinking through armchair problem-solving, I apply to adventure poetics arguments made by critics about the pedagogic potential of rhetoric and narrative in other contexts. These arguments concern the use of literary language to cultivate the kind of flexibility and ingenuity distinguishing excellence in the arts of practice, ranging from the craft of the mariner to the skills of politicians, doctors, and thieves. This ingenuity is much harder to teach than specific competences—the kind of competences that are delineated in treatises on practical seamanship. Iser, for example, argues that eighteenth-century novels hone the reader's ethical faculty when the narrator withholds judgments on characters and their behavior, stimulating the reader to come up with a view of her own. Victoria Kahn suggests that Machiavelli uses rhetoric as an instrument to teach the flexibility needed for the Renaissance prince to excel in the exercise of power. In *Machiavellian Rhetoric: From the Counter-Reformation to Milton*, Kahn explains how Machiavelli plays rhetorical games with his readers to cultivate their cunning, making his treatise a succession of thought-experiments for learning, where real-life interests are not immediately at stake. With Robinson Crusoe's new poetics of adventure, Defoe has found a way to stimulate ingenuity, exploiting techniques constitutive of the novel form, including the forward flow of narrative as well as attention to particularity, information, and detail.

THE MARITIME PICARESQUE: PROFILES IN CRAFT

Robinson Crusoe initiated a wave of maritime adventure fiction across
the 1720s to 1740s in Great Britain and France. I call this subgenre the
"maritime picaresque," because it has an important fictional antecedent
in the picaresque novel, which depicts an itinerant adventurer-hero and
his or her struggles for survival on the margins of the world, as has
been noted by Giancarlo Maiorino.[61] In the Spanish fiction discussed by
Maiorino, the *picaro*'s cunning is the popular common sense of the dominated oppressed by social inequality, who lack the possibility for upward
mobility. The itinerant mariner, in contrast, ventures into the Edge zone
with craft in active pursuit of knowledge, adventure, and surplus value.

The eighteenth-century maritime picaresque does not compare in expanse or endurance to the boom in sea fiction that will occur in the nineteenth century described in chapter 4. But it does include novels beloved
by readers of the time. Defoe himself wrote some subsequent sea voyage novels, as did authors well known for their picaresque novels back
on land, like Alain René Le Sage, the Abbé Prévost and Tobias Smollett.
There were also maritime picaresque novels by William Rufus Chetwood.
Chetwood's Captain Robert Boyle, Defoe's Captain Bob Singleton, Le
Sage's Captain Robert de Beauchêne, Prévost's Capitaine Robert Lade,
and Smollett's Roderick Random all bear a family resemblance to Robinson Crusoe, but they are not his double. All are forged in the crucible
of craft, but different novels highlight different aspects of craft's multifaceted capacity, both as regards the skills it bundles together as well as
regards its ethical instability, with its potential to be used for good, bad,
or amoral action outside the law. Thus, the collectivity essential for craft
will be the focus of Defoe's *Life, Adventures & Piracies of the Famous
Captain Singleton*, taking a different path through craft from the heroism of the solitary Crusoe on his desert island. In Le Sage's novel about
the pirate Beauchêne, in contrast, those skills of craft associated with the
heroism of the warrior are emphasized, and his novel models craft as
the capacity of the proud aristocrat. To conclude, then, here are a few of
the profiles in craft found across the maritime picaresque's pages. From
these profiles, it should be evident that craft's multifaceted nature has
a poetic advantage: enabling it to generate a range of protagonists and
plots able to accomplish different kinds of cultural and ideological work.

CRAFT'S COLLECTIVE: CAPTAIN BOB, QUAKER WILLIAM, THE INGENIOUS CUTLER, AND MANY OTHERS

Robinson Crusoe is a heroic individual, able to survive in complete isolation, which, I have suggested, is an ideological transformation of the

collective agency characterizing the craft of the sea. Defoe gives craft its collective due in *The Life, Adventures & Piracies of the Famous Captain Singleton* (1720), which, Jody Greene has observed, would have made for a very different account of the rise of the novel if Ian Watt had used it as his tutor text.[62] When Captain Bob Singleton, the title character, is abandoned on the island of Madagascar, he joins a company of fellow mutineers, who have rebelled against their captain on a return journey from Goa to Lisbon. Their equivalent to the ship's toolbox in *Robinson Crusoe* are tools, including guns, carpenters' tools, doctors' instruments and medicines that the captain allows them to take with them in leaving them on an island amidst "savages" and "wild beasts."[63] The company then manages to make it to mainland Africa and trek to the western coast in order to find passage to Europe. Across this dangerous journey into the unknown of the African contintent, they survive by pooling their heterogeneous skills as well as by making use of local knowledge of native peoples met along the way. The ship's "ingenious cutler" makes trade jewelry by melting down and refashioning coins. A sailor who had been a cook's assistant can pickle meat without "cask or pickle," using saltpeter and the sun. A local met on the coast of East Africa comes up with a way to make a ship watertight in the absence of tar and pitch by his knowing preparation of the sap from an indigenous tree. Captain Bob is the manager who excels at organizing these different skills. His friend and adviser, the Quaker William, offers cunning in religious as well as earthly affairs, giving Captain Bob, for example, the spiritual salve to clear his conscience and enjoy the fruit of his ill-gotten gains.

From Captain to Designer: Robert Boyle

Rufus Chetwood was a contemporary of Defoe who authored imaginary voyage narratives and maritime adventure fiction. Like *The Life and Strange Surprising Adventures of Robinson Crusoe*, *The Voyages and Adventures of Captain Robert Boyle* (1726) also has a mariner adventurer-hero who is a paragon of craft. Robert Boyle is the son of a sailor who was lost in a shipwreck on the Scilly rocks that left only one man alive, a detail that recalls the shipwreck of Cloudesley Shovel, though Chetwood sets his novel in the preceding century. In delineating Captain Boyle's craft, Chetwood emphasizes Boyle's pragmatic imagination, which lets him overcome difficulties, and emphasizes the state-of-the-art aspect of craft's expertise in jury-rigging and manipulating technology. Boyle gets his start apprenticed to a watchmaker, a profession that capitalizes on his "good mechanical Head."[64] When he then is kidnapped and put on a vessel bound for the New World, Boyle discovers his "Inclination" for the sea and masters "the Mathematicks, as also the Work of a Sailor."[65] Taken prisoner and enslaved in Sallee, Boyle, like Robinson Crusoe, applies his craft to survival in a dangerous frontier zone beyond European control.

During the captivity of Robert Boyle, Chetwood explores the potential to apply craft to activities and social relations on land. With Boyle's efforts to curry favor with his master, the equivalent of Crusoe's jury-rigging on the deserted island turns to landscape architecture. While in captivity, Boyle ingratiates himself by designing and manufacturing a lovely garden, replete with statues of Neptune in his chariot of sea horses, surrounded by four Tritons. "Gardening was what I always took delight in, both Theoric and Practic," Boyle tells us.[66] Chetwood's transformation of craft onshore to the skills of the designer is prescient of later centuries, when the engineer will join the crafty mariner among the heroic forgers of modernity, where he or she remains into our present. Like the mariner, the engineer works in Edge zones back on land, pushing the limits of design, materials, and techniques in quest of their supersession. And like the mariner, he or she uses compleat skills crossing the divide between theory and practice.

In Chetwood's novel, Boyle eventually uses the ruses of craft to escape in the company of a beautiful fellow captive, the Englishwoman Mrs. Villars. His picaresque career then spans the oceans of the globe, and even crosses paths with the historical figure of William Dampier.

CRAFT OR FEMININE WILES: MRS. VILLARS

One notable difference between Chetwood's novel and the maritime adventure fiction of Defoe entails Chetwood's expansion of adventures to include adventures in love. Entangling episodes of maritime danger with adventures of passion, love, and sexuality, Chetwood's novel compares the dangers offered by each. Adventures of love traffic in dangers as menacing as any encountered on the oceans of the globe, from the time Boyle's master castrates the young lawyer who is having an affair with his wife, when the master discovers the pair having sex. Indeed, Chetwood portrays the homosocial relations of the maritime world as safe in contrast to the violence induced by passion. Thus, after his punishment, the lawyer turns castrato, and Boyle meets him again in the company of William Dampier, making the most of his singing voice. Boyle tells the clerk's story to Dampier, and while at first, the castrato appears upset, by the end, he is in a good humor, and the company "ended the Day in Mirth and Jollity."[67]

Different kinds of practical reason are in the balance as Chetwood compares adventures of love and seafaring, revealing some differences in women's and men's specific domains of practical expertise. Boyle's female counterpart, Mrs. Villars, first enters adulthood as "a Woman of Business," managing her father's overseas trade.[68] However, Mrs. Villars must then call on a passive, seemingly enfeebled cunning that is the ruse of those in dominated social positions. While men navigate physical danger from the environment and people alike with craft, women exercise a more dissimulative resourcefulness in withstanding the violent advances of men.

CRAFT WITHOUT PERFORMANCE: ROBERT LADE

We know the Abbé Prévost for his picaresque novels set on land. However, Prévost was also keenly interested in the maritime world. He edited a fifteen-volume collection that appeared over 1746–1759, the *Histoire générale des voyages*, condensing accounts of celebrated historical voyages across the age of global sail. Prévost also wrote fictional works of the maritime picaresque. *La Jeunesse du Commandeur* (1741) is about the "imprudence" rather than "prudence" of a younger son who runs away to sea corrupted by his taste for maritime travel literature. In the course of cruising around the Mediterranean, the young commander-to-be establishes the contours of prudence by folly and miscalculations, many incited by love, as the Abbé Prévost, like Chetwood, experiments with fusing the adventures of craft with those of love and gallantry.

The craft of the hero of Prévost's *Les Voyages de Capitaine Lade* (1744) is, in contrast, fully accomplished. The Englishman Captain Robert Lade partakes of what Prévost's preface frames as a thirst for profit and adventure characterizing the citizens of Britain. As the title of his narrative suggests, Lade adventures across the oceans and globes of the colonial world, driven by ambition and the quest for gain. In his journey, he crosses mariners famous from the nonfictional literature on the sea, and in a nod to Defoe, Lade even includes a journal selection from Alexander Selkirk, whose name, he tells us, is in fact Selcrag, which gives Lade the chance to include his own version of Selkirk's tale. In this pastiche, as well as throughout Lade's narration, Prévost evinces his familiarity with the poetics of historical mariner-authors. In detailing the deeds of the ship's company, he has Lade use the collective "we" of craft. When Lade reflects on the attention of mariner-writers in details to the craft, he observes that it is typical of journals of seamen to "focus rather on the position of spots, the descriptions of coasts, ports, bays and waters, than the physical and moral history of the countries that he visits."[69] Indeed, at moments, Lade adheres so closely to the mariner's professional concerns that he almost flips over into a parody reminiscent of the storm sequence in *Gulliver's Travels*. One such moment is when Lade imports unmodified into the narration a table of the latitudes and longitude of all "remarkable" spots of the west coast of the Americas, from California down to the southern coast of Chile, in a table that goes on for a number of pages.[70]

But despite Lade's consummate seamanship, Prévost's narrative *tells us* about the deeds of craft rather than, like Defoe, *showing* the work of craft in action, which is an aesthetic effect essential to Defoe's adventure performance. The distinction between Prévost's telling and Defoe's showing can be illustrated by the treatment of a storm in each work. The storm in the *Voyages du Capitaine Lade* occurs when Lade has gone to West Africa to acquire gold and his ship is caught in "the most horrible tempest that one can have an idea of from history or from Mariners' narratives."[71] Such superlatives do nothing to show the substance of mariners' work, nor draw the reader into this work through engaging their own pragmatic imagination. Though Lade alludes to "all the art of our seamen," he only does so to say it was "exhausted," so that "nothing was sadder to see, & the Captain & all the Crew, lying face down against the Ship's deck, sometimes rolling upon each other, or bumping into each other at each shock the vessel received from the waves, & with their only hope in God."

In *Robinson Crusoe*, in contrast, the storm that will wreck Crusoe's ship eventually does reduce the mariners to the end of their art, but not before Defoe has detailed their work of the craft. At the same time, Defoe's choice is selective and focuses on aspects of the craft that will be important to cunning reading. Thus, his concern in the storm is its effect on the ship's course. The storm, he tells us, begins about twelve days after "we past the Line . . . and were by our last Observation in 7 Degrees 22 Min. Northern Latitude, when a violent Tournado or Hurricane took us quite out of our Knowledge; it began from the South-East, came about to the North-West, and then settled into the North-East, from whence it blew in such a terrible manner, that for twelve Days together we could do nothing but drive . . . scudding away before it" (31–2). When, on the twelfth day, "the Weather abating a little, the Master made an Observation as well as he could, he found that he was in about 11 Degrees North Latitude, but that he was 22 Degrees of Longitude difference West from *Cape St. Augustino*; so that he found he was gotten upon the Coast of *Guinea*, or the North Part of *Brasil*, beyond the River *Amozones* toward that of the River *Oronoque*" (31–2).[72] With all these workmanlike details, Defoe is describing the craft of navigation. At the same time, he is proffering information that will be useful for the work of the cunning reader. This information helps answer the question about the whereabouts of Crusoe's island that the novel's hero can discover only many years later into the novel's plot.

WARRIOR CRAFT: ROBERT CHEVALIER, PIRATE CAPTAIN

The pirate Robert Beauchêne, who is the hero of Alain René Le Sage's *Les Avantures de Monsieur Robert Chevalier, Dit de Beauchêne, Capitaine de flibustiers dans la nouvelle France* (1732) is an enterprising adventurer, like Lade and Crusoe. And his deeds, too, are steeped in the ethos of craft from the narrative's preface, which I am citing from the English translation of the novel in 1745. Via his bookseller, Beauchêne justifies to his reader "the Infinity of minute Details of the Rencounters in which he commanded; for according to his Notions, a Captain of a Privateer, nay a common Master of a Ship, ought to have the same Prudence, Courage, and Address, in the Conduct of their Affairs, as an Admiral has in his."[73] But Beauchêne, whom Le Sage drew from a historical model, gives his own twist to craft as well, stemming from his colonial origins. Beauchêne is raised by what Le Sage paints as the proud, courageous, and bloodthirsty Iroquois on the Canadian frontier. As a result of this formation, Beauchêne exhibits a warrior version of craft that resembles the valor of a medieval knight, despite his obscure origins, in contrast to the technologically adept craft of the jury-rigging Lade or Crusoe.

Much of La Sage's novel is devoted to the power of Beauchêne's craft, enabling him to thrive in the wild zone "beyond the line"—to cite Carl Schmitt's term for the New World territories and oceans discussed in the introduction; the zone where "the [European] struggle for land–appropriations knew no bounds. Beyond the line was an 'overseas' zone in which, for want of any legal limits to war, only the law of the stronger applied. . . . This freedom meant that the line set aside an area where force could be used freely and ruthlessly."[74] In this wild zone, individuals struggle continuously to at once create and to enforce the conditions of their recognition, in a frontier version of Hegel's master–slave dialectic. Beauchêne's warrior prowess allows him to excel at this contest, enabling him to compel respect in the absence of any established social order. With Beauchêne's craft of valor, implicit in his family name—Knight [*Chevalier*]—Le Sage has framed the New World beyond the line as the inheritor of feudal times, drafting a new form of modern romance, with the swashbuckling pirate as its star.

BOLDNESS TO HELL: CAPTAIN EDWARD TEACH, AKA BLACKBEARD

The pirate's mastery of craft is the lesson of the sensational *A General History of the Pyrates* (1724), a wildly successful collection of pirate biographies that scholars believe to have been coauthored if not written by Defoe. When its putative author, Captain Johnson, justified the book, he contrasted the disreputable deeds of his protagonists with the usual exemplary heroism that made lives worthy of literary record. Johnson noted nonetheless that his subjects excelled in a version of craft: "Bravery and Stratagem in War." Such excellence "make[s] Actions worthy of Record;

in which Sense the Adventures here related will be thought deserving that Name."[75] Though this collection is not a novel, it is worth mentioning three of its profiles in craft, which show the widely differing possibilities for instantiations of this compleat capacity, encompassing both evil and emancipation. Captain Johnson himself noted the likeness of his biographies to "a Novel" apropos of the female pirates Anne Bonny and Mary Read, who, however, were historical figures, in a fusion of fact and fiction characteristic of craft's romance of practice.[76]

In all the annals of craft, there is no figure (with the exception of Ahab) who better exemplifies the untempered exercise of what I have called "resolution" than Captain Edward Teach, aka Blackbeard (figure 2.4). Blackbeard, in his biographer's words, evinced "uncommon Boldness and personal Courage," but he applied it in thoroughly immoral contexts, showing: "to what a Pitch of Wickedness, human Nature may arrive, if its Passions are not checked." When Teach turned his wickedness against his crew, he offered a pathological example of the importance of force to compel recognition in the world "beyond the line." "One Night drinking in his cabin with *Hands* [the ship's master], the Pilot, and another Man; *Black-beard*, without any Provocation, privately draws out a small Pair of Pistols, and cocks them under the Table. . . . When the Pistols were ready, he blew out the Candle, and crossing his Hands, discharged them at his Company; *Hands*, the Master, was shot thro' the Knee, and lam'd for Life . . . Being asked the meaning of this, he only answered, by damning them, that if he did not now and then kill one of them, they would forget who he was."[77] Johnson details Blackbeard's "extravagant" "Frolicks of Wickedness," which include challenging his crew to join him in making *"a Hell of [our] own"* to see how long *"we can bear it."* With this design, Blackbeard closed up all the hatches in the Hold, "filled several Pots full of Brimstone," and other "combustible Matter," sets it on fire, and "so continued till they were almost suffocated," "pleased that he held out the longest," when he finally opened the hatches for air.[78]

THE CRAFT OF FREEDOM: CAPTAIN MISSON

The proto-socialistic Captain Misson, also a subject of Johnson's biographies, is at the antipodes of Johnson, seeking to create on earth a Utopia out of craft, rather than a living Hell. The key to craft's utopia for Misson is its liberal promise to form the basis of an elite distinguished by merit and work. Misson first intimates craft's meritocracy when he rejects the career of the sword open to him as the younger son of wealthy nobility, and instead adopts the more workmanlike way of the sea, not only learning the science of navigation but "always one of the first on a Yard

Figure 2.4. Captain Edward Teach, aka "Blackbeard." Note the similarity in his depiction to the portrait of Robinson Crusoe on the barren beach of his island (figure 2.1). Both stand on the shore, decked with their weapons, against a background depicting a ship. The water serving as Blackbeard's backdrop is coastal, in contrast to the wild sea framing Crusoe. Pirates favored coastal waters, where they used small, maneuverable crafts and exploited the shallows against more cumbersome deep sea vessels. Coastal waters also gave them nooks and crannies to hide in, aiding their guerrilla tactics. "Blackbeard, the Pirate," illustration in Captain Charles Johnson, *A General History of the Pyrates* (London: T. Woodward, 1726). Courtesy of the John Carter Brown Library at Brown University.

Arm, either to Hand or Reef, and very inquisitive in the different Methods of working a Ship," which made him a "compleat sailor."[79] While on his travels in Rome, Misson meets a deist priest, Carracioli, who disillusions him with the "subtle enterprising Genius," of organized religion.[80] Though the narrator frames Carracioli as "ambitious" and "irreligious," he nonetheless spurs Misson to shape a renegade pirate community founded on principles of complete liberty and equality, including the abolition of slavery.[81] Its culmination is the foundation of an island society baptized "*Libertalia*," whose cosmopolitan people, hailing from across cultures of the early modern maritime crucible, are called *Liberi*, in keeping with Misson's desire that "in that might be drown'd the distinguish'd Names of *French, English, Dutch, Africans, &c.*"[82]

HEROINES OF CRAFT: ANNE BONNY AND MARY READ

Women are generally barred from acceding to craft's empowered agency in the masculine fraternity of the sea. But Captain Johnson includes the biographies of two cross-dressing female pirates, Anne Bonny and Mary Read, who wield weapons and their wits to outdo their male brethren. In their dazzling, if brief, career, they underscore that craft is fundamentally a capacity of merit, available to anyone who can excel in its diverse arts. Johnson's edition includes an illustration of Bonny and Read brandishing swords, which emphasizes the two women's ability to exploit male embodiment, down to their five-o'clock shadows (figure 2.5). At the same time, the two resourceful heroines have no hesitation reclaiming their female embodiment in the struggle for survival. This switch occurs when Bonny and Read are captured with their other male shipmates, who are hanged. Bonny and Read, in contrast, plead pregnancy and are pardoned.[83]

CRAFT AND VIRTUE: RODERICK RANDOM

Craft is an amoral capacity that can serve vice as well as virtue—most often vice, in the case of Captain Johnson's notorious subjects. The attempt to accommodate craft to virtue is challenging, and worth a novel of its own. This novel is Tobias Smollett's first novel, *The Adventures of Roderick Random* (1748), a picaresque novel with extensive sections on life at sea.

Smollett's hero, Random, is an illegitimate child of a gentleman and his poor relation, as inured to hardship as any picaresque hero from his childhood. Random is saved from destitution only by a kindly uncle, who is a sailor. When Random's uncle kills his Captain in a duel and then

Figure 2.5. Anne Bonny and Mary Read, also notorious pirates. Like Blackbeard and Crusoe, they stand on the shore, decked with their weapons, against
a coastal background with ships. Their figures and hairstyles are feminine,
but they have stubble on their faces, as if they were hermaphrodites, and their
poses are bold and open. The meritocratic craft of the sea is available to anyone
who has the ability—and the opportunity—to learn and master its demanding
capacities, even women. "Anne Bonny and Mary Read," illustration in Captain
Charles Johnson, *A General History of the Pyrates* (London: T. Woodward,
1726). Courtesy of the John Carter Brown Library at Brown University.

deserts, Random is left to make his career relying on his wits, thrown
into the picaro's struggle to eke out an existence. Picaresque cunning is
exported to life at sea, when Random eventually gets a place in the British
Navy as a surgeon's mate, and his travels will include a detailed account
of serving on a British naval vessel fighting the Spanish in the New World.
The Navy is a perfect instance of the kind of authoritarian structures
where sailors—in particular, those before the mast—call on popular cunning just to survive. At the same time, Random's life as a member of the
fraternity of craft is fused with his education into the arts of a humane
and skillful surgeon.[84] Since antiquity, the doctor has been cited as an
example of virtue in the practical arts, more ethically upstanding than the
navigator, to whom he is compared.[85]

In this novel of Smollett's almost thirty years after *Robinson Crusoe*,
the reward for the mariner's craft is not profit from overseas adventure,
as it was for the heroes of Defoe. Rather, a marriage, fortune, and moral

improvement all crown Random's wandering career, and though he rises tempered by the wild world beyond the line, he ultimately renounces its amoral temptations. Random serves honorably in the British Navy, which helps him form a steady character and in the end enables him to win the heart of a wealthy gentlewoman. In Random's words, echoing her genteel judgment, "the miseries I had undergone, by improving the faculties both of mind and body, qualified me the more for any dignified station."[86]

Random's fate is that of the maritime picaresque itself. Following *Roderick Random*, the maritime adventure novel will yield in the second half of the eighteenth century to novels set on land about the pleasures and desires of civil society. This territorialization applies to adventure novels, as well as novels of manners, until James Fenimore Cooper revitalized the sea adventure novel in 1824.

CHAPTER 3

Sea Adventure Fiction, 1748–1824?

THE YEARS BETWEEN Smollett's *Roderick Random* (1748) and James Fenimore Cooper's *The Pilot* (1824) span a period of vibrant innovation in the novel. During this time, writers in Western Europe pioneered some of the most important genres in the history of the form. These poetics include the different members of the family of the novel of manners, such as the novel of worldliness, the domestic novel, and the novel of education, as well as the sentimental novel. The picaresque novel flourished on land leading to a slapstick form in France, *le roman gai*, and the picaresque loosened the stays of the novel of manners, yielding libertine fiction. Tales of ghosts and the Gothic novel shadowed the Enlightenment, whose moral and epistemological principles were turned to action in *le roman philosophique*. And in 1814, with *Waverley*, Walter Scott invented a type of historical fiction that was to launch the novel to a major role in shaping modern cultural nationalism across Europe and the Americas in the nineteenth century.

The world's oceans similarly remained a frontier of modernity during this span. 1748–1824 was the era that saw the systematic exploration of the Pacific, in expeditions commanded by Anson and Bougainville, La Pérouse, Cook, and Vancouver, among others. Along with accurate charts, these explorations yielded knowledge of the South Pacific and its inhabitants, and Cook went a long way to demystifying the idea that the South Pole was home to an inhabitable Great Southern Continent. The invention and dissemination of Harrison's chronometer permitting the calculation of longitude at sea and the conquest of scurvy are just a few more highlights from the maritime frontier across these years.

Professionals eagerly awaited news of such innovations, and so did general readers, as the maritime book trade boomed. Philip Edwards is speaking of the entire eighteenth century when he observes that along with the serious professional audience for sea voyage literature, "there were not enough scientists, navigators, entrepreneurs and politicians to buy books in the quantities that would keep publishers in funds. It was the general public who made voyage-narratives so profitable to publish."[1] Alongside the narratives of historical explorers, readers perused shipwreck narratives, ranging from narratives about the wreck of His Majesty's Ship *The Wager* in Anson's expedition (1740–1744) by some of its survivors, including John Bulkeley and John Cummins, Alexander Campbell, Isaac Morris, and John Byron, to Owen Chase's account of the disaster that befell the whaleship *Essex* in 1819. Readers bought historical accounts of routine sea voyages by travelers other than mariners, like the dying Henry Fielding's *Journal of a Voyage to Lisbon* (1755) or the naturalist Bernardin de Saint-Pierre's *Voyage à l'Isle de France* (1773). They also consumed collections that included summaries of famous voyages across the history of ocean travel, like Tobias Smollett's *Compendium of Authentic and Entertaining Voyages* (1756), the Abbé Prévost's fifteen-volume *Histoire générale des voyages* (1746–1759), and Jean Louis Hubert Simon Desperthes's *Histoire des naufrages* (1788–1789).

Given this ferment around the novel, the sea, and the maritime book in 1748–1824, one would expect novelists of the time to continue to expand the library of sea adventure fiction. Yet the maritime picaresque was abandoned—at least, that is the conclusion to draw from the well-remembered novels of the time. The absence is puzzling, and it may be that there are collections I have overlooked—this chapter could well be a stub awaiting emendations. In any event, James Fenimore Cooper noted the fact that sea novels faded after Smollett, when Cooper vaunted how he had renewed the genre in a preface to his *The Red Rover*.

To note the absence of seafaring as a subject driving adventure plots is not to say that the maritime world entirely disappeared from the pages of the novel genre.[2] Across the different novels being practiced in the years between Smollett and Cooper, seamen and sea travel make occasional appearances, in one of two ways. The maritime world can serve as a reservoir of character types.[3] In Fanny Burney's *Evelina*, for example, the pranks of the gruff, coarse Captain Mirven enliven country and city society's bland gentility. The British Navy is populated by two social types in the novels of Jane Austen, who was a sister of not just one rear admiral, like Fanny Burney (James Burney), but of two (Charles Austen and Francis Austen). The aristocratic "*Rears* and *Vices*" are one type wittily characterized by Mary from *Mansfield Park*, ward of the scandalous rear admiral.[4] Staël's Lord Nelvil in *Corinne*, too, is a dissolute aristocratic mariner, dallying with an extraordinary entertainer in Italy, before breaking her heart to marry the proper young lady who serves his family's interest. The honest young man from impoverished background who rises through his own merit is the other type. In *Mansfield Park*, Fanny's brother William is an appealing embodiment of vigorous young manhood, as is the seasoned Fredrick Wentworth, hero of *Persuasion*. These active, forthright characters offer an attractive alternative to the etiolated aristocrats who can be romantic leads in domestic fiction, as in novels like Burney's *Evelina*, or even Fanny's beloved Edmund in Austen's *Mansfield Park*.[5]

Across the years 1748–1824, maritime travel also continues to be used as a plot convention to precipitate encounters between characters. This use of seafaring dates back to the romances of antiquity, where global ocean travel could provide connections between episodes and bring into contact emissaries of distant and sometimes clashing worlds. In classical romance, this contact was dangerous and chaotic. The sea harbored alluring or vicious figures and forces that diverted the character from his or her intended goal. The Sirens and nymphs play such a role in *The Odyssey*, and pirates in Heliodorus's *Ethiopian Romance* recur to divert sea voyagers from their intentional destinations. Both these romances inspired the inventors of the novel when they were translated into the vernacular in the early modern period.

The world beyond the line of the eighteenth-century maritime picaresque contained echoes of the chaotic encounters precipitated by sea voyages in romance. In novels penned later in the century, in contrast, oceans and seas facilitate more organized narrative and social interactions, even while retaining the possibility of deadly shipwreck. To embark on the Atlantic and Mediterranean, as well as the Indian Ocean, during these years was to connect across difference. Françoise de Graffigny's *Lettres d'une péruvienne* (1747) starts the process of integrating a captive Inca princess into aristocratic French society during an Atlantic crossing, when the princess herself captivates a French aristocrat. In Frances Brooke's *History of Emily Montague* (1769), which has been called the first Canadian novel, the love between the Montreal settler Emily Montague and the English Colonel Rivers spans the Atlantic. Almost fifty years later, in Scott's *The Pirate* (1821), virtuous country gentility and a pirate susceptible to reform meet along the Scottish coast.

Such cross-ocean connections perform cultural work, even as they stimulate the plot of novels both in England and in France. In *The History of Emily Montague*, epistolary exchange across the Atlantic provides ample opportunity for delay and miscommunication but also forges the affective bonds of a civil society scaled to the global British empire. As the letters portray customs ranging from those of the Hurons and the Canadian settlers to London high society, they set norms of nature and virtue that can unify the different groups of the empire into a graded spectrum of manners and morals. In Scott's *The Pirate*, in contrast, the energy draws in toward the homeland, and the dashing Cleveland is redeemed through love and puts his supranational craft in the patriotic service of the British Navy.

On the French side of the literary Channel, cross-ocean travel is also an occasion to meld disparate values in a socially productive way. In *Lettres d'une péruvienne*, for example, the ocean periphery conveys an exotic character back to the core, and her uncorrupted virtue and simplicity provide a salutary corrective to the overly artificial French aristocracy. In Bernardin de Saint-Pierre's *Paul et Virginie* (1786), the aristocratic Virginie, born and raised on the Ile Maurice, is sent away from home and her childhood love, Paul, to perfect her lady's education in France. The distance across oceans tests and affirms their bond, despite the fact that Paul is déclassé and born out of wedlock, before Virginie dies in a shipwreck on her return, within sight of land, because she is too modest to remove her clothes.

Among the naturalist Bernardin's works, as I have mentioned, is his nonfictional overseas travel narrative that included a visit to the Ile Maurice of *Paul et Virginie*. The *Voyage à l'Isle de France* follows the conventions of nonfictional sea voyage narrative closely, offering remarkable occurrences of danger and remedy, from seasickness to destruction of the vessel. Saint-Pierre narrated these adventures in plain style, and organized information day by day, echoing the 24-hour frame of reference of a ship's log. Saint-Pierre's familiarity with overseas travel and travel narrative, yet his refusal to call on this familiarity in *Paul et Virginie*, is a confirmation that writers were not penning maritime adventure fiction because they lacked knowledge about seafaring or maritime travel literature. Nor had they forgotten *Robinson Crusoe*, which remained beloved by readers. Indeed, Jean-Jacques Rousseau deemed *Robinson Crusoe* the only book needed to educate the young lad Emile, cultivating resourcefulness and the values of artisanal labor.

SOME CONJECTURES

When James Fenimore Cooper explained the hiatus between Smollett and his own *The Pilot*, he laid both the credit and the blame on Smollett's overwhelming mastery. In his words, "Smollett had obtained so much success as a writer of nautical tales, that it probably required a new course should be steered in order to enable the succeeding adventurer in this branch of literature to meet with any favour."[6] Cooper's hypothesis is that of an author, emphasizing his literary feat. My own line of speculation draws on recent critical scholarship concerning the novel's cultural work in the period 1748–1824.

These years coincide with the moment when the novel was engaged in unifying the nation as an imagined community in the English and French traditions at issue in my study. Across different strains of the novel of manners, courtship plots, notably, were used to integrate different social classes and regions into a single nation, as well as to situate nations within an international republic of culture, through defining European "types" against one another. The fate of Roderick Random to be secured on shore in a happy marriage to a gentlewoman is indicative of what is to come. This will be a similar fate of mariner characters when they show up in novels, be it Scott's criminal pirate, Cleveland, in *The Pirate*, or Jane Austen's upstanding officer, Frederick Wentworth, in *Persuasion*. The maritime picaresque would be hard to transform to achieve such a centripetal project. Its rambling disposition pulls it outward from civil society toward comportment that navigates risk on the Edge zones of the globe, in the world beyond the line.

A related problem posed by the maritime picaresque to the novel's cultural work in these years involves the mariner's ethos of craft. Along with imagining the modern nation, critics have shown how the novel across the later eighteenth and early nineteenth century helps forge a new set of dominant values by melding middle-class values of virtue and nature with aristocratic values of status and blood. In this cultural mythmaking, the courtship plot plays an important role. But the mariner's job to rove troubles the domestic closure of a happy courtship plot. The value of craft itself moreover has a dubious, unstable relation to virtue and no connection to birth, since it is an ethos grounded in work. In certain respects, the connection of craft to skilled work makes it a value appealing to the middle class. At the same time, the middle-class ethos of work is inimical to the aristocracy, constitutively a leisure class. From this perspective, craft, if taken up, would drag the novel away from its ability to forge an alliance between aristocracy and bourgeoisie, which novel critics have argued as one of the cultural roles of the novel in the second half of the eighteenth century. The ethos of work is, however, a way to accommodate middle-class and working-class values. This potential may help explain the renewal of sea fiction in the middle of the nineteenth century, when the aristocracy's role on the stage of world history dwindled, and the novel turned to making sense of the relation between now hegemonic middle classes and lower classes seeking access to middle-class rights and privileges.

One question from a feminist perspective is whether the absence of maritime novels in 1748–1824 was shaped by the novel's pervasive association at this time with feminized sociability. There was a sociological component to this association: the female reading public expanded. And there was an ideological component: the feminization of private life was part of how middle-class ideology established the distinction between public and private spheres, and private life was an important part of the novel's domain. The masculine work of the sea and maritime adventures could be hard to accommodate to the processes of feminization so visible in the novel in the seventy-five years between Smollett and Cooper. However, this speculation could be countered with Henry Tilney's answer to Catherine Morland apropos of her schematic division between novels for ladies and books for gentleman: "the person, be it gentlemen or lady, who has not pleasure in a good novel, must be intolerably stupid."[7]

A final thought, from the perspective of the book trade: novelists had a hard time drafting works as exciting and remarkable as historical accounts in the era when Europeans navigated and charted the Pacific. Novelists would need to wait until the remarkable news from the sea slowed down; it was at sunset, like Hegel's owl of Minerva, that the sea novel once more set sail.

• • •

While maritime adventure fiction lay dormant in the years 1748–1824, the sea was being actively reimagined in other aesthetic media and genre. In the ensuing interlude, "The Sublimation of the Sea," I describe that process of reimagination. Today, we think of the ocean as an elemental, wild zone devoid of human life. In fact, however, this notion is another name for the sea's disappearance as a theater of craft in the development of the Enlightenment/Romantic sublime.

The sublime was the expression of a distinctively modern notion of aesthetic grandeur. The sublime broke with ornate, stylized patterns of magnificence, in the name of a new kind of elevation: the elevation procured by witnessing spectacles of overwhelming power, be they of sublime "glory" or "gloom," to use the art critic John Ruskin's terms apropos of the painter J.M.W. Turner.[8] The sea was an ideal example of the terrifying sublime. At the same time, the Enlightenment episteme drew a sharp distinction between aesthetics and work. The sea could be rethought in sublime terms only by being transformed into a wild space of raw, natural power, disconnected from the human agency of craft.

In keeping with the elevated status of the sublime, the literary genres for the elaboration of the sublime were elevated as well. These genres were not the mariner's prose of work, nor even the polite novel, but rather philosophy and poetry, which are the textual basis of my argument in the following interlude. As we will see, landscape painting, too, played a role in the process of disconnecting wild natural seas from human work. Romantic landscapes of the ocean are in fact not originary, presocial landscape but rather pointed constructions, replacing the information-rich genre paintings of maritime life in early modern art.

Within literature, narrative poetry is the medium where the sea undergoes sublimation. As I argue in the following interlude, the sublime vision of the sea emerges in *Paradise Lost* of Milton, who elevated seventeenth-century accounts of the maritime frontier into epic poetry. Narrative poetry, if not specifically epic, would continue to be the medium for delineating the sea across its sublimation. Indeed, even after the process is completed, Romantic poets like Byron and Coleridge used narrative poetry to repopulate the empty seas with creatures of their imagination, on a voyage devoid of craft.[9]

Though the following interlude breaks with my attention to the novel, it tracks a cultural reimagination of the sea so profound it will affect maritime adventure fiction, when James Fenimore Cooper reinvigorated the sea novel in the 1820s. While the sublime's empty seas were not historically accurate, their abstract vacancy stimulated novelists' fertile imagination. In chapters 4 and 5, you will see nineteenth-century authors of sea fiction repopulate the empty seas of the sublime with a more diverse, even extravagant, spectrum of protagonists than the adventurers, renegades, and castaways of the eighteenth-century maritime picaresque—even female, like Lieutenant Murray Ballou's Fanny Campbell, the female pirate, or supernatural, like the Flying Dutchman and the Mephistophelean pilot Schriften, in Captain Marryat's *The Phantom Ship*.

The Sublimation of the Sea

"*Od' und leer das Meer*"
—Tristan in Richard Wagner's *Tristan und Isolde*,
cited from T. S. Eliot's *Wasteland*[1]

Transgressing the Boundaries

The "sublime" is a distinctive aesthetic of modernity, customarily defined as the pleasure offered by spectacles of overwhelming power. It was first formulated by Longinus, a classical Greek author, in a treaty titled *Peri Hypsos*, "on elevated writing." In Longinus's account, sublime or elevated style included figures of speech and thought so powerful that listeners would forget they were listening to oratory, lose their critical distance, and be "transported." Though these practices were diverse, they shared the fact that they represented extremes of power and emotion. Longinus encompassed excesses of elevation and destruction: the sublime's "glory" and "gloom," to take up the phrase of John Ruskin apropos of a master of the sublime in painting, J.M.W. Turner.[2]

The glorious face to the sublime for Longinus was God's creative word as recounted in the Hebrew Bible. The passage "Let there be light," he suggested, combined simplicity with magnificence of thought. At the gloomy end of the spectrum were scenes that Longinus was less comfortable theorizing, though they fill his treatise, because they are "terrifying; yet from another point of view they are . . . altogether impious and transgress the boundaries of good taste."[3]

Among Longinus's examples of transgressive and impious sublime images, he repeatedly cited portrayals of what the mariners of modernity would call remarkable occurrences at sea. Thus, he mentioned a storm simile used by Homer to capture a warrior's superior strength in battle:

> He rushed upon them, as a wave storm-driven,
> Boisterous beneath black clouds, on a swift ship
> Will burst, and all is hidden in the foam;
> Meanwhile the wind tears thundering at the mast,
> And all hands tremble, pale and sore afraid,
> As they are carried close from under death.[4]

Explaining why this image grips us, Longinus spoke of content: the gripping, as well as apt, details as Homer "draws a picture of men avoiding
destruction many times, at every wave." Homer reinforced such a representation of mortal peril with a violent use of syntax that strained beyond
the limits of acceptable practice. Longinus writes that Homer "forces and
compels into unnatural union prepositions which are not easily joined
together when he says *'from under* death.' He has tortured his line into
conformity with the impending disaster, and by the compactness of his
language he brilliantly represents the calamity and almost stamps upon the
words the very shape of the peril: 'they are carried from under death.'"[5]

Implicit in Longinus's formulation of the sublime is the aesthetic interest of crossing beyond the line—the limits of life in the case of the seafarers and the limits of rhetoric and syntax for the poet. As an aesthetic
shaped by the experience of limits and their transgression, the sublime
emerged from one of the central concerns of classical tragedy—the limits
of the human—even as it violated the respect for limits that is a familiar
hallmark of classical thought. Aristotle's poetics would be an example
of the classical respect for limits in the domain of literary criticism. He
is concerned with how tragedies adhere to ideal patterns, rather than
searching for innovations that break the mold. Longinus does not theorize the value of venturing beyond the line, whether apropos of rhetoric
or the wild ocean. Nonetheless, in registering its power, Longinus distinguishes an aspect of the sublime that will make it one of the—if not
the—defining aesthetic of modernity.

Longinus's treatise was disregarded by European aesthetics until the
early modern period. It was brought to critical attention with its translation into the vernacular, and notably with *Du Sublime, ou du Merveilleux
dans le Discours: Traduit du Grec de Longin* [Treatise on the Sublime and
Marvelous in Discourse Translated from the Greek of Longinus] (1674),
by Nicolas Boileau, a critic who played a preeminent role in defining
the neoclassical aesthetic. In Boileau's preface to his translation, he used
Longinus to identify that there were other kinds of forceful representations that could move audiences beyond magnificence and pomp of conventional high style. As Boileau observed, "sublime style always calls for
great words; but the Sublime can be found in a single thought, a single
figure, a single turn of phrase."[6] With this observation, Boileau effected
the fundamental transformation of the sublime in its modern renewal,
from a qualification of style to a matter of content and thought.[7]

As Boileau attempted to characterize the nature of such forceful representations, the term "sublime" alone seemed not to suffice. In the title
of his translation, he coupled the sublime with the marvelous, an expansion he reiterated in his preface, adding as well the terms "extraordinary"
and "surprising." Boileau pronounced, "It is important to know that by

sublime, Longinus does not mean what Orators call sublime style, but rather the extraordinary and the marvelous qualities [*cet extraordinaire et ce merveilleux*] that make a work delight us, transport us, carry us away [*enlève, ravit, transporte*]." And again, "We must understand by the sublime in Longinus the extraordinary, the surprising, and, as in my translation, the marvelous in discourse."

Marvelous, extraordinary, surprising: to catch the character of the sublime, Boileau casts a semantic net including terms then in contemporary circulation for mariners' discoveries and dangers in the Edge zones of the maritime frontier. While the term "marvelous" was applied to the wonders found in New Worlds, "extraordinary" and "surprising" recurred as synonyms for remarkable dangers at sea. Less than a decade before Boileau, John Milton, the poet subsequently acknowledged as founder of modern sublimity, would use the mariner's comportment amidst such dangers to model the kind of empowered agency that strives to go beyond the limits, to the point of overthrowing God.

SATAN ON THE BEACH

Milton's *Paradise Lost*, first published in 1667, contains scenes of both sublime gloom and sublime glory. Sublime glory radiates from Milton's portrayal of heaven and paradise; sublime gloom envelops the rebellious Satan's fall. When Milton described the hostile regions of Satan's new sublunary empire, critics have noted that they were modeled on the harsh conditions discovered by maritime explorers on the wild seas beyond the line—in particular, the Arctic wastes. Ian MacClaren, for example, specifies that Milton's portrayal of a "frozen continent" discovered by Satan's devils echoes the Arctic wastes portrayed in *The Strange and Dangerous Voyage of Captaine Thomas James* (1633) popular in Milton's time.[8] In Milton's reworking, James's arctic wastes become a continent of sublime gloom indeed:

> ... dark and wild, beat with perpetual storms
> Of whirlwind and dire hail which on firm land
> Thaws not but gathers heap and ruin seems
> Of ancient pile. All else deep snow and ice,
> ... The parching air
> Burns frore and cold performs th' effect of fire.[9]

Satan's devils come upon this continent bound on a "bold adventure."[10] In their roving dispositions, they resemble navigators who sought the Northwest passage or plumbed other Edge zones of the globe beyond the bounds of European knowledge and technology.[11]

The maritime frontier shapes the sublimity of Satan's fall not only as concerns his new empire, but in how Milton characterizes Satan's empowered agency. When Satan plunges from Heaven, he falls into a sea of fire, and Milton figures him first as a monster of the deep, Leviathan. This monster, however, soon reveals the countenance of a compleat mariner, cool head "uplift above the wave and eyes / That sparkling blazed," radiating resolution.[12]

To anatomize the comportment of Satan amidst such dangers, we can go down the checklist of craft. As he falls, Satan is in dire danger, "Prone on the flood." But he is not alone; he has "the companions of his fall o'erwhelmed / With floods and whirlwinds of tempestuous fire . . . welt'ring by his side."[13] As the compleat mariner, he evinces strategic optimism amidst such disaster. He incites his crew to make for a "dreary plain," beyond the "the tossing of these fiery waves," to seek "What reinforcement we may gain from hope, / If not what resolution from despair."[14] Satan then supplements such resolute words with embodiment, lifting himself up to flit across the ocean surface and land on an unknown shore. There, he discovers "dry land" that proves to be "burning," and his "uneasy steps" are "not like those steps / On Heaven's azure . . . and the torrid clime / Smote on him sore besides, vaulted with fire." Persisting amidst suffering, Satan exhibits the mariner's patience and endeavor: "Nathless he so endured, till on the beach / Of that inflamèd sea he stood."[15] Milton reinforces this association of Satan on the beach with the bold mariner by turning Satan's spear into the mast supporting great ambitions of nautical adventure: "His spear (to equal which the tallest pine / Hewn on Norwegian hills to be the mast / Of some great admiral were but a wand)."[16]

Unlike the compleat mariner, however, whose professional persona projects prudence toward the mighty and treacherous ocean, Satan crowns his craft by self-consciously reveling in its power. When Satan and his mates touch the shore, their first action is to "glory . . . to have scaped the Stygian flood / As gods and by their own recovered strength / Not by the suff'rance of Supernal Pow'r."[17] It is with this attitude of defiant confidence that Satan then starts the mariner's task of surveying and charting the newly discovered shores: "'Is this the region, this the soil, the clime,'/ Said then the lost archangel, 'this the seat / That we must change for Heav'n, this mournful gloom / For that celestial light?'"[18] Having Satan and his crew defy Providence and vindicate their own empowered agency, Milton implies the potential sedition to a theological worldview of the mariner's craft, though Satan's bold defiance contrasts with the uneasy accommodation of survival and salvation in mariners' own accounts.

THINGS UNATTEMPTED YET IN PROSE OR RHYME: MILTON THE
JURY-RIGGER

Satan on the beach is a path-breaking navigator, discovering the brutal
conditions of his new, sublunary realm. His creator, Milton, is an explorer as well. From the opening line of his epic poem, "[b]old, and sublime," Milton figures his "advent'rous song," as eschewing the middle
way: "with no middle flight intend[ing] to soar / Above th' Aonian mount
while it pursues / Things unattempted yet in prose or rhyme."[19]

To pursue things unattempted is to surpass what has gone before. One
important intertext for the scene of Satan on the beach is a moment from
Camões's *Lusaíds* when Vasco da Gama first steps on new, unexplored
lands, after he has accomplished the feat never before achieved by European navigators of rounding the Cape of Good Hope. At this moment of
discovery, da Gama shows himself entirely devoted to his craft, seeking
to fix his bearings, in contrast to Satan's self-conscious pride.[20] Da Gama
does this by wheeling out the astrolabe that he had not been able to sta-
bilize on the ship's pitching deck:

> But I, eager to know where I was,
> Stayed on the sandy beach with the pilots
> To measure the sun's height, and use our art
> To fix our bearing on the cosmic chart.[21]

The astrolabe is a cumbersome technology from the late medieval period.
It is replaced in the sixteenth century by the portable cross-staff and back-
staff, subsequently refined into the sextant that was to remain a foundational tool until GPS superceded celestial navigation in the mid-1990s.

Satan has a more up-to-date optical instrument at his disposal when he
first lands. This is the newly invented telescope, which will revolutionize
modern science. To lend his Biblical protagonist this state-of-the-art technology, Satan's creator, Milton, relies on poetic jury-rigging using figurative language. Camões simply describes da Gama's gesture, exemplifying
his ambition to narrate strategy and action without embellishment in a
romance of practice.[22] Milton, in contrast, endows Satan with his telescope via an obscure heroic simile. The simile concerns how Satan throws
his shield behind him as he struggles to the beach. When he does this, its

> ... broad circumference
> Hung on his shoulders like the moon whose orb
> Through optic glass the Tuscan artist views
> At evening from the top of Fesolè

Or in Valdarno to descry new lands,
Rivers or mountains in her spotty globe.[23]

When we unknot the strands of this simile, we are incited by Milton to reflect on the relations among technological innovation, craft, science, and human defiance of a theological worldview.

Milton scholars explain the "Tuscan artist" as Galileo, who was one of the telescope's pioneers. Milton was in fact supposed to have looked through Galileo's telescope in the company of the scientist, while Galileo was under house imprisonment by the Inquisition.[24] Among Galileo's goals in tracking the movement of celestial bodies—in this case, the satellites of Jupiter—was to find a way to use the heavens to solve the question of calculating longitude at sea. If the moon as viewed by Galileo through his telescope, then, is Satan's halo, this halo is made visible by scientific knowledge partnering with the mariner's practical reason with the aim of pushing the boundaries of knowledge by charting the heavens and the globe.

As Galileo's persecutors grasped, the potential of such scientific exploration is a thorough supersession of the theological cosmos, starting from the ability of astronomy to disprove the religious belief that sun and moon orbit around the earth (viz Galileo's "and yet, it moves"). It is thus fitting that Milton's ambiguous syntax enables a second, stranger reading where the moon, and by substitution, Satan's halo, becomes the subject and looks back at its viewer on earth, which has become the object. For though verisimilitude leads us to read the line in accordance with historical fact, the grammar of the simile is obscure. What if it is "the moon / whose orb / Through optic glass" views "the Tuscan artist"? The reversible syntax opens the possibility that the orb of the moon, and by metonymy, Satan, becomes the subject of the gaze, returning it back at the earth. With such creative jury-rigging, through the literary tools of the poet—simile, syntax, and a more fantastic exercise of the imagination than the mariner's conjecture—Satan takes possession of the telescope and adds it to his arsenal.[25]

Milton, of course, does not liken his own explorations in *Paradise Lost* to the fall of Satan into chaos and gloom. Rather, Milton strives upward toward sublime glory and the heights of the Muses. (Indeed, throughout the sublime lineage, sublime elevation is associated with rising upward toward the divinity, while sublime gloom dives into the abyss and spreads out across the vast unbounded landscape of the sea.) Along with his striving upward to the divinity, Milton intones a suitably pious moral: to "justify the ways of God to men."[26] However, though Milton may seek to soar upward, he shares with Satan and with the figure of the navigator the interest in transgressing limits. This interest contains the potential, even if not realized, to overthrow the theological worldview.

The sublime similarity between vanguard navigator and adventurous artist was noted by the painter Jonathan Richardson in *An Essay on the theory of painting* (1725). For Richardson, the artist was sublime in pushing beyond limits pursuing the expansion of poetic technique: "The sublime disdains to be trammelled, it knows no bounds, it is the sally of great geniuses and the perfection of human nature."[27] In such striving, the artist and the navigator were brethren, voyaging to new worlds. "Who knows what is hid in the womb of time!" Richardson declared. "Another may eclipse Rafaëlle; a new Columbus may cross the Atlantic ocean, and leave the pillars of that Hercules far behind. . . . 'So should the Artist, warm'd with Heav'nly Fire, / To a perfection yet Unknown aspire.' [Pope] This is the great rule for the sublime."[28]

The Low Sublime of Piracy

If Satan has kindred ennobled in his culture, like the mariner and artist, working in the dynamic Edge zones of modernity, Satan on the beach has more notorious brethren in the early modern maritime corpus as well. These are the brethren of the coast, pirates, who ply the world beyond the line with bold resolution, "gaining immense booty and committing unspeakable atrocities."[29] The language is from Alexandre Exquemelin's *The Buccaneers of America*. Published in the same decades as Boileau's translation of Longinus, Exquemelin's book launched the modern romance with the pirate's resolute willingness to go to the limits and beyond. In the passage I have quoted, Exquemelin is characterizing the most violent figure in his narrative, whom he likens to the devil for his cruelty. This comparison came at a moment when L'Olonnais was trying to extract intelligence from resistant Spanish prisoners. As they demurred, he became "possessed of a devil's fury, ripped open one of the prisoners with his cutlass, tore the living heart out of his body, gnawed at it, and then hurled it in the face of one of the others, saying, 'Show me another way, or I will do the same to you.'"[30]

Captain Johnson, too, used comparisons to the devil to characterize terrifying pirate violence in his *General History of the Pyrates* (1724). One of Johnson's particularly diabolical figures was Captain Edward Teach, aka Blackbeard. A pirate's pirate, Teach compelled admiration for his terrible deeds from fellow pirates, Johnson noted, for a person "who goes the greatest Length of Wickedness, is looked upon with a kind of Envy amongst them, as a Person of a more extraordinary Gallantry." Even his pleasures were "Frolicks of Wickedness . . . so extravagant, as if he aimed at making his Men believe he was a Devil incarnate." I have previously cited his challenge to his crew to make a "*Hell of [our] own*," in the hold of his ship.[31]

The destructive transgressions of L'Olonnais, Blackbeard, and their brethren are at the other end of the spectrum from the creative striving of Richardson's artists pursuing perfectability, or the acquisition of knowledge sought by the mariner at his most heroic. But they certainly go beyond the bounds, being "altogether impious and transgress[ing] the boundaries of good taste," to return to Longinus's understated phrase. Byron would recognize the kinship between pirates and more elevated strivings of the modern spirit when he dignified them to embody the existential pursuit of freedom in the Romantic gentrification of the work of the sea.

The Pleasure of an Unknown Navigation

Critics pondering the sublime had no difficulty explaining the exaltations of sublime elevation. But they struggled with the sublime pleasures taken in experiences that were terrifying, though they also returned repeatedly to their power. Since oceans were theaters of sublime terror, in contrast to mountain landscapes, associated with elevation toward God, ocean landscapes offered an occasion for such questions. Thus, John Dennis, writing in 1704, emphasized the distinctive sublime emotion of "enthusiastic terror" accompanying scenes of "thunder, tempests, raging seas, inundations, torrents," along with witchcraft, monsters, earthquakes, and other extraordinary physical occurrences.[32] When Addison pondered why the sight of the ocean should have the power to induce sublimity, his version of Dennis's "enthusiastic terror" was "agreeable horror." In *The Spectator* of September 20, 1712, Addison declared, "of all objects that I have ever seen, there is none which affects my imagination so much as the sea or ocean. I cannot see the heavings of this prodigious bulk of waters, even in a calm, without a very pleasing astonishment; but when it is worked up in a tempest, so that the horizon on every side is nothing but foaming billows and floating mountains, it is impossible to describe the agreeable horror that rises from such a prospect."[33] Linking the ocean's sublimity with the feelings aroused on a ship during a storm, Addison implicitly makes the connection between the perception of sublimity and the fear for life arising from mortal danger. The mariner's response would be to encounter such conditions with the resolution, strategic optimism, and other protocols of craft. But the sublime lineage would exchange that optimism, along with the struggle for survival, for the pleasures of terror.

Indeed, terror would become the basis of the sublime itself, when Edmund Burke capped half a century of speculations on agreeable horror with his *Philosophical Enquiry into the Origins of Our Ideas of the Sublime and Beautiful* (1757). There, he explained the function of such terror from the viewpoint of the idle spectator. Such experiences, Burke speculated, were good for the soul, and particularly salutary for those who suffered from melancholy.[34] With the spectacle of terror, the sublime stimulated the passion of self-preservation, and thus invigorated leisured aesthetes, who had no immediate experience of dangers.[35] In Burke's formulation, then, the sublime aesthetic offers an elevated version of the delights of *Robinson Crusoe* for the armchair sailor, who shadows Crusoe's struggles in her imagination.

In journals and published accounts, maritime explorers who grappled with the ocean's actual dangers were reticent that they took any pleasure in the terrifying aspects of their profession. Indeed, they rarely spoke of pleasure at all, representing themselves as entirely consumed with the work of craft and service to their mission. One exception to this reticence is offered by Cook when he meditated in his journals on the allure of "an unknown Navigation": "Was it not for the pleasure which naturly results to a Man from being the first discoverer, even was it nothing more than sands and Shoals, this service would be insuportable especialy in far distant parts, like this, short of Provisions and almost every other necessary."[36] Strikingly, at this moment, Cook speaks of navigation's pleasures in distinctly nonproductive terms, rather than as serving Enlightenment perfectibility, worldly power, or capitalist profit. He calls this allure "natural," which is to say difficult to conceptualize, and indicates that it is deeply compelling.

Perhaps Cook was able to articulate nonproductive pleasure distinctive to his work of maritime exploration because he was composing his journals in the 1760s and 1770s and was in some measure shaped by the aesthetic of the sublime. We can detect echoes of the sublime delineation of landscape at a few striking moments in what is otherwise his completely workmanlike adherence to plain style. One such moment is the previously cited description when Cook attempts to give a sense of the overwhelming, unimaginable aspect of the Great Barrier Reef that almost destroys him. At that point, Cook uses a vocabulary of sublimity to emphasize the failure not just of craft but of thought confronting the hitherto unimagined danger: "A Reef such as is here spoke of is scarcely known in Europe, it is a wall of Coral Rock rising all most perpendicular out of the unfathomable Ocean, always overflown at high-water generally 7 or 8 feet and dry in places at low-water; the large waves of the vast Ocean meeting with so sudden a resistance make a most terrible surf breaking mountains high especially as in our case when the general trade winds blowes directly upon it."[37] Note the sublime adjectives "vast," "unfathomable," and "terrible," in what is otherwise the mariner's plain style. With this recourse to sublimity, Cook shows us how, in a reversal, the sublime has returned from the realm of aesthetics, where it offered afterimages of the terror provoked by confronting the dynamic limits of modernity, to the mariners who practice these forbidding spaces in the physical world. By the time Cook drafts his journals, the sublime offers the discourse to express those aspects of modernity's fascination with going beyond the limits that cannot be explained by instrumental yields, but entails a more ambivalent—gloomier?—fascination.

The gloomy pleasures that attend the often painful efforts to work at the limits and beyond was a subject of reflection for theorists and poets of the sublime in the Romantic and post-Romantic lineage, who sometimes approached this problem through the theme of the voyage. I have mentioned, for example, how Baudelaire was fascinated by the compulsion to journey, and took it up in the concluding poem of *Les Fleurs du mal*, "Le Voyage." Now that the sublime's connection to the transgression of limits has been constellated with the mariner's journey, we can understand why Baudelaire ends with the figure of a ship captained by Death, and why in this journey, Baudelaire launches the crew beyond the very boundary between glory and gloom. "To Hell or Heaven," spleen or ideal, "what does it matter"? *Beyond good and evil* to find "something *new*."[38]

THE SUBLIME OCEAN: WHAT STRIKES THE EYE

Across the eighteenth century, the qualification of sublime was increasingly applied by philosophers and writers to the ocean cut off from work. When Joseph Addison evaluated the sea as sublime at the century's opening, he could still stipulate that it was best experienced as sublime when on board a vessel.[39] He wrote, "[a] troubled ocean, to a man who sails upon it, is, I think, the biggest object that he can see in motion, and consequently gives his imagination one of the highest kinds of pleasure that can arise from greatness."[40] But across the next decades, the sublime view from shipboard would disappear.

In 1747, for example, John Baillie noted two aspects of seafaring that disqualified the sea as known in practice from being sublime. First, the sublime was incompatible with everyday experience and eroded by familiarity: "The grandeur of the heavens seldoms affects us, it is our daily object, and two or three days at sea would sink all that elevated pleasure we feel upon viewing a vast ocean." And second, in actual navigation, the concern for personal safety would too great: "There ever enters in the description of storms . . . some small degree of dread, and this dread may be so heightened (when a person is actually in one) as entirely to destroy the sublime."[41] Burke would make this point made about sublime terror more generally. In Burke's words, when "danger or pain press too nearly, they are incapable of giving any delight, and are simply terrible; but at certain distances, and with certain modifications, they may be, and they are delightful, as we every day experience."[42]

The disconnection of work at sea from the sublime ocean belongs to the more general Enlightenment view that art should not be connected to business or instrumental reason. For Addison's contemporary, Shaftesbury, the sublime was to be removed from business. Thus, he puts characterizations of sublimity in the mouth of the "philosophical rhapsodist" Theocles, when Theocles takes retreat in pastoral leisure, "Ye fields and woods, my refuge from the toilsome world of business."[43] In the view of Theocles, the sublime is in nature divorced from human agency and indeed from life itself. Theocles accordingly finds the pinnacle of the sublime by looking up to the barren mountain tops, declaring, "But behold! through a vast tract of sky before us, the mighty Atlas rears his lofty head, covered with snow, above the clouds . . . space astonishes. Silence itself seems pregnant; whilst an unknown force works on the mind, and dubious objects move the wakeful sense."[44] When Shaftesbury does paint the ocean, tellingly, it is not in the context of the aesthetic of the sublime. Rather, he represents it as a realm of grotesque life, with, it should be said, a good deal of distaste. Thus, Shaftesbury inveighed against sea voyage narratives for their portrayals of "monstrous *Brutes*" ("some *enormous Fish*, or *Beast*") and "yet more *monstrous Men*": "*he* is ever compleatest, and of the first Rank, who is able to speak of Things the most *unnatural* and *monstrous*."[45]

Immanuel Kant would make explicit that the problem in using the ocean as a figure of sublimity was its powerful association with biology, knowledge, and work. In his "Analytic of the Sublime" from *The Critique of Judgment* (1790), Kant writes:

> if we are to call the sight of the ocean sublime, we must not *think* of it as we [ordinarily] do, as implying all kinds of knowledge. . . . For example, we sometimes think of the ocean as a vast kingdom of aquatic creatures, or as the great source of those vapors that fill the air with clouds for the benefit of the land, or again as an element which, though dividing continents from each other, yet promotes the greatest communication between them; but these furnish merely teleological judgments. To call the ocean sublime we must regard it as poets do, merely by what strikes the eye.[46]

The separation between aesthetics and instrumental reason articulated by Kant is essential to the Enlightenment episteme.

Shaped by this Enlightenment view, the aesthetic of the sublime would yield the wild ocean, a terrifying domain of uncontained nature, which remains the vision of the ocean that springs to mind when we think of this realm today. So powerful is this aesthetic that critics and cultural historians generally treat the sublimated sea and the birth of the ocean as new subject matter for art and literature. In his introduction to *The Oxford Book of the Sea*, Jonathan Raban, himself well versed in the craft as a mariner-author, muses on the curious fact that while the early modern world is chock-full of maritime figures, the sea heaves into view as an object of aesthetic contemplation only with Romanticism. For Raban, that is to say, the sublimation of the sea across the eighteenth century is the invention of the sea in art and literature. From the perspective of the early modern lineage of craft, this invention is rather a shift from a depiction of the ocean known in the intimacy of human practice to the ocean as "space itself."[47]

The cultural historian Alain Corbin, too, registers what I call the sublimation of the sea when he discusses the new aesthetic appreciation of the elemental ocean that gripped leisure travelers in the second half of the eighteenth century in *The Lure of the Sea*. Before 1750 he writes, it was rare to find "admiration expressed for the infinite expanse of the waves or the delight that arises from a visual analysis of actual substance; nowhere did anyone express a desire to feel the powers of waves or the touching coolness of the sands against his body . . . [or to enjoy] the brightness or transparency of the water."[48] But from the vantage point of the sublimation of the sea, what seems like the elemental ocean, deriving from nature, is in fact a socially constructed ocean, one purged of knowledge that comes from hands-on practice, along with dirty bilge water and people at work. Nathaniel Colson's chart of the kinds of sand that lie at the bottom of the Channel reproduced in chapter 1 (figure 1.7) epitomizes the useful, textured knowledge that disappears in the smooth, evacuated sea achieved by the Enlightenment sublime.

DARK-HEAVING, BOUNDLESS, ENDLESS, AND SUBLIME

Following the evacuation of the sea, Romantic writers are eager to repopulate it with characters and creatures of the imagination. When Coleridge constructs the sea as an archaic, enchanted realm ruled by spirits and superstition in *The Rime of the Ancyent Marinere*, to utilize the spelling of the work's original title, it is important to bear in mind that at the same time, the real seas were in the vanguard of science, technology, communications, and commerce. For Baudelaire and Rimbaud, the adventure of the sea will be internalized, whether it is the "monstrous, boundless sea" of Baudelaire's urban uncanny in "Les Sept Vieillards [Seven Old Men]" or the surreal interior landscapes navigated by Rimbaud in *Le Bateau ivre* [The Drunken Boat]. T. S. Eliot wanted to use the extreme edges of the ocean to figure the sterility of modernity's pursuit of progress in the fourth section of *The Wasteland*, whose draft recounted a shipwreck of fishermen setting out from Eliot's native Cape Cod. Ezra Pound, however, was unsympathetic to the ocean as a territory of modernity and deemed the section too bad even to edit, leaving us with only the eight lines on Phlebas the Phoenician, that treat the ocean as an archaic realm, in the manner of Coleridge.

George Gordon, Lord Byron, had some personal knowledge of the craft. He was a yachtsman and the grandson of John Byron, the author of *The Wreck of the Wager*, from Lord Anson's circumnavigation of the globe (1740–1744). But when Byron summoned up the ocean into verse, it was the ocean purified of human agency: "[d]ark-heaving;—boundless, endless, and sublime / —The image of Eternity—the throne / Of the Invisible," as Byron put it in *Childe Harold's Pilgrimage*.[49]

As the Romantics reinvigorated iconic figures from early modern scenarios of craft and launched them onto these evacuated seas, they turned the work of the sea into existential striving. This is the transformation, certainly, worked by Byron on the pirate. In his Byronic incarnation, following the French and American Revolutions, the pirate's watchword becomes existential freedom—not the amoral right to navigate freely across the world's oceans that defines the freedom of the seas, but rather the unbounded right to life, liberty, and happiness, along with the pursuit of (other people's) property:

> O'ER the glad waters of the dark blue sea,
> Our thoughts as boundless and our souls as free,
> Far as the breeze can bear, the billows foam,
> Survey our empire, and behold our home!
> These are our realms, no limits to their sway—
> Our flag the sceptre all who meet obey.
> Ours the wild life in tumult still to range
> From toil to rest, and joy in every change.[50]

Attending this democratic, existential impulse, the pirate's shocking cruelty is muted, and he sometimes takes on the overtones of a noble outlaw à la Robin Hood.

After Byron created the pirate as an existential hero, this figure would fascinate a post-Romantic lineage from Rimbaud to William Burroughs.[51] The lineage culminates in the postmodern celebration of anarchic rebellion, deterritorialization, and mobility, epitomized by a pirate manifesto for the end of the twentieth century, *The Temporary Autonomous Zone, Ontological Anarchy, Poetic Terrorism*, by one Hakim Bey.[52] But the seas for Bey's pirates, despite their rebellion against Enlightenment epistemologies, remain the smooth, empty seas of the Romantic sublime.

A STORM WOULD HAVE BEEN SOME CONSOLATION

The sublimation of the sea is a process that occurred in the visual arts as well as in literature. Writing in 1712, Addison counseled authors to follow the example of "Great Painters [who] do not only give us Landskips of gardens, groves, and meadows, but very often employ their pencils upon sea-pieces."[53] Addison referred here to maritime genre painting that flourished in the seventeenth century, where the sea's portrayal was from the vantage point of its practice. In *A Small Dutch Vessel close-hauled in a Strong Breeze* (1672) by Willem van de Velde the Younger, the might of the elements, wind, and waves is not only inseparable from but indeed accentuated by the maneuvers taken by the vessels (figure Int.1). The sea is treated similarly in *Ships Driving onto a Rocky Shore in a Heavy Sea* (c. 1703), by Willem van de Velde the Younger's son, Cornelius, who lived in England and was Addison's contemporary (figure Int.2). The image is replete with specific information about the kind of vessel, the shape of the waves, and the texture and quantity of white water. Similarly, the image delineates the rigging of the vessel, showing the maneuvers taken by mariners in this heavy weather.

Compare the rich information about the sea and maneuvers taken by mariners in gale conditions to Caspar David Friedrich's *Monk by the Sea* (1809; figure Int.3). In this picture, sea and sky are almost all we see, a vision reinforced by the solitary viewer painted into the scene. But sea and sky are present not as a theater of craft, but rather as empty elements to be filled with the viewer's imagination. Friedrich in fact initially had two ships in the vista, but he eventually painted them out to increase the scene's feeling of desolation. That he succeeded is evident in the response of Marie von Kügelgen, who observed in 1809 to a friend that the picture represented "[a] vast endless expanse of sky . . . still, no wind, no moon, no storm—indeed a storm would have been some consolation for then one would at least see life and movement somewhere. On the unending sea [*ewige Meeresfläche*] there is no boat, no ship, not even a sea monster, and in the sand not even a blade of grass, only a few gulls float in the air and make the loneliness even more desolate and horrible."[54] The Romantic evacuation of the sea epitomized by Friedrich's painting entails not only removing human agency from the content of the scene but also evacuating the informational function of marine landscapes. Marine landscapes had this function not only in genre painting, but also in the images made by mariners to record views of unknown coasts in the course of navigations, such as the images by William Hodges, the artist on Cook's second expedition, as in this pen and ink sketch of Dusky Bay (figure Int.4).

Figure Int.1. Sky and sea are an occasion for Willem van de Velde the Younger to study color, form, and light, but the painting also offers detailed information about the specific conditions of the sea and the vessels, as well as their maneuvers. The National Gallery website notes: "The black and white striped flag at the masthead of the 'galjoot,' the small gaff-rigged vessel in the foreground, may indicate that it comes from the area around the island of Texel. She may well be a pilot going out to assist an incoming ship. In the middle distance is a large ship with a Dutch pennant." Cited at *http://www.nationalgallery.org.uk/paintings/willem-van-de-velde-a-small-dutch-vessel-close-hauled-in-a-strong-breeze*; consulted December 2009. Willem van de Velde the Younger, *A Small Dutch Vessel close-hauled in a Strong Breeze* (c. 1672, oil on canvas). Courtesy of Art Resource, © National Gallery, London.

THE MARINER AS UNCOUTH ORPHEUS: FALCONER'S SHIPWRECK

As with any cultural process, the sublimation of the sea occurred unevenly. One of the latest artifacts resisting the process is *The Shipwreck* (1762) by William Falconer. Falconer was a mariner, and besides being a poet, he was an author of a major piece of practical literature of seamanship, *An Universal Dictionary of the Marine*, first published in 1769

Figure Int.2. This storm scene by Cornelius van de Velde, like the scene by the painter's father (figure Int.1), both offers a painterly opportunity for studying the possibilities of the medium and gives precise details on the meteorological conditions and their effect on the ships. The National Maritime Museum website identifies these ships as "East Indiamen" and describes the conditions of the ships in precise nautical language: "On the left another ship is shown in more detail, pitching in starboard-bow view in the violent sea with its sails furled, except for the fore-course which billows out of control. Figures can be seen on the deck, their raised arms indicating that they are attempting to take it in hand." Available at *http://www.nmm.ac.uk/mag/pages/mnuExplore/PaintingDetail.cfm?ID=BHC 0985&letter=S&search=painting*; consulted December 2009. The website also speculates that the scene may depict the Great Storm of 1703. As I mention in chapter 2, Defoe took this storm as the occasion for penning *The Storm: Or, A Collection Of the most Remarkable Casualties and Disasters Which happen'd in the Late Dreadful Tempest Both By Sea and Land* (1704). Cornelius van de Velde, *Ships Driving onto a Rocky Shore in a Heavy Sea* (c. 1703?, oil on canvas). Courtesy of the National Maritime Museum, London.

and reprinted at least six times in the years following its publication. The full title shows the work's aim to cover the terminology needed in the variegated skills that make up the knowledge of the craft, ending with an acknowledgment of craft's collectivity. On the title page of the 1769 edition, we read:

Figure Int.3. In comparison to the information offered by the sea scenes of genre painting, Caspar David Friedrich's sea is empty, and indeed, he even painted out two ships to enhance its effect of desolation. Caspar David Friedrich, *Monk by the Sea* (1809, oil on canvas). Courtesy of Bildarchiv Preussischer Kulturbesitz, Art Resource, on behalf of the Nationalgalerie, Staatliche Museen zu Berlin, Berlin.

An Universal Dictionary of The Marine or, a Copious Explanation of The Technical Terms And Phrases Employed In The Construction, Equipment, Furniture, Machinery, Movements, and Military Operations of a Ship. Illustrated with Variety of Original Designs of Shipping, in different Situations; Together with separate Views of their Masts, Sails, Yards, and Rigging. To which is annexed, a Translation of the French Sea-Terms and Phrases, collected from the works of Mess. du Hamel, Aubin, Saverien, &c.

Falconer perished at sea the year of its first publication.

Though Falconer's poem *The Shipwreck* "enjoyed a vast popular reputation as the greatest marine poem in language until well into the nineteenth century," this popularity is hard to understand today.[55] Raban registers the poem's illegibility when he comments on Falconer's awkward efforts to "marry the theories of Addison and Burke to actual shiphandling in an actual storm," in a poem that "bristles with technical nauticalia at the same time as it wallows fashionably in delightful horror."[56] The missing piece in this explanation is the cultural logic that would make descriptions of craft and sublime landscape coexist. Falconer

Figure Int.4. William Hodges was the artist on Cook's second voyage. As the *Resolution* surveyed Dusky Bay off what is now called New Zealand, Hodges drew "the bay from various angles . . . offer[ing] a means of orientation to parallel the charts produced by Cook's officers." In Cook's view, "'Mr Hodges has drawn a very accurate view both of the North and South entrance as well as several other parts of this Bay, and in them hath delineated the face of the country with such judgment as will at once convey a better idea of it than can be expressed by words.'" Watercolor was used by expeditions for such records in action because it dried quickly. Quotations from John Bonehill, "Hodges and Cook's Second Voyage," in *William Hodges 1744–1797—The Art of Exploration*, eds. Geoffrey Quilley and John Bonehill (New Haven: Yale University Press for the National Maritime Museum, 2004), 82. William Hodges, *Dusky Bay, New Zealand* (1773, watercolor). Courtesy of Mitchell Library, State Library of New South Wales.

is trying to show his audience not only the dangerous conditions at sea that occasion sublime terror, but also the mariner's work struggling to overcome them. Such a portrayal of craft would have been the flip side of any portrayal of remarkable dangers in nonfictional narratives or maritime adventure fiction.

The sublime contours of Falconer's landscape are evident when Falconer first introduces his subject as a realm, where "hostile elements tumultous rise / And lawless floods rebel against the skies / Till Hope expires, and Peril and Dismay / Wave their black ensigns on the watery way."[57] The sublimity of the artist's own strivings is also evident at the poem's beginning, where Falconer makes his bid for poetic glory as extending the epic in new directions. With *The Shipwreck*'s portrayal of the destruction of a merchant vessel in the Mediterranean, Falconer tells his audience that he aims "A scene from dumb oblivion to restore / To fame unknown, and new to epic lore!" (I, 38–39). This new scene is seamen at work, down to importing the "terms uncouth, and jarring phrases" (I, 85). These terms uncouth are the words of art identifying different parts of the ship and maneuvers essential for command at sea that Wye Salton-stall dubbed "technological" in his preface to Captain John Smith's *Sea Grammar* of 1627.

Falconer vaunts his project even as he deprecates his lack of literary skills and his use of uncouth technical language:

> His verse no laurel-wreath attempts to claim,
> Nor sculptur'd brass to tell the poet's name.
> If terms uncouth, and jarring phrases, wound
> The softer sense with inharmonious sound,
> Yet here let listening sympathy prevail,
> While conscious Truth unfolds her piteous tale! (I, 83–88)

Though Falconer is a mariner, not a poet, he speaks "truth" and appeals to "sympathy," basic human values worth more than the "sculptur'd brass" and "laurel-wreath" rewarding literary art. In implying the truth of his work as more valuable than the artifice of the professional *littérateur*, Falconer is in the vein of Camões boasting the superiority of his narrative of truth over to Homer's fables, as well as mariner-authors like Dampier and Cook, who boast in a more back-handed way—through apology—about their professional expertise. Later in *The Shipwreck*, Falconer is less modest about his ambitions. He compares his efforts to the bold exploration of the classical adventurer Orpheus, willing to sail to the depths of Hell and phrase a song to move its ruler:

> When sacred ORPHEUS, on the Stygian coast,
> With notes divine implor'd his consort lost;
> Tho' round him perils grew in fell array;
> And fates and furies stood to bar his way:
> Not more adventurous was th' attempt, to move
> The powers of hell, with strains of heavenly love,
> Than mine, to bid th' unwilling muse explore
> The wilderness of rude mechanic lore. (II, 398–405)

With "rude mechanic lore," Falconer refers to the particular challenge posed to his effort by the technical, specialized details of maritime labor. What is difficult about this task is not the rude sounds of the terms but rather their recondite, technical precision. Who but someone familiar with the work of the sea will know what it means when, "Now down the mast the sloping yard declin'd, / Till by the jears and topping-lift confin'd" (II, 388–89)? An experienced mariner, Falconer is so knowl-edgeable about the work of the sea that he can give many details about the specific dangers, adding to a vindication of seamen's work and hero-ism. These maneuvers are, however, too specialized, and only a reader with at least some familiarity with the work of the sea could understand their narration.

To make these specialized maneuvers comprehensible, Falconer comes up with the technique of using running footnotes to detail the parts of the ship and the meaning of maneuvers (figure Int.5). In the third edi-tion, from 1769 that I cite from, there are no footnote numbers, but a footer offers a prose gloss beneath the dramatic action in the poetic verse, though by the early nineteenth century, this gloss was being laid out as back matter. Here is an example from the 1769 edition of the interplay between performing description and prose gloss apropos of how sails are furled as the gale intensifies. Canto 2, lines 385 ff. run as follows:

> At last to furl the courses they consent.
> That done, to reef the mizen next agree,
> And try beneath it, sidelong in the sea.
>
> Now down the mast the sloping yard declin'd,
> Till by the jears and topping-lift confin'd.
> The head, with doubling canvas fenc'd around,
> In balance, near the lofty peek, they bound.
> The reef enwrapt, th'inserted knittles ty'd,
> To hoist the shorten'd sail again they hy'd
> The order given, the yard aloft they sway'd;
> The brails relax'd, th'extended sheet belay'd,
> The helm its post forsook, and, lash'd a-lee,
> Inclin'd the wayward prow to front the sea.

The footer apropos of line 387 runs: "To try, is to lay the ship with her side nearly in the direction of the wind and sea; with the head somewhat inclined to the windward; the helm being laid a-lee to retain her in that position. See a further illustration thereof in the last note of this Canto." And apropos of line 389: "The topping-lift, which *tops* the upper end of the mizen-yard (see note 257, p. 61); this line and the six following describe the operations of reefing and balancing the mizen." Even as Fal-coner seeks to retain the connection between the work of the sea and the sublime experience of the sea's terror, his separation between the prose of work and the poetry of sublime spectacle indicates how hard it is to hold the two together. In this disjunction, the details of work are graphi-cally subordinated to aesthetic effect, being consigned to the bottom of the page.

That done, to reef the mizen next agree,
And try beneath it, fidelong in the fea.
    Now down the maft the floping yard declin'd,
Till by the jears and topping-lift confin'd.
The head, with doubling canvas fenc'd around, 390
In balance, near the lofty peak, they bound.
The reef enwrapt, th' inferted knittles ty'd,
To hoift the fhorten'd fail again they hy'd.
The order given, the yard aloft they fway'd;
The brails relax'd, th' extended fheet belay'd. 395
The helm it's poft forfook, and, lafh'd a-lee,
Inclin'd the wayward prow to front the fea.
                    F   When

V. 387. To try, is to lay the fhip with her fide
nearly in the direction of the wind and sea, with the
head fomewhat inclined to the windward; the helm
being laid a-lee to retain her in that pofition. See a
further illuftration of this in the laft note of this
Canto.

    V. 389. The topping-lift, which *tops* the upper end
of the mizen-yard (fee note 257, p. 54.); this line and
the fix following defcribe the operation of reefing and
balancing the mizen. The reef of this fail is towards
the lower end, the knittles being fmall fhort lines
ufed in the room of *points* for this purpofe (fee note
132, 148. p. 46, 47.); they are accordingly knotted
under the foot-rope, or lower edge of the fail.

    V. 396. Lafh'd a-lee, is faftened to the lee fide.
See note 130. p. 45.

Figure Int.5. While elevated sentiments and rhetorical figures billow aloft in
verse in *The Shipwreck* by the mariner author William Falconer, the workmanlike definitions of craft run along the bottom of the page in prose. Page
from William Falconer, *The Shipwreck* (Philadelphia: Thomas Dobson, 1788).
Courtesy of the John Carter Brown Library at Brown University.

TURNER WAS IN THIS STORM

I have framed Falconer's effort to retain the sea as the theater of craft as reactionary, holding onto an earlier cultural construction that the sublimation of the sea was sweeping away. At the same time, Falconer's adventure using terms of art also looks forward to a further transformation of the sublimated sea, when Romanticism returns to the sea as the breeding ground for literary and artistic modernism. In this transformation, the sea is reclaimed as a theater of work. However, the artist or poet's interest is not in offering a romance of maritime practice per se, but rather in drawing a parallel between the craft of the mariner and the craft of the artist or writer, engaged in exploring uncharted domains of representation and thought.

With the desublimation of the sea as a figure of artistic creativity, maritime subject matter becomes a vehicle for some of the first forays into artistic modernism. We can see this process under way in a series of early-nineteenth-century sea scenes painted by Joseph Mallord William Turner. The first is one Turner had been asked to paint for the Duke of Bridgewater as a pendant to a storm scene by the Dutch maritime artist Willem van de Velde the Younger in the Duke's collection (figure Int.6). The van de Velde picture was *Ships in a Stormy Sea*, 1671–1672, which is to say an image contemporary with van de Velde's *Small Dutch Vessel close-hauled in a Strong Breeze* (see figure Int.1) also c. 1672 and similar in composition.[58]

The picture Turner painted for this commission was *Dutch Boats in a Gale: Fishermen Endeavouring to Put Their Fish on Board*, which was first exhibited in 1801. Turner's *Dutch Boats in a Gale* is in continuity with Dutch maritime art, showing Turner's skill at giving information on the work of the sea, along with using the storm as an occasion to portray atmosphere, elements, and movement.[59] In Turner's *Dutch Boats in a Gale,* as in van de Velde's paintings, the drama of the scene is inseparable from its information concerning the conditions of the vessel's navigation. The painter reveals the direction and power of the gale from the aspect of waves, sails, and clouds. All three pictures as well convey the mariners' activity responding to these conditions, though Turner does not delineate an authoritative mariner as in van de Velde's piece, where a figure indicates his command of the situation with an outstretched arm. Rather, Turner's workers of the sea are more humble fishermen, struggling to keep their catch and their ship amidst the violence of wind and waves.

Turner's erasure of the specificity of the mariner's art and amplification of the might of the wild sea in *Dutch Boats in a Gale* is writ large in *The Shipwreck*, a painting first exhibited four years later, in 1805, that may, indeed, have been directly inspired by Falconer's poem, newly

Figure Int.6. *Ships in a Stormy Sea* is another storm scene by Willem van de
Velde the Younger c. 1672. This image hung in the collection of the Duke of
Bridgewater in J.M.W. Turner's time, and the Duke commissioned Turner to
paint a sea scene that would be a companion piece for van de Velde's work. The
result was Turner's *Dutch Boats in a Gale: Fishermen Endeavouring to Put their
Fish on Board*, first exhibited in 1801. Willem van de Velde the Younger, *Ships
in a Stormy Sea* (1671–1672, oil on canvas). Courtesy of the Toledo Museum of
Art. Purchased with funds from the Libbey Endowment. Gift of Edward Drum-
mond Libbey, 1977.62.

republished at the time (figure Int.7).[60] Rather than offering the maneuvers of mariners in response to a critical situation, Turner asks viewers
to contemplate the human drama of the moment when their vessel is in
the process of sinking, its broken carcass bobbing in the background.
What maneuvers there are heroic, but not specific to navigation and
seamanship; rather they are the efforts of a small fishing vessel to rescue
survivors in a longboat.

    The Shipwreck's turn away from the mariner's craft might seem to be
part of the sublimation of the sea described across this chapter. Yet at the
same time, in Turner's picture, the mariner's craft ebbs to reveal skilled
labor of another kind. In *The Shipwreck*, Turner details the waves with

Figure Int.7. Turner's *The Shipwreck* (1805) may have been directly inspired by William Falconer's poem of the same name, newly republished at the time Turner finished the painting. In *The Shipwreck*, Turner also was dialoguing with conventions of maritime art—in particular, Dutch maritime art of the early modern period. Compare the Dutch images to Turner's *Shipwreck* and note Turner's purified focus on the elemental power of nature and the human struggle with its might. J.M.W.Turner, *The Shipwreck* (1805, oil on canvas). © Tate, London, 2009.

a textured, highly visible brushstroke, revealing the painter's oils. With such a transformation, these waves start to call attention not only to the materiality of painterly technique, but also to the power of Turner's vision and execution.

Turner mines this parallel between the craft of the mariner and the art of the painter throughout his portrayal of sublime conditions encountered at sea. One exemplary work is the *Snow Storm—Steamboat off a Harbour's Mouth Making Signals in Shallow Water, and going by the Lead. The Author was in this Storm on the Night the Ariel left Harwich,"* first exhibited in 1842 (figure Int.8).

As the title indicates, Turner cultivated the myth that he had gone out on this boat to experience the storm firsthand, lashed to the mast like a

Figure Int.8. In the narrative around *Snowstorm—Steamboat off a Harbour's Mouth Making Signals in Shallow Water, and going by the Lead. The Author was in this Storm on the Night the Ariel left Harwich,* Turner cultivated the myth that he was a roving Odysseus. While Odysseus had himself lashed to the mast to overhear the mortally dangerous singing of the Sirens, "Turner claimed that, at the age of sixty-seven, 'I got the sailors to lash me to the mast to observe it (the storm); I was lashed for four hours and did not expect to escape, but I felt bound to record it if I did.'" However, it appears that "[N]o ship called the Ariel ever sailed from Harwich." Cited on page 23 of Miquette Roberts, *The Unknown Turner. Notes for Teachers*, with contributions from Catherine Cullinan, Colin Grigg, and Joyce Townsend, published online by the Tate Britain (*http://www .tate.org.uk/britain/turner/tp_unknownturner.pdf*; consulted June 2009). The *Ariel* was, however, the name of a historical ship commanded by John Paul Jones that performs a maneuver requiring consummate craft in *The Pilot* by James Fenimore Cooper, a celebrated novel of the American Revolution that rejuvenated sea fiction in 1824. While the off-kilter viewpoint of this painting does intimate seasickness, James Hamilton suggests in *Turner and the Scientists* that in fact Turner modeled the visuals of the storm on the patterns of iron filings illustrating the presence of electromagnetic waves, as shown by Turner's contemporary, Michael Faraday (see figure Int.9). When Turner structured his painting invoking the latest developments in modern science, he revealed the hidden natural forces at the basis of the compass technology that inaugurated global navigation. J.M.W. Turner, *Snowstorm—Steamboat off a Harbour's Mouth Making Signals in Shallow Water, and going by the Lead. The Author was in this Storm on the Night the Ariel left Harwich* (1842, oil on canvas). © Tate, London, 2009.

modern-day Odysseus. Note that Turner transformed the Odysseus legend in a fashion consistent with the sublime in its modern iteration, and specifically as capturing the enterprise to push the boundaries of ever expanding knowledge. Odysseus jury-rigged a way to plumb enchantment and overhear divine song. Turner, in contrast, braves deadly elements to achieve a close-up view of extreme natural conditions that would yield information enriching his artistry.

This parallel between the craft of navigator and artist continues in Turner's treatment of the waves, similar to *The Shipwreck*. However, the artist's hand comes to the foreground of the picture not for its expressive brushstrokes, as in *The Shipwreck*, but rather for a pattern taken from contemporary science. In *Turner and the Scientists*, James Hamilton observed that Turner modeled the swirling waves and weather on the pattern made by iron filings in the presence of a magnet, thereby illustrating the lines of force it organized in electromagnetic fields (figure Int.9).[61] Turner learned of this pattern from Michael Faraday's *Experimental Researches in Electricity* (1831), state-of-the-art science of his time.

The pleasures of the sublime, so runs philosophical discourse, are the pleasures taken in experiences of overwhelming force, epitomized by the spectacle of wild nature. In Turner's sublime snowstorm, the artist's effort to recreate these experiences for the spectator yields to the artist's ability to diagram the workings of force in the physical world, using vanguard science. This inversion of the sublime—from forceful experience to a diagram of force—also yields another paradigm for representation than images that limn the visible face of the world. This kind of representation reveals the physical properties of the subject matter represented, which themselves become integral to the image's organization.

In the case of the ship in a snowstorm, Turner makes visible, specifically, the force field that moves the compass, the revolutionary technology at the basis of the modern ability to navigate and chart the vast and obscure oceans of the globe. From the vantage point of the subsequent history of art, Turner's patterns shift the viewer's attention away from the drama of the storm towards modernist abstraction. But from the vantage point of maritime modernity, his reference to magnetism recalls that navigators used abstract techniques to represent the physical world centuries before modernist art.

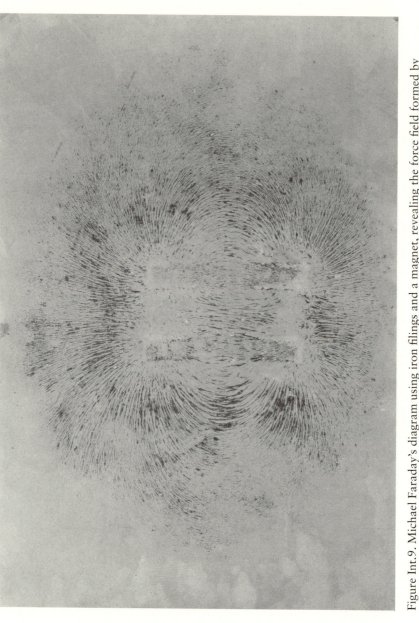

Figure Int.9. Michael Faraday's diagram using iron filings and a magnet, revealing the force field formed by invisible electromagnetic waves. Turner followed Faraday's research, which was in the vanguard of science of the time. "Magnetic Experiment by Michael Faraday." Image reproduced courtesy of The Royal Institution, London, Bridgeman Art Library.

CHAPTER 4

Sea Fiction in the Nineteenth Century:
Patriots, Pirates, and Supermen

> To you, the bold searchers, researchers, and whoever embarks
> with cunning sails on terrible seas . . .
> —Friedrich Nietzsche, *Thus Spoke Zarathustra*[1]

THE PERIPHERY WRITES BACK

After a seventy-five year hiatus, the maritime novel was reinvented by
James Fenimore Cooper, with *The Pilot*, published in January 1824.[2]
Depicting the exploits of John Paul Jones privateering off the coast of
Scotland during the American Revolution, *The Pilot* was quickly and
enthusiastically received in a transatlantic literary field.[3] British readers
were among Cooper's biggest fans, *The Pilot*'s celebration of the American Revolution notwithstanding, and Cooper's publisher was worrying
about how to protect his edition from British piracies by the end of 1824.
A four-volume French version of *The Pilot* appeared in 1824, reprinted
in 1824, 1825, 1826, 1827–1829, and beyond. *Der Lootse* appeared in
German in 1824. The novel was first published in Italian in 1828–1829,
in Swedish in 1831, in Spanish in 1832, in Dutch in 1835, and in Portuguese in 1838. After *The Pilot*, Cooper penned *The Red Rover* (1827),
portraying the British hunt for a glamorous rebel pirate off the American
seaboard in the middle of the eighteenth century. With just these two
transatlantic best-sellers, Cooper had put sea fiction back on the map of
influential narrative genres.

In the space of ten years, Cooper's poetics were taken up and reworked
by writers in the United Kingdom, France, and the United States. They
shifted from an innovation to an established international practice—a
"traveling" genre.[4] Thomas Philbrick observes, "By 1831 the sea novel
was well under way in England; Marryat had published *Frank Mildmay*
in 1829 and *The King's Own* in 1830. Michael Scott had begun serial
publication of *Tom Cringle's Log* in 1829, and William Neale's *Caven-
dish* appeared in 1831."[5] Captain Marryat also conceived of sea tales
aimed at youths, a form of the sea novel that lives to this day. In France,
Eugène Sue, better known for inventing the urban mystery genre with *Les*

Mystères de Paris, got his start with the novellas *Kernok le pirate* (1830) and *El Gitano ou les contrebandiers espagnols* (1830), followed by the full-length novels *Atar-Gull* (1831), *La Salamandre* (1832), and *La Vigie de Koat-Vën* (1833).[6] Contemporaries recognized that these narratives across national boundaries formed a unified genre, which had a number of names in its day: sea tale, sea romance, sea novel, nautical novel, naval novel, *le roman maritime*. My term to unify these works will be "sea fiction," since the genre includes both full-length novels and shorter tales.

After sea fiction's European consecration, the genre returned back across the Atlantic to widespread practice by U.S. authors in the later 1830s and 1840s.[7] Within fifteen years of sea fiction's invention, novels with high literary ambitions took their point of departure from sea fiction's poetics. Though sea fiction would lose the prestige of novelty by the 1850s, adventure authors would continue to include the form in their quiver across the nineteenth century and beyond. Rudyard Kipling, Robert Louis Stevenson, Jack London, and Rafael Sabatini all penned influential examples of the genre. "When your [Patrick] O'Brians are out, recommend Marryat," counsels *Library Journal* at the turn of the twenty-first century.[8]

Sea fiction's prestige and influence make it one of the preeminent transatlantic literary forms of its era. Novel scholars have certainly discussed extensively individual masterpieces, such as Melville's *Moby-Dick* and Hugo's *Les Travailleurs de la mer*, but the works' immediate generic horizon is at best mentioned in passing. Rather, these literary monuments sit, sometimes awkwardly, within a narrative of the nineteenth century as the century that perfected historical realism.

When Gesa Mackenthun ponders literary criticism's refusal to admit Cooper's sea fiction into "the American national canon," in contradistinction to his frontier novels, she points out that "America's foundational narrative is a continental one, its setting the wilderness of the frontier."[9] Despite this myth-making, however, Cooper in fact made his fame with *The Pilot* before the Leatherstocking cycle, and continued to write sea fiction until the end of his career. Cooper's contemporaries needed no reminding about his attention to the sea. Balzac captured the reigning view in his time, when he wrote that Cooper "is . . . the only author worthy of comparison to Walter Scott," not only for his ability to "idealize the magnificent landscapes of America," but for his ability to "paint the sea and seaman."[10] While Europeans writers and readers admired Cooper's frontier novels, Cooper's *sea fiction*, not the Leatherstocking tales, was the poetics that traveled intact to be practiced across the Atlantic.[11]

As Mackenthun's statements make clear, critics working on the American novel in the first half of the nineteenth century are a notable exception to the pervasive neglect of the sea novel as a major international form. Their attention has been spurred by the importance of seafaring themes for canonical authors such as Poe and Meville. Philbrick explains that *James Fenimore Cooper and the Development of American Sea Fiction* "grew out of my conviction that *Moby-Dick* is too often thought of as the first appearance of the sea in American literature."[12] Attentive to the processes of decolonization shaping American literature, Americanists also grasp the transatlantic scale that reveals sea fiction's literary and cultural impact. When Cooper reanimated sea fiction, American authors and readers defined the distinctiveness of the American tradition with an intense, if ambivalent relation to European writers, readers, and literary institutions. As the case of sea fiction shows, the flow went both ways.

The international perspective evinced by such Americanists working on the first part of the nineteenth century differs from the Eurocentrism of critics who survey the novel's poetic development from the other side of the Atlantic. Their focus on European authors accurately reflects the literary geography of narrative innovation in the century and a half before *The Pilot*. During a long eighteenth century spanning from *La Princesse de Clèves* of Madame de Lafayette (1678) to the historical fiction of Scott (late 1810s), new forms of the novel were indeed initiated by Western European authors, particularly those of the Channel zone. To credit Western European authors with forging the poetics of modern narrative in the era 1678–1824 is not to say that they were insulated from historical processes of globalization. The new eighteenth-century studies have drawn attention to the impact of overseas colonialism on European literature and culture, including how European inventors of the novel "novelized" (to use Bakhtin's words) the textual genres that emerged from the practices of empire.[13] Recent studies of the European reception of *The Thousand and One Nights* have also made visible how innovative novelists of Europe shaped the modern novel absorbing poetics from non-European contexts.[14] There is nonetheless a difference between European writers who novelize European global contact and Cooper's invention in a former colony of a narrative poetics that was imported intact by Western Europe. Cooper's invention of sea fiction is a significant event in what might be called Western *geopoetical* relations: an innovation from what was then the "periphery" of the international literary field so influential as to take root as a genre in the Western European narrative "core."[15] The shift in the global balance of narrative innovation inaugurated by Cooper would accelerate in the twentieth century, when influential subgenres of the novel include socialist realism, from the USSR, and magical realism, from Latin America.

To diagram the basic poetic matrix of nineteenth-century sea fiction, I use Cooper's *Pilot*, so influential in the United States—"the first, and still . . . best of nautical novels," in the words of the *Atlantic Monthly* from

1859—as well as abroad—"one of the most splendid novels of Cooper," was the view in 1838 of Alexandre Dumas.[16] After sketching Cooper's model, this chapter ends by showing the continuity of Cooper's basic patterns in its adaptation by the two most influential authors responsible for launching sea fiction in Western Europe: Captain Frederick Marryat in the United Kingdom and Eugène Sue in France.

A DIFFERENT COURSE

In his 1823 preface to *The Pilot*, Cooper started by invoking the novels of Smollett, but though he "has navigated the same sea as Smollett, he has steered a different course."[17] To define that course, Cooper pointed the reader toward the historical novel, a genre then at the apogee of contemporary prestige, from his novel's title, *The Pilot*, which self-consciously echoed Sir Walter Scott's *The Pirate* of 1821. In the 1823 preface, Cooper stressed his debt to Scott in the setting of a mythical moment in the foundation of the U.S. nation—specifically, "the daring and useful services of a great portion of our marine in the old war" (3–4). Portraying the Revolutionary period, Cooper moreover took a subject that in 1824 was approaching the sixty-year remove that Scott suggested as ideal for a novel devoted to "men rather than manners" in the preface to *Waverley* (1814). At the same time, Scott's novels do of course evince an ethnographic interest in manners, as Scott himself was the first to acknowledge: "[s]ome favourable opportunities of contrast have been afforded me, by the state of society in the northern part of the island at the period of my history, and may serve at once to vary and to illustrate the moral lesson."[18] In his 1823 preface, Cooper also stressed his aim "to exhibit, in his imperfect manner, a few traits of a people who, from the nature of things, can never be much known" in delineating "those scenes which belong only to the ocean" (3).

When Cooper positioned himself as the descendant of Smollett and the imitator of Scott, he aligned himself at once with a recognized past master of the maritime novel and the most famous novelist of the time. In this positioning, he fits cultural sociologist Pierre Bourdieu's model for how an emerging writer breaks into the literary field. In order to validate a new practice, the newcomer places this practice under the aegis of established positions, which can be individuals, movements, groups, or poetic practices, such as literary genres. That both Smollett and Scott were British makes clear the continued prestige of the British literary tradition for Cooper, notwithstanding his subject matter of the American Revolution.

Bourdieu's model also fits Cooper's gesture when he penned retrospective prefaces to *The Pilot* in 1849 and to *The Red Rover* in 1850. Now at the apogee of his fame and the prestige of the nautical novel, Cooper in the 1850 preface to the *Red Rover* boasted of his feat renewing sea fiction after Smollett had "obtained so much success as a writer of nautical tales" that any "succeeding adventurer" could only renew the genre with "difficulty."[19] In the 1849 preface to *The Pilot*, Cooper also clarified that his allusions to Scott were meant as polemic, not praise. This preface criticized Scott for his ignorance of maritime society, despite Scott's pretensions to accuracy. In fact, "the secret of [*The Pirate*'s] success was to be traced to the power of creating . . . *vraisemblance*." In his own novel, in contrast, Cooper offered "truer pictures of the ocean and ships than any that are to be found in the Pirate" (5).

As Cooper elaborated the "truer pictures" conveyed in his novel, he emphasized his interest in sharing the practical knowledge of the sea. Cooper instructed the readers of *The Pilot* that, "as every practical part of knowledge has its uses, something has been gained by letting the landsman into the secrets of the seaman's manner of life" (7). When Cooper described the technical knowledge of seafaring as "secrets," he reprised the early modern term for knowledge of a guild or craft that was applied to the mariner's expertise. Hence the presence of "secrets" in titles of practical manuals, like *The Seamans Secrets*, by John Davis, whose aim was not to lay "downe the cunning conclusions apt for Schollers to practice upon the shore, but onely those things that are needfully required in a sufficient seaman."[20] Cooper's preface further emphasized the practical accuracy of his depiction by underscoring that the novel's information derived from his own experience in the navy and that he had vetted his manuscript with an old messmate, who treated "the whole matter as fact," offering criticisms which were "strictly professional, and perfectly just" (7).

Performance of His Duty

As regards Cooper's practice, Cooper's poetic matrix in fact does take off from Smollett, utilizing the structure of episodes found in the eighteenth-century maritime picaresque.[21] Like *Roderick Random* or, for that matter, *Robinson Crusoe*, Cooper initiates the reader into the seaman's life through adventure episodes constructed of challenges, most often dangers, which characters overcome performing the mariner's craft. Cooper also followed the practice used both in nonfictional and fictional maritime adventure of devising an exemplary individual who would embody craft in its multifaceted mastery. In *The Pilot*, the exemplary individual is the Revolutionary hero John Paul Jones, the pilot of the novel's title.

The Pilot performs Jones's mastery of craft from the time he first steps onto the boards of Cooper's narrative. At the novel's opening, set during the American War of Independence, the rebellious colonials are privateering off the Scottish coast in the name of their emergent nation. Jones has been called aboard their vessel, the *Ariel*, to navigate a treacherous strait called the Devil's Grip. Navigation of a vessel through "the breakers and shoals at midnight" would in any case be difficult. Cooper increases the perils by putting Jones in command of a frigate, which, Cooper instructs his land readers, is a "huge ship" (50). Across his series of adroit maneuvers in response to extraordinary danger, Jones exhibits all the facets of the mariner's craft previously delineated.

The embodied nature of craft, for example, emerges in Jones's demeanor of command that inspires confidence and obedience in his crew, which Cooper repeatedly distills to a single word: calm. At the beginning of the navigation, Jones gives "the required directions in those still, calm tones, that formed so remarkable a contrast to the responsibility of his situation," a "contrast" that seals the authority of command, and that is a textbook example of the mariner's demeanor in danger (51). As the gale starts to howl, Jones "thunder[s] forth his orders," where necessary, in order to rise "above the tempest," at once "steady and calm, and yet so clear and high as to reach every ear" (53). When calm mutates to cool at the most dangerous moment of the navigation, Cooper underscores that a calm demeanor characterizes the thought processes of the commander as well as his physical aspect. Even as the vessel seems to threaten to dash upon the rocks of the narrow detroit that offers exit to the open sea, Jones maintains "those cool tones that are most appalling in critical moments, because they seem to denote most preparation and care" (51).

In explaining calm as "preparation and care," the narrator aligns it with protocol, a set of practices regularized and honed by collective experience. The pilot is attentive to protocol from the episode's beginning: "tack your ship, sir, tack your ship; I would see how she works, before we reach the point, where she *must* behave well, or we perish" (50). Throughout the episode, the narrator saturates Jones's maneuvers with terms that qualify protocol in the semantic field of craft. As Jones patiently works his way through the straits, coming up as close to land as he can, falling off, and tacking again, the narrator speaks of his "prudence or skill" (53). Jones himself emphasizes another aspect of craft dependent on experience, local knowledge: "I have the advantage of knowing the ground well" (41).

To clear the Devil's Grip, the *Ariel* must round the outermost point of the narrow passage, thwarted by the tide, as the winds increase to a gale. How to gain enough speed so as to avoid being swept into the rocks? Jones responds with a bold, unorthodox maneuver, evincing "resolution," that raises competence and skill to the consummate craft of the compleat mariner. This maneuver is "hard driving"—laying on canvas in heavy winds, despite the danger of destroying sails and mast:

"There is no more tacking or box-hauling to be done tonight," said the Pilot. "We have barely room to pass out of the shoals on this course . . ." "If we had beaten out the way we entered!" exclaimed Griffith, "we should have done well." "Say, also, if the tide would have let us do so," returned the pilot, calmly. "Gentlemen, we must be prompt . . . That topsail is not enough to keep her up to the wind; we want both jib and mainsail." "'Tis a perilous thing, to loosen canvass in such a tempest!" observed the doubtful captain. "It must be done," returned the collected stranger; "we perish, without it—see . . . already . . . the sea casts us to leeward!" . . . The orders of the lieutenant were executed almost as soon as issued, and every thing being ready, the enormous folds of the mainsail were trusted, loose, to the blast. There was an instant when the result was doubtful; the tremendous threshing of the heavy sail, seeming to bid defiance to all restraint, shaking the ship to her centre; but art and strength prevailed, and gradually the canvass was distended, and bellying as it filled, was drawn down to its usual place, by the power of a hundred men. . . . "She feels it! she springs her luff!," . . . "the light opens from the hom-moc already; if she will only bear her canvass, we shall go clear!" (54–55)

In opting for hard-driving, despite its dangers, Jones employs a maneuver that exhibits "the captain's experience and knowledge of his ship."[22] Jones's knowledge is particularly impressive, since Jones has just come on board the frigate for the first time and tested it with only a few tacks before taking on the Devil's Grip.

When the powerful gale blows even the jib from the "bolt-ropes," Jones lets the vessel luff. Officers, crew, and readers hang in suspense, all hoping that the ship has gained enough momentum to clear the land, as Jones steers deftly through the narrow, treacherous exit to the channel. "At length the ship reached a point, where she appeared to be rushing directly into the jaws of destruction, when, suddenly, her course was changed, and her head receded rapidly from the wind" (56). From Odysseus navigating Scylla and Charybdis to Cook extricating his ship from the Great Barrier Reef, finding the path out of the impasse—the *poros* out of the aporia, to use the Greek term resonant with philosophical significance—has crowned the agency of the compleat mariner. William Gilmore Simms praised the adventure of the Devil's Grip in 1842 as an example of Cooper's ability to "rivet" readers. In this episode, Cooper's "Prometheus in action" evinced "[t]he courage that looks steadily on the danger, however terrible; the composure that never swerves from its centre under the pressure of unexpected misfortune;— the knowledge that can properly apply its strength, and the adroitness and energy, which, feeling the force of a manly will, flies to their task, in instant and hearty obedience."[23] Courage, composure, applied knowledge, adroitness, collective execution: the capacity, in short, that I have called "craft." Simms's review captures the portrayal of heroism that Cooper's contemporaries most appreciated about this novel and about Cooper's sea fiction more generally.

In *The Pilot*, the narrator's phrase for Jones's excellence in action is "the performance of his duty" (51). As the novel's succinct title, *The Pilot*, suggests, the protagonist claims the reader's interest as a pattern of professional expertise. This model of protagonist differs from the protagonists in the novel of manners across its subgenres. In such subgenres as the historical novel, the domestic novel, as well as the Gothic and sentimental fiction, all popular at the time of Cooper, readers are engaged by protagonists' complex, multilayered subjectivity. The characters are expressions of their environment and background, but at the same time, protagonists in novels of manners have distinctive interiority. The first lines of Jane Austen's *Emma* present "Emma Woodhouse, handsome, clever, and rich, with a comfortable home and happy disposition [who] seemed to unite some of the best blessings of existence." Austen continues by setting up the limitations of Emma's character, which give her the potential to grow and to transform: "The real evils indeed of Emma's situation were the power of having rather too much her own way and a disposition to think a little too well of herself." [24]

When Cooper first introduces Jones, in contrast, all the reader learns is that Jones is a "small man in a drab pea-jacket," a garment that is the badge of his profession (15). An American lieutenant adds several pages later that Jones has the "small bur-r-r" of a "man who was born on the other side of the Atlantic" (30). This laconic presentation is all that is needed for a character who interests the reader with his professional performance. Cooper continues to deck Jones in the garb of work when Jones steps into the full light of the reader's scrutiny as he begins navigation of the Devil's Grip, his face hidden under a "hat, that had seen much and hard service," revealing only Jones's "calm blue eye," that will prove to have a "keenness of vision" seeming to "exceed human power" (33, 54). Even details that contribute to shaping a protagonist's personality in a novel of manners serve the performance of craft in Cooper's adventure pattern. Jones's Scottish origins, for example, matter because they give him the local knowledge to navigate the Devil's Grip, not because they explain any singularities of personality.

In drafting a character whose identity inheres in his performance across the novel, Cooper continues the long-standing adventure protocol for character. In adventure fiction from its prehistory in classical romance, as I have discussed, adventure challenges test the constancy of the protagonist's identity. Thoughts, feelings, background, and status fade in comparison to what the protagonist achieves in action. In medieval adventure, for example, the stake of adventure performance is to demonstrate that birth is valor. In Cooper's sea fiction, adventure performance vindicates the Promethean protagonist of craft, whose origin is irrelevant to his capacity. As Jones puts it "coldly" when initially questioned about his background: "It is but of little moment where a man is born, or how he speaks . . . so that he does his duty bravely, and in good faith" (30).

The model of heroism as the successful performance of dangerous deeds contrasts with the heroism of deep subjectivity found in the novel of manners. However, Cooper's novels do have features of the novel of manners—specifically, the historical novel—which is not surprising, given Cooper's engagement with Scott in *The Pilot*'s prefaces, whether as model to be imitated or dismantled. Cooper surrounds his Prometheus in action with secondary characters who are a gallery of types of the maritime tribe. At the same time, Cooper refunctions the presentation of social types to serve the performance of craft.

Even as characters like Long Tom Coffin and Boltrope embody different social types found at sea, they embody different facets of craft, a capacity that may be glamourized in the figure of the exceptional individual but that is in fact collective. The use of different characters to embody different facets of craft dates to Daniel Defoe's *Captain Singleton* and to Captain Bob's motley pirate crew. In nineteenth-century sea fiction, from the time of Cooper, this crew will explicitly be associated with the different functions of seamen on a professional sailing vessel, even one that plies the trade of piracy, as in Cooper's second sea novel, *The Red Rover*. In *The Pilot*, Long Tom Coffin embodies the can-do, completely experiential, traditional side to craft. Born on the water, lacking any formal education, the powerful, gnarled old harpooner and gunner has an intuitive feel for the weather, the conditions, the maneuvers, and how they should be executed. His intuitive grasp shows that the mariner's local knowledge does not belong to a single region or sea, but rather is at home at the level of the oceans of the globe. He is paired with the unimaginative, upright sailing master Boltrope, who embodies craft as protocol, the exact and punctilious execution of orders.

These two homely characters, vital to the work of the sea, contrast with the novel's romantic leads, the upright, ready, enthusiastic young officers Griffith and Barnstable, serving American freedom. Griffith and Barnstable speak to the professional fraternity of craft, its good will, and the process of training that is needed to achieve the mastery of a character like Jones. The crewmembers of the vessel are not just tools to be used by the master mariner, but part of the craft and essential to performance. Accordingly, when Jones assumes command of the *Ariel*, Cooper is explicit that Jones must earn it by showing its crew that he is a consummate master of the craft, the craft that is theirs as well as his.

In Cooper's words, Jones's authority "can only be acquired, under such circumstances, by great steadiness and consummate skill" (454).

THE ONLY CLASS OF MEN WHO NOWADAYS SEE ANYTHING LIKE STIRRING ADVENTURE

In novels by Smollett, Chetwood, Le Sage, or Prévost, as well as Defoe, a mariner's training gave the protagonist the tools to adventure and survive in the Edge zones of the expanding early modern world. Cooper's mariners, in contrast, are all "heart and soul, devoted to their profession," in the words of an 1824 review of *The Pilot* from the *New-York Mirror*.[25] The maritime picaresque placed work at the center of the story, but the interest of this work was inseparable from the extreme situations where it was required for survival. In Cooper's renewal of the genre, these arduous conditions turn to the more routine but nonetheless dangerous work at sea, involving "the seaman's manner of life" (7).

The contrast between *The Pilot*'s adventures of maritime labor and the maritime picaresque's more heterogeneous adventures at the edges of modernity is evident from the titles of the founding works in each genre. Even taking account of the differences in title conventions between 1719 and 1821, the move away from the world beyond the line to the mariner's profession emerges from Cooper's succinct identification of his subject by his protagonist's line of work, *The Pilot*, in contrast to *The Life and Strange, Surprising Adventures of Robinson Crusoe, of York, Mariner: Who lived Eight and Twenty Years, all alone in an un-inhabited Island on the Coast of America, near the Mouth of the Great River of Oroonoque; Having been cast on Shore by Shipwreck, wherein all the Men perished but himself. With An Account how he was at last as strangely deliver'd by Pyrates*. Cooper's professionalization of craft involves the kind of challenges that befall his character, the characters themselves, and the geography of their adventure. As Defoe's title suggests, the maritime picaresque launches its protagonists across the unknown edges of the world's oceans and coasts. In nineteenth-century sea fiction, the theater of action is the high seas and the surf of shores that may be remote or exotic, but they are not necessarily the zones of modernity on Edge.

The maritime picaresque thrived in the eighteenth century, when Europeans still had not explored large areas of the terraqueous globe—notably, the Pacific Ocean. By the time Cooper penned *The Pilot*, the globe's blank spaces had contracted to the polar regions. Edgar Allen Poe accordingly sent his narrator to the South Pole in his send-up of three centuries of maritime exploration in *The Narrative of Arthur Gordon*

Pym of Nantucket (1838). Islands off the map were another geography used in nineteenth-century sea fiction when writers did want to preserve or at least dialogue with the maritime picaresque's romance of craft in the Edge zones of the world. Floating islands, too, defied European world maps and would fascinate Poe and Melville, as well as Verne. For readers familiar with the maritime book, such novels are stuffed with playful allusions to all its different genres, from practical manuals to pirate biographies. Robert Louis Stevenson rewrote the island off the map as an island with a treasure map in *Treasure Island*.[26]

The decline of the romance of path-breaking navigation by the time of Cooper was spurred by advances in science and technology. The conquest of scurvy and the ability to calculate longitude at sea are just two examples of innovations of the later eighteenth century that drastically improved the safety of navigation. But as the glamour of exploration dissipated, it became possible to recognize that the craft exercised in the more routinized work of the sea had adventures and heroism of its own. Melville made this point in his preface to *Typee*, when he suggested that even if commonplace for mariners, work at sea appears remarkable for "fire-side people." In Melville's words, "Sailors are the only class of men who now-a-days see anything like stirring adventure; and many things which to fire-side people appear strange and romantic, to them seem as common-place as a jacket out at elbows."[27] By the end of the century, the working era of sail, too, would be past. But when Cooper wrote, sailing ships were if anything more efficient and better designed than ever, even with steam on the horizon. From the end of the nineteenth century, Conrad notes the "pathos" of this era: "when the sailing ships and the art of sailing them reached their perfection, they were already doomed."[28]

THE CAPACITY FOR WORK . . . IN MOMENTS OF DOUBT AND DANGER

In the review by Simms previously cited, the critic wrote that Cooper shows "*the capacity for work* . . . the sort of manhood upon which all men rely in moments of doubt and danger."[29] Underscoring that the adventures of craft are the adventures of professional seamen engaged in work at sea, Cooper's sea fiction participated in a discourse on work that flourished in advanced capitalist nations of the world across the nineteenth century. This discourse, crossing philosophy, political philosophy, nascent sociology, ethnography, and the arts, emerged as a way to make sense of the disruption of traditional forms of labor accompanying industrialization and urbanization. The discourse on work also emerged in conjunction with liberal democratic ideals and helped further claims for political enfranchisement by the newly identified working classes.

Considered in historical context, the mariner's compleat agency contrasts starkly with the contours of industrial labor, and in particular with its dehumanizing effect so eloquently described in the socialist tradition. In Marx's description, the division of labor in the factory was an important element in this degradation. As a result of industrial practices, the worker participated in only one small part of the labor process. She was disconnected from the outcome of her activity, and from her bond to other workers that would be nurtured in the collective process of artisanal production. Another element of this degradation was the wholesale abstraction of labor as part of capitalist commodification. When labor itself became a commodity, the experience of labor was emptied of significance, flattened, and quantified. Split off from the human who performed it, work became mystified in such degraded conditions, reappropriated only in the irrational allure of merchandise.

The compleat capacity of craft contrasts with the degraded labor of industrial production in a number of ways. It is, first of all, an integrated knowledge that involves coordinating a range of faculties and skills, both mental and physical. In *The Human Condition*, Hannah Arendt differentiates among phsyical labor, the work of fabrication, and action; craft unites these different facets to human production. In addition, craft is permeated by a rich, articulated experience of time missing in industrial labor. Craft requires training and experience and is always contending with unforeseen situations; part of the work of craft is to produce time, in the calculation of longitude; craft also engages time as the timing of the effective maneuver, encompassing patience, regularity, and opportunity. The capacity to get time on one's side and make it an ally is essential to the difficult enterprise of navigating great forces beyond human control with imperfect technologies. Last, craft is inseparable from collectivity, since mariners work a vessel that could not be manned by a single individual. In scenes like navigating the Devil's Grip, Cooper shows the capacity of craft to bond together captain, officers, and crew. They remain connected to each other and to the entire labor process from start to finish, even as they fulfill a set of differentiated tasks allocated by expertise.

Performing an integrated vision of labor, Cooper's sea fiction shifts the cultural work of the genre. In the eighteenth-century maritime picaresque, the trials of craft confirmed the demeanor that offered the best chance of success in the risky endeavors at the edges of capitalism, science, and technology. In the nineteenth century, during the take-off of industrial capitalism, sea fiction used craft to dignify work. With its performance of skilled labor, sea fiction offered a message of democratic empowerment, translatable to other fraternities—and sororities, moreover, for female readers like George Sand and Charlotte Brontë admired Cooper's sea novels as well.

At the same time, the democratic message is tempered to make a place for hierarchy, even if its order derives from capacity, rather than from birth. Shipboard life, in Cooper's portrayal as in reality, is a deeply hierarchical structure. The emphasis on mariners as part of a profession helps justify this hierarchy as essential to efficient performance. With the dedication of everyone on board the *Ariel* across rank and job function—the captain and pilot, the lieutenants Barnstable and Griffith, the harpooner Long Tom Coffin, down to the midshipman Merry—Cooper also shows that hierarchy need not be degrading, if hierarchy is an expression of collective wisdom; if it serves a function; if workers are respected for their specific skills; and if they are bound together by common interest. The pirate community on the Rover's superb craft the *Dolphin* in Cooper's second piece of sea fiction, *The Red Rover*, offers another vision fusing hierarchy and democracy. Decisions are made in common, and loot is shared. At the same time, the community needs a leader to command decisively in moments of danger, and at these times, the commander's authority is absolute.

Cooper's heroic portrayal of the profession of mariner is further freighted with democratic potential in diverging from one of the essential aspects of labor so important in the ideology of capitalism. As Marx describes labor in *Capital*, humans use technology to extract value from Nature. Not only does man oppose "himself to Nature as one of her own forces," he does so "in order to appropriate Nature's productions in a form adapted to his own wants."[30] The compleat craft of Cooper's mariners is, in contrast, a kind of work that procures survival without surplus. The upshot of the *Ariel*'s bravura navigation of the Devil's Grip is that the ship and its company are safe to pursue the British another day. True, in the end, Cooper's mariners serve the cause of American independence, and this cause is critical to sea fiction's ideology, as I will subsequently discuss. This idealized aim of founding a new democracy, however, is qualitatively different from value-added operations of capitalist production. Both maritime historians and literary critics have compared the work on the ship to the factory and observed that novelists like Melville and Conrad critique industrial labor with their depictions of shipboard life.[31]

From the perspective of Marxian literary analysis, novelistic genres offer imaginary solutions to intractable problems that permeate the social totality. A good indication that a critic has isolated the intractable problem at issue in a genre is that the issue orients other contemporary genres as well. Certainly, the dehumanizing quality of industrial labor was addressed with other forms of the novel contemporary with sea fiction, such as the industrial novel that flourished in Britain in the midcentury. A comparison between maritime fiction and Victorian industrial fiction also illustrates the specificity of sea fiction's response. Novels like *Alton Locke*

(1850), *Hard Times* (1854), and *Mary Barton* (1848) portray the degradation of industrial labor with sentimental strategies. Delineating the harsh
conditions that workers endure, they ask readers to sympathize with the
sufferings of their characters. In doing so, industrial fiction solicits a sympathetic community that could then undertake the work of improving society. Sea fiction, in contrast, asks readers to identify with active workers
rather than remaining passive spectators. As readers follow the episodes of
danger and remedy, they take on the challenges confronting the mariners,
share their apprehension, admire their prowess, and are diverted while
gleaning some sense of the technical details of maritime life.[32] Integrating
readers into an imaginary community of labor, sea fiction's performance
of craft not only entertains and instructs readers about the practical life
of the sea, as was Cooper's intention, but it also ennobles the struggles of
the everyday, inciting readers to become the equivalent of the compleat
mariner in navigating their own lives and work.

Charles Kingsley offered a criticism of such romanticism in *Alton
Locke*, whose hero of the title begins the novel writing Byronic narrative
poems seeking to rehabilitate a Byronic corsair into "a pious sea-rover"
of the Pacific "with a crew of . . . uncommonly fine fellows," all "manly
and jolly."[33] A turning point in the novel occurs when Locke's friend, a
bookseller, punctures the heroic images of the sea and counsels Locke
to turn his attention to the London poor. Unacknowledged in the bookseller's disdain for the romance of seafaring is the fact that the mariner's
craft is a genuine ethos rather than false consciousness: the ethos of a
long tradition of skilled and heroic labor.

Alton Locke takes the bookseller's advice. But the career of Locke's
creator moved in the reverse direction. Kingsley followed *Alton Locke*
with *Westward Ho!*, a two-part historical novel set in the era of Sir Francis Drake. The first part of *Westward Ho!* occurs on land, until a failed
courtship plot sends to sea two brothers, one an accomplished politician
and courtier, the other a bluff, plain sailor. The triumph of the sailor
is already intimated in his attention to craft couched in plain style as
he prepares for his voyage: "Whereon Frank [the courtier brother] sent
Drake a pretty epigram, comparing Drake's projected leat to that river
of eternal life whereof the just would drink throughout eternity . . . ,
Amyas [the mariner] took more heed of a practical appendage to the
same letter, which was a list of hints scrawled for his use by Captain John
Hawkins himself, on all sea matters, from the mounting of ordnance
to the use of vitriol against the scurvy, in default of oranges and 'lim-
mons.'"[34] Kingsley continues to draw on the semantic field of craft once
the sailor is in his element. Frank "watched with astonishment how the
simple sailor, without genius, scholarship, or fancy, had gained, by plain

honesty, patience, and common sense, a power over the human heart, and a power over his work whatsoever it might be . . . The men looked up to him as infallible, prided themselves on forestalling his wishes, carried out his slightest hint, worked early and late to win a smile from him; while as for him, no detail escaped him, no drudgery sickened him, no disappointment angered him." [35]

His Love of Liberty May Be Questionable

Cooper's heroic portrayal of the mariner is of its age not only in its interest in anatomizing work, but in its contextualization of craft as an expression of professionalism. The word "profession" recurs in the novel, in critics' reviews, and in Cooper's prefaces, applied to the subject of his book, to his audience, and to the professional mariners that Cooper consulted to guarantee his novel's saltwater accuracy. Craft may resist industrial labor, but at the same time, when Cooper moors maritime labor to professionalism, he binds it firmly to his present. As important studies on the rise of professionalism have shown, professionalism is part of the modern standardization and division of labor that also is exemplified by the factory system. Like the factory system as well, professionalism works in tandem with disciplinary power, also emerging to dominance in the first half of the nineteenth century.

When the maritime picaresque's ethos of craft is reborn under the aegis of professionalism, shifting historical context transforms the meaning of an old motif. In particular, professionalism transvalues the ethical ambiguity of craft. As we have seen, the possibility for self-serving, if not criminal, behavior is a concern raised by the kind of excellence in action characterizing work. This possibility is voiced in philosophers' suspicion of practical reason, since Aristotle's *Nicomachean Ethics*. In the eighteenth-century maritime picaresque, authors from the time of Defoe are straightforward about craft's potential for evil as well as for good. Among its crafty mariners, we meet the slaver Crusoe, the pirate Singleton, the buccaneer Beauchêne, and so on. In *The Pilot*, too, the protagonist serves self-interest. The narrator makes clear that Jones finished his career as a mercenary in the navy of Catherine the Great, pursuing ambition. In the words of the former lieutenant, Griffith, now risen to honorable and vigorous happy middle age in the new American republic, Jones's "love of liberty may be . . . questionable; for if he commenced his deeds in the cause of these free States, they terminated in the service of a despot!" (422). The Red Rover, the hero of Cooper's second nautical novel of that name, is a similarly dubious character. The Rover, aka

Captain Walter Heidegger, dies for American independence in the novel's epilogue. However, the drama depicted in the novel concerns his career as a pirate, cruising for profit up and down the Eastern seaboard.

At the same time, these characters' ethical shadows serve to throw into relief the power of their professionalism. In the ideology of professionalism, individuals are held accountable for their excellent performance, and the surrounding personal context is comparatively unimportant. From this vantage point, dubious characters make good professional heroes, for they evince the difference between professional excellence and virtue in private life. In *The Mirror of the Sea*, we remember, Joseph Conrad was eloquent that the ethos of work was distinct from traditional notions of virtue. "The moral side of an industry . . . is the attainment and preservation of the highest possible skill on the part of the craftsmen. Such skill . . . may be called the honor of labor."[36] In the novel of manners, ethical virtue is an important ideal. While heroes like Cooper's Pilot and the Red Rover cannot be measured with this standard, they nonetheless are upholding an ethos of their own.

WE DO NOT LIKE THE AUTHOR'S DOMESTIC PAINTING SO WELL

If the power of Cooper's novels lies in their performance of the honor of labor, this focus may help explain their anemic love plots, often noted by critics of his time. Set back on land, these love plots detail how able young men win virtuous young ladies, and are an intermission from the performance of craft. In *The Pilot*, two valiant American naval officers, Barnstable and Griffith, court the cousins, Kathleen and Cecilia, whose guardian removes them from North America to the Scottish coast. In *The Red Rover*, the capable Wilder, whose birth and morals are uncertain throughout much of the novel, finally proves his ethical virtue, together with his social status that enables him to win the well-born Gertrude. Concerning the love plots in *The Pilot*, the Victorian journalist Leigh Hunt opined: "We know enough of the sea, and of the dangers of it, to take more than an ordinary interest in the most celebrated passage of this novel: and we have read few things that have left upon us a more lasting impression. We do not like the author's domestic painting so well."[37] The Western historian Francis Parkman was more direct: "[T]he reader is apt to pass with impatience over the long conversations among the ladies at St. Ruth's, and between Alice Dunscombe and the disguised Paul Jones, yet he is amply repaid when he follows the author to his congenial element. The description of the wreck of the Ariel, and the death of Long Tom Coffin, can scarcely be spoken of in terms of too much admiration."[38] When the *Atlantic Monthly* announced its view of *The Pilot* as the first and still the best nautical novel in 1859, it added: "we say this in full recollection of its brace of stupid heroines."[39]

Given the prestige of the novel of manners in the 1820s, it is not surprising that Cooper included elements of its poetics in his pattern. But to include is not necessarily to approve: What does his citation of the courtship plot convey? What if critics' dissatisfaction registered Cooper's position-taking against this type of plot, and specifically its use by Scott? From Richardson's *Pamela* (1740) on, the courtship plot was an agent of compromise and social reconciliation, reforming the rake, persuading aristocracy about the appeal of middle-class virtue, and subsequently teaching Romantic youths to recognize the importance of social norms. Scott's courtship plots function similarly, in the process accommodating older values of rank and blood with middle-class norms of nature, reason, and virtue.

As Lukács observed, the protagonist of these plots is a middle-of-the-road hero, in no way exceptional, who embodies social expectations.[40] Cooper has equivalent protagonists: Griffith and Barnstable in *The Pilot* are Ivanhoe's nautical brothers. Cooper's consummate mariners, in contrast, reject virtue defined as moral norms, though they adhere to the honor of their profession. Cooper accordingly does not entangle protagonists like Jones and the Rover in the courtship plot or its work of social compromise; nor does he use it to bend their craft to ethical virtue. To put this from the vantage point of Cooper's delineation of character: his compleat mariners step onto the deck of the novel as they leave it, consummate supermen of craft.

Cooper's refusal to entangle Jones or the Rover in a love plot is a sharp contrast with the fate of the compleat mariner, Cleveland, in Scott's historical novel, *The Pirate*. Cleveland falls in love with the beautiful, imaginative, virtuous Minna, a love that Minna returns. Marriage is not an option for the pair since "[t]he hawk pairs not with the dove; guilt matches not with innocence," in the words of Norna, the mad and magical woman who turns out to be Cleveland's mother.[41] Nonetheless, Minna's love spurs Cleveland to abandon his pirate associates and enlist in the navy, where he distinguishes himself with "honourable and gallant conduct."[42] When he is killed "leading the way in a gallant and honourable enterprise," Minna can thank Heaven with eyes "streaming with tears, that the death of Cleveland had been in the bed of honour."[43] While Jones dies at the end of *The Pilot*, Griffith pronounces the ambivalent eulogy that, "[h]is devotion to America proceeded from desire of distinction, his ruling passion, and perhaps a little also from resentment at some injustice" (422). Cooper's Rover of his second sea novel is more comparable to Cleveland, since he takes up the cause of American independence at the end of *The Red Rover*. However, he does so not for love but rather for motives that are not spelled out—we can surmise because he aligns American independence with the value he places on personal freedom.

George Sand noted the constitutive equivocation about the motives of Cooper's protagonists, whether they acted "in the name of their country or with an eye to their own fortune."[44] Sand offered this observation in an article comparing Cooper and Scott. For Sand, such equivocation revealed that Cooper's characters were motivated by "the adventurous spirit of the men who sailed in search of new worlds, their untroubled energy among the unheard-of-dangers of the great ocean voyages, of the capture of bounty and settlement in the dreadful solitude of distant islands."[45] Sand viewed these embodiments of global modernity as characters superior to the society of their time, which is why Sand gave her preference to Cooper over Scott, in ranking these "two great poets of the middle class."[46]

The Colonial Has Liberated Himself

In the lines from Byron's *The Corsair*, quoted in the interlude, the opening song of the pirates celebrates their freedom to move across the world's ocean: "O'ER the glad waters of the dark blue sea, / Our thoughts as boundless, and our souls as free, / Far as the breeze can bear the billows foam, / Survey our empire and behold our home! / These are our realms, no limits to their sway."[47] In her article comparing Cooper and Scott, Sand also noted the importance of untrammeled mobility to Cooper's protagonists. These characters "stepped out over every reef in the universe; over snowfields as readily as volcanoes, everywhere conquerors of primitive life, of nature itself in its most formidable vastnesses."[48]

The ability to navigate without constraint across what was commonly called the "trackless ocean" depended on the mariner's consummate craft. The mariner's mobility also depended on conventions of international law. As I have discussed, from the seventeenth century, European powers agreed to treat the seas as a zone where all had the right to move freely, regardless of aim. The freedom of the seas differs markedly from the kind of freedoms at issue in liberal and democratic political projects. Liberal and democratic freedoms depend on citizenship in the nation, while freedom of movement on the oceans is available to anyone on the globe. In keeping with its global scale, the freedom of the seas is an amoral right. It makes no judgments about right and wrong reasons for navigating. The right to unobstructed movement on the surface of the world's oceans extends to mariners exploring new lands, slavers, refugees from religious persecution, merchants, navies warring with each other, and privateers like Jones. Nor does the right to freedom of the seas have any connection to individuals' claims to happiness, justice, self-determination, or any of the other values associated with freedom in its liberal-democratic uses. The only exception made for the enjoyment of freedom of the seas pertained to pirates. While privateers and navies were authorized to kill and profit under the aegis of sovereign states, pirates' unregulated and self-interested predation made them "enemies of all human kind."

Freedom of the seas played a central role in the eighteenth-century maritime picaresque. Adventuring across the oceans of the globe was the prerogative of the protagonists of Defoe, Chetwood, Le Sage, etc., if they could survive in the harsh Edge zones of expanding modernity. The motives driving characters like Crusoe, Beauchêne, and even Random, are generally profit, occasionally vindication of rank, and also the existential pull of "rambling," viz Crusoe, whose "Head began to be fill'd very early with rambling Thoughts."[49] When Cooper renews sea fiction, in contrast, he moors freedom of the seas to patriotism. Jones serves the emergent American republic privateering off the Scottish coast, and even Captain Heidegger, the Red Rover, will end by putting his roving in the service of the American Revolution. American reviews of the time looked away from the protagonists' amoral exploits and emphasized Cooper's patriotism. In fact, the full sentence in the previously quoted opinion of the *New-York Mirror* runs that Cooper's mariners are "heart and soul, devoted to their profession *and their country*" (my emphasis).

The specificity of American nationalism in the 1820s clarifies why Cooper would celebrate patriotism with novels about mariners exercising the freedom of the seas. As Philbrick and Santraud have observed, the ability to trade freely across the oceans was an important ground for the American Revolution. Cooper, indeed, explicitly opened his novel by criticizing the British for refusing to recognize this right. The novel's first sentence unifies the United States and Europe around the Atlantic: "A single glance at the map will make the reader acquainted with the position of the eastern coast of the island of Great Britain, as connected with the shores of the opposite continent. Together they form the boundaries of the small sea, that has for ages been known to the world as the scene of maritime exploits, and as the great avenue through which commerce and war have conducted the fleets of the northern nations of Europe" (9). Though transport should circulate freely on this "great avenue," it was historically obstructed by "the islanders [who] long asserted a jurisdiction [on this "disputed ocean"], exceeding that which reason concedes to any power on the highway of nations" (9).

The British obstruction of freedom of the seas was a vital question for the United States not only at the time Cooper set his novel but when it was composed, within a decade after the War of 1812 defending American freedom of navigation.[50] Between the War of 1812 and the 1850s, more-over, American nationalism was a "maritime nationalism," in Philbrick's words. Cooper himself commented on the "[the] tendency to the sea, which the American has manifested since the earliest of the colonial establishments."[51] An 1827 review of Cooper's *The Prairie* shows how tightly contemporaries bound up patriotism with seafaring when it cast Cooper as "A sailor and an American. . . . His *Pilot* is truly a Tale of the Sea;—'native and enured into that element.'"[52]

This view of the sea as American destiny was internationally recognized. In the words of Alexis de Tocqueville in 1835, the Americans "are driven to take over the seas as the Romans were to conquer the world."[53] Tocqueville extended this vocation from the United States to Americans, who had world-renowned reputations as mariners. In Tocqueville's words, "[t]he European sailor ventures upon the open seas with caution . . . The American disregards these precautions and braves these dangers." Americans triumphed due to "intellectual and moral reasons." Tocqueville indeed likened American mariners' bravura to heroism, concluding that "Americans endow their way of trading with a kind of heroism."[54]

Americans' reputation as compleat mariners was an important part of maritime nationalism, at home as well as abroad. The *North American Review*'s comments on *The Pilot* identify republican freedom and the mariner's craft as the twin foundations of American national values and then suggest that craft is the more compelling of the two: "We have a commonplace, hackneyed sort of enthusiasm, on the subject of liberty, republic, principles, etc. . . . But on the subject of our naval skill and prowess . . . we are, yet, real enthusiasts. This is a string to which the national feeling vibrates certainly and deeply; and this string the author has touched with effect."[55]

If Cooper was able to renew the maritime picaresque, a form that had been abandoned for seventy-five years, in 1823, his success is hence shaped by the political and ideological specificities of his position as an American writer. Critics generally understand the cultural work of the novel in the years between Smollett and Cooper as incorporating readers into the nation as an imagined community, in Benedict Anderson's memorable phrase. Transactions between virtue and status were essential to creating this nation, fusing the values of the old ruling class, the aristocracy, with the values of the emergent ruling class, the middle class. The contribution of the novel to imagining the modern nation could explain why writers abandoned the maritime picaresque. How could a genre celebrating the supranational value of freedom of the seas and the amoral freedom of craft be put to work securing the boundaries and ideals of the nation? From the American vantage point, in contrast, maritime values were of direct national interest.[56] Under the capable leadership of Jones, the *Ariel* offers the microcosm of an ideal society not just of professionals but of patriots, joined by the bonds of work, and pursuing American freedom, the common good.

Note how Cooper updated the vision of the globe from the eighteenth-century maritime picaresque, as well as its supranational portrait of craft. In December 1823, one month before *The Pilot's* publication, the Monroe Doctrine codified a decade of reflection on the role that the United States should take with regard to the European struggles to control the New World. In Carl Schmitt's account of European geopolitics, the Monroe Doctrine articulated the end of the New World as the world beyond the line. With the establishment of independent republics like the United States, Colombia, and Argentina, the New World was transformed into the Western hemisphere, peopled by countries with their own interests. In Schmitt's explanation, these countries occupied the moral high ground, a high ground recognized in Europe as well. The world beyond the line became the "unspoiled New World"—no longer a state of nature according to Hobbes but rather one according to Rousseau: "a sphere of guaranteed peace and freedom," separated "from a sphere of despotism and corruption," as "the new West claimed to be . . . the true Europe."[57] Cooper claimed this moral high ground for his crafty mariners pursuing American independence. Their pursuit was approved by republican Europeans. We have seen Sand express her preference for Cooper over Scott, and in an anonymous review in *Le Globe*, Sainte-Beuve objected to Scott's supposed "impartiality" that in fact was the mask of "the Tory Baronet." In contrast, "Cooper writes as citizen and as philosophical man at the same time. In him one finds human reason that is remarkably free of prejudice, enlightened moral feeling, profound faith in liberty, in equality, in religion, in his country, in the dignity of human nature . . . one recognizes in Fenimore Cooper the noble type of an American republican."[58]

With the nation modeled on a shipboard fraternity soldered by craft, sea fiction idealizes a vision of the modern nation forged and maintained by the bonds of skilled work. Virtue and blood have potential to serve the nation, but they are activated and mobilized only as craft, as elements in its collectivity. The American collectivity bonded by skilled work differs from the imagined community produced in the novels of Austen or Scott. For both these authors, as more generally in the novel of manners, work plays no role in the use of a courtship plot to subdue conflicts between classes and social groups. Love, taste, insight, and the vindication of virtue help integrate feudal notions of value, emphasizing status, blood, and privilege, with middle-class ethics. But while John Paul Jones is of Scottish origin and serves a rebel army, there his similarity with Fergus MacIvor ends. As Sainte-Beuve put it, "whilst never ceasing to belong to the family of the Scottish novelist, he has pursued an independent path,—and the colonial has liberated himself."[59]

A Deep Blood-Red Field: The Price at Which I Am to Be Bought

It is important that the skilled work bonding Americans into a nation is supranational in scope, plied on the oceans of the globe. Craft is a value well suited to a country that viewed its identity from its inception as a "nation among nations," to cite the title of Thomas Bender's recent book, emphasizing the importance of a global, and specifically, overseas perspective for American studies.[60] This appeal of craft as a capacity in the global arena contrasts with the difficulties it presented for British and French authors in their novels delineating and insulating the contours of the nation as an imagined community.

At the same time, craft's orientation at once to the nation and the globe is fraught. Jones's global origins initially lead the *Ariel*'s crew to doubt his commitment to the American cause, a doubt that will be reinforced by the fact that he ends his career in service to a "despot." When the Rover first meets Wilder, he presents the *Dolphin*'s crew as a global workforce of desperadoes: "There was not a maritime nation in Europe which had not its representative among that band of turbulent and desperate spirits. Even the descendant of the aboriginal possessors of America had been made to abandon the habits and opinions of his progenitors" (777–78). At the novel's end, nonetheless, this desperate crew puts its superior capacity in service of the American cause of independence, implying allegorically the vital, if rough, heterogeneity of the new American nation.

In the final instance of Cooper's pattern, patriotic freedom then turns out to be a value that can be accommodated with sea fiction's honor of labor, in contrast to the ethical virtue of the courtship plot; however, this accord occurs not through compromise and reconciliation, as in the novel of manners, but rather through unstinting expenditure of blood. Cooper's sea fiction abounds in the deaths of its charismatic characters. In their deaths, they purify the mariner's craft of its potential for self-interest or evil-doings, as well as show the mortal danger of the seaman's life. The anthropologist Georges Bataille understood sacrificial bloodshed as one example of "expenditure": nonproductive activity that is essential to the creation of sacred values. Bataille wrote, "Cults require a bloody wasting of men and animals in *sacrifice*. In the etymological sense of the word, sacrifice is nothing other than the production of *sacred* things."[61] Bataille included abstract values like glory and honor among these "sacred things"; republican freedom is one such abstraction.

When Cooper's hero dies on the novel's stage at the end of *The Red Rover*, the Rover explicitly shifts his credo from freedom understood as individualism into freedom understood as American liberty. Throughout the novel, the Rover sails under the blood-red flag that he has inherited from Byron's Corsair Conrad. The Rover's flag is "a deep, blood-red field, without relief or ornament" (509). The Rover tells Wilder, "'I like it better than your gloomy fields of black, with death's heads and other childish scare-crows. It threatens nothing; but merely says, 'Such is the price at which I am to be bought'" (509). Red is the color of blood, and thus symbolizes the universal common denominator of humanity; contrasting with the blue blood of the aristocracy. But the novel makes good on individualism's democratic potential only when the Rover dies for American freedom instead of gain, shrouding himself in the American flag in a deathbed apotheosis. "With a supernatural effort, his form arose on the litter; and, with both hands elevated above his head, he let fall before him that blazonry of intermingled stripes, with its blue field of rising stars, a glow of high exultation illumining every feature of his face" (868).

In *The Pilot*, too, Cooper sacrifices characters in the cause of freedom, including the consummate seaman, gunner, and harpooner Long Tom Coffin and the unimaginative but competent sailing master Boltrope. If bodies sanctify the soil of a nation, *The Pilot* claims the ocean for the United States by burying these dedicated mariners in the "trackless waste." At the same time, unlike the bodies of heroes who are buried in a nation's soil, sanctifying its territory, those of Coffin and Boltrope are absorbed without a trace. "[N]o memorial in the midst of the ever-rolling waters" is left "to mark the place of their sepulture" (413).

When Melville portrayed shipboard society in his first sea novels, such as *White-Jacket*, he attacked sea fiction's political myth-making. Rather than an idealized community of craft, Melville hammered home in this novel about life on a man-of-war that the navy is a brutal hierarchy ruled by force, flagrantly at odds with American ideals. Melville's narrator declares, "Our institutions claim to be based upon broad principles of political liberty and equality," but "a sailor . . . shares none of our civil immunities; the law of our soil in no respect accompanies the national floating timbers grown thereon, and to which he clings as his home. For him our Revolution was in vain; to him our Declaration of Independence is a lie."[62]

THE OBSCURITY OF FACTS CLOUDED BY TIME

Seafaring was perceived as essential for the United States in Cooper's time because it was the motor of America's commercial destiny. Cooper noted the U.S. mercantile spirit as a challenge to a writer who would pen a romance concerning the beginnings of the American nation à la Walter Scott. Philbrick observes, "the exalted and ideal tone of romance," the narrative genre used to make a myth of history; however the commercial bent of "American maritime history rendered such a tone absurd."[63] Cooper noted this conflict in his 1850 preface to *The Red Rover*, which explains that he invented the legend of the Red Rover because the "staid character of the [American] people ... especially ... that portion of them ... most addicted to navigation" yielded little that would confer the "peculiar charm" that is the privilege of a "work of the imagination." The preface linked this charm to mystery, specifically the obscurity of "facts clouded a little by time" (429).

Cooper does make one exception to America's lack of romance in this preface, which is "the career of Kidd" (429). In the text of *The Red Rover*, Cooper suggests that the romance of piracy derives from another kind of obscurity, not the obscurity of facts, but rather the obscurity of motives. Thus, Mrs. Wyllis's reflections on the Rover: "Even those tales of the time, which recounted the desperate acts of the freebooter, with wild and fanciful exaggerations, did not forget to include numberless instances of even chivalrous generosity" (750). In Cooper's sea fiction, the obscurity of romance emanates from the ethical instability of craft and it lends mystery to the private history of an individual rather than of a nation. Such mystery, encompassing a character's obscure background as well as his or her obscure motives, characterizes the Pilot as well as the Red Rover and works synergistically with the lack of attention in adventure poetics to a character's complex psychology. Alexandre Dumas registered the atmosphere of mystery around the Pilot's past, using images conjuring poor visibility, when he commented that Cooper left his hero's career outside the exploits in the American Revolution unrepresented, from the "clouds surrounding his birth" to "the obscurity of his death."[64] While troubling the patriotic foundations of the United States, craft's ethical ambiguity lends an atmosphere of romance to America's practical, commercial origins and character.

BREATHLESS INTEREST: FROM PERFORMING TO GRIPPING DESCRIPTION

In contemporary reviews, critics assimilated Cooper's keen knowledge of sea life with his vivid techniques for involving the reader in its portrayal. "The ocean is truly his element—the deck his home," declared the review in the *New-York Mirror*, evoking Cooper's ability to make his readers "see the waters—the ships—the manning of the yards—the heaving of the lead—the very cordage of the vessels. Every movement—from that of the tracking of the frigate to the launching of the whaleboat, is visible to our eyes, and we actually take part in the proceedings and conversations of the crew." In admiring how "[e]very thing is done nautically," the review noted that Cooper had a way of delineating events "with a truth and force, and generat[ing] such a breathless interest, that De Foe himself is, in some respects, thrown at a distance by our author."[65] This appreciation of Cooper recurred throughout contemporary reception, down to the phrase "breathless interest."

The critic from the *New-York Mirror* is right that Cooper substantively transformed Defoe's narrative games at the level of information into a new poetics of suspense. In Defoe's paradigm, I have argued, episodes solicit a cunning reader who organizes the information offered and problem-solves with the protagonist. In Cooper's transformation of such readerly protocol, the reader is still asked to problem-solve along with the protagonist. However, Cooper draws on Gothic techniques for creating reader identification with the protagonists in danger. In the process, he makes the dangers palpable, heightening their emotional urgency.[66]

The Gothic asks the reader to sympathize with protagonists negotiating zones of danger that are also zones of mystery. In the Gothic, indeed, dangers are inseparable from obscurity, an obscurity that is sometimes visual and physical, always epistemological—to the point of the existence of either the danger or the mystery itself being shadowy and doubtful. The dangerous mysteries are tied at once to place and to family history, in an expression of aristocratic values. The role of the Gothic protagonist is to explore and resolve the mysteries, and the reader shares his or her efforts and pains. At the end of the Gothic narrative, often after hundreds of pages, the power of Enlightenment prevails. Finding the cause of the mysteries dispels their danger and relegates to the past feudal values, a regime of force, and a religion of mystification and superstition.

The role of the narrator in such a narrative built around the communication of information is to move this process of discovery along and simultaneously to delay it. In this interplay, the Gothic thus picks up the cybernetic games of eighteenth-century adventure fiction, launched by the maritime picaresque. At the same time, the Gothic saturates these dangers with terrifying affect, learned from sentimental and pre-Romantic aesthetics. From sentimental fiction, the Gothic takes strategies for portraying the protagonist's palpable, embodied emotions. From pre-Romanticism, the Gothic takes the literary delineation of picturesque and sublime weather and scenery. Gothic authors press these delineations into the service of a delay in revealing answers. Even as such descriptions function in the forward movement of the narrative, they function at the level of reader involvement, coloring events with emotion for the protagonist and, by sympathetic identification, for the reader. Hesitation and uncertainty are other effects used by the narrator to involve the reader and delay revelation of the mystery. In the Gothic, the protagonist is torn between a rational explanation for strange occurrences that may be less menacing than they might appear—and an emotional and sometimes superstitious response, suggesting them as deadly and even supernatural.

Cooper picks up on all these Gothic techniques and applies them to dangers of a different order. The dangers do not stem from the dark secrets of blood and land but rather are extreme weather, shoals and coasts, hostile beasts and men. In keeping with this transformation, the secret becomes the expedients of craft, the previously mentioned trade use of secret in the sense of the early modern *The Seamens Secrets*. To discover the secret of Cooper's sea fiction becomes a challenge for practical reason in quest of the effective expedient, rather than pure reason, seeking the hidden truth of the Gothic.[67]

Cooper's application of Gothic techniques to narrate danger is evident in the scene depicting Jones's seamanship in the Devil's Grip. As the ship negotiates the treacherous waters, readers are incited to identify with characters' responses to the terrifying might of the sea. In the Gothic, most of these responses are in the mind of the protagonist, a narrative poetics that the Gothic takes up from first-person epistolary fiction. Cooper, in contrast, cues the reader to the protagonist's judgments through citing his spoken words. In the case of the Pilot, these cues walk a fine line between evincing the mariners' cool and intensifying the readers' anxieties. Jones, the compleat mariner, is also given to melodramatic statements like "here we get the true tide and the real danger" (51) or "Now is the pinch . . . if the ship behaves well, we are safe—but if otherwise, all we have yet done will be useless" (54).

Jones's ability to remain calm amidst such danger contrasts with other characters of the shipboard community. Sometimes they speak, but at times, Cooper draws on the ability of the third-person omniscient narrator to reveal their gestures and bare their feelings. As Jones mentions the danger, Cooper hints that the crew's uneasiness breaks through their professionalism: "nothing but the habits of the most exact discipline could suppress the uneasiness of the officers and men within their own bosoms" (48). Despite his experience, "the quarter-master at the cun gave out his orders . . . in deeper and hoarser tones than usual" (51). After Jones lays on sail successfully, "A moment of breathless astonishment succeeded the accomplishment of this nice manœuvre" (53), and then, "the hardy mariners, knowing that they had already done all in the power of man, to ensure their safety, stood in breathless anxiety, awaiting the result" (56). Silence is as powerful in conveying anxiety as commentary. While the crew watch Jones try to clear the point in the final maneuver, "[n]o noise proceeded from the frigate to interrupt the horrid tumult of the ocean."

"Twenty times, as the foam rolled away to leeward, the crew were on the eve of uttering their joy, as they supposed the vessel past the danger; but breaker after breaker would still heave up before them, following each other into the general mass, to check their exultation." When the vessel makes it round the point and it is clear that Jones has triumphed, "[T]he seamen were yet drawing long breaths, and gazing about them like men recovered from a trance" (56).

When critics complemented Cooper on his ability to inspire "breathless interest," from the *New-York Mirror* on, their words echo Cooper's emphasis on strained breathing within his scenes of maritime danger. Cooper learned this emphasis from the Gothic, where breathing is the transition from emotion and thought to sensation. When the heroine of Ann Radcliffe's *Mysteries of Udolpho*, Emily Saint-Aubert, believes she has seen a ghost, she "trembled, breathed with difficulty" as "an icy coldness touched her cheeks."[68] The delineation of landscape to block resolution of the mystery is another technique Cooper adapts from the Gothic repertoire. As "the hardy mariners . . . stood in breathless anxiety, awaiting the result" of Jones's final piloting, Cooper delays its revelation by delineating a sublime seascape:

> At a short distance ahead of them, the whole ocean was white with foam, and the waves, instead of rolling on, in regular succession, appeared to be tossing about in mad gambols. A single streak of dark billows, not half a cable's length in width, could be discerned running into this chaos of water; but it was soon lost to the eye, amid the confusion of the disturbed element. Along this narrow path the vessel moved more heavily than before, being brought so near the wind as to keep her sails touching. (56)

The sublime tone of "chaos" and "confusion" is Gothic as well.[69] In other landscapes, Cooper translates the Gothic's fondness for chiaroscuro into the lighting of scenes at sea.[70] "All the lanterns had been extinguished on the deck of the frigate . . . and as the first mist of the gale had passed over, it was succeeded by a faint light that was a good deal aided by the glittering foam of the waters . . . The land could be faintly discerned, rising like a heavy bank of black fog, above the margin of the waters, and was only distinguishable from the heavens, by its deeper gloom and obscurity" (48). From the swerve through the Gothic, Cooper transforms what I have called "performing description" apropos of the eighteenth-century maritime picaresque into what I will call "gripping description," thinking of Jones's opening navigation of the Devil's Grip.

In his preface to *The Pilot*, Cooper took pride in the fact "that the work would be more likely to find favour with nautical men, than with any other class of readers." In contrast, "[t]he Pilot could scarcely be a favourite with females," a large part of the novel-reading public, since the author's "aim was to illustrate vessels and the ocean, rather than to draw any pictures of sentiment and love" (7). Given how much Cooper takes from the Gothic, a genre associated with women, Cooper's professed disdain for his female readers is a strategy of disavowal. Certainly, Cooper's contemporaries, both male and female, found his portrayals of maritime danger gripping even if they knew nothing of the sea.[71] In the words of R. H. Dana Jr., author of *Two Years Before the Mast* (1840), "[t]housands . . . follow . . . [its] minute nautical manœuvers with breathless interest, who do not know the name of a rope in the ship; and perhaps with none the less admiration and enthusiasm for their want of acquaintance with the professional detail."[72] Dana, who learned so much from Cooper himself, puts his finger on Cooper's skill at fusing Gothic suspense with the kind of technical information on maneuvers, including the specialized language of the sea. Indeed, in gripping description, nonspecialist readers can enjoy technical language as an effect of obscurity. Technical language slows down the narrative and heightens suspense. In this process, specialized depictions of work take over the narrative function of crumbling castles and intimidating mountain scenes in the Gothic. The obscurity of technical language both intimates and blocks information, suggesting the force and power of men who can maneuver such intricate technologies, even as the specifics of these maneuvers remain vague.

At the same time, Cooper's epigraph to *The Pilot* pitched his work to "landsmen," and nonspecialist audiences do glean information about seafaring from his scenes of maritime danger, though they do not fully understand the technical terms. Such knowledge is in keeping with the yield of performing description as practiced by Defoe. From the scene of the Devil's Grip, for example, landsmen learn that the frigate is a comparatively massive craft—that to navigate against the wind entails a number of tacks, as well as a maneuver called "backing the sails," that tacking is an arduous business requiring precision on the part of the steersman and those mariners manipulating the sails, that laying on sail is a bravura maneuver, etc. Cooper's gripping descriptions hence work for two different kinds of audiences, which is part of the technique's success. While an audience familiar with the sea appreciates the truth of Cooper's portrayal and seeks to outmaneuver him, a nonspecialist audience enjoys a suspenseful introduction into the world of maritime performance. Subsequent adventure fiction will take Cooper's gripping description beyond the sea to communicate other bodies of technical expertise.

With gripping description, Cooper goes well beyond any use of specialized knowledge found in the eighteenth-century maritime picaresque—with the exception of the second voyage of *Gulliver's Travels*, whose incomprehensible literal transcription of pages of a practical manual is precisely the point of Swift's parody. As this specialized language indicates, Cooper has transformed Defoe's manner of framing Crusoe's challenges so that the solution could be intimated by common sense, even if a technical piece was needed to make it precise. In Cooper's pattern, in contrast, there is only technical expertise, and the aspects pitched to nonspecialist readers are the Gothic protocols for creating suspense.

One nineteenth-century critic called Cooper the first to "extract . . . a dramatic interest from the log book, and suspend . . . the hopes and fears of his plot upon the maneuvering of a vessel."[73] Using "dramatic" and "log book" in the same sentence, this critic registers how far Cooper's Gothic strategies have taken him away from the mariner's plain style.[74] Compare, for example, Cooper's techniques of reader involvement in the Devil's Grip with Cook's narration when the *Endeavour* first strikes the Great Barrier Reef. While the extraordinary danger of a hitherto unimaginable reef might offer an opportunity for dramatic emphasis, Cook's narration is instead compressed. No description of emotion or landscape, and no figures of speech or thought dramatize the danger. No psychological details summon up the feelings of captain or crew in desperate circumstances; no descriptions of landscape stress the sublimity or terror of the scene. Even the narration of technical maneuvers shares this compression. The only technical language used refers to expedients that play an important role in the struggle to stave off shipwreck; other technical terminology is left out as too routine to bear mention. As a result of such compression, Cook has gotten the *Endeavour* off the reef before the reader has had time to process the heroism of the deed.

To gauge the influence of Cooper's gripping description, compare how Verne reworked Cook's deed of craft in his own nonfictional account of Cook's voyage. In contrast to Cook's compression, Verne has learned from nineteenth-century sea fiction the importance of dilating the time between a danger and its remedy. To manufacture suspense, Verne adds to Cooper's melodramatic repertoire his own fondness for the technique of embroidering worst-case scenarios. "Terrifying choices!" Verne specifies as the rising tide lifts the vessel off the reef:

If the vessel was freed, it would sink as soon as it was no longer held up by the rock; if it remained stranded, it would soon be destroyed by the billows, which were tearing apart its ribs! And there were not enough longboats to take all the crew to shore at the same time! Was it not to be feared in these circumstances that discipline would be trampled on? Who could guarantee that a fratricidal struggle would not take the disaster to the point of no return? And even if a part of the sailors made it to the coast, what fate was waiting for them on an inhospitable

beach, where their nets and firearms would barely enable them to procure food? What, moreover, would become of those who should have
stayed with the ship?[75]

All these scenarios are nowhere in Cook but rather Verne's dramatic
imagination, summoning up a litany of disasters found across the maritime corpus of shipwreck and survival.[76]

To experience suspense, all a reader of sea fiction needs is literacy, sensations, and the fear of death. Suspense is thus a more democratic entertainment joining a community of readers than the earlier cybernetic
challenges of the maritime picaresque, which solicited cunning readers
who enjoyed testing their ingenuity. The pleasures of suspense are also
more democratic than the affect solicited by sentimental fiction, which
invited readers of taste, feeling, and morality to join the sentimental community. If Cooper's suspense pattern creates "breathless interest," the
reader's labored breathing is a bodily expression of sea fiction's accessi-
bility, for to draw breath is the basic requirement of staying alive. It also
includes the reader in the social microcosm of the ship, for "breathless"
interest is precisely the condition of the characters themselves, like the
"breathless anxiety" of the mariners on board the *Ariel* at the most critical moment of the navigation (56).

The essence of suspense is life threatened by death, and the medium
of the struggle is time. In grappling with the elements, adventure at sea
often understands time as the challenge of "temps," in the French sense:
time and weather, to which it adds expanse. In the first bravura navigation in *The Pilot*, the *Ariel* races against the storm and tide in the Devil's
Grip; Jones's last feat will require contending with fog, as well as engaging a British ship. Whether the obstacle is weather, tide, human, or beast,
the dilation of time over space produces the chase, the core adventure
scenario of Cooper's sea fiction. With the sequence of the chase, Cooper
invents a powerful narrative mechanism, gripping the reader as it simultaneously vindicates sea fiction's ideological investment in movement, another name for enjoying the freedom of the seas.

Even as the readers of sea fiction are joined with the democratic bond
of suspense, they identify with the mariner who comes up with remedies to survive extraordinary danger. Joining the ordinary reader with
the superior individual, sea fiction's community of suspense can glorify a
proto-fascist ideology, as well as ennoble every person's struggles for survival in daily life. This identification of ordinary reader with consummate
mariner in gripping description procures a sense of power, and a sense
of pleasure in danger as well. Cooper's Rover glories in suspense as the
privilege of the elite individual strong enough to look death in the face. In
the Rover's words, "I love suspense; it keeps the faculties from dying, and

throws a man upon the better principles of his nature. Perhaps I owe it to a wayward spirit, but to me there is sometimes enjoyment in an adverse wind" (719). With the term "suspense," the Rover names a keen aesthetic pleasure that would have been unthinkable for Captain Thomas James, shipwrecked in Hudson's Bay and struggling in the throes of the Arctic winter. There is also no such pleasure expressed by Cook in his journals when he looks into the jaws of destruction. For Cook, the only aesthetic moment singled out is the indescribable pleasure in the thrill of discovery, be it of nothing more than barren sands.

Nautical Novels: Mesty . . . You Are a Man

Captain Frederick Marryat was responsible for launching sea fiction in the United Kingdom with *The Naval Officer or, Scenes and Adventures in the Life of Frank Mildmay* (1829). But this first novel translating Cooper's pattern across the Atlantic is a generic hybrid in comparison to Marryat's version of the "nautical novel," fully realized in *Mr. Midshipman Easy* (1836), arguably the most popular among Marryat's more than twenty sea novels and the only one "never to go out of print."[77] *Mr. Midshipman Easy* bears the name of its protagonist, Jack Easy, a gentleman's son. Jack is encouraged to go to sea by a distant family relative, a ship's Captain, to cure him of his French revolutionary ideals, which Jack has absorbed uncritically from his hare-brained father. Enrolled in "the rough school" of the Navy, to cite the master's mate on board Jack's first posting, the *Harpy*, Jack will eventually abandon his belief in innate human equality and recognize that the best social order is a meritocracy.

As the master's mate, Mr. Jolliffe sums up the moral of *Mr. Midshipman Easy*, "The service is a rough, but a good school, where everybody finds his level—not the level of equality, but the level to which his natural talents and acquirements will rise or sink him" (82). By the novel's conclusion, Jack adopts this moral as his own: "To suppose all men were born equal, is to suppose that they are equally endowed with the same strength, and with the same capacity of mind, which we know is not the case. I deny it from Scripture, from which I could quote many passages; but I will restrict myself to one—the parable of the Talents: 'To one he gave five talents, to another but one,' holding them responsible for the trust reposed in them. We are all intended to fill various stations in society, and are provided by Heaven accordingly" (303).

But if we look more closely at its details, the novel does not make a vigorous case for Jack's Bildung at sea.[78] First of all, as Jack's own tongue-in-cheek pun taking talents for capacity rather than money might intimate, the "rough, but . . . good school" of the Navy turns out to be a corrupt hierarchy rewarding rank and wealth rather than merit. Marryat's narrator underscores this point in introducing the *Harpy*'s first lieutenant, "Mr Sawbridge . . . a good officer, one who had really worked his way up to the present rank, that is to say, that he had served seven-and-twenty years, and had nothing but his pay" (41). Jack Easy exemplifies what Sawbridge sums up as the "cleaner," "more gentlemanly," and "more useless" midshipmen, lacking Sawbridge's ethos of duty and service.[79]

The other problem with the view that the novel shows Jack's Bildung pertains to its protagonist. True, Jack does eventually abjure his French Revolutionary ideals, but these ideals are empty stereotypes from the time Jack introduces them clowning from the security of his upper-class position.[80] And true, Jack acquires a passable notion of seamanship in his service, but it could not be compared to the craft of Jones or the Rover, or even Cooper's Griffith, Barnstable, or Wilder. Rather than capturing the reader's interest for his acquisition of craft, Jack claims our attention for his entitled willingness to get himself into scrapes, mock authority, and test the limits of hierarchy. When Jack is called home to administer his family fortune at the novel's end, his patron, the Governor of Malta, puts Jack's case frankly. Note how "adventure" has been transformed to designate immature scrapes when the Governor declares to Jack, "you have a wonderful talent for adventure . . . but, if I understand right from Captain Wilson, you were brought into the profession because he thought that the service might be of use in eradicating false notions, rather than from any intention or necessity of your following it up as a profession" (290).[81]

Jack is a gentleman picaro. But Marryat, himself a naval officer, is not a writer to underplay danger at sea. Jack's goodwill and strength would yield little beyond some schoolboy pranks, if Jack did not have the guidance of a compleat mariner, though one who is pointedly not recognized with a corresponding rank in the British Navy. This compleat mariner is a black sailor, Mesty. Forged in the crucible of the Black Atlantic, Mesty is described with a satirical mixture of stereotypes as a "curious anomaly," claiming the birth of an Ashanti warrior, with a "spare-built, yet muscular form," and a long, proud face "by no means common with his race," graced with a Roman nose and thin lips. Mesty speaks English with the Irish brogue of "emigrant labourers at New York," "dashed with a little Yankeeism" (53). Mesty decides to journey to Great Britain from New York, after having heard that slavery had been abolished there, by escaping and stowing away on a merchant vessel. Upon arrival, he enrolls on a man-of-war. As the narrator subsequently specifies in a more humanitarian tone, Mesty "had been a great man in his own country; he had suffered all the horrors of a passage in a slave ship; he had been sold as a slave twice; he had escaped—but he found that the universal feeling was strong against his colour, and that on board of a man-of-war he was condemned, although free, to the humblest of offices," which is to say the ship's cook (65).

Even as Marryat's portrayal of Mesty relies on racial stereotypes, the novel at the same time portrays Mesty's extraordinary capacity. Jack and Mesty have become friendly because they instinctively recognize each other's worth. They cement their bond when they are on a cutter separated from their squadron in battle, which they commandeer for a little "holiday." To redeem their spree, they capture a Spanish prize, which, however, proves to be more of a challenge than anticipated. In this exploit, Mesty shows himself "foremost in everything," from securing the ship to subduing the mutiny that ensues (94). Jack will subsequently rely on Mesty's craft to guide his adventures not only at sea but also on land. Thus, for example, Mesty clears the way for Jack's success with a Spanish beauty by murdering the enemies of her father.

Mesty shows himself master of all aspects of craft, from patience and protocol to creative jury-rigging, as for example, when the rest of the crew desert their prize to go drinking on an island, and Mesty discovers the means to force their capitulation:

A narrow piece of salt pork had been left at the gangway; Jack, without knowing why, tossed it overboard; being almost all fat, it sank very gradually: Jack watched it as it disappeared, so did Mesty, both full of thought, when they perceived a dark object rising under it: it was a ground shark, who took it in his maw, sank down, and disappeared.

"What was that?" said Jack.

"That ground shark, Massa Easy—worst shark of all; you nebber see him till you feel him"; and Mesty's eyes sparkled with pleasure. "By de powers, they soon stop de mutiny; now I hab 'em." (104)

Seizing opportunity and turning the shark's danger to salvation, Mesty comes up with the plan of stealing the mutineers' boat when the mutineers are drunk on the island, giving them the choice of submission or a swim through shark-infested waters.

As in the eighteenth-century maritime picaresque, too, we shadow Mesty's solutions to challenges using performing description. Thus, information about the ground shark, like Crusoe's goats, is given as it is in the process of being used. One passage from the novel can show how technical Marryat can be in his performing description, like Cooper introducing his readers into the specialized language of the sea. In the course of taking the Spanish ship, Mesty "left four men abaft, and went forward on the forecastle, examined the cable, which was *coir* rope, and therefore easily divided, and then directed the two men forward to coil a hawser upon the for-grating, the weight of which would make all safe in that quarter, and afterwards to join them on the quarter-deck" (94).

With adventures forging a bond between Jack and Mesty, Marryat, like Cooper, offers adventures performing craft that yield community across social distinction joined by the bonds of work. Meritocracy is its standard: Jack recognizes Mesty's superiority and offers him a bond above his society's racism after Jack and Mesty subdue the mutiny through Mesty's cunning. At that point, Jack declares, "Mesty, that you have been a prince, I care little about . . . but you are a man, and I respect you, nay, I love you as a friend" (109). At the same time, Jack's break with racism only goes so far. He provides Mesty with his final job in the novel, as his own servant, a job that is more comfortable, but as far below Mesty's extraordinary capacity as Mesty's functions in his Majesty's service.

With its consolidation of a meritocratic community that yet preserves hierarchy, *Mr. Midshipman Easy* is doing ideological work as specific to Great Britain as Cooper's republican fraternity is to the context of the United States. We saw Cooper's Jones declare, "It is but of little moment where a man is born, or how he speaks . . . so that he does his duty bravely, and in good faith" (30). In the fraternity of Jack and Mesty, in contrast, birth and background matter. Their alliance models a kinder, gentler form of social inequality, where rank acknowledges merit and is softened by compassion and common sense. This gentle social inequality is in keeping with the ideals of liberal reformers of his time, and Marryat self-consciously directs his portrait at the Navy, an organization that, he spells out throughout his novels, does not live up to its meritocratic ideal.[82] In chapter XXI of *Mr. Midshipman Easy*, Marryat reiterates that here, as in past novels, he takes issue with how naval officers abuse their power toward their inferiors, while the "greatest charm attached to power is to be able to make so many people happy" (180). Beyond the Navy, Britons were enmeshed in questions of how to reform British electoral districts to expand the voting base at the time the sea novel took off in Great Britain. These questions were addressed but not resolved in the Reform Bill of 1832, and they would continue to resonate across the middle decades of the nineteenth century, when the nautical novel was at the apogee of its prestige.

Marrayt's novel is further removed from Cooper's democratic community of seamen in that the anchoring bond of its community joins a British gentleman and a character who is by birth an African prince. With this depiction, the novel yields the cross-cultural elite to govern Britain's overseas empire. At the same time, the novel implies that the bond is somewhat nerve-wracking due to Mesty's distance from European ethics. In the character of Mesty, Marryat spins out the amoral side to craft that is one of its qualities across its history and steeps it in racial Othering. Mesty is referred to as "the artful black" (277), and his menace emanates from his full name, Mephistopheles Faust. Mesty kills Jack's enemies in a chapter subtitled, "[i]n which Mesty should be called throughout Mephistopheles, for it abounds in black cloaks, disguises, daggers, and dark deeds" (281). Though parodic, comedy here, as so often, has more than a shred of truth. Mesty's threat remains discernable in the novel's final word on Mesty's fate in Jack's service. "Mesty held his post with dignity, and proved himself trustworthy," the narrator informs the reader, opening the door to other possible outcomes, even as he seems to confirm Mesty's reliability (337).

At the same time, Marryat is fascinated by the amoral if not immoral menace of craft, and returns to it in other novels, where it is also the attribute of European seaman. This menace is perhaps most dramatic in his fantastic sea novel, *The Phantom Ship* (1839). In Marryat's version of the Flying Dutchman legend, Philip Vanderdecken is an upright young man who roams the seas of the globe, in quest of his father, to help his father's soul find peace. While Philip is a Barnstable-, Griffith-, or Wilder-type character, his father is on the way to Ahab, endowed with resolution but not prudence, who is cursed for vowing to bring his ship around Cape Horn "in defiance of storm and seas, of lightning, of heaven, or of hell, even if I should beat about until the Day of Judgment."[83] Neither Philip nor his father is the compleat mariner in this novel. Rather this role is filled by a diabolical adversary in Philip's quest: the ageless one-eyed pilot Schriften, "although small, neatly made," with "an air of superiority . . . which almost impressed you with awe."[84] Philip crosses oceans, fights battles, contends with mutinies, and survives storms, typhoons, and shipwrecks, until at the end of his life, he forgives Schriften, thereby inadvertently stumbling on the way to free his father's soul by reclaiming craft for humanity and ethics.

COMPARATIVE SEA FICTION: SOME FEATURES OF TRAVELING GENRES

In genres, poetic patterns reach beyond the practice of an individual author to be adopted by a community of readers and writers. Their social appeal suggests that they fulfill a collective need, performing some kind of cultural or ideological work. This collectivity can exist at a number of different scales, including an international literary field. Across the history of the novel, the international literary field has been shaped by a range of genres that travel from one national context to another, not only translated but also adapted by local writers to local literary tradition and society. These genres include picaresque fiction, adventure fiction, Gothic fiction, historical fiction, realism—and sea fiction, whose travels in the nineteenth century are markedly more international than the eighteenth-century maritime picaresque.

Genres that travel across space, like genres that endure across time, must be able to address social and/or literary questions that are transportable, that can speak to divergent publics or a public defined in its diversity, dispersion, and heterogeneity. In the case of nineteenth-century sea fiction, the key to its transportability is its performance of craft. This appeal of craft is overdetermined. The mariner's craft itself is a capacity that is legible and compelling across cultures involved in maritime globalization, viz the international nature of the maritime corpus where craft is delineated in the early modern era. Because of its glamour, craft has ideological usefulness as well, in offering imaginary solutions to problems of other kinds. As a kind of skilled labor, craft is well suited to represent the process of work and the social status of the worker, central concerns of political and social debate in the middle decades of the nineteenth century across nations at the forefront of capitalist modernization, where sea fiction enjoys popularity. At the same time, as we have seen in the eighteenth-century maritime picaresque, craft's flexibility lets it modulate to generate a range of plots that can express different values. Thus, this chapter has shown craft to found a new democratic republic in Cooper, while for Marryat, it justifies a tempered class system and forges the alliance to rule Britain's overseas empire.

A similar stability and adaptability characterizes the cultural work that can be accomplished with sea fiction's interest in the freedom of the seas. Freedom of the seas, the freedom of unimpeded movement, is a foundation of international law. It is of national importance for countries in the vanguard of globalization; and it is at the same time a value that is sufficiently complex to generate different plots and adapt to different cultural contexts. In the case of the United States, as exemplified by *The Pilot* and *The Red Rover*, freedom of the seas is at stake in the rebellion against social constraints and is essential to the commercial destiny of the new American nation. In the case of Great Britain, as exemplified by Marryat's *Mr. Midshipman Easy*, Jack and Mesty embody freedom of the seas in their carnival of ossified rank and social pretension. At the same time, the novel is justifying Britain's imperial reach when it makes the proving ground for their free circulation the oceans of the globe. In *Mr. Midshipman Easy*, those seas happen to be the Atlantic and Mediterranean; in Marryat's *The Phantom Ship*, the hero's chase for the *Flying Dutchman* encircles the earth. Catherine Gallagher identifies the imperial overtones to such a version of the free seas in her analysis of the nautical novels of Marryat's compatriot, Michael Scott. There, she declares that the nautical novel would be "the right place to find" a notion of British subjectivity as "a phenomenon of extra-territorialization." In this context, national identity "would name not a place but a world order of unobstructed movement."[85]

When Marryat translated Cooper's poetics to Great Britain, the British novel was dominated by genres whose fundamental imaginary scale was the nation, such as the historical novel, the domestic novel, and the novel of manners. As Gayatri Spivak and Edward Said, among others, have suggested, this national focus helped elide Britain's participation in the violent aspects of global commerce, such as the slave trade and imperialism. In a novel like *Mansfield Park* or *Jane Eyre*, overseas colonies drive the action, but they remain too disruptive of the novel's liberal ideology and soft vision of power to take center stage.[86] The dangers of sea adventure, in contrast, offer a safer way for British novelists to reconnect the nation with the globe.[87]

Sea fiction's simultaneous stability and flexibility are evident in the form's narrative poetics, as well as in its defining cultural values. The kernel of sea fiction's narrative sequence is an adventure built of a danger and the search for a solution that involves the reader in simulating craft. This formula is simple, enabling sea fiction to travel light. As a result, authors have flexibility concerning other aspects of the novel that are not essential to its narrative structure, giving them poetic points of entry to insert this traveling form into other host literary traditions.

Marryat finds one poetic point of entry in his narrative voice. While Cooper's narrator at times sounds like Walter Scott and at times mixes Gothic and plain style in gripping description, Marryat returns to the maritime picaresque. Marryat prefers performing description over gripping description, as in the details on how Mesty captures the prize ship and negotiates the mutiny quoted earlier. In the previously quoted descriptions of Mesty, we can also see how Marryat returns to Smollett's distinctive mixture of satirical and humanitarian attitudes toward life at sea. Mesty is presented first satirically—as a "curious anomaly"—and then with the sympathetic voice of humanitarian narrative—specifying that Mesty "had been a great man in his own country; he had suffered all the horrors of a passage in a slave ship" (65). Marryat's narrator explicitly points the reader to his debt to Smollett from his novel's first introduction into the world of his own picaro from comically clueless parents. Mrs. Easy, Jack's mother, becomes pregnant after eleven years of marriage, he tells us, and cannot quite believe that it is not "a mistake, like that of Mrs. Trunnion in the novel," which is to say, Smollett's *Adventures of Peregrine Pickle* (4–5). There is literary position-taking at work in Marryat's regression. While Cooper boasted that his novels steered "a different course" from his illustrious forbear, Marryat reminds readers about the vital contribution of British authors to the maritime novel.

The Smollett-like mixture of satire and horror is also evident in the narrator's descriptions of violence. Like Smollett, Marryat does not shy away from detailing the abuse of the body at sea, and his tone veers abruptly from horror to comedy, or even mingles the two. Such is the case of the death of Mr. Pottyfar, mortally wounded in taking a Russian frigate toward the novel's end. Even in extremis, Mr. Pottyfar "had contrived . . . to reach a packet of the universal medicine, and had taken so many bottles before he was found out, that he was one morning found dead in his bed, with more than two dozen empty phials under his pillow, and by the side of his mattress. He was not buried with his hands in his pockets, but when sewed up in his hammock, they were, at all events, laid in the right position" (256).

In the case of death at sea, such a difference in narrative voice is not a question of mere literary convention but yields a difference in cultural work. Recounted with a mixture of violence and satire, mariners' deaths do not sanctify the birth of a new republic, as in Cooper. Rather, the violent death of Mr. Pottyfar is one more incident in *Mr. Midshipman Easy's* carnival of social order. Carnival levels social difference, reminding readers of the basic human level of the body, but does not abolish it. Marryat's carnival is thus one more expression of his poetics' investment in a tempered version of hierarchy.

Cultural work that is at once internationally resonant and flexible, as well as poetics that are at once stable and adaptable: these features of sea fiction also enable Cooper's poetics to travel and be taken up in France.[88]

Le Roman Maritime: Heroes of Evil

When Eugène Sue first "tried the luck of the French novel on the ocean," in the words of his contemporary, the critic Sainte-Beuve, Sue credited his efforts to the inspiration of Cooper.[89] Sue described his admiration for Cooper's sea fiction in a preface penned when Sue's first two maritime novellas, *Kernok le pirate* (1830) and *El Gitano* (1830), were published together under the title *Plik et Plok*. Congratulating Cooper on introducing a new vibrant subject for the novel and distinguishing Cooper's "deep patriotic idea," Sue proposed to delineate France's own "glorious naval exploits almost unknown in Paris."[90] In return for a copy of *Plik et Plok*, Cooper expressed satisfaction that "another *practical* [Cooper's emphasis] man has taken up the cause of the sea, which . . . has not yet received the attention it merits."[91] Cooper encouraged Sue in his project to reinvigorate interest in the French Navy: "a great step will have been made towards this important object, when the young and daring spirits of the nation shall find public attention strongly attracted to that arm of national renown."[92]

Among Sue's maritime novels, the most widely admired was the full-length *La Salamandre* (1832), devoted, in Sue's words, to "the naval mariner."[93] Sue's contemporary, Honoré de Balzac, voiced the dominant critical opinion, when he singled it out for its "principle of duration and of life [*principe de durée et de vie*], and these fundamental beauties, which will lead people to say about it for a long while: 'this is a remarkable work.'"[94] The mariner protagonists of *La Salamandre* are the seasoned upright Lieutenant Pierre and his teenage son, Paul. Raised at sea, Paul offers the portrait of the compleat mariner as a young man: "good, brave, bold, generous . . . of medium height, but slender, flexible and graceful," with "his bold, free, and frank . . . demeanor," a jutting forehead, aquiline nose, a pronounced chin that gave him "an expression of pride and arrogance," and deep-set black eyes, "lively, piercing, witty" (319).

Pierre and Paul are called upon to exercise their craft in extreme danger when the *Salamandre* runs aground on the sandbar of Terim. At this juncture, Sue shows that he, like Cooper, knows how to pit his reader's hopes and fears on the maneuverings of a vessel. Here is one moment from Sue's gripping description, at the end of the chapter "Incertitude [Uncertainty]":

'Well!' said Pierre anxiously to Bouquin, leaning over the chain-wales. How much?' 'Eighteen fathoms, lieutenant,' said the seaman in pulling up the sounding lead. There was briefly on the impassive face of Pierre a rapid expression of pain, resignation and despair. However, he jumped onto the quarter-deck and commanded with his usual calm [*sang-froid*]. Only his short, hurried, urgent tone announced that the maneuver was of great importance. "Get the bonnets ready to haul down!" he shouted, "and "head up into the wind, helmsman. Bouquin, what is the depth?' 'Fifteen fathoms, lieutenant.' (458–59)

As Bouquin counts down the diminishing depth, suspense intensifies, in a version of Cooper's chase, turning movement through space into a race against time. Sue echoes Cooper's pattern too in soliciting the reader's emotion by showing Bouquin's anxiety breaking through the veneer of studied professional calm. Even such a demanding critic as Théophile Gautier praised *La Salamandre* for "its style [and] drama," as well as for its "philosophical intention, information [*la donnée*], and genre."[95]

But the mariner's craft proves impotent in the face of a shipwreck provoked not by conditions beyond human agency, but rather by incompetence. The fault belongs to the ship's commander, the Comte Merval, a doddering aristocrat recalled by the Restoration to naval service from the depths of a tobacco shop. If Sue's intention with his maritime fiction is to celebrate the untold glories of the French navy, *La Salamandre* is a bizarre way to go about this project. Not only does Sue set the novel in the Restoration, when France's naval prestige is at a low point; the plot of *La Salamandre* recalls the historical wreck of the *Méduse* in 1816. Like the case of *La Salamandre*, *La Méduse* ran aground under the command of an incompetent aristocrat, Duroy de Chaumareys, recalled by the Restoration from the desk job of customs official. Like *La Salamandre*, as well, the survivors of *La Méduse* drifted at sea on a raft without provisions, resorting to cannibalism before being rescued. Sue, who had served as an assistant to a ship's doctor for six months in the French Navy, consulted medical reports for details of the sufferings of survivors from the *Méduse*.[96]

Amidst these historical echoes, there is a fictional figure who is able to snatch victory from the jaws of defeat. This figure is a passenger, the handsome, blasé nobleman, Szaffie, suffering from *le mal du siècle*, and whom Sue explicitly designates, like a compleat mariner, as a "superior man [*homme supérieur*]." But Szaffie's victory is not in the arena of craft; it concerns the practical reason that manipulates men, not ships. One of the chosen of society, Szaffie has there garnered only a "bitter sadness," and "deep discouragement" (407), leading him to a Satanic revolt, where he turns his extraordinary capacity to destroying the lives of others: "killer of the spirit, Szaffie wanted to murder the soul and not the body" (408).

The shipwreck in *La Salamandre* is not of Szaffie's doing, but he uses it to further his scheme to corrupt Paul's beloved, the beautiful and naive Alice. When Alice dies as the survivors of the shipwreck drift on a raft, she pronounces Szaffie's name in a delirium of starvation, and shows Paul that Szaffie has stolen her love. Through that, Szaffie seeks to corrupt Paul, and thereby to initiate Paul into his nihilistic credo of disenchantment: "But when one no longer has a heart, when, withered and dried up, it is dead, senseless, and cold, then one can challenge society [*le monde*] and its disappointments, for then this heart is only a corpse, to be exposed to social tortures, which one mocks" (452).

After the survivors are rescued, the empire of Szaffie's moral corruption expands. Paul's father, Pierre, is then condemned for a nobly motivated insubordination to the ship's incompetent captain, in a desperate hope of saving the vessel, an insubordination that the valiant but overly punctilious Pierre is the first to own. Facing his father's execution, Paul receives a demonic proposal from Szaffie that they form an elite society outside the law, in a territorial version of a pirate fraternity, dedicated to predation at the heart of the highest society: "Listen, Paul. You are handsome and brave; you have the most terrible motives to hate society [*le monde*] that fate ever gathered over the head of a man. Your need for revenge must be inexorable and keen. . . . Come join me, Paul! I can open for you a wide and great career among positions and men; we will still find there a powerful means of acting on humanity, we will dominate men from a frightening height" (501–2). Paul, however, refuses Szaffie's offer, and shows the impotence of craft by taking his own life, as his father is executed.

Szaffie is a hero of evil. To cite a maxim of La Rochefoucauld that Sue places at the head of a chapter in *Atar-Gull*: "There exist heroes of evil as well as of good."[97] In Sue's novel, *Atar-Gull*, the seemingly obsequious but actually vengeful enslaved African Atar-Gull is also such depicted as such a hero, although the social injustice spurring his revenge gives it a more understandable motive than Szaffie's Romantic *ennui*. As Atar-Gull plots and executes a perfect revenge on the man who enslaved him, Sue starts his translation of craft from the sea to land. Other heroes of evil in Sue's maritime novels include the pirates Kernok and El Gitano and the slave trader, Captain Brulart. In *La Vigie de Koat-Vën*, the amphibious Count Henri de Vaudrey is at sea, "a compleat mariner," and also "brave, handsome, witty," but he is a destructive seducer when it comes to women: "if he had to confess to the chaplain on board, he could have said: 'My father . . . I have done it all'"[98] (583).

The failure of craft in *La Salamandre* is as specific to France's failed naval fortunes as the mariner's mastery is specific to the naval prowess of the United States and Great Britain in novels by Cooper and Marryat. Beyond France's maritime defeat, craft's failure in Sue signifies his refusal to vindicate the heroism of work, though the emergence of the working class onto the stage of politics was occurring in France, as it was in the United Kingdom and the United States, at the time. The years of Sue's sea fiction are, for example, the years when French utopian socialism gives a modern meaning to the notion of the proletarian. But Sue turns away from Cooper's portrayal of craft as resistance to dehumanizing labor. In Sue's version, the nonproductive productivity of navigation turns to the *Salamandre*'s destruction and Szaffie's nihilism.

At the same time, under Sue's pen, craft's failure yields another kind of literary success. Taking up Cooper's renewal of sea fiction, Sue transports his poetics back to land and applies them to the novel of manners. In the British context, sea fiction offers a way to open up the horizon of the novel of manners and connect the cultural work of the novel to the globe. For Sue, Cooper's poetics introduce a way to conceive of the chaos of post-Revolutionary society. Sue's insight, crystallized in *Atar-Gull* and elaborated in subsequent sea novels, is that once hierarchies guaranteed by God and blood crumble, society becomes like the ocean, a turbulent, murky, fluid realm of forces that cannot be controlled by any individual or even a social group. This chaos contains its version of extraordinary dangers—shoals, monstrous creatures, stormy weather, pirates—and its successful navigation requires something like the mariner's craft. Sue drew attention to *La Salamandre*'s engagement with a traumatized present in the preface, framing his work as an expression of "our extinguished faith, our destroyed beliefs, our used-up souls, our decrepit civilization, our base selfishness [*égoïsme*]" (1323). Balzac recognized *La Salamandre*

as expressing post-Revolutionary malaise, framing Szaffie as the personi-
fication of his "entire century," with its "complete *disillusionment* . . . the
dull and inevitable effect of the depravity of our blasée society, deadened
to all belief."[99]

When Sue articulates craft as the capacity of heroes of evil, he, like
Marryat, confirms the flexibility of sea fiction to adapt to local context,
both literary and political. Emphasizing craft's potential for wrong,
though efficient action, Sue pits his heroes of evil against virtuous characters, in an echo of the plots of popular melodrama.[100] Melodrama was
an invention of the French Revolution, reforging a shattered national and
political community as a community of theatergoers who came together
suspended on the sufferings of virtues in distress, even as they delighted in
the villains' excess of evil. Melodrama is thus a solution from Sue's own
literary tradition for how to procure the democratic pleasure of suspense,
even when the mariner's performance of craft has failed.

Yet *La Salamandre* does not adapt the melodramatic aesthetic unmodified. In particular, Sue paints his virtuous characters as struggling so ane-
mically to survive that suspense over their fates is attenuated, leaving no
counterweight to Szaffie's diabolical machinations. As a result, the nature
of the reader's involvement changes as well. While melodrama solicits sympathy for its suffering characters, Sue's novels, in contrast, invite the reader
into a community similar to the one that Szaffie offered to Paul. Come join
with the characters who have superior knowledge of corrupt society, Sue
invites his readers, and you too can dominate society from the comforts of
your armchair, reading about crimes, performing them in thought, but not
even asked to participate in their actual (if fictional) execution.

In inciting the reader to join with other superior individuals, Sue opens
a meritocratic community quite different from the democratic community of suspense bonding readers together in the Devil's Grip, or on the
Terim sandbank. The figures with superior knowledge—whether Szaffie or the narrator—belong to a rarified community of elite individuals
who dominate the chaos of French post-Revolutionary society in their
ability to understand it. The tension in this novel between a democratic
aesthetics of suspense and a meritocratic aesthetics of epistemological
mastery gives aesthetic expression to political and social challenges of the
novel's time. The tension between democracy and meritocratic liberalism
shaped the uneasy compromises of the July Monarchy instigated by the
Revolution of 1830, the year when Sue first adapted Cooper's sea fiction
to France. Balzac, for one, recognized the interest of Sue's coupling of an
aesthetics of suspense with an aesthetics of knowledge, and went on to
apply it in his own fiction.

In realism, part of this epistemological mastery involves understanding the types of post-Revolutionary society. Both Balzac and Théophile

Figure 4.1. Eugène Sue likened his satire of the old aristocracy in *La Salamandre* to the caricatures by Henri Monnier. In this caricature from 1828, four years before *La Salamandre*, Monnier portrays the ossification of the old aristocracy in their high-society salons. The old aristocracy may bore itself comfortably to death in its salons (viz Stendhal's *Le Rouge et le noir*), but Sue's novel transports them to the global theater of action, where their paralysis unleashes shipwreck and cannibalism. *Le Faubourg Saint-Germain*, after Henri Monnier, engraved by François Seraphin Delpech (1828, color lithograph). Image reproduced courtesy of The Bridgeman Art Library.

Gautier praised Sue's interest in social types when they reviewed his novel in the early 1830s. Social types are present in Cooper's novels too, used by Cooper to show the different human traits used in work at sea. At the same time, Sue adapts Cooper to the French context, not only because his ill-fated ship showcases types of French post-Revolutionary society but also because he echoes the way they are portrayed in contemporary French social observation. Sue used a tone mixing irony and satire that evoked the journalistic genre of the physiologies, as Gautier observed, a minor nonfictional genre of French social commentary in the 1820s, which Balzac penned before writing novels on contemporary French society. Not only Gautier, but Sue himself invoked his debt to the physiologies, when he compared the novel's portrait of the Comte Merval to the caricatures of Henri Monnier (figure 4.1). Sue also linked his biting tone to France's

Figure 4.2. In Géricault's rendition of the historical shipwreck that was the model for Sue's *La Salamandre*, the empty seas of the sublime have become a theater of horror. They offer the spectacle of suffering, violence, and death, while ships are recalled only as debris, and the sea is devoid of any working vessels. Théodore Géricault, *Le Radeau de la Méduse* (1819, oil on canvas). Courtesy of Réunion des Musées Nationaux/Art Resource, on behalf of the Musée du Louvre, Paris.

post-Revolutionary malaise in his preface to *La Salamandre*. To imagine a new society arising from the ashes of the Revolution is to "take death for life, the sardonic laugh and the stammering of the old person on his deathbed for the cooing of a child who smiles at existence" (1323).

Sue's adaptation of Cooper's sea pattern in light of French literary conventions and social context extends to his treatment of violence. Sue's maritime novels are full of physical and psychological cruelty, bloodshed, and torture, well beyond any violence in Cooper. Sue's contemporaries noted the "implausible horror" of Sue's imagination, to cite Balzac's comment on a struggle in the agonies of shipwreck between the delirious Paul and his father Pierre for a crust of bread.[101] In the preface to *Atar-Gull*, addressed to Cooper, Sue indeed apologized for this horror, expressing the "terrible fear to pass for a *vile [abominable] man*, creating horror for pleasure" (1316). Sue's explanation apropos of *Atar-Gull* was that this horror did justice to the horror of the slave trade. At the same time, the horror is pervasive throughout Sue's maritime (and other) fiction. What Sue does not spell out is that sensational horror ran throughout popular French spectacles in the wake of the Revolution, spectacles like melodrama, as well as the phantasmagoria. Such sensational horror also marks the painter Théodore Géricault's rendition of the historical shipwreck inspiring Sue's *La Salamandre: Le Radeau de la Méduse* (1819) (figure 4.2).[102]

ALL THOSE WHO DO NOT LIKE TO LIVE WITHOUT DANGER

Antonio Gramsci commented that the popular version of the Nietzschean doctrine of the superman originated in late ("low") Romanticism, transmitted through Balzac and Dumas.[103] The patron of low Romanticism, Lord Byron, moreover, was an avid sailor, author of poems celebrating life on the high seas. He was also the grandson of the career naval officer John Byron, author of *The Wreck of the Wager*. But there is nothing like the adventures of craft in Byron's narrative romances.

Vautrin and Monte Cristo are the inheritors of Cooper's Rover and Jones, as reworked in Sue's Szaffie. Balzac's Vautrin is Szaffie, divested of his Romantic Satanism, down to Vautrin's offer to Rastignac and then to Lucien de Rubempré, echoing Szaffie's demonic offer to Paul.[104] Before penning *Le Comte de Monte Cristo*, Alexandre Dumas made no secret of his admiration for Cooper, writing a sequel to *The Pilot*, *Le Capitaine Paul*, whose pretext was Cooper's lack of details on Jones's biography. The Count of Monte Cristo also recalls Paul from Sue's *La Salamandre*, who has chosen the life of revenge over suicide. The mariner Edmond Dantès is wrongfully imprisoned to a living death by Restoration society, but with his escape through death by water from the Chateau d'If, Dantès takes the mariner's craft onshore and returns to punish those who have wronged him, as well as to reward the good, under the alias Sinbad the sailor. At the end, his debts with land-based society accomplished, this superman beyond good and evil resumes his maritime career, sailing off into the horizon with the oriental beauty, Haydée, who bears the name from Byron's poem of the beautiful daughter of a Greek pirate in love with Byron's hero Don Juan.

Despite Gramsci's distinction between the low superman of Byron transmitted to Dumas and Balzac and Nietzsche's more sophisticated philosophy, Nietzsche himself was fond of the romance and adventure of the sea. Indeed, Gramsci is pointing us to Nietzsche's cultural inspiration in the heroism of the mariner when Gramsci picks up on the superman's possession of what turn out to be qualities of the compleat mariner through his readings of nineteenth-century adventure fiction. Nietzsche's superman revels in his maritime genealogy when Nietzsche frames him with figures of speech that come from the discourse of craft.[105] Nietzsche writes that Zarathustra "was a friend of all who travel far and do not like to live without danger," whom he addresses as "the bold searchers, researchers, and whoever embarks with cunning sails on terrible seas."[106] Zarathustra fashions himself as "fond of the sea, and all that is of the sea's kind," claiming "the delight in searching which drives the sails toward the undiscovered . . . the seafarer's delight."[107] Like the compleat mariner, Zarathustra seeks to push the edges of knowledge in quest of their supersession. Like the mariner, he does so with curiosity and boldness, evincing strategic optimism—in the figure of Zarathustra, Champlain's "gay resolution" turns to what Nietzsche elsewhere calls "gay science." Nietzsche's adventurer Zarathustra explores, however, not the globe but rather the psyche, and in particular, human reason, which philosophers have wrongly envisaged as contemplative but which Zarathustra recognizes as essentially practical and embodied. Zarathustra seeks to transform pure into practical reason, however, not by turning away from philosophers' questions, but rather by melding thought with action. To stimulate this fusion, Nietzsche conceives of a new form of philosophical writing that operates like adventure. His Zarathustra uses tricky rhetoric and figuration, forms of thought and expression that are extreme challenges for the flexible, creative, jury-rigging ingenuity of his cunning reader.

CHAPTER 5

Sea Fiction beyond the Seas

> And now we rushed into the embraces of the cataract, where
> a chasm threw itself open to receive us. But there arose in
> our pathway a shrouded human figure, very far larger in its
> proportions than any dweller among men. And the hue of the
> skin of the figure was of the perfect whiteness of the snow.
> —Edgar Allen Poe, *The Narrative of Arthur
> Gordon Pym of Nantucket*[1]

THE ROUTINIZATION OF THE SEA

To diminish the dangers and uncertainty attending navigation had been
the ambition of governments, scientists, and mariners across the era of
global sail. Every chart of a hitherto unknown coast was a contribution.
So were new technologies. The sixteenth-century cross-staff for taking
the angle of the stars was perfected across centuries into the modern
sextant. Refinements in ship design allowed ships to sail progressively
closer to the wind, giving them the ability to utilize more varied conditions. Modernization accelerated in the second half of the eighteenth century. In 1759, Harrison perfected the chronometer, enabling calculation
of longitude at sea. Scientists figured out the cause of scurvy by the end
of the eighteenth century. The British Navy was the first systematically to
implement the proactive use of foods containing vitamin C. The safety
and reliability of sea travel intensified with the replacement of sailing by
steam in commercial and military navigation.[2] Fifty years after Robert
Fulton's navigation of the Hudson in 1807, steamship travel was well on
its way to supplanting sail.[3] In 1838, two English steamships crossed the
Atlantic in fourteen days, followed by Cunard's establishment, with an
1840 crossing, of a Liverpool-Boston line.

As maritime transport became safer and more predictable, its importance in global communications, passenger travel, and freight transfer increased.[4] At the same time, another name for the routinization of the sea
is the demise of craft. As craft faded, the compleat mariner started to lose
his cultural prestige. Sea fiction's adventure poetics were still in splendid working order in the middle of the nineteenth century. But they celebrated a kind of work that increasingly seemed archaic. Some adventure

novelists depended on the fact that the zenith of craft was still within collective memory. Novels like Robert Louis Stevenson's *Treasure Island*, Rudyard Kipling's *Captain Courageous*, Erskine Childers' *The Riddle of the Sands*, or Jack London's *The Sea Wolf* combed the maritime world in search of overlooked frontiers for craft. But for novelists interested in the dynamic Edges of modernity, sea fiction was a form that had lost its function.

This moment of danger proved a moment of opportunity.[5] As the working age of sail receded, this chapter argues, Herman Melville, Victor Hugo, and Joseph Conrad reworked sea adventure fiction to dramatize skilled work in other Edge zones that, like the maritime frontier, were murky, unknown, and risky, but that were qualitatively different: situated at the level of language and the human psyche, rather than the physical world.[6] In such a modernist turn, Melville, Hugo, and Conrad, each in their own ways, framed art and thought as modernity's incompletely charted frontiers, which it was the novelist's task to explore. The adventurous novelist supplanted the mariner. Indeed, in his preface to *The Nigger of the "Narcissus,"* Conrad would call the novelist a "worker in prose," and speak of the "workman of art."[7]

The starting points of Melville, Hugo, and Conrad alike for such a modernist transformation of sea fiction were classic sea adventure plots about the work of the mariner contending with remarkable dangers at sea. Like other sea adventure authors of their time, all three novelists sought underexplored corners of the maritime world to test their protagonists—whaling for Melville, the biology and geology of a remote outer reef for Hugo, and the psychological pressures of shipboard life for Conrad. Yet as these writers tested their protagonists, they started to chip away at craft's capacity and prestige. In the process, the crafty mariner started to submit to another kind of figure who emerged from the shadows: the narrator of his story. Plumbing the obscurity of language and thought with narrative, the narrator/novelist opened a new arena for the cunning reader, inviting her to join along in the search for meaning and clarity, rather than in problem-solving survival.

From the vantage point of traditional literary history, the literary art of Melville, Hugo, and Conrad has little to do with the popular novels of Jules Verne. From the vantage point of maritime modernity, in contrast, all these authors respond similarly—with the invention of new narrative forms—to the same crisis at the juncture of the novel and the supersession of craft. But while Melville, Hugo, and Conrad pursued things unattempted yet in the domain of the novel, Verne did not tamper with sea fiction's powerful adventure poetics, but rather used them to move from existing technologies and charted spaces to the edges of modern innovation and beyond. In Verne's new science fiction pattern, sea fiction's adventures in problem-solving enabled fiction to unlock frontiers of modernity currently unreachable through state-of-the-art science and technology.

A BAKED BABY, BY THE SOUL OF CAPTAIN COOK!

Melville came to maritime fiction through his personal experience whaling and in the merchant marine. He also came to it through his fondness for the maritime book, alluding to its many genres throughout his novels.[8] This makes for some extraordinary characters, such as the sailor Mad Jack Chase, noble captain of the topmast in *White-Jacket*, who can recite from memory maritime poets ranging from Luís Vaz de Camões to Byron. In contrast to hearty brown Mad Jack, the poor Sub-Sub librarian introducing *Moby-Dick* belongs to "that hopeless, sallow tribe which no wine of this world will ever warm."[9] But the sallow Sub-Sub is even more familiar with the maritime corpus. He fishes his quotes on cetology from such diverse texts and genres as Purchas's collection of voyages and narratives of Arctic explorations, circumnavigations by Schouten and Cowley, explorations by Cook and Scoresby, "Narrative of the Globe Mutiny," and literature, including *Paradise Lost*, Falconer's *The Shipwreck*, and Cooper's *The Pilot*, among a range of sources.

From his first work, *Typee*, Melville indicates some disturbance in the capable ethos of craft. *Typee*'s preface enticed readers with claims of a renegade's true sojourn among beautiful South Seas cannibals, framed in the discourse of maritime adventure. This "curious adventure," the narrator boasted, would divert even sailors, to say nothing of armchair sailors, with the doings of the "singular and interesting people" of *Typee*.[10] Throughout the novel, synonyms for the remarkable occurrence recur, until its closing assurance that the narrator's "strange appearance and remarkable adventure occasioned the liveliest interest" for the mariners on board the vessel that rescued him (252–53). Chapter 7's headings suggest that the remarkable occurrences divulged in *Typee* will be a castaway narrative à la Robinson Crusoe: "The other side of the Mountain. Disappointment. Inventory of Articles brought from the Ship. Division of the Stock of Bread. Appearance of the Interior of the Island. A Discovery. A Ravine and Waterfalls. A sleepless Night. Further Discoveries" (41).

But *Typee* hardly depicts a shipwrecked mariner's bravura feats. If anything is extraordinary about *Typee*'s adventures, it is the protagonist's complete abnegation of craft, along with its voluntaristic ethos of agency. A physical injury immobilizes the hero, but he hardly resists a slide into delightful, passive indolence. When he has abandoned himself to the point of being hand-fed at a feast, "masticating a morsel

182 • Chapter 5

that Kory-Kory had just put in my mouth," his fellow renegade, Toby, ironically underscores his extraordinary passivity with "amazing vehemence": "'A baked baby, by the soul of Captain Cook!'" (95). Through repeated intimations of the Marquesans' cannibalism, Melville creates suspense with sea fiction's adventure pattern of danger and remedy. But the danger is more a question hovering over the entire narrative than a specific series of problems to be solved. Why is the narrator being treated so well? Do these cannibals excel in hospitality or are they softening up the narrator for a tasty meal?

Melville continued to set up readers for a plot offering the performance of craft and then frustrate their expectations throughout his writings of the 1840s. Sometimes, he teases by layering on evocations of different kinds of sea fiction and other maritime genres within a single work. His first maritime novel, *Redburn*, for example, at moments evokes the chronicle of life before the mast recently made famous by Richard Henry Dana Jr. At other moments, it is redolent of the eighteenth-century maritime picaresque. The hapless Wellingborough Redburn recalls a hero of Smollett, for example, in his slapstick mishaps, framed with tongue-in-cheek chapter headings.

But for all the different opportunities for the performance of craft in *Redburn*, it does not occur. Thus, to take the example of how Melville jams his picaresque citations, Redburn is no resilient adventurer like Roderick Random. Rather, he is a melancholic, and the subject of his fixation, from his childhood fascination with a little glass ship contained in a glass bottle on the mantle of his childhood home, is the eighteenth-century maritime picaresque's gritty but fulfilling world. This ship, Redburn recounts, provoked his "insane desire" to smash the container in order to enter into its charmed cosmos.[11] Redburn here evinces what Flaubert called a "retrospective concupiscence" for maritime life, alluring because it promises rich experience that contrasts with the grinding misery and circumscribed opportunities of Redburn's impoverished present. "Talk not of the bitterness of middle-age and after life; a boy can feel all that, and much more, when upon his young soul the mildew has fallen" (16). Dust is the precipitate of the eighteenth-century picaresque's gritty romance of practice in Redburn's mildewed, melancholic perception. Dust textures the scene in the bottle, and it textures, too, the eighteenth-century books that Redburn finds on the *Highlander*, at first obscuring the title of Adam Smith's *Wealth of Nations*, which Redburn comes upon together with a book with a generic early modern nonfictional sea title: "an account of Shipwrecks and Disasters at Sea" (98).

Once shipped aboard the *Highlander*, a merchant vessel making a routine Atlantic crossing, Redburn's melancholy affronts the harsh, unforgiving daily work of life at sea. This disappointment would not in itself necessarily tweak the maritime novel, either the eighteenth-century maritime picaresque or nineteenth-century sea fiction. From Crusoe's first voyage, violently ill and terrified in a small gale, heroes have been lured to sea by the empty romance of sea fantasy, only to jettison it rapidly in place of sea fiction's empowered romance of practice. But Redburn refuses to undergo such productive disenchantment. When set to the most menial tasks like picking oakum, he cheers himself by "repeating Lord Byron's Address to the Ocean, which I had often spouted on the stage at the High School at home" (135).

From such stubborn tenacity, Redburn does achieve fleeting moments of satisfaction that nurture his pathology. On a "ramble into the country," for example, Redburn meets "three charmers" and finds himself talking "Addisonian English" (230, 235). The afternoon culminates in a meal of "souchong, and . . . such buttered muffins [as] never were spread on the other side of the Atlantic. . . . And there they sat—the charmers, I mean—eating these buttered muffins in plain sight. I wished I was a buttered muffin myself" (235). Dallying in a fantasy of being ingested by these charming cannibals, Redburn offers another version of the hero's passive erotic abandonment in *Typee*. Craft is in trouble in Melville's sea fiction of the 1840s.

THE FIRST *MOBY-DICK*: WHAT A PICTURE OF UNPARALLELED INDUSTRY AND DARING ENTERPRISE!

When Melville drafted *Moby-Dick* at the end of the 1840s, whaling was an ideal subject for a rousing sea novel. The industry was at the height of its prestige and was one of the few contemporary theaters of maritime action at the time that required compleat craft.[12] Sailing ships were used by whalers to explore the most remote byways of the globe in their pursuit of the deadliest catch. As Ishmael remarks, "For many years past the whale-ship has been the pioneer in ferreting out the remotest and least known parts of the earth. She has explored seas and archipelagoes which had no chart, where no Cook or Vancouver had ever sailed. . . . All that is made such a flourish of in the old South Sea Voyages, those things were but the life-time commonplaces of our heroic Nantucketers" (909–10). With whaling, Melville had moreover grasped a perfect industry to celebrate internationalism and patriotism, in keeping with the nineteenth-century practice of sea fiction pioneered by Cooper. In this global enterprise, Americans competed with and often bested the British.

That whaling was the subject for an epic sea novel was a point made in *Mocha Dick: or the White Whale of the Pacific*. This novella, by the prolific and popular author of sea fiction, J. N. Reynolds, was published eleven years before *Moby-Dick or The Whale*, to cite the full title, in 1839. *Mocha-Dick* offers a harpooner's yarn about slaying a wily old white whale. At the end of *Mocha Dick*, a frame narrator stressed this industry as worthy of an epic of American global power. "Could we comprehend, at a glance, the mighty surface of the Indian or Pacific seas, what a picture would open upon us of the unparalleled industry and daring enterprise! What scenes of toil along the coast of Japan, up the straits of Mozambique . . . Sail onward, and extend your view around New Holland, to the coast of Guinea; to the eastern and western shores of Africa, to the Cape of Good Hope; and south, to the waters that lash the cliffs of Kergulan's Land, and you are ever upon the whaling–ground of the American seaman." [13]

What critics have called the first *Moby-Dick*, from reviews in Melville's time, was the sea novel about whaling that Reynolds called for but did not write himself. When Evert A. Duyckinck reviewed Melville's *Moby-Dick* when it first appeared, he distinguished, "Book No. I . . . a thorough exhaustive account admirably given, of the great Sperm Whale. The information is minute, brilliantly illustrated . . . has its level passages, its humorous touches, its quaint suggestion, its incident usually picturesque and occasionally sublime." [14] Before the existence of the medium of film, to say nothing of the TV series, *Deadliest Catch*, written narrative was indeed one of the best technologies to represent such remote and dangerous industries, completely inaccessible to armchair audiences. It also was a good technology for conveying information about remote animals of the underwater world. For the sperm whale above all other whales, Ishmael observes, "his is an unwritten life" (934).

This first *Moby-Dick* then is a classic sea novel, subjecting heroic mariners to extraordinary dangers on the maritime frontier of their age. Fittingly, Ishmael stresses the remarkable occurrence as the proper epistemological frame to understand his project. In particular, he cautions armchair readers against mistaking "the realities of the whaleman" for "fabulous narrations" due to their ignorance (987), or scoffing "at Moby Dick as a monstrous fable, or still worse and more detestable, a hideous and intolerable allegory" (1011). From the vantage point of the maritime remarkable occurrence, the white whale's "unwonted magnitude," "remarkable hue," and "unexampled, intelligent malignity" make him a worthy foe, summoning the full measure of craft (988).

In constructing the trials of craft in this first *Moby-Dick*, Melville draws on several important aspects of sea fiction's poetics. One is to organize *Moby-Dick*'s adventures as a chase, in the use of the ship's movement through space–time as a technique of dramatization pioneered by Cooper. Indeed, the novel is one long chase, portraying an industry where mariners circle thousands of leagues round the globe. And then when the white whale is found, the chase has just begun—viz the titles of the novels' final climactic chapters: "The Chase—First Day"; "The Chase—Second Day"; "The Chase—Third Day."

Melville also adheres to sea fiction in drafting characters that lay a professional rather than psychological claim to our interest, assembling the different facets of craft in the different personalities of the crew. Starbuck excels in prudence. Stubb never misses an opportunity for strategic optimism. Flask evinces protocol's power to put a great deal of skill at the disposal of even the most unheroic of men. Captain Ahab excels in resolution, ready to sail to the depths of Hell to pursue his quarry. The harpooners, Daggo, Tashtego, and Queequeg, are models of embodiment.

But taken together, the ship's company does not add up to the sum of craft, commanded, as they are, by a perverted captain who is all resolution. And no other seaman steps in with compleat craft to remedy Ahab's lack. Starbuck is too prudent to challenge his commander, despite his immense competence and lucidity as to the coming disaster: "I am game for . . . the jaws of Death . . . if it fairly comes in the way of the business we follow; but I came here to hunt whales, not my commander's vengeance. How many barrels will thy vengeance yield thee even if thou gettest it, Captain Ahab? it will not fetch thee much in our Nantucket market" (966). Stubb has optimism and protocol but little else. Bulkington could be the novel's perfect mariner and his fellows' beacon—only no sooner has he been introduced than he mystifyingly recedes.

Among all the crew, Queequeg comes the closest to the superman of sea fiction, and the reader could imagine him galvanizing the crew to survival, if only his narrator would allow him a starring role. Sea fiction aficionados of the time might detect in Queequeg's biography echoes of Mesty, another dark-skinned prince, in Marryat's *Mr. Midshipman Easy*. But the Bulkington problem plagues Queequeg as well. Despite his eminent capacity and his charisma in the chapters on shore, Queequeg's role recedes when the *Pequod* sets sail. And yet, the narrator tantalizes us with what might have been, when Tashtego loses his footing and falls into the sperm-whale head. Queequeg, prompt, bold, and inventive, dives in after him and finds a way to save him by jabbing a hole in the sinking head under water. Fishing Tashtego out from destruction in these lifeless jaws, Queequeg effects "the deliverance, or rather, delivery of Tashtego," in a feat of life-giving jury-rigging (1161). Queequeg's coffin similarly jury-rigs survival, turning to Ishmael's life preserver in the final catastrophe.

Queequeg's unsustained burst of heroism adds to the reader's frustration. The *Pequod* sinks not only because no crewmember is resolute enough to challenge his commander, but because the novel's author thwarts the potential of his capable characters. In the destruction of the *Pequod*, not only Ahab fails on his contractual obligations, but also

Melville breaks his contract with the reader of sea fiction.[15] With the failure of craft, what becomes of sea fiction's cultural work?

The Second Moby-Dick: That One Portentous Something

Ahab's broken contract yields destruction: "concentric circles seized the
lone boat itself, and all its crew, and each floating oar, and every lance-
pole, and spinning, animate and inanimate, all round and round in one
vortex, carried the smallest chip of the Pequod out of sight" (1406).
"Now small fowls flew screaming over the yet yawning gulf; a sullen
white surf beat against its steep sides; then all collapsed, and the great
shroud of the sea rolled on as it rolled five thousand years ago" (1407).
Melville's broken narrative contract yields a tale. "*Epilogue*: 'And I only
am escaped alone to tell thee'" (1408).

Joseph Conrad: "The yarns of seamen have a direct simplicity, the
whole meaning of which lies within the shell of a cracked nut. But Marlow was not typical."[16] "Not typical" is the device of Ishmael, an indifferent seaman, but a remarkable narrator. It is also the device of the second
Moby-Dick—not a narrative of remarkable occurrences but rather the
remarkable occurrences of narrative. Melville's remarkable poetics transgress poetic and generic expectation, across all the different scales of the
novel. They are visible at the level of the sentence, propelled by what Casarino calls a "syntactical rush"—"a syntax of deferral and liminality—a
syntax that unfolds at one and the same time by overcoming limits and
by adding new ones further along."[17] At the macro-level, Melville melds
sea fiction with a literary genre transgressing established conceptual categories. This genre is the literary anatomy, described by Samuel Otter in
its most ambitious and expansive sense as a "heterogeneous, omnivo-
rous, encyclopedic, rhetorically experimental, stylistically dense form."[18]
Another way to think of this movement to the limits and beyond is as a
voyage into the unplumbed regions of the mind, rather than of space. Ishmael's conceptual and rhetorical transgression is a metaphysical voyage,
more specifically, whose mission is to explore, in the words of Richard
Brodhead, "the state of the world and our place in it."[19]

The transfer of adventure to the domain of speculation opens the
human psyche as one of modernity's new frontiers. Even before Ishmael,
the turn of sea adventure narratives inward can be dated to Edgar Allen
Poe's *Narrative of Arthur Gordon Pym of Nantucket* (1838). From Pym's
first captivity and near-death in the hold of the ship, Poe translates the
remarkable occurrences of navigating the Edge zones of modernity to
the liminal states of the human psyche. Poe's novel retains, however, the
frame of sea fiction's adventure poetics, even if pushed to their limits. At

the novel's end, Pym is carried along into the warm, milky seas of the still uncharted South Pole, which turn out to be haunted with a disturbing psychic vibe. The traveler's narrative breaks off abruptly and disturbingly with the creepy vision of an undefined phantom form cited in this chapter's epigraph.

As Melville's Ishmael yokes the adventures of craft with the adventures of speculation, he employs narrative practices encompassed by the aesthetic of the sublime. But not sublime like the Romantic seas, suppressing the human agency of work to liberate the sea's power as an aesthetic image. Rather, *Moby-Dick* is sublime returning to the early modern parallel between the search for novelty on the part of an innovative artist or writer who resembles the vanguard navigator. To recall Jonathan Richardson: "The sublime disdains to be trammelled, it knows no bounds, it is the sally of great geniuses, and the perfection of human nature." "Who knows what is hid in the womb of time! Another may eclipse Rafaëlle; a new Columbus may cross the Atlantic ocean, and leave the pillars of that Hercules far behind." [20] Modeling Ishmael's inquiry on the mariner's skilled labor, Melville suggests that the arduous questions of epistemology and ontology demand highly skilled, compleat work as well. As appropriate for a narrator desublimating the sea, Ishmael is contemptuous of romantic, melancholy, and absent-minded young men, who are sent up to the masthead to look for whales but instead cite parodies of Byron: "Roll on, thou deep and dark blue ocean, roll! / Ten thousand blubber-hunters sweep over thee in vain." "'Why, thou monkey,' said a harpooneer to one of these lads . . . 'Whales are as scarce as hen's teeth whenever thou art up here'" (961).

Early in the novel, Melville offers an image for *Moby-Dick*'s renewal of the early modern parallel between the craft of the vanguard navigator and the work of the artist—in this case, the narrator, with the novelist in the background. When Ishmael comes to the Spouter Inn, he finds a painting that he dates to the early modern era: the time of the "New England hags." But this "very large oil-painting" has been "so thoroughly besmoked, and every way defaced, that in the unequal cross-lights by which you viewed it, it was only by diligent study and a series of systematic visits to it, and careful inquiry of the neighbors, that you could any way arrive at an understanding of its purpose" (805). In Ishmael's characterization, this "boggy, soggy, squitchy picture . . . enough to drive a nervous man distracted" possesses a "sublimity" of a very distinctive sort: "indefinite, half-attained, unimaginable sublimity . . . that fairly froze you to it, till you involuntarily took an oath with yourself to find out what that marvellous painting meant" (805). When Ishmael attempts to make its subject out, it starts by sounding like an early modern maritime genre painting, and turns through a series of speculations to the quest for meaning, without a particular content. "It's the Black Sea in a midnight gale.—It's the unnatu-ral combat of the four primal elements.—It's a blasted heath— . . . It's the breaking-up of the ice-bound stream of Time. But at last all these fancies yielded to that one portentous something in the picture's midst. *That* once found out, and all the rest were plain" (805).

The work of the sea is Ishmael's starting point in speculating on the boggy, soggy, squitchy picture, as in his speculative forays more generally. In *Moby-Dick*, the empowered agency of the crafty mariner gives way to the novelist's work constructing images to pursue the difficult activity of philosophical speculation. The parallel is meaningful. Like craft, specula-tion is hard work; and it too traffics in great murky zones of overwhelm-ing forces where uncertainty is high. And like craft, speculation emerges from the wisdom of a skilled collective, yet requires resolution, patience, and jury-rigging when existing knowledge and technologies fail confront-ing the unknown. The mariner's craft hence permits Melville to highlight aspects of philosophical exploration that fall outside conventionalized accounts of rational method.

When Ishmael uses the work of whaling to approach metaphysical speculation, figurative language plays an important role in his practice. Ishmael's use of figures of speech as a way to think through epistemo-logical problems is transgressive of the usual protocols of speculation in philosophy. Philosophers have historically mistrusted figurative lan-guage, credited with the ability to trick. Not only does Ishmael use fig-urative language to pursue philosophy; he so intertwines the work of whaling and speculation throughout the adventures of *Moby-Dick*, that the two become inseparable, bound even closer than any kind of figura-tion, for the reader can no longer treat one domain as a substitution for the other.[21]

The boggy, soggy, squitchy picture does this, and another good example of such a tight bond is the chapter "The Monkey–Rope." The title refers to the lifeline of the harpooner—in this case, Queequeg—who oversees the flensing or stripping of the whale from the perilous position of the dead whale's back on the rolling sea. Ishmael holds the rope to belay Quee-queg in the event of an emergency. Because Ishmael is tied to his fellow, Queequeg became "my own inseparable twin brother; nor could I any way get rid of the dangerous liabilities which the hempen bond entailed" (1135). Ishmael then passes from the specific instance of the monkey rope to human community. To cite Ishmael, "So strongly and metaphysi-cally did I conceive of my situation then, that while earnestly watching his motions, I seemed distinctly to perceive that my own individuality was now merged in a joint stock company of two." "And yet still further pondering . . . I saw that this situation of mine was the precise situation of every mortal that breathes; only, in most cases, he, one way or other, has this Siamese connexion with a plurality of other mortals" (1135). How are the different figures of interconnection—the monkey–rope, the stock company, and the Siamese twin—related, and how do they illuminate the bonds of dependence in human community? Trying to reconcile the paradigms of bonds in each figure, the reader in *Moby-Dick* is invited to apply a version of cunning reading.

With an important difference, however: while the cunning reader of sea fiction usually contemplates pragmatic matters, Ishmael poses a problem that at its basis is an ethical one: what kinds of bonds form the warp and woof of human community? The cunning reader becomes an ethical reader, more in line with the reader of the novel of manners discussed by Iser and others. Yet in identifying with Ishmael, she does not find herself framed as a liberal ethical reader in the comfort of her armchair. Whatever answer Ishmael may open the way to, it is important that its starting point is craft's collectivity. Ethics in *Moby-Dick* is not defined as relations among atomistic subjects, but rather is a mode of human relation whose starting point is social bonds formed in work—tempered in the mutual interdependency of the struggle for survival.

The ethos of collective interdependency so preoccupies Ishmael that he extends it to the way in which he makes sense of his sublime, obscure figures of art. As Ishmael contemplates the boggy, soggy, squitchy picture, he is bringing craft's techniques of problem-solving to a nonpragmatic task. But, unlike Robinson Crusoe, who subjected philosophical contemplation to craft's problem-solving and found an answer, Ishmael complicates the problem more and more by introducing term after term. This process of making comparison after comparison creates a kind of collectivity of literary figures. To make sense of such a crowd of figures that Ishamel has drawn out of the obscure, sublime painting, requires, in Ishmael's words, "diligent study and a series of systematic visits to it [the painting], and careful inquiry of the neighbors" (805). *Moby-Dick* is a novel that pursues the sublime transgression of convention, specifically the conventions of sea fiction, which is an adventure associated throughout the Romantic lineage with a creator's individual genius. And yet at the same time, Melville unfolds this exploration through a narrator who makes sense of the world, and art as well, through work in a collectivity.

THE FIRST *WORKERS OF THE SEA*: THE GLORIFICATION OF WORK

Victor Hugo was steeped in the maritime world when he took sea fiction's trials of skilled labor from seafaring to poetics in his *Travailleurs de la mer* (1866), which I will be citing in its translation *Toilers of the Sea*; however, a more accurate translation would be "workers of the sea."

Hugo, unlike Melville, had never worked at sea. He was, however, an amateur sailor and avid reader of maritime literature across its history, including the accounts of the "great mariners and pirates of the past," as well as "the sea novels of Fenimore Cooper, and above all those of . . . Eugène Sue."[22] At the time Hugo wrote *Toilers of the Sea*, he was living on the Channel Islands, in political exile from the Second Empire, with "the ocean at my window."[23]

Hugo's fascination with ocean life perhaps helped him to grasp the sea as a continued frontier of modernity in the 1860s, even when its cultural visibility was starting to fade. In *The Condition of the Working Class in England* (1844), Frederick Engels had turned his back on the spectacle of ship traffic on the Thames to explore the poverty of urban workers, a focus that would characterize much cultural theory of the second half of the nineteenth century.[24] Hugo, in contrast, unified his novels about the urban proletariat with his depiction of work at sea. In the preface to *Toilers of the Sea* (1866), Hugo painted this novel, along with *Notre-Dame de Paris* (1831) and *Les Misérables* (1862), as a three-paneled triptych to different aspects of human "struggles": with religion, with society, and with nature. All three struggles pitted human freedom against a determining fatality, which Hugo qualified as *ananke*, using the Greek word he had already highlighted in *Notre-Dame*. "In *Notre-Dame de Paris* the author denounced, "the *ananke* of dogmas"; in *Les Misérables*, he indicated "the *ananke* of laws," and in *Toilers of the Sea*, "he indicates the third," which he calls "the *ananke* of things." Nature, the material world, "obstacles . . . under the form of the elements": these synonyms in Hugo's preface designate the human struggle to wrest subsistence from the *physis*. "[I]t is necessary for him to live, hence the plow and the ship."[25]

When Henry James reviewed *Toilers of the Sea* in *The Nation* the year it appeared, he commented wryly on Hugo's grand rhetoric of fatality, applied to "what a writer less fond of magnificent generalizations would have been content to describe as 'a tale of the sea.'"[26] As James indicates, Hugo's ornamental rhetoric is unexpected in a novel about the work of the sea, which should rather employ gripping description and the novelist's rendition of the mariner's plain style. However, James's insight that Hugo's novel celebrates the same subject matter as sea fiction is accurate. Hugo put the goal of *Toilers of the Sea* yet more straightforwardly in his first notes for the preface of the novel, which declared: "Work can be epic."[27] And indeed, we have seen that the craft exercised by the mariner has been a fit subject for epic poetry in modernity from Camões to Falconer; Hugo seeks to import craft's epic implications into the novel.

Toilers of the Sea, like *Moby-Dick*, is a novel that binds several books between its covers. Among these books, I focus here only on two: the centerpiece of the novel recounting a great deed of craft and Hugo's transformation of it into a modernist exploration into the dynamism of poetic imagery. The deed of craft involves the tricky salvage of a steamboat engine wedged in a remote offshore reef during shipwreck, which Hugo narrates with sea fiction's poetics of problem-solving. The engine merits the deed because of its worth: "A steamboat was a prodigious novelty in the waters of the channel in 182–," when the novel is set (100).

Unlike *Moby-Dick*, where supermen are wanting, Hugo offers a hero at the level of his challenge. He names the novel's section describing the engine's salvage after this hero, "Gilliatt the Cunning" (263). Gilliatt is a poor man who lives from fishing but who is a "born pilot" (79) with "rare science as a mariner" (80). Hugo has drawn this perfect mariner with all the aspects of craft, including his countenance, marked by the "proud, vertical wrinkle which indicates the bold and persevering man" between his eyes (78). His skills are compleat: "a joiner, a blacksmith, a cartwright, a caulker, and even a bit of a machinist" (82). Beyond skill and competence, Gilliat has the compleat mariner's "inventive and powerful . . . dexterity," enabling him to thread a path through the unyielding, overwhelming forces of nature (78). Hugo explains, "An Indian fable says: 'One day Brahma asked force, "Who is stronger than you?" She replied "Adroitness." . . . Of ordinary stature and ordinary strength, he [Gilliatt] was able . . . to lift the burdens of a giant, and to perform the prodigies of an athlete" (78).

The title of Hugo's novel is in the plural: *Toilers of the Sea*. Indeed, supermen would seem to abound in *Toilers of the Sea*, in contrast to *Moby-Dick*, which frustrates the reader looking for a superman of craft. Gilliatt salvages the engine for another worker of the sea, Mess Lethierry. A "redoutable sailor" who is also cut according to the pattern of the compleat mariner, Lethierry had "navigated a great deal" and "[n]o one knew the seas as he did" (89). Like Gilliatt, his expertise is compleat: "He had been cabin-boy, sailmaker, top-man, helmsman, boatswain's mate, boatswain, pilot, and captain" (89). Lethierry shows the overlap between the compleat mariner and the entrepreneur when he successfully launches the first steamship connecting Guernsey and mainland France, which he names *La Durande*. Yet Lethierry never serves profit alone, risking his life to save people who shipwreck on the island's treacherous coasts.

When Lethierry discovers at the age of sixty that he can no longer himself lift the anvil of the Varclin forge, weighing 300 pounds with one arm, Clubin, "a skilfull and capable mariner" takes over piloting *La Durande* (121). Clubin is described as the "*alter ego*, the double of Mess Lethierry," and his compleat mastery recalls that of Lethierry as well as Gilliatt, down to Hugo's similar syntax for describing it. Clubin is a "clever stower of cargo, a handy man aloft, a careful and able boatswain, a robust helmsman, an experienced pilot, and a bold captain" (121). In delineating Clubin, Hugo emphasizes that he possesses "all the talents which risk, perpetually undergoing transformations, demands": "He was prudent, and he sometimes pushed prudence even to daring, which is a great quality at sea. His fear of the probable was tempered by his instinct of the possible" (121).

Clubin, however, has no responsibility to others, not even the man who employs him, and devises a plan to betray Lethierry. Carrying a large sum of money owed to Lethierry, Clubin decides to wreck "accidentally" *La Durande* on the Hanways, a reef near shore, and swim away with his ill-gotten gains. Is it evidence for craft's collective character that Clubin miscalculates when he plots alone, although he is described as "one of those mariners who face danger in a proportion known to themselves, and who know how to extract success from every adventure," as well as being a "renowned swimmer" (121)? Confused by a fog, though he is seasoned to such conditions, Clubin mistakes a formidable remote outer reef, the Douvres, for Hanways reef. His plan gone awry, Clubin is stranded on the Douvres, along with the shipwrecked steamboat, and there becomes the prey of a giant octopus. And it is on the forbidding Douvres reef that Gilliatt, alone battling the elements, will perform his great deed of craft, salvaging the steamboat engine, in an attempt to win Lethierry's beautiful daughter, Déruchette.

Despite the novel's cast of capable mariners, they exercise their craft in isolation. Lethierry navigates *La Durande* on his own as long as he is able. Clubin succeeds Lethierry, but never navigates with him, and then betrays him. Gilliatt is a social outcast. His mysterious aura along with his extraordinary knowledge of the elements lead his fellow islanders to confer on him the epithet "crafty [*le malin*]," which is not just praise but also expresses their suspicion. Ostracized by his fellow islanders, Gilliatt lacks comrades and performs his deed in isolation. Captain Cook and his crew struggling to save the *Endeavour* from the Great Barrier Reef look almost solaced in their ability to rely on one another in mortal peril, compared to Gilliatt's brutal solitary struggle with the Douvres.

Gilliatt has been compared to Crusoe in his isolation, but in fact, his historical significance is quite different. Defoe created a single heroic mariner to dramatize a capacity anchored in a collectivity. Hugo, in contrast, portrays his hero's isolation as the consequences of mechanization. Lethierry and Clubin navigate alone because the *Durande*'s powerful engine replaces the crew needed to work the sails. Indeed, this solitude induced by mechanization facilitates Clubin's betrayal of Lethierry, because he needs only to dupe one assistant. This assistant is the helmsman, Tangrouille, whom Clubin has persisted in employing despite—or, as it then turns out, because of—his alcoholism. The telos of *La Durande* is the vast, depopulated container ship of the turn of the twenty-first century.

While Lethierry rescued shipwrecked travelers and mariners, Gilliatt's struggle is with an engine and a reef. Hugo, fertile in plots, might conceivably have given Gilliatt aid, but in isolating him with a reef—nature—and an engine—technology—Hugo distills work to its solitary essence in the mechanical age. At least that is how Marx conceived of the essence of labor in his famous portrait in *Capital* cited in chapter 4, which Marx published just three years after *Toilers of the Sea*. Unlike Marx's pattern of the worker, however, Gilliatt still can apply craft in this struggle. His body parts are not disjointed but rather all endowed with different keen capacities and work together as part of his embodied reason. Craft takes on the wreck of mechanization and triumphs just as it is being snuffed out, sufficiently creative to jury-rig expedients that mimic mechanization as well. [28] Gilliat shows his skill as a "machinist" when he jury-rigs a system of pulleys to winch the engine off the reef, for example, anticipating an invention from the 1860s when the novel is written, not the 1820s, when the novel is set: "The very ingenious adjustment of this burton possessed some of the simplifying qualities of the Weston-pulley of to-day" (322).

Description on the Reef: Never Has Writing Gone So Far

No matter how heroic the deed, the ethos of craft is in decline when the collectivity of skilled mariners disappears. This collective dimension to craft, what Conrad called the "bond of the sea," was important in nineteenth-century sea fiction, with the form's portrayal of shipboard societies. In French sea fiction, I have suggested, the bond was starting to unravel with Sue's heroes of evil. But these individualistic heroes are exceptions, set off against the ship's crew. In Hugo's novel, in contrast, collectivity has been jettisoned. Without collectivity, the novelist loses a great resource for creating plots. The different facets to craft can be represented as different aspects to the crew of seamen, and their interpersonal relations help generate problems and solutions, on Melville's *Pequod*, as on the *Ariel* in Cooper's *The Pilot*.

Hugo nonetheless manages to come up with an extraordinary feat of craft worthy of the annals of sea fiction, using the harsh and challenging environment alone. The entire second part of the novel that narrates Gilliatt's great deed, *Gilliatt le malin*, is as much a description of an extraordinarily dangerous terrain as it is of an action, or rather space and action are inseparable from each other, from the first book of this second part, aptly titled "The Reef [*L'Ecueil*]." The reef is one of the most inhospitable terrains for humans of the marine environment, perhaps with the exception of the polar wastes. It is also the site of dramatic shipwrecks and salvages that historically have stretched mariners to the full display of their craft, as Hugo well knew, having read the voyages of Captain Cook avidly from boyhood. For Gilliatt's epic deed, Hugo has taken a well-known reef close to home, that mariners normally would avoid. However, under the wrong conditions, as imagined by the capable novelist, this reef can turn into an obstacle as formidable as any met in the Edge zones of the world.

In this first *Toilers of the Sea*, the adventures of Gilliatt on the Douvres reef proceed according to sea fiction's adventure formula of trials testing the craft of the mariner, which the cunning reader problem-solves in imagination, at the level of information. This series of trials begins at the moment Gilliatt approaches the reef. Methodical and farseeing, Gilliatt's first challenge, even before how to get the engine off the reef, is where to overnight in what will certainly be a time-consuming operation. "It was imprudent to locate himself on the Durande. It was an extra load, and instead of adding weight to the vessel, the important point was to lighten it. . . . To be outside of it, yet near it; that was the problem" (285–86). This problem leads Gilliatt to reconnoiter the wreck and the reef from the vantage point of use: in search of a shelter.

As Gilliatt considers the reef from the vantage point of shelter, Hugo enumerates its physical aspect using sea fiction's well-established technique of performing description to show aspects of the environment as they are being put to use. "Where was he to find a shelter under such conditions. . . . Only the two Douvres remained. They seemed hardly habitable. A sort of excrescence on the upper plateau of the great Douvre could be distinguished from below. . . . Perhaps there was a hollow in this rock. A hole in which to hide one's self" (286–87). Exercising the mariner's pragmatic imagination, Gilliatt conjectures a shelter in the rock at the flattened summit of the great Douvre, but this inaccessible location only poses another problem. "But how was he to reach the plateau? how was he to ascend that vertical wall, as dense and polished as a pebble, half covered with a sheet of viscous hairweed, and having the slippery aspect of a surface that has been soaped?" (287). Gilliatt then exercises some impressive skills at technical climbing. He will manage to anchor a grapnel on the little Douvre, swing from it across an 8- or 10-foot gap, and then, after some setbacks, climb up a rope to its summit, where "[n]othing but what had wings had ever before set foot." On arriving there, Hugo underscores that Gilliatt has successfully exercised the mariner's pragmatic imagination, stating, "Gilliatt's conjecture had, moreover, been correct" concerning the possibility of a shelter on the summit (289). The statement is Hugo's equivalent for Gilliatt of Crusoe's "[a]s I imagin'd, so it was," when Crusoe spied the indraft allowing him to steer his cache from the ship's wreckage to shore.

Throughout the adventure of the engine's salvage, Hugo breaks the reef down into a series of problems and solutions, which then pose new problems in Crusoesque fashion, problems that he moreover amplifies with all obstacles from weather and terrain at his disposal. To the challenge of prying the engine off the reef, Hugo adds the obstacle of a storm and the reef's deadly inhabitant, the octopus. But as Hugo develops these problems, he starts to shift from following the techniques of sea fiction, as regards his use of description. And here his novel veers off into new poetic territory. Henry James was picking up on Hugo's deviation of sea fiction to explore new image practices when he commented, "M. Victor Hugo is a poet, and he embarks upon the deep in a very different spirit from the late Captain Marryatt. He . . . touches at foreign lands whose existence has never been suspected; and he makes discoveries of almost fabulous importance."[29]

Hugo's deviation of sea fiction starts through taking performing description in the direction of the descriptions in realist novels, then a form of the novel at the apogee of its prestige. With its encyclopedic aims, realist description deviates from performing description in offering details that serve pure knowledge rather than a particular, pragmatic problem. In the section on Gilliatt's challenge to find a place to overnight, for example, Hugo adds details on the reefs' geology and history that illuminate their formation:

> Upright rocks with flat summits, like the great Douvre and "the Man" [another reef in the novel] are decapitated peaks. They abound in the mountains and in the ocean. Certain rocks, above all, those which one meets with in the open sea, have notches like trees which have been hacked. They have the appearance of having received a blow from an axe. They are, in fact, subjected to the vast movements to and fro of the hurricane, that wood-chopper of the sea. . . . The Roque-au-Diable (Devil's Rock) at Guernsey, and the Table in the valley of Anweiler, present this singular geological enigma under the most surprising conditions. (286)

Hugo draws details here and elsewhere from the emerging science of oceanography, inaugurated with Matthew Maury's *The Physical Geography of the Sea* (1855), and he draws as well from Jules Michelet's more idiosyncratic *La Mer* [The Sea] (1861). True, in *Toilers of the Sea*, in contrast to the realist novel, the encyclopedic details ultimately will be brought back round to the pragmatic demands of adventure. The geological digression ends, for example, with Gilliatt's conjecture that the outcropping could contain a niche to shelter. But such descriptions, nonetheless, start to take the novel away from craft and details enabling its performance, offering the reader instead omniscient knowledge and reflections on natural history.

Hugo's description of the reef contains yet another kind of description even more removed from performing description and its pragmatic imperatives, which I will call transforming descriptions. Such descriptions, more characteristic of poetry than the novel, start from material details and then glide along a series of images to transmute the material world into figures of thought and imagination.[30] Thus, when Hugo describes the architecture of the reef, he moves from its geology to its enigmatic lighting, which becomes "the glaucous light from the eye of a sphinx" (309). The moving water becomes "movements of a mysterious dance." The passage continues, emphasizing the ghostly aspect of the reef, and finally turns this natural space into a "wondrous palace where Death sat contented" (310).

Similarly, when Hugo describes the creatures on the reef, he is not concerned with presenting them as a challenge to practice (performing description) or anatomizing their different species (encyclopedic, realist, description), but rather transforms the *physis* into a figure of the imagination—not the pragmatic imagination of the mariner, but rather the phantasmagorical imagination of the poet. Passages like the following abound: "Frightful swimming swarms prowl about, doing their work. It is a hive of hydras. The horrible is there, the imaginary." Hugo continues, "[t]o look into the depths of a sea is to behold the imagination of the Unknown. It is to see it from the terrible side" (205). When James commented on the upshot of Hugo's image voyage into new realms, he noted how the effect of this exploration was for Hugo to dematerialize the nature he seemed to be describing. In James's words, "[n]ever . . . has mere writing gone so far: that is, never was nature so effectually ousted from its place, in its own nominal interest."[31] Never has writing gone so far: we are on the terrain of the sublime, in the early modern sense of achieving things unattempted yet in prose or rhyme. In the second *Toilers of the Sea*, as in the second *Moby-Dick*, figurative language becomes a way to travel in the realm of phantasm. These phantasms are Hugo's "discoveries of almost fabulous importance" noted by James.[32]

If this novel is, indeed, as Hugo framed it, an epic of work, his narrative hence does not just perform the heroism of craft, as in a conventional novel of sea fiction. It also showcases another kind of skilled work: the work of the poet exploring with description in search of what James calls discoveries of fabulous importance.[33] In employing description, Hugo uses an aspect of poetics that across history has been a site in literature where writers draw attention to work, in general, and to their own literary artifice, in particular. Philippe Hamon makes this observation, pointing out several different ways in which description is an aspect of poetics highlighting work. Description uses the technical terms from specialized domains of work, and participates in the more general conceptual work of systematic knowledge. It is also an occasion for the writer to show off his ability to "work on the lexicon."[34]

The telos of Hugo's adventure taking the image to the limits and beyond in the history of the avant-garde is "the poetic adventure" of surrealism, striving to bridge the divide between imagination and reality into a new reality, a surreality.[35] This adventure is prepared by Rimbaud's transmutation of sea adventure fiction into the adventures of the lyric "I" cast away on the seas of the image in *Le Bateau ivre* [The Drunken Boat]: "And henceforth, I swam in the Poem / of the sea steeped in stars and milky, / Consuming green blue sky; where, waterline pale / And ravished, a thoughtful drowned person, sometimes floats down."[36]

CRAFT AND DREAD

When the second *Toilers of the Sea* deviates Gilliatt's deed of craft into exploration through the image, Hugo uses this exploration to analyze psychic experiences essential to the maritime frontier.[37] Throughout his transforming description, Hugo explores the psychic impact of working in these extreme zones of nature. This impact is understated if not ignored in the maritime corpus, which is terse about personal experience, and reticent about any details that have no immediate practical relevance. The mariner's inner life only breaks through tantalizingly at moments such as Cook's brief comments on the sterile pleasures of an unknown navigation.

Making Gilliatt a dreamer, as well as a compleat mariner, Hugo chooses a hero who registers this impact, though Gilliatt himself is inarticulate, and the verbalization of his sensations is left to the narrator. In Hugo's account, both the allure and the terror of extreme spaces lie in the experience they offer of existential dread: the enigma of the *physis*, sunken in its senseless, unredeemed materiality, what Hugo in the novel's preface called "the *ananke* of things." Gilliatt is sensitive to this dread before his struggle with the reef, at home in his bed, when he wakes up at night feeling "strangely moved" (331). In this chapter on the terrors of the night, Hugo calls the night an experience of "fathomless promiscuousness," where species and categories are crossed without any finished final form, and which "causes mineralization to vegetate, vegetation to live," and so on (333). Hugo declares, "[e]verywhere the incomprehensible; nowhere the unintelligible" (335). Everywhere "the formidable question: Is this Immanence a Being?" Does sunken matter have a soul, does it have meaning? Does it have morality? Where is God in the creation? "Where does destiny begin? Where does nature end?" "All this . . . weighed upon Gilliatt. Did he understand it? No. Did he feel it? Yes" (335–36).

The unfathomable promiscuity of sunken matter, in Hugo's delineation, characterizes the reef that is the theater of Gilliatt's epic struggle.

It characterizes the architecture of the reef between land and sea, and it characterizes the reef's dwellers, "[m]onstrous creatures": "[v]ague lineaments of antennae, tentacles, gills, fins, yawning jaws, scales, claws, nippers, float there, quiver, grow huge, decompose, and are effaced in the fatal transparency" (205). Such incomprehensible promiscuity characterizes the storm that is the challenge, and beyond Gilliatt's specific struggle, it characterizes the ocean that is the medium of his craft: "Of all confusions, the ocean is the most indivisible and the most profound. . . . It is the universal recipient; a reservoir for fecundation, a crucible for transformations. It amasses, then disperses; it accumulates, then sows; it devours, then creates. It receives all the sewers of the earth, and converts them into treasure. It is solid in the iceberg, liquid in the wave, impalpable in effluvium," and so on (279).

Gripped with dread before the enigma of chaotic, generative matter, the question for humans, Hugo states, is "How is one to move under their convergence?" (335). No metaphysical answers are forthcoming, but Gilliatt cuts the Gordian knot and responds to dread with practice. In Hugo's existentialist delineation, the possibility of remediating metaphysics with action is the allure of an unknown navigation or any other great deed of craft. True, Gilliatt's ostensible motive for undertaking his salvage is to win a pretty young girl, which is part of the novel's sentimental, framing plot. But once on the reef, he does not give her further thought. Rather, his struggle is with the *physis*, and when he triumphs, he taunts the clouds, likened to an epic hero, with "ironical joy for militant intelligence to prove the vast stupidity of these furious forces" (408–409).

Hugo's emblem of the sickening materiality of the *physis* is the giant octopus, also called a devilfish, landlord of the reef. "Compared with it, the hydras of old are laughable. . . . The octopus has no musclar organization, no menacing cry, no breastplate, no dart, no pincers," etc. (415–16). Hugo goes on to abstract this giant octopus with his transforming description, calling such creatures a torment for the philosopher and "blasphemies of creation against itself" (420). Without an explanation, the octopus is generative possibility itself without morals or reason: "terrible matrix" of "the Possible" and "shadows converted into monsters. To what purpose? What end does this serve?" (420).

Although the octopus's existence cannot be comprehended philosophically, this particular octopus threatening to destroy Gilliatt can be killed by the crafty mariner who knows its weakness, like Gilliatt. This weakness is its head, and Gilliatt plunges his knife in at just the right moment with a knowing turn of the hand. The octopus can also be subdued by being represented. Hugo included his own ink and wash image of "La Pieuvre [The Octopus]" in the sheaf of images he composed around the themes of *Toilers of the Sea* (figure 5.1).

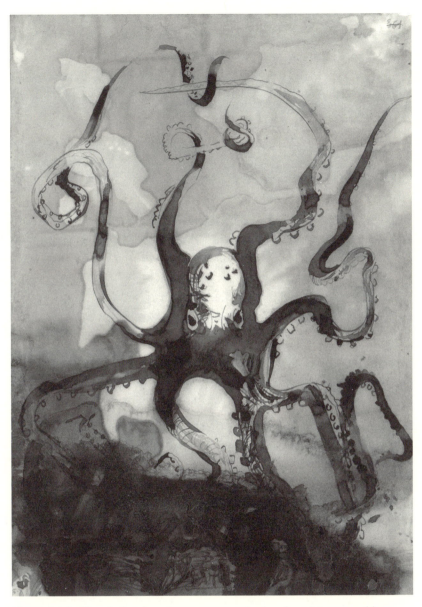

Figure 5.1. In Hugo's drawing, the octopus, cerebral and sensitive, resembles his creator to the point of signing Hugo's initials with his tentacles—and the octopus's preferred medium of defense is the writer's dark ink. While artists on historical voyages of exploration used watercolor to seize quickly the contours of unfamiliar landscapes, Hugo used watercolor to delve into his dark and mobile fantasy. "The sublime is below," Hugo observed (quoted by Georges Didi-Huberman, "Victor Hugo: Ombres, Vents, Vagues," available at *http://www.atopia.tk/index.php?option=com_content&task=view&id=74&Itemid=61*; consulted June 2009. Victor Hugo, *La Pieuvre* (c. 1866, pen, brush, brown ink, and wash on cream paper). Courtesy of the Bibliothèque Nationale de France.

Here, Hugo transforms the octopus into a reflection of the writer or artist, cerebral and sensitive (in contrast to other illustrators of the novel, such as Gustave Doré, who would render the octopus as a demonic monster). The analogy is thought-provoking. Like Hugo's octopus, the artist or writer undertaking the sublime search for new territories, becomes a figure with the potential to shed ethics, devoted to pure possibility. Hugo reinforces this parallel between sublime creator and terrifying octopus by having his octopus protect itself with its cloud of dark ink, which is the medium used by Hugo for his literary representation. Hugo, moreover, asserts his dominance over this formidable creature, who also offers his likeness by having the octopus do homage to its creator, with two intertwined tentacles that trace Victor Hugo's initials.

THE ONLY SEAMAN OF THE DARK AGES WHO HAS NEVER GONE INTO STEAM

Melville and Hugo invented the modernist novel from sea fiction, responding to the decline of craft. A consequence of the routinization of ocean travel, the decline of craft was sealed by the transition from sail to steam. Joseph Conrad was a mariner who turned to a career as a writer because he detested the quality of steam travel, and above all how steam took the art and adventure out of the work of the sea. In *A Personal Record*, Conrad recounts the prophecy of his examiner who accorded his certificate as master mariner: "[y]ou will go into steam presently. Everybody goes into steam." Conrad responds, "There he was wrong. I never went into steam—not really. If I only live long enough I shall become a bizarre relic of a dead barbarism, a sort of monstrous antiquity, the only seaman of the dark ages who had never gone into steam—not really."[38] Conrad's use of the term "antiquity" is at once ironic and telling concerning the pace of technological innovation—the working age of sail has only just disappeared, and yet its knowledge is as irrelevant as if it dated to the remote past. Antiquity is also the term Marlow, Conrad's seaman narrator, uses in *Heart of Darkness* to designate craft as it appears in the age of steam. When Marlow finds "*An Inquiry into some Points of Seamanship* by a man Towser, Towson—some such name," a "simple old sailor," he dates this "amazing antiquity" to the 1820s, which is to say when the working age of sail was still at its height. Though its knowledge is a relic—or precisely because of it—the volume glows with "a singleness of intention, an honest concern for the right way of going to work, which made these humble pages, thought out so many years ago, luminous with another than a professional light."[39]

Instead of going into steam, Conrad went into writing, though not without giving steam a try. Conrad was a mate for five months in 1887 on a coasting steamer, the *Vidar*, which sailed in the Eastern seas. He also sought work as a pilot on the Suez Canal, though without finding a position. In 1890, Conrad signed up as a riverboat pilot on the Congo River. He received a medical discharge in 1891, ill with malaria and disgusted with colonial violence. While out of work, Conrad started the manuscript that was to become *Almayer's Folly*. His last professional position at sea was as chief officer on a comfortable sail-driven passenger ship traveling between London and Adelaide. During this voyage, Conrad made the acquaintance of John Galsworthy, one of the ship's passengers, who was at the time "a young man just down from Cambridge, and supposed to be becoming a lawyer."[40] Looking back on that meeting over thirty years later, Galsworthy described Conrad in terms that could have been lifted from the man who was to become his friend and share with him the bond of literature. "He was a good seaman. Watchful of the weather, quick in handling the ship; considerate with the apprentices . . . With the crew he was popular; they were individuals to him, not a mere gang; and long after he would talk of this or that among them . . . Many evening watches in fine weather we spent on the poop. Ever the great teller of a tale, he had nearly twenty years of tales to tell . . . He was extraordinarily perceptive and receptive."[41]

Conrad had been enamored of literature of the sea from his boyhood. In *A Personal Record*, Conrad dates his "first introduction to the sea in literature" to the proofs of his father's translation of Hugo's *Toilers of the Sea,* that Conrad "read to him [Apollo, Conrad's father] aloud from beginning to end, and to his perfect satisfaction, as he lay on his bed, not being very well at the time."[42] Conrad denigrates "the sea-life of light literature" when he describes how it feeds the imagination of Lord Jim, his male Bovary, prompting dreams of "saving people from sinking ships, cutting away masts in a hurricane, swimming through a surf with a line; or as a lonely castaway, barefooted and half naked, walking on uncovered reefs in search of shellfish to stave off starvation . . . confront[ing] . . . savages on tropical shores, quell[ing] . . . mutinies on the high seas, and in a small boat upon the ocean . . . [keeping] up the hearts of despairing men—always an example of devotion to duty, and as unflinching as a hero in a book."[43] In "Tales of the Sea" (1898), in contrast, Conrad was more respectful of sea fiction, specifically that penned by Marryat and Cooper: "Perhaps no two authors of fiction influenced so many lives, and gave to so many the initial impulse towards a glorious or a useful career. Through the distances of space and time those two men of another race have shaped also the life of the writer of this appreciation."[44]

Conrad credits mariners' historical accounts of their navigations with pushing him into his first career as seaman, which was indeed an exceptional choice for a citizen of Poland. In "Geography and some Explorers," Conrad points to "books of travel and discovery" that made the sea for him "a hallowed ground." Such books "peopled it with unforgettable shades of the masters in the calling which, in a humble way, was to be mine, too."[45] Upon assuming his first command in the South Pacific, Conrad writes of channeling a maritime collective unconscious: "all of a sudden, all the deep-lying historic sense of the exploring adventures in the Pacific surged up to the surface of my being."[46]

In the course of that command, Conrad went so far in his homage to Cook as to set his sails to follow in Cook's wake. When planning a voyage from Sydney to Mauritius, Conrad tells us, he petitioned for a route that was not conventional and required some tricky navigation, in order to sail through the Torres Straits between Australia and New Guinea that Cook had put on the map of the world's oceans. To his surprise, his employers agreed. In the course of this passage through the Torres Straits, Conrad passed what he called a "hallowed spot [an island], for I knew that the *Endeavour* had been hove to off it in the year 1762 [sic] for her captain, whose name was James Cook, to go ashore for half an hour. What he could possibly want to do I cannot imagine. Perhaps only to be alone with his thoughts for a moment. The dangers and the triumphs of exploration and discovery were over for that voyage. All that remained to do was to go home, and perhaps his great and equable soul, tempered in the incessant perils of a long exploration, wanted to commune with itself at the end of its task. It may be that on this dry crumb of the earth's crust which I was setting by compass he had tasted a moment of perfect peace."[47]

THE EXTRAORDINARY COMPLICATION BROUGHT BY THE HUMAN ELEMENT

Conrad's first tale of the sea, *The Nigger of the "Narcissus,"* was the third novel of his career, following two works of imperial adventure fiction. Conrad oriented the reader toward expecting a work of sea fiction from this work's subtitle, taking the generic tag *A Tale of the Sea*, first used by Cooper in his path–breaking *The Pilot—A Tale of the Sea*.[48] From the perspective of nineteenth-century sea fiction, *The Nigger of the "Narcissus"* appears an attempt to renew the form by mining the psychology of mariners. Delineation of psychology pervaded other subgenres of the novel in the second half of the nineteenth century. It was, however, a less explored frontier for sea adventure fiction.

Hugo had moved the sea novel in the direction of psychology when he deviated the performance of craft into exploring the psychic allure of the terrifying unknown. Hugo was interested in the psychic experience of the frontier. Conrad, in contrast, focused on the psychology of mariners aboard a working vessel on routine voyages on the high seas. Here, he also brought into the sea novel material from nonfictional sea literature—not, however, the heroic accounts of exploration, but rather the literature about quotidian life at sea made famous by Richard Henry Dana Jr.'s *Two Years Before the Mast* (1840). It was the frictions and tensions of daily life that interested Conrad, and he drew his characters accordingly, deviating them into shadowy quirks and pathologies from their delineation in sea fiction as either supermen or embodiments of professional types. In Conrad's words, the "interest" is "not the bad weather but the extraordinary complication brought into the ship's life at a moment of exceptional stress by the human element below her deck," to cite from Conrad's "Author's Note" to *Typhoon*.[49]

When *The Nigger of the "Narcissus"* appeared, critics agreed that what made this narrative remarkable was its ordinariness: "an account of an ordinary voyage made by an ordinary sailing ship from Bombay round the Cape to the Thames [where] [n]othing particular happens."[50] But though the events certainly do not compare to the chases found in Cooper or the shipwreck devolving into cannibalism in Sue's *La Salamandre*, Conrad's quotidian focus does enfranchise the irrationalities of human behavior for the adventure of the sea. On the voyage of the *Narcissus*, interactions among the disturbingly charismatic, malingering James Wait and the repulsive, incompetent, work-dodging Donkin produce fear-mongering and superstition that inflame the crew almost to the point of mutiny. In the blunt assessment of old Singleton, upholder of old-fashioned craft on the *Narcisuss*: "Ships are all right. It is the men in them!"[51]

Bringing to the foreground the subtleties of psychology, Conrad claims for sea adventure fiction a new repertoire of adventures worth narrating—not only situations of crises, like near-mutiny, which he does include, but also achievements that would seem too minor to be included among sea fiction's usual roster of its deeds. When the *Narcissus* is foundering on its side in the midst of a storm, the life-saving achievement is the cook's ability to jury-rig a way to make coffee, in a performance deemed nothing short of "'meeraculous'" (51). The minor miracle of a cup of coffee rallies the crew abandoned to "hopeless resignation." "Had we been saved by his recklessness or his agility, we could have at length become reconciled to the fact; but to admit our obligation to anybody's virtue and holiness alone was as difficult for us as for any other handful of mankind" (51). Their morale restored, captain and crew struggle to the rising sun and right the ship in maneuvers that Conrad details with a mariner's precision, using the poetics of gripping description.[52]

In taking the psychopathology of everyday life on board ship as his subject, Conrad pursues the translation of adventure scenarios to the territories of the mind found throughout literature of the second half of the nineteenth century, in fiction (the detective story) and even in poetry (Baudelaire and Rimbaud). At the same time, Conrad does so without interiorizing the adventure itself. Rather, Conrad explores the juncture of thought and emotion that shapes performance at sea. Virginia Woolf noted this aspect of Conrad's achievement when she compared his sea fiction to the novels of Cooper and Marryat, whose heroes' craft seemed to flow effortlessly. As Woolf put it, Conrad speaks with a "double vision . . . at once inside and out. To praise their silence one must possess a voice. To appreciate their endurance one must be sensitive to fatigue."[53] What Woolf calls Conrad's double vision allows Conrad not only to develop some of the adventures of seafaring unacknowledged by the discourse of craft, but it also allows him to anatomize the mariner's pragmatic imagination, which is, after all, part of the human element below deck. A number of his sea tales offer case studies that help conceptualize its delicate balance of creativity and realism, exhibited in performance but difficult to abstract.

In *Typhoon*, for example, the extraordinary storm of the title threatens a ship captained by a man "entirely given to the actuality of the bare existence," with "just enough imagination to carry him through each successive day, and no more" (4). Until the storm of *Typhoon*, Captain MacWhirr's minimal imagination was an asset to him. But it almost kills him when MacWhirr drives his ship into a terrible typhoon by failing to project a storm beyond his ship's capacity, even as the pragmatic imagination should note the ship's barometer in freefall and the ship heaving in violent swells. The dangers of the storm are, in contrast, imagined not only pragmatically but melodramatically by MacWhirr's first mate Jukes. In the teeth of the typhoon, Jukes scares himself into trying to jump overboard, but is saved by MacWhirr, whose insensitivity is an asset in the midst of terrifying conditions, and indeed, MacWhirr batters his way through the storm with the aid of the persevering engineer Rout.

Jukes's melodramatic despair in the grip of the typhoon is cut from the same cloth as the flights of fancy endangering craft in *The Secret Sharer*. Here, the extraordinary occurrence anatomized by Conrad is the responsibility of the first command. As the young captain struggles to assume the mantle of his office, he falls into a fantasy of sympathy for a stealthy criminal sailor, Leggatt, who steals on board. Far from refusing this mysterious visitor or seeking to bring him to justice, the young captain shelters Leggatt in his cabin. The story's glimpses of the chief-mate and crew's interest in the bizarre behavior of their commander keeping to his cabin would be the material for a comic send-up of sea fiction, if the captain's narcissistic identification with Leggatt did not almost lead him to run his ship aground.

Only in this situation of imminent danger does the young commander succeed in calling on his pragmatic imagination, just in the nick of time. Sizing up the situation, he "remembered only that I was a total stranger to the ship," and drops the other uses of stranger that have circulated through the novella: "the secret stranger ready to depart," and that he is, in his words, a "stranger" to himself. Recalled to his duty, the young commander gives the order to bring the ship about, scanning some way to gauge whether the order has been a success, since the land's distance is difficult to judge in the dark. Is the ship moving? The captain anxiously casts about for some marker. And then he sees the hat he lent Leggatt, bobbing "[w]hite on the black water. . . . Now I had what I wanted—the saving mark for my eyes." Fancy is abandoned for craft as the captain "watched the hat—the expression of my sudden pity for his mere flesh. It had been meant to save his homeless head from the dangers of the sun. And now—behold—it was saving the ship, by serving me for a mark to help out the ignorance of my strangeness. Ha! It was drifting forward, warning me just in time that the ship had gathered sternway. 'Shift the helm,' I said in a low voice."[54]

THE DEPLORABLE DETAILS OF AN OCCURRENCE

Struggling with the psychological intricacies of danger, the mariners in many tales by Conrad manage to salvage their craft, even if their heroism is ordinary, in contrast to the supermen of nineteenth-century sea fiction. The ethos of craft emerges intact in *The Nigger of the "Narcissus,"* *Typhoon*, *The Secret Sharer*, and *Youth*, among others. In *Lord Jim*, in contrast, the last residue of this novel's conformity to sea fiction is in its subtitle, *A Tale*. Despite the resonance of this generic tag with Cooper, the Red Rover's elegant, dexterous *Dolphin* has no affinity with the ramshackle steamship *Patna*, "old as the hills . . . eaten up with rust worse than a condemned water-tank" (53). The dashing Rover would never have recognized even his caricature in the *Patna*'s monstrously overweight, cowardly, opportunistic New South Wales German captain. When that patron saint of craft, Crusoe, makes his appearance in *Lord Jim*, it is not as the capable Crusoe transported from his own era to Conrad's present, but Crusoe as he would have looked had he managed to stay alive until the end of the nineteenth century, an amazing antiquity disoriented on a busy street corner. The character Robinson is "[a]n emaciated patriarch in a suit of white drill, a solah topi with a green-lined rim on a head trembling with age," deaf, and supporting himself with "both hands on the handle of an umbrella," dragged along by a petty unscrupulous entrepreneur with plans to make money from guano on a sterile, sun-baked remote desert island (163).

Rather than the remarkable occurrences of craft, the first part of *Lord Jim* is an effort to piece together what Marlow calls "the deplorable details of an occurrence" (80). Marlow coins this phrase in the course of trying to put his finger on his fascination with the case of dereliction of duty on the *Patna* that is the subject matter of the first part of the novel. "Why I longed to go grubbing into the deplorable details of an occurrence which, after all, concerned me no more than as a member of an obscure body of men held together by a community of inglorious toil and by fidelity to a certain standard of conduct, I can't explain" (80). Marlow muses, "Perhaps, unconsciously, I hoped I would find that something, some profound and redeeming cause, some merciful explanation, some convincing shadow of an excuse" (80). This excuse would be a way for Marlow to salvage "the solidarity of the craft": "Don't you see what I mean by the solidarity of the craft? I was aggrieved against him [Jim], as though he had cheated me of a splendid opportunity to keep up the illusion of my beginnings, as though he had robbed our common life of the last spark of its glamour" (139).

The *Patna* affair grips all members of the maritime profession who come into its orbit in *Lord Jim*. The facts of the case are not what are gripping. The seamen's dereliction of duty is obvious, and with the exception of what hit the *Patna*, any factual disputes are cleared up. There is one, notably, so situation-specific that it telegraphs to the reader Conrad's own immersion in the work of the sea, and hence raises the question of the quarry of this novelist who had, despite his own craft, forborne to offer the reader a classic sea adventure novel. The cowardly officers abandoning their ship said they saw nothing in the darkness, leading them to think it was sunk, while the survivors testify to the fact that there was still light on board. The disparity is clarified by one of the nautical assessors, Captain Montague Brierly, aka Big Brierly—"the captain of the crack ship of the Blue Star line" who "had never in his life made a mistake, never had an accident, never a mishap" (85). Brierly shows his craft—and his creator Conrad's knowledge of the sea, as well—when Brierly recalls the optical effect that would be had from viewing just the ship's hull from a boat low in the water in the dark.

According to Marlow, "[w]hether they knew it or not," what drew all the sailors of the port to the trial was an "interest that . . . was purely psychological—the expectation of some essential disclosure as to the strength, the power, the horror, of human emotions," a disclosure that, however, never comes (84). As for Brierly, at the time of the trial, Marlow speculates he was bored or exasperated. What Brierly himself tells Marlow is, "[t]his is a disgrace. We've got all kinds amongst us—some anointed scoundrels in the lot; but, hang it, we must preserve professional decency . . . We are trusted . . . I don't care a snap for all the pilgrims that ever came out of Asia, but a decent man would not have behaved like this to a full cargo of old rags in bales. We aren't an organised body of men, and the only thing that holds us together is just the name for that kind of decency. Such an affair destroys one's confidence" (93). If Brierly is in fact speaking his mind, he finds this loss of confidence devastating, for he commits suicide by jumping overboard from his ship shortly after a last punctual round of duties. Indeed, the *Patna* affair emanates an "uncanny vitality" on what Marlow calls "the fellowship of the craft": "it seemed to live . . . in the minds of men, on the tips of their tongues . . . years afterwards, thousands of miles away, emerging from the remotest possible talk" (144). "*Impossible de comprendre* [impossible to understand]," is the view of the courageous French lieutenant who helped pilot the foundering steamship to safety, concluding "so that (*de sorte que*) there are many things in this incident of my life (*dans cet épisode de ma vie*) which have remained obscure" (145, 147).

The trial ends, but Marlow's fascination with Jim does not. In the remainder of the novel, we follow Marlow reconstructing and reviewing the events from Jim's short life many years later, trying to salvage some vestige of craft but to no avail. In the dereliction of duty on the *Patna*, Jim shows himself unable to improvise in contending with unforeseen situations, which is the hallmark of craft. Jim goes on to make the same mistake in the very different circumstances of his romance with Patusan: miscalculating about Brown in letting him escape, thereby provoking Dain Waris's death, and, in the end, stubbornly offering himself to Doramin's bullet, rather than escaping with his girlfriend for further adventures.

There is a historical explanation for Marlow's inability to make sense of Jim's obscurity. Jim is the bearer of a message Marlow does not want to hear, but Jim is its symptom rather than its cause. There is no spark of glamour illuminating Jim because craft has disappeared. It has, however, disappeared at the level of a historical conjuncture, rather than as a circumstance specific to Jim's personality.

Marlow himself still clings to "the last spark of . . . [the] glamour [of craft]" (139). Searching in vain for its residue, Marlow combs through the facts of Jim's case. This search arrests the forward movement of classic sea adventure fiction and sends the cunning reader toward events in the past. Marlow's search blocks the gripping aspect to sea fiction's episodes of danger and remedy, and makes the struggles of the protagonist, like that of the reader, only about coordinating information. There is something of detective work about the effort shared by Marlow and the reader, with the difference that unlike the masterful Sherlock Holmes, Marlow flounders in perplexity, without a satisfying result. No wonder then that when Marlow employs a lexicon around craft, its terms have lost their precision and circulate like an incantation to summon what has been lost. Thus, the phrase "one of us," that, in the words of Cedric Watts, encompasses variously "'a fellow-gentleman', 'a white gentleman', 'a white man', 'a good seaman', 'an outwardly-honest Englishman', 'an ordinary person' and 'a fellow human being'" (notes to *Lord Jim*, 354).

To Make You See: Conrad's Maritime Modernism

From the vantage point of craft, *Lord Jim* is the prelude to *The Mirror of the Sea*, where Conrad pronounces craft's eulogy with eloquence. At the same time, Marlow's stubborn search for an extinct capacity results in a narrative poetics that launches the novel into uncharted waters. It yields Marlow's narrative obscurity, the signature of Conrad's modernism. That Marlow is an obscure narrator is a critical commonplace. What is added by noting the maritime frame is that Conrad's seaman narrator brings to the demise of craft techniques that he has learned in the course of the mariner's work of navigation, achieving orientation from partial information.

Marlow asks his questions following the trial of the *Patna*, whose inquiry into competing versions of events is standard operating procedure in voyages where there was a dereliction of duty, as famous mutiny cases make clear. That there is no official log to refer to is professionally accurate. In merchant voyages, record-keeping was sloppier than in military and government contexts; no surprise that there is little formality in the case of the *Patna*, "owned by a Chinaman, chartered by an Arab, and commanded by a sort of renegade New South Wales German" (53).

But beyond the trial, the narrator Marlow's approach coordinating different kinds of partial information so as to render phenomenal obscurity intelligible is the foundation of navigation, which permits transport across the trackless ocean. Conrad underscores the importance of the mariner's struggle with obscurity to yield sight, by which he means at once vision and intelligibility. In *The Mirror of the Sea*, he remarks, "To see! to see! . . . is the craving of the sailor."[55] Drawing a parallel between the mariner and "the rest of blind humanity," Conrad continues, "To have his path made clear for him is the aspiration of every human being in our beclouded and tempestuous existence. I have heard a reserved, silent man, with no nerves to speak of, after three days of hard running in thick south-westerly weather, burst out passionately: 'I wish to God we could get sight of something!'" The struggle to wrest sight, in the sense at once of vision and intelligibility, is also represented, in Conrad's preface to *The Nigger of the "Narcissus,"* as the task of the novelist, whom he styles "the worker in prose" (146). "My task which I am trying to achieve is, by the power of the written word . . . to make you *see*" (147). Conrad's use of the phrase "make you" here is ambiguous. Does Conrad seek to present phenomena so vividly that the reader will grasp them? That is one dominant critical account concerning what is called Conrad's impressionism. But what if "make you see" is meant to compel the reader to participate in the processes of wresting intelligibility from obscurity; to shadow the kind of processes Marlow applies to the case of Jim?

What critics have noted as Marlow's obscurity is in fact Conrad's narration incorporating fundamental precepts of information processing from navigation. To grasp this similarity, I rely on Hutchins's *Cognition in the Wild*, analyzing the navigational processes of the Sea and Anchor Detail on the USS *Palau*, sailing off San Diego in the 1980s. Now, the technologies on the *Palau* differ from those used at the time of Conrad; however, both are part of the same era in navigation that spans from the introduction of the marine chronometer until GPS. Even with the marine chronometer permitting the calculation of longitude at sea, the navigator lacked any immediate information about the ship's position once out of sight of land. To figure out this position, the navigator made a series of partial observations. These observations included calculations like measuring the angles of the planets to gauge the ship's latitude and comparing the time when the sun was at its zenith (noon) on any day to noon back in Greenwich to gauge the ship's longitude. They also included cross-checking the measurements with estimations of where the ship should be based on its course by the compass, along with estimations about speed, adjusted for current and drift. To such calculations, they added observations of flora, fauna, and any known physical features, as well as measurements of depth and examination of the sand at the bottom of the ocean.

This process of cross-checking partial information so fundamental to navigation is one in which "the ship's situation" is to be "represented and re-represented," to use Hutchins's words. The goal of such a process is what Hutchins calls, "the *propagation of representational state* across a series of *representational media*."[56] In other words, evidence in different kinds of media—compass bearings, depth, celestial calculations—need to be aligned so that they all give the same answer as to location. This process may sound straightforward, but calculations are made by people using sensitive technologies and, like any human process, subject to error. Sometimes, there are minute differences in these calculations that need to be reconciled. In reconciling such differences, the pragmatic imagination, though significantly less important than before the chronometer, steps in. The need to make sense of such gaps is part of the reason why navigation before GPS was viewed as an activity that was at once science and art. If the results are off, even by a minimal amount, they can result in the few feet that separate a deep channel from a dangerous shoal.

This craft of lining up partial observations across different media to yield an accurate calculation of orientation is essential to *Lord Jim*. It is essential to the novel's adventures, which portray Marlow combing through the facts of Jim's case and of Jim's life, trying to salvage some shred of the mariner's ethos of craft. Marlow also seeks to coordinate different kinds of partial information in his narration of the events of the plot, and indeed in conjuring the phenomenal world itself. This work of giving accurate though obscure and partial findings, which must then be reconciled by the narrator and by the reader shadowing his perceptions, is what Ian Watt called Conrad's "delayed decoding."[57] In this version of cunning reading, however, the challenge is no longer survival on the world's remote waters and coasts—it is to understand the world and events depicted in narrative.

To see how Conrad transfers the work of navigation to narration, we can take the example of a scene explicated by Watt to exemplify Conrad's delayed decoding. In the scene, Marlow portrays how he first meets Jim, a meeting precipitated by a misunderstanding. Jim confronts Marlow, misconstruing a statement made by a man speaking to Marlow. The statement is "Look at that wretched cur," which Jim takes to apply to himself, when it in fact applies to a dog (94). However, Marlow does not narrate this miscommunication in straightforward fashion. Rather, Marlow starts off with partial information about different aspects of the misunderstanding using the different devices by which fiction creates its referential illusion—setting, character, dialogue, etc.—and only eventually coordinates them to produce an explanation.

In surveying the setting, for example, Marlow first uses the device of description, portraying the mangy dog in question hunting for fleas. He then turns to dialogue, with the words between Marlow and Jim that intimate a grave insult. Interior monologue is added when we enter Marlow's mind with his "supernatural efforts of memory," to recall the misunderstanding, while there is interference in obtaining this information from the surrounding world: "I was hindered by the oriental voice within the court room" (97). Such interference from the environment is a common problem in the work of collecting information at sea: in the midst of a fog, for example, it is difficult to gauge when the sun is at its zenith and hence obtain a calculation essential to longitude. The interference recurs throughout Marlow's collection of partial information of different kinds. Tellingly, when Marlow scans Jim's face trying to read character from it, he compares it to bad weather, the conditions when the navigator's observations are disrupted: "a darkening sky before a clap of thunder, shade upon shade imperceptibly coming on, the gloom growing mysteriously intense in the calm of maturing violence"(95). Indeed, throughout his struggles to grasp Jim's character, Marlow will emphasize Jim's similarity to those foggy or stormy conditions at sea that impede information-collection in navigation. Hence, the recurrence of statements like, "I don't pretend I understood him. The views he let me have of himself were like those glimpses through the shifting rents in a thick fog—bits of vivid and vanishing detail, giving no connected idea of the general aspect of a country. They fed one's curiosity without satisfying it; they were no good for purposes of orientation" (99).

In the scene of the wretched cur, in contrast to the more general problem of Jim's character, however, Marlow does eventually succeed in lining up all the details across different representations and grasping the misunderstanding. Once the misunderstanding has been clarified, it can be dispelled. Even in clarification, there is double-checking, as in navigation. To bolster his denial that he called Jim a cur, Marlow not only describes his intent but points Jim toward the actual dog. "'Don't be a fool,' I cried in exasperation. . . 'I've heard' . . . 'Don't be a fool,' I repeated. 'But the other man said it'. . . At last his eyes followed downwards the direction of my pointing finger. He appeared at first uncomprehending, then confounded, and at last amazed and scared as though a dog had been a monster and he had never seen a dog before. 'Nobody dreamt of insulting you,' I said" (97–98).[58]

Lord Jim is Conrad's last novel narrated by Marlow, who has worked his way in the course of his trilogy from the adventures of craft to the adventures of information coordination and comprehension. In this movement, Marlow's narratives progressively abandon the thrilling adventures of classic sea fiction. In subsequent novels, Conrad would draft adventure plots reinvesting cunning reading with suspense. Only five years after the Marlow trilogy, Conrad published the first of what were to be his two works of spy fiction, a genre where the chase after information becomes an essential motor of the adventure.[59] Conrad nods to the superseded world of craft in *The Secret Agent*, by putting the destruction of an emblem of navigation at the center of the novel's plot, in the sense of story. The terrorist plot, in the sense of criminal activity, takes aim at the Greenwich observatory, epicenter not only of astronomy but also of the prime meridian that anchors the calculation of longitude, which is one crucial measurement essential in the information coordination of navigation.

Critics explain the significance of Conrad's obscurity that I have called the struggle for intelligibility in a number of different ways. One explanation is that Conrad's obscurity calls attention to the craft of writing. Another is that this obscurity makes us reconsider the familiar by presenting it as strange. Yet another is that such obscurity conveys a sense of time that is phenomenological, to name just a few. From the vantage point of the work of the sea, another explanation might be pedagogical, to train armchair sailors, in keeping with the professorial bent of Marlow, who boasts of turning out "youngsters enough in my time, for the service of the Red Rag, to the craft of the sea, to the craft whose whole secret could be expressed in one short sentence, and yet must be driven afresh every day into young heads till it becomes the component part of every waking thought—till it is present in every dream of their young sleep!" (75).

Through making Marlow's struggle for intelligibility a problem in the narrative, Marlow, and through him, Conrad, starts to challenge the cunning reader. Conrad does not do so, however, in the quest of helping armchair sailors learn the art of navigation: the case of Jim is not a story-problem like those found in practical treatises on seamanship discussed in this study's first chapter and parodied by Conrad in *Heart of Darkness* and *Typhoon*. Rather, Conrad asks the reader more generally to exercise her pragmatic imagination to search for solutions, in a more challenging version of the entertaining invitations to problem-solve initiated by Defoe in *Robinson Crusoe*.

Such thought games, as I have explained, have historically been used to help foster the ability to improvise creatively in the face of the unforeseen, one constitutive aspect of craft, as of other arts of action, that is difficult to teach. These games used in professional contexts: Conrad, indeed, portrays himself as undergoing such pedagogical problem-solving at the level of the pragmatic imagination in his own education as a mariner. This portrayal occurs in a lengthy description of his examinations for his certificates at the Marine Department of the Board of Trade, where an examiner places him "in a ship of a certain size, at sea, under certain conditions of weather, season, locality, etc., etc.—all very clear and precise," orders him to tell him how "to execute a certain manœuvre," and then starts to inflict problem after problem on the "imaginary ship" that "seemed to labour under a most comprehensive curse" until "long before the end I would have welcomed with gratitude an opportunity to exchange [it] into the *Flying Dutchman*."[60] In *Lord Jim*, however, Conrad is not in the business of turning out readers to qualify for service to "the Red Rag." Purged of maritime specificity, Conrad's effects of narrative obscurity offer the reader the chance to exercise her pragmatic imagination, without a specific aim beyond the process of reading itself.

Indeed, this search without a specific end may be just the point of Conrad's pedagogy of obscurity. In the preface to *The Nigger of the "Narcissus*," speaking of his own "work" in prose, Conrad reiterates the obscurity of the artist's task (artist in the sense of someone involved in creation, poesis): "the aim of art . . . like life itself, is inspiring, difficult—obscured by mists. It is not in the clear logic of a triumphant conclusion; it is not in the unveiling of one of those heartless secrets, which are called the Laws of Nature. It is not less great, but only more difficult" (148). Transmuting maritime adventure fiction into the artist's exploration of a murky realm—a boggy, soggy, squitchy scene—in search of . . . something, Conrad dissociates adventure from an immediate practical aim. With his notion of the work of art as a noninstrumental exploration of a land veiled in mists, Conrad picks up the Kantian idea of art—purposive form without purpose. For Kant, this notion qualifies the effect generated by the finished artwork. For Conrad, in contrast, literary exploration is conceived as a dynamic and ongoing process joining artist and cunning reader.

"To make anything very terrible, obscurity seems in general to be necessary," Edmund Burke remarked of the art of the sublime. Like Melville's Ishmael, Conrad's Marlow tells a tale that reconnects the sea of work to the sublime by making sea adventure the occasion to explore other foggy Edges than those of the globe: the obscure realms of language and of the mind. Conrad offers, of course, his own figure for the boggy, soggy, yet portentous something, when he describes the untypical, eery atmospheric effect of Marlow's tale in *Heart of Darkness*, radiating "a glow [that] brings out a haze" in the twice-refracted, evocative yet obscuring light of the spectral illumination (9).

VERNE'S SCIENCE ADVENTURE FICTION: TO BOLDLY GO . . .

Jules Verne, too, mobilized sea fiction's poetics to explore other Edge zones of modernity beyond the seas; however, these Edges were not the reflexive, modernist domains of language and thought. Instead, Verne was interested in new physical geographies that could become the future equivalents of the maritime frontier, as well as the scientific technologies that would make them practicable.

If Verne turned to sea fiction to imagine modernity's potential geographical and technological frontiers, it is in part on account of sea fiction's subject matter. In contrast to some land-locked theorists of modernity in his era, Verne grasped the vitality of the maritime case, and modeled emerging frontiers by intensifying some of its salient traits. Verne also, as I will subsequently explain, took from sea fiction its powerful poetics, which, unlike Melville, Hugo, or Conrad, however, he was not interested in dismantling. Rather, Verne capitalized on their potential to bring remarkable occurrences beyond the bounds of ordinary readers to life through depicting them as challenges that required skilled labor—labor that the reader is invited to share at the level of the pragmatic imagination. Verne turned this potential to inventing science adventure fiction, a new form of adventure novel that would achieve an unprecedented international success, starting with the novels of Verne himself. Verne is, according to the UNESCO *Index Translationum*, the "fifth most-translated author of all time (after the collective works of Walt Disney Productions, Agatha Christie, the Bible, and Lenin)."[61]

We can see Verne transmuting sea fiction into science adventure fiction from his first novels, which include a journey to the core of the earth in *Journey to the Center of the Earth* (1864), a space trip in *From the Earth to the Moon* (1865), and a panorama of the ocean's floor in *Twenty Thousand Leagues under the Sea* (1869). Though Verne's novels do not broach self-reflexive questions about the art of the novelist, like the modernist sea novels discussed in previous sections, they are self-conscious about sea fiction's rich tradition. *Twenty Thousand Leagues under the Sea*, notably, is filled with send-ups and allusions both to specific sea novels and to generic conventions.

The plot of the novel turns, of course, on the invincible submarine *Nautilus*, a technology that Verne did not need much imagination to extrapolate, since he drafted it on the eve of its realization.[62] What Verne did extrapolate from the maritime case, however, was what was distinctive about the submariner's modernity. First of all, he understood the modern importance of the right to global mobility implied in the freedom of the seas, which the *Nautilus* took to a new level. *Mobilis in mobile* is aptly chosen as the motto of this craft with its dazzling speed and maneuverability, able to conquer the oceans of the globe by unlocking below the sea's surface a realm of comparatively easy transport, untroubled by weather and the dangers of hidden reefs. In its global hypermobility, Verne's *Nautilus* does away with the resistance of the sea so daunting to mariners. He also intimates the increasing abstraction of space that poststructuralist theorists, such as Deleuze and Guattari, as well as Paul Virilio, have noted as an aspect of late modernity.[63] For Deleuze and Guattari, as for Virilio, the endpoint of this process is a "strategic submarine, which outflanks all gridding and invents a neonomadism . . . The sea, then the air and the stratosphere, become smooth spaces again, but, in the strangest of reversals, it is for the purpose of controlling striated space more completely."[64] Carl Schmitt, too, is following in the wake of Verne's enhancement of the freedom of the seas into a more abstracted global mobility when Schmitt notes maritime existence as a waystation on the way to the increasingly abstract conditions of late modernity, which he calls a planetary regime of space dominated by the total rootlessness of modern technology; what Schmitt also calls "an industrial-technical existence."[65]

With the supranational identity of the *Nautilus*'s crew, too, Verne presciently extrapolates from the maritime case. Seamen shared a supranational identity, rooted in the bond of maritime work, which was distinct from their identities deriving from affiliations rooted in family, nation, and other territorial communities. This supranational identity is enhanced in Verne's submarine novel to the point of supplanting any other political or civil affiliation. For Nemo, his global identity makes him a superman, above the law, while his crew seems about to leave behind not only terrestrial affiliation but individuality, if not personhood itself. In contrast to the picturesque, differentiated members of a ship's company in classic sea fiction, Nemo's crew is a faceless group of efficient workers, harbingers of industrial-technical existence, and specifically of the disappearance of individuals from the work of the sea in the automated tanker ship of our time.

If the qualities of maritime modernity help Verne intimate a level of industrial-technical existence that will be its successor, the poetics of sea fiction give him the way to endow his vision with imaginative life. Before Verne, Mary Shelley had grasped the mariner as a model for the dynamic spirit of modern explorations in science and technology, when she framed Frankenstein's experiments in bioengineering with the tale of an explorer striving to reach the North Pole in *Frankenstein, or, The Modern Prometheus* (1818). And Shelley had relied on sea fiction's poetics of performability in the invention process of Victor Frankenstein until she asked the reader to suspend disbelief when Frankenstein crossed from assembling inanimate body parts to the monster's animation. At that point, Shelley then turned to a sentimental poetics to persuade readers as to the existence of her new android—depending on the eloquence of the monster and the tragedy of his ethical choices to win the reader's sympathy, rather than on sea fiction's performability effect.

Verne, in contrast, uses sea adventure fiction's poetics of performability to cross from existing technologies and charted spaces to the edges of modern innovation and beyond. To give conviction to his science fantasies, Verne organizes his narrative according to sea fiction's pattern of a challenge followed by problem-solving. As in sea fiction, as well, Verne uses the organization of challenge followed by problem-solving both to structure an individual episode and to string together these episodes at the macrolevel of the novel's plot.

From the opening lines of *Twenty Thousand Leagues under the Sea*, Verne turns his new nonexistent technology into a series of problems to be solved. Indeed, much of *Twenty Thousand Leagues under the Sea* is one long buildup to its existence, from the enigma of the submarine when it is first introduced: as "a strange event, an unexplained and inexplicable occurrence."[66] Posed as a problem, the submarine's identity can then be explained. Verne strings this explanation out across the novel's opening chapters, as the distinguished professor of ocean sciences, Arronax, invites the reader to join him in his search for an answer. The cunning reader identifies with Arronax, piecing together partial information, until Arronax meets up with the craft itself and becomes its prisoner. Once on board the *Nautilus*, Verne does not shy away from applying sea fiction's formula of challenge and problem-solving to explaining its mechanism. These solutions are rigorously based on scientific information of Verne's time.[67] Michel Serres is one of the critics for whom this accuracy marks the limits of Verne's vision. However, from the point of view of cunning reading, this accuracy indicates Verne's concern to make his submarine operable, in keeping with sea fiction's poetics of performability.

Also serving performability is Verne's frequent practice of surrounding such operable facts with details that Barthes would call "the effect of the real." These details are mentioned to convey a sense of existence rather than because they help to accomplish actions. In setting down such details, Verne often follows a hierarchy through three levels of operability: existing technologies, those plausible through their analogy with the existing, and the fictive whose workings he wants to make persuasive.[68] In the chapter "All by Electricity," for example, Verne prefaces Nemo's explanation of the *Nautilus*'s workings with descriptions of three kinds of instruments: (1) "usual navigational equipment," "such as the thermometer, which tells me the temperature inside the *Nautilus*; the barometer, which measures the weight of the air and hence forecasts changes in the weather," and so on; (2) existing instruments not usually found on ships adapted for underwater navigation, such as a pressure gauge, with "a new kind of sounding instrument"; and (3) "other instruments," whose use cannot be imagined, which are the prelude to "a few things" explained by Nemo about how the submarine works (76–77).

In the process of conjuring imaginary technologies to life, Verne gives useful information, both in word and illustration, about existing technologies. Useful information is also offered in explaining how imaginary technologies should run. This information is in keeping with the didactic function envisioned for Verne's novels by his publisher, Hetzel, who included them in his magazine popularizing knowledge, the *Magasin d'éducation et de récréation*."[69] Such didactic moments are, however, often static in comparison to the gripping description of maneuvers in Cooper or Marryat. Details no longer drive the action forward and the capacities of the submarine are explained, rather than performed. Thus, Nemo shows the capacities of the *Nautilus*'s hull to Arronax:

"These two hulls are constructed from steel plates with a density 7.8 times that of water. The first hull is no less than 5 cm thick, and weighs

394.96 tons. The keel alone, which is 50 cm high by 25 cm wide, weighs 62 tons; and the total weight of the keel, the second envelope, the engine, the ballast, the various fixtures and fittings, and the bulk-heads and internal braces is 961.52 metric tons, which, when added to 394.96, gives the required total of 1,356.48 metric tons. Am I clear?" "Perfectly," I replied. (83)

Though such descriptions may not be compelling, they do further an aspect of Verne's poetic challenge in building a plot from purely imaginary technologies. Verne must first create his technologies before they can be used, in contrast to sea fiction, which mobilizes technologies actually in existence, even if the landlubber reader does not understand them.

Verne further concretizes his imaginary technologies with another tactic of performability from sea fiction: the propagation of representational states across representational media. In the case of *Twenty Thousand Leagues under the Sea*, most notably, this propagation occurs as a play between descriptions and different forms of illustrations to supplement the information in the narrative. Verne's 118 illustrations expand exponentially on a practice already used by Defoe, who included representations in different genres to perform the existence of Crusoe's island in *Robinson Crusoe* and its sequels (portrait of Crusoe on shore, map of the island, map of Crusoe's circumnavigations; see figures 2.1 to 2.3). With the advent of mass reproducibility, image inclusion becomes much easier, and Verne utilizes such representation and re-representation across genres to take us from the familiar to the fantastic. He juxtaposes the genres and views that would be familiar from the history and representation of life at sea with illustrations melding actual with fantasy technologies, actual with imagined spaces, as well as depicting realities that exist only in his mind. Thus, the map (figure 5.2) and the frigate *Abraham Lincoln* (figure 5.3) are routine images in the contemporary practice of the sea. Captain Nemo taking observations with a sextant at noon offers a scene familiar from the work of the sea as well, except that here the scene is set on the deck of the imaginary submarine (figure 5.4). By the time we get to the underwater promenade in the Crespo Forest, we are fully immersed in the domain of imaginary technology, such as the imaginable, but as of yet unrealized, diving suit and aqualung, which Ned Land, the "man of masts and sails" (Conrad) skeptically contemplates in the illustration "I was ready to go" (figure 5.5).

Once Verne has secured his submarine's existence with the poetics of performability, he can go on to test its capacities in classic adventure form. A good example of gripping description occurs during Nemo's conquest of the South Pole.[70] In the course of leaving the scene of his triumph, Nemo meets "an enormous block of ice, an entire mountain,"

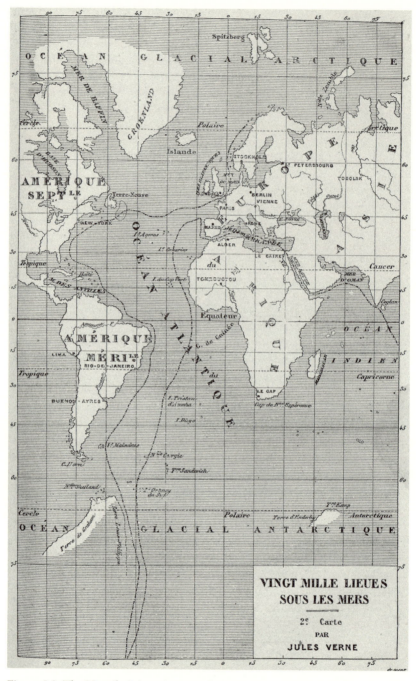

Figure 5.2. The *Nautilus*'s imaginary underwater voyages are traced on a world map, by then a familiar convention of surface sea voyage narratives. Second map, illustration by Alphonse de Neuville and Edouard Riou, in Jules Verne, *Vingt Mille Lieues sous les mers* (Paris: Hetzel, 186–?) Courtesy of the Harry Ransom Humanities Research Center, University of Texas at Austin.

Figure 5.3. The *Abraham Lincoln* is a recognizable ship of its era, and the scene gives no indication of its fabulous quarry. "The frigate *Abraham Lincoln*," illustration by Alphonse de Neuville and Edouard Riou, in Jules Verne, *Vingt Mille Lieues sous les mers* (Paris: Hetzel, 186–?). Courtesy of the Harry Ransom Humanities Research Center, University of Texas at Austin.

Figure 5.4. A familiar scene from daily life at sea—except for the mariner's garb and his observation platform. "Captain Nemo measuring the sun," illustration by Alphonse de Neuville and Edouard Riou, in Jules Verne, *Vingt Mille Lieues sous les mers* (Paris: Hetzel, 186-?). Courtesy of the Harry Ransom Humanities Research Center, University of Texas at Austin.

Figure 5.5. Ned Land, the man of mast and sails, skeptically inspects the future of technology. "I was ready to go," illustration by Alphonse de Neuville and Edouard Riou, in Jules Verne, *Vingt Mille Lieues sous les mers* (Paris: Hetzel, 186–?). Courtesy of the Harry Ransom Humanities Research Center, University of Texas at Austin.

that slips itself underneath the *Nautilus* and pushes the submarine into a "tunnel of ice" (315, 317). When the tunnel is blocked on all sides, Nemo and his companions find themselves encased in "an impenetrable wall of ice" (320). Nemo will then call upon his compleat craft: first, trying ice-mining, next, boiling water in his craft's engines to thin it further, and finally, turning danger to remedy by ramming the submarine against the bottom of the ice cube to dislodge an ice shard that will shatter the icy ceiling above. Across this labor, Verne also uses gripping description and thereby includes the reader in the stress. As the submarine runs out of air, Arronax gives a tongue-in-cheek description of what really would happen if the reader experienced breathless interest: "At about three in the afternoon, the feeling of anguish in me grew to an overwhelming degree. Yawns dislocated my jaws. My lungs worked fast as they searched for the combustive gas indispensable for breathing, now more and more rarefied," and so on for another page and a half until "[m]y face was purple, my lips blue, my faculties suspended. I could no longer see, I could no longer hear. All idea of time had vanished from my mind" (326–28).

Verne's success with readers testified to the achievement of his formula. Théophile Gautier was enthusiastic when he reviewed the *Voyages et aventures du capitaine Hatteras* in 1866. Differentiating Verne's travel narratives from imaginary voyage narratives, Gautier observed that "[i]f they have not really been achieved, and even if we still cannot achieve them, they present a scientifically rigorous possibility, and the most daring are only the paradox or extreme case deriving from a well-recognized truth." Indeed, Gautier explicitly compared Verne's manner of achieving this effect to the mariner's journal that, I have argued, Defoe used to invent the poetics of adventure in maritime adventure fiction. Gautier indeed proceeded to name the novel where Defoe originated the practice. Gautier called Verne's narrative "exact and detailed like a ship's log [that] creates the conclusive [*l'absolue*] sense of reality. Maritime mathematical and scientific techniques and technologies [*technicité*] used soberly in the appropriate situation give such a stamp of truth to this fantastical Forward that we cannot convince ourselves that he has not achieved his voyage of exploration. When Hatteras takes stock of the events, no ship's captain would find anything to rewrite, and so it is for even the smallest detail. Only Robinson's journal, drafted by de Foe, achieves this level of plausibility [*vraisemblance*]."[71]

CRAFT'S DAY OFF

As a proponent of symbolism, what would Gautier have made of other descriptions in Verne's subsequent *Twenty Thousand Leagues under the Sea*, which take the poetics of performability to unpragmatic domains?

Nowhere does the mariner's plain style make allowances for a promenade through the beauties of the underwater realm, like the promenade through the forest of Crespo: "Words are inadequate to recount such marvels! When even the artist's brush is incapable of depicting the unique effects of the liquid element, how could a pen begin to portray them?" (108). Nonetheless, Arronax does his best to describe the luxuriance of Nemo's underwater realm of refracted illumination: "The sun's rays struck the surface of the waves at an oblique angle, and the light was decomposed by the refaction as if pasing through a prism. It fell on the flowers, rocks, plantlets, shells, and polyps, and shaded their edges with all the colours of the solar spectrum. It was a marvel, a feast for the eyes, this interweaving of coloured tones, a true kaleidoscope of green, yellow, orange, violet, indigo and blue, the complete contents of a crazy colourist's palette!" (109). This enjoyment is not the province of the professor alone. Nemo is a connoisseur of the fine arts of life, and throughout the *Nautilus*, there are touches that speak to Nemo's inventive elegance, whose goal is pleasure and harmony, rather than utilitarian performance. It is impossible to think of any historical master of craft, or Crusoe, for that matter, devising a meal of savory sea turtle fillet, a ragout of dolphin liver, preserved sea cucumbers, a dessert cream from whale milk sweetened with sugar made from a kind of seaweed (fucus), and finished off with a cigar made of golden leaves from a seaweed that naturally produces nicotine.

What is the function of such whimsical moments that have nothing practical to contribute to the existence of the *Nautilus* or its ability to travel through the sea?[72] They could be redeemed for sea fiction's pragmatism. George Basalla argues that technological dreams are an important dimension to technological innovation, and he sees these dreams as generated not just by technologists but by science fiction, including "Jules Verne's submarines and spacecraft."[73] For Basalla, such dreams are the signature of technologies taken to the limits of existing practices and beyond in quest of perfectibility. Basalla writes that technological dreams "epitomize the technologists' propensity to go beyond what is technically feasible" and "provide an entry into the richness of the imagination and into the sources of the novelty that is at the heart of Western technology."[74]

But there is a less instrumental answer to the question as well. Across the adventure of the sea, practical matters have taken center stage. Though creativity and imagination are part of craft, the compleat mariner deploys them to instrumental ends. In such moments as the underwater banquet and the forest at Crespo, Verne gives the pragmatic imagination a day off, freeing it to improvise, unconcerned with expediency and aim. At the beginning of the lineage of maritime adventure fiction, Defoe harnessed adventure fiction to the mariner's craft to try to tame the excesses of the projecting spirit. Verne's science fiction at the other end of this history ends by liberating the type of impracticable schemes that Defoe wanted

Jack Aubrey, Jack Sparrow, and the Whole Sick Crew

WHEN CONRAD WROTE, craft was fading, but its empowered agency was within cultural memory. Across the twentieth century, even the memory of craft would disappear. Prudence, sea legs, and the pragmatic imagination remain essential for safe navigation, for professional seamen, and for pleasure boaters as well. And ocean transport remains essential to our global infrastructure. But it is only when something goes drastically wrong that we even read news of the ships criss-crossing our terraqueous globe, let alone recall the skills of their operators.

At the same time, to "boldly go where no man has gone before," to cite the motto of Captain James Kirk and the crew of the Starship *Enterprise*, remains constitutive of our modernity. And in our time, too, we continue to glamourize the work of navigating high-risk zones at the Edge; zones of flux, danger, and destruction. Astronauts, hackers, and financiers have been some avatars of the mariner in the later twentieth century. So, too, have scientists, though the practice of zones on Edge remains in our time, as in the era of global sail, divorced from humanitarian or ethical aims. The leisure pursuit of extreme sports, and the journalism depicting it, from *Outside Magazine* to the catalogs of the outdoor clothing and gear company Patagonia, offer an attenuated form of craft's allure.

The afterlife of craft is visible as well in the thriving genre of popular adventure fiction. From Verne's *Journey to the Moon*, space adventure fiction extended to the universe sea fiction's trials of craft. Both detective fiction and spy fiction, too, take up the field of information as one of the Edge zones of our time, represented in the United States by the novels of Tom Clancy, John Grisham, and Michael Crichton. In the United States, space travel and spy fiction met the exploding frontier of cybernetics to yield cyberfiction. William Gibson's *Neuromancer* (1984) and Neal Stephenson's *Snow Crash* (1992) are two examples of a genre where sea adventure fiction's poetics of problem-solving become warped and nonlinear, flexing to a frontier at the intersection of virtual reality, the psyche, and futuristic space. In such a world, the problem-solving of the cunning reader becomes folded in upon itself as well. This nonlinear time-space is well adapted to the illusionistic power of cinema, spectacularly on display in Larry and Andrew Wachowski's *The Matrix* (1999).

Indeed, from the dawn of the twentieth century, film has proved a medium well-suited to conjure the action-driven pattern of sea fiction's adventure formula, whether in warped or classic form. To take the case of sea fiction alone, already in the silent era, Hugo's *Toilers of the Sea* was adapted multiple times, as it would be in the era of sound. *Moby-Dick*, too, has gone through a number of film versions, starting with Millard Webb's silent *The Sea Beasts* (1926) starring John Barrymore. The novels of Verne have been adapted, emphasizing both their whimsy and their thrills, from the pioneer Georges Méliès's 1902 *Le Voyage dans la lune* to Eric Brevig's *Journey to the Center of the Earth* (2008). Twentieth-century authors have continued to pen sea novels that made captivating popular films, viz the novels of Sabatini that Michael Curtiz would adapt, such as *The Sea Hawk* and *Captain Blood*.

Writers pushing at the edges of their art, too, have used sea adventure novels as a jumping off point for experiments in narrative and thought since the later nineteenth century. Throughout these novels, both characters and adventure poetics go AWOL, abnegating their performances of craft. In the last decades of the nineteenth century, the French naval officer Julian Viaud, who used the pen name Pierre Loti, set novels in seafaring milieus—the British Navy, amidst Breton and Basque fishermen—but refused dangers at sea or the performance of craft. Instead, his novels freeze adventures at sea to plumb the layered, nonlinear time of fantasy, which Loti ornaments with exotic details. Thus, *Aziyadé, Extrait des notes et lettres d'un lieutenant de la marine anglaise entré au service de la Turquie le 10 mai 1876 tué dans les murs de Kars, le 27 octobre 1877* (1879) starts with an English naval officer who goes AWOL in Constantinople on a voyage of sexual discovery. This voyage leads him to love a beautiful harem girl along with a handsome young man, and eventually to fight against his country in the Turkish Army. Another upright naval officer who explores his fanasy frontiers of gay love is Lieutenant Seblon in Jean Genet's *Querelle de Brest* (1953). Behind his demeanor of craft, Seblon is wracked by gay desires he cannot openly avow, in Genet's complex rewriting of Melville's late novella *Billy Budd, Sailor*, which remained unpublished until 1924.

Bohemian social rebellion along with a rebellion against adventure narrative's illusions disrupt sea adventure in Thomas Pynchon's *V.* (1963), a spy novel of sorts, starring a seaman hero, Benny Profane, member of a bohemian group of social renegades who baptize themselves the Whole Sick Crew. The Polish Stanislas Lem uses sea adventure fiction's plot of problem-solving to launch his capable men of action into rogue voyages beyond the line in science fiction. In *Solaris*, which takes to outer space the creepy ending of Poe's *Narrative of Arthur Gordon Pym of Nantucket*, the sublime space of the universe folds into a sea of pain, sucking the astronaut hero, a pattern of his profession, into a voyage exploring the torments of his memory. This sublime fusion of outer space with the psyche figures prominently in the film made of Lem's novel *Solaris* by Andrei Tarkovsky.

Craft is also AWOL due to forces beyond the astronaut's conscious control in Arthur C. Clarke's *2001: A Space Odyssey* (1968), as in the film adaptation by Stanley Kubrick. In the novel *2001*, practical reason is betrayed by the technology that is usually its willing servant, when the computer Hal takes on a life of its own. Like the mysterious planet's sea of pain in Lem's *Solaris*, Clarke's marvel of artificial intelligence launches the astronaut Bowman, the twenty-first century Odysseus, not only beyond the longing to return home but also beyond any life marked by earthly clock-time, perhaps into the exploration of post-Newtonian four-plus dimensions? In Kubrick's film adaptation of the novel, cinematic technology is deviated from its willing service as well—in this case, the service to realistic illusion. Rather than projecting a plausible world, Kubrick's space sequences catapult the viewer into visual trips at the juncture of space travel, hallucination, and exploration of non–realistic optical effects made possible by the film medium.

Outer and inner space also fuse as the voyage landscape in twentieth-century classics where sea fiction's poetics of problem-solving address death as the final frontier. Ernest Hemingway's *The Old Man and the Sea* (1952; part of a "sea trilogy" he never finished), takes the occasion of a fisherman's struggle with a monstrous beast to depict danger and the horizon of death as defining the human condition. The dangerous route of a mail plane over Argentina offers a similar occasion in *Vol de nuit* (1931) by Antoine de Saint-Exupéry, who himself disappeared over the Mediterranean while flying with the Allied Forces in 1944.

Classic sea adventure fiction, too, remains popular into the turn of the millennium.[1] Sea adventure series have proved particularly appealing to children and adolescents across the twentieth century, both classics like *Treasure Island* and contemporary historical works. The most famous twentieth-century series include C. S. Forester's books following the career of Horatio Hornblower, from his start as a midshipman, along with Arthur Ransome's *Swallows and Amazons* series, inaugurated in 1930, where heroic maritime adventures explicitly are scaled to child's play. In such tales, young readers of the twentieth century, too, enjoy the heroism of resourcefulness and the ethos of skilled work, which is, after all, the reason Rousseau recommended *Robinson Crusoe* to his pupil Emile in 1762 in the novel entitled *Emile, or on Education*. The *Tintin* series by Hergé consists of graphic novels that capitalize on sea adventure fiction's poetics of problem-solving utilized in spy fiction. The armchair sailor's playful games with information take on color and shape in the travels of the resourceful Tintin and his friend, the bumbling sailor Captain Haddock. Coloring books of notorious pirates are a spin-off of adventure literature at sea that offer children the chance to imagine a world where labor is heroic and yields self-gratification. As they tint the woodcuts of Captain Teach and Anne Bonny wielding pencils and markers, children enjoy pirates' transgressions as coloring beyond the lines.

The romance of piracy has remained alive for grownups as well, cultivated in cinema, as in popular culture. Arguably the most radically revisionist pirate movie is Ulrike Ottinger's feminist *Madame X*, the pirate queen (1977), who storms the masculine bastion of craft with the pirate's carnival of social norms, and reclaims it in the name of female pleasure. Gore Verbinski's *Pirates of the Caribbean* (2003) offers the pirate carnival to mainstream audiences, introducing comedy into the serious business of work at sea. Captain Jack Sparrow, inseparable from his eccentric portrayal by the actor Johnny Depp, would have been a worthy profile in craft for the eighteenth-century Captain Johnson, had Johnson admitted humor into his violent cosmos, where piratical transgressions are prosecuted in deadly earnest. The incompleat mariner Sparrow/Depp, in contrast, makes a carnival of practical reason, with his venal mockery of craft that somehow achieves its aim, epitomized by his compass that does not point North yet that can lead to the heart's desire. Embodiment, a quality possessed in spades by Depp's Sparrow, is an essential element of his appeal. In our era when so much human contact has become mediated and abstract, audiences soak up the aura of the human body along with the Caribbean sun, which emanates from Jack's camp articulation, his wild hair, smudged makeup, and tattered bohemian fashion peppered with rum, dirt, and sand.

On the honorable side of the world beyond the line, the reputable, upright Captain Jack Aubrey carries the standard of sea adventure fiction into our present. His creator, Patrick O'Brian, depends on the gulf between the heroic era of global sail and our present for the success of a poetics that produced twenty-plus sea novels. Criss-crossing the oceans of the globe during the Napoleonic Era, Jack Aubrey and his friend, the doctor-spy Stephen Maturin, meet with remarkable occurrences at sea that O'Brian has lifted from the maritime book, both fact and fiction, across its history. Through the end of the nineteenth century, this appropriation would have been piracy, for such books and deeds were legend. With the eclipse of the global age of sail, O'Brian's plunder becomes historical salvage.

Of course, in our time, there remain readers knowledgeable in the history and practice of sail, and part of O'Brian's success is that he can write on two levels, a tactic of sea adventure authors from the time of Cooper. Those conversant in the history of the sea and/or sailing enjoy recognizing familiar knowledge in unfamiliar contexts, while most audiences, in the previously cited words of Dana on Cooper, "follow . . . [its] minute nautical manœuvers with breathless interest, who do not know the name of a rope in the ship; and perhaps with none the less admiration and enthusiasm for their want of acquaintance with the professional detail."[2] To initiate these nonspecialist audiences into the bygone work of the sea, O'Brian provides technical explanation and framing, far more extensive than that offered by Cooper or other previous sea adventure authors. O'Brian further eases ignorant readers into sea fiction's adventures of craft by inviting them through the now more familiar gate of the novel of manners. His series hinges on the interest of Aubrey and Maturin, characterized as private individuals, with psychological strengths, weaknesses, and depths, rather than portrayed as patterns of their profession. O'Brian also leavens sea fiction's performance of craft with the novel of manners' domestic details. This domestication extends from the life of sailors home on land to shipboard habits. There, dangers at sea are interspersed with the homey scraping of amateur string-playing and whiffs of the mariner's substantive if somewhat indigestible comfort meals, including porridge, rusty bacon, Irish soda bread, and the like.

But though the approach is from the novel of manners, the path leads, in O'Brian's skillful management, to the empowered agency of craft contending with remarkable occurrences at sea. One last example, then: the ending drama of *The Thirteen Gun Salute*, which O'Brian has taken from a historical source it would by now be redundant to name. In this drama, Captain Aubrey's ship, the *Diane*, runs ashore on an uncharted reef in the Southern Pacific. To cite Captain Aubrey: "We have struck an unknown, uncharted reef at high water. We are now aground. . . . There is a strong likelihood that by lightening her we may float her off the reef at the next high tide. . . . In any event we are about to lower down the boats."[3] What follows is a heroic struggle: "All day they lightened ship. . . The pumping went on all the time. . . . The best bower, backed with the smaller stream anchor, they lowered carefully." As Aubrey and his crew struggle to heave the *Diane* off the reef, they are engaged in an "arduous, complex task," one that involves "very severe and often highly-skilled labour day and night with peaks of intensity at full tide as extreme as anything Jack had known."

Notes

INTRODUCTION: SEAFARING ODYSSEUS

1. G.W.F. Hegel, *Hegel's Philosophy of Right*, trans. and notes by T. M. Knox (New York: Oxford University Press, 1967), 151. First published in 1821.

2. E.G.R. Taylor, *The Haven–Finding Art, A History of Navigation from Odysseus to Captain Cook* (London: Hollis & Carter, 1971), 40.

3. Georg Lukács, *The Theory of the Novel*, trans. Anna Bostock (Cambridge, MA: MIT Press, 1974), 88.

4. Lukács, 41. Lukács's influential insight has subsequently been applied by critics to both the eighteenth- and nineteenth-century European novels of education and maturation discussed in *The Theory of the Novel*, as well as to novels extending into our time from across the globe, including works by Toni Morrison, V. S. Naipaul, and Gabriel García Márquez, among many others.

5. Theodor Adorno and Max Horkheimer, *Dialectic of Enlightenment*, trans. John Cumming (New York: Continuum Books, 1972), 46, 61.

6. Other useful theories of adventure fiction include Jacques Rivière's *Le Roman d'aventure* (Paris: Editions des Syrtes, 2000) and Jean-Yves Tadié's *Le Roman d'aventures* (Paris: Presses Universitaires de France, 1982). For studies of adventure literature related to sea fiction, see, among others, Martin Green's *Dreams of Adventure, Deeds of Empire* (New York: Basic Books, 1979); Michael Nerlich's *Ideology of Adventure*, trans. Ruth Crowley (Minneapolis: University of Minnesota Press, 1987), 2 vols.; and Andrea White's *Joseph Conrad and the Adventure Tradition* (New York: Cambridge University Press, 1993).

7. See Mikhail Bakhtin's argument in "Forms of Time and of the Chronotope in the Novel," in *The Dialogic Imagination: Four Essays*, ed. Michael Holquist, trans. Caryl Emerson and Michael Holquist (Austin: University of Texas Press, 1981), 84–258.

8. Francis Bacon, "The New Organon," in *The New Organon and Related Writings*, ed. Fulton H. Anderson (Indianapolis: Bobbs-Merrill, 1984), 118.

9. Joseph Conrad, *The Mirror of the Sea* (Marlboro, VT: Marlboro Press, 1988), 64.

10. Jonathan Lamb, *Preserving the Self in the South Seas 1680–1840* (Chicago: University of Chicago Press, 2001), 49.

11. To note that armchair sailors reveled in the romance of work at sea is not to say that work on a sailing ship had anything romantic about it. Working conditions were brutal, mortality was high, and the ship was a violent, authoritarian environment. As Samuel Johnson famously put the matter, "No man will be a sailor who has contrivance enough to get himself into a jail; for being in a ship is being in a jail, with the chance of being drowned"; moreover "[a] man in a jail

has more room, better food, and commonly better company." James Boswell, *The Life of Samuel Johnson*, ed. David Womersley (New York: Penguin, 2008), 186.

12. For an overview of the maritime print corpus, see John Hattendorf's "*The Boundless Deep . . .*" (Providence, RI: John Carter Brown Library, 2003). See as well my essay "Historical Fiction," in *Oxford Encyclopedia of Maritime History* (New York: Oxford University Press, 2007), vol. 3, 2–7.

13. In using historical sea voyage narratives to understand the mariner's mystique, I am focusing on works by Dampier, Cook, and others, which literary and cultural historians have more frequently utilized for their portrayals of first encounters between Europeans and indigenous peoples and to understand the history of colonialism. My aim in shifting the focus is to attend to understudied aspects of this corpus; its delineation of work, drawing attention to the role played by embodied reason in the history of modernity.

14. "One of the most expensive books" of the mid-seventeenth century was Sir Robert Dudley's *Dell'arcano del mare* (Florence, 1646), "the first sea atlas to include charts for the entire world based on the Mercator projection," as well as "instruction in navigation techniques, drawings and diagrams on ship architecture, and even naval tactics for use in warfare." Hattendorf, 94, 93.

15. "According to O.H.K. Spate, voyages outstripped divinity as the most popular form of print in the first part of the Eighteenth Century." Conference statement for the History of the Maritime Book Conference, hosted jointly by Princeton University and the National Maritime Museum, Greenwich, UK, October 4–5, 2002. Available at *http://www.princeton.edu/~maritime/*; consulted June 2008. The "Term Catalogues of 1668–1709 show voyages to have been the most popular genre of literature published then, and that this was a new popularity," Martin Green tells us in *Dreams of Adventure, Deeds of Empire*, 71.

16. On the shifting criteria for mimesis and the importance of this aesthetic in the rise of the novel, see, for example, Michael McKeon's *The Origins of the English Novel, 1600–1740* (Baltimore: Johns Hopkins University Press, 1987) and Catherine Gallagher's *Nobody's Story: The Vanishing Acts of Women Writers in the Marketplace, 1670–1820* (Berkeley: University of California Press, 1994).

17. In Italian literature, for example, Emilio Salgari was a master of maritime adventure fiction, which he started writing for newspaper serialization in the late nineteenth century. His countryman, Rafael Sabatini, wrote sea novels in the early twentieth century, though he wrote in English rather than his native Italian. Sabatini's novels included the 1922 *Captain Blood: His Odyssey* (Washington, D.C.: Regnery Publishing, 1998), which Michael Curtiz made into the legendary movie starring Errol Flynn. In the nineteenth century, the reach of maritime adventure fiction extended to the transatlantic Spanish-speaking world. Benito Pérez Galdós penned a historical novel about Trafalgar (1873), *Trafalgar: La Corte de Carlos IV*, ed. Dolores Troncoso (Barcelona: Critica, 1995). On pirate novels in nineteenth-century Latin America, see Nina Gerassi-Navarro, *Pirate Novels: Fictions of Nation Building in Spanish America* (Durham, NC: Duke University Press, 1999).

18. Conrad, *The Mirror of the Sea*, 64.

19. Daniel Defoe, *Robinson Crusoe*, ed. Michael Shinagel (New York: W.W. Norton, 1994), 220. The novel is in fact titled *The Life and Strange Surprising*

Adventures of Robinson Crusoe of York, Mariner, and I will refer to it in this fashion when the title's wording belongs to my argument.

20. Certainly, journalists, doctors, teachers, scholars, factory workers, farmers, valets, coal miners, and thieves tread across the novel's stage. Novels dignify them, however, as protagonists through the events of their biographies; their educations, loves, births, and deaths, as well as their struggles for self-realization.

21. Elaine Scarry, *Resisting Representation* (New York: Oxford University Press, 1994), 65. Catherine Gallagher's *The Industrial Reformation of English Fiction* (Chicago: University of Chicago Press, 1988) confirms the extent to which workers' lives are at issue when workers figure as protagonists in novels, rather than a dramatization of the labor process itself. Bruce Robbins also reveals nineteenth-century realist and domestic novels' lack of attention concerning the processes of labor in *The Servant's Hand* (Durham, NC: Duke University Press, 1993), though he makes a different point: that this oversight indicates the culture's ideological blindspot concerning industrial labor.

22. Conrad, *The Mirror of the Sea*, 20.

23. Victor Hugo, *Les Travailleurs de la mer*, ed. Yves Gohin (Paris: Gallimard, 1980), 593.

24. Victor Hugo, *Toilers of the Sea*, trans. Isabel F. Hapgood (New York: Signet Classics, 2000), xiii.

25. See Giancarlo Maiorino, *At the Margins of the Renaissance: Lazarillo de Tormes and the Picaresque Art of Surviva*l (University Park, PA: Penn State University Press, 2003).

26. On the emergence of the domestic novel from women's how-to literature, see, for example, Nancy Armstrong's *Desire and Domestic Fiction* (New York: Oxford University Press, 1987).

27. Lukács, *The Theory of the Novel*, 36.

28. The terrestrial bias of novel studies has never extended to specialists who work on maritime literature, such as Robert Foulke, Thomas Philbrick, and Monique Brosse in France. But theorists have not connected such erudition with more general inquiry into the novel's cultural significance.

29. Allan Sekula, *Fish Story* (Düsseldorf: Richter Verlag, 2002), 48.

30. Maritime issues figure prominently amidst the essays collected in *The Global Eighteenth Century* (Baltimore: Johns Hopkins University Press, 2005), edited by Felicity Nussbaum, a beacon in the new eighteenth-century studies. The contributors to the collection *Fictions of the Sea. Critical Perspectives on the Ocean in British Literature and Culture* edited by Bernhard Klein (Farnham, Surrey, UK: Ashgate Press, 2002) use the maritime perspective and a transnational focus to rethink the British literary tradition across its long history. These are just two among numerous recent important works that connect the general debates currently shaping the field of literary and cultural studies with expertise that used to be the province of maritime specialists. Other works include *Preserving the Self in the South Seas, 1680–1840* (Chicago: University of Chicago Press, 2001), by Jonathan Lamb, which connects the writings of mariners first charting the Pacific with political, epistemological, and poetic discourse being elaborated simultaneously in Europe. Cesare Casarino's *Modernity at Sea: Melville, Marx, Conrad in Crisis* (Minneapolis: University of Minnesota Press, 2002) examines the use

made of sea novels by modernist writers like Melville and Conrad to expose the contradictions of late capitalist modernity. Ian Baucom explores the impact of the slave trade in shaping a melancholy Romantic lineage in *Specters of the Atlantic: Finance Capital, Slavery, and the Philosophy of History* (Durham, NC: Duke University Press, 2005). Anna Neill explores how maritime adventurers were recuperated for imperial and capitalist projects in *British Discovery Literature and the Rise of Global Commerce* (New York: Palgrave, 2002). At the time I was finishing this manuscript, Hester Blum's *The View from the Masthead* appeared (Durham, NC: University of North Carolina Press, 2008), portraying American sea fiction in the antebellum period. So did Christopher Miller's *The French Atlantic Triangle: Literature and Culture of the Slave Trade* (Durham, NC: Duke University Press, 2008), where maritime writings and issues figure prominently at the scale of a multi-lingual Atlantic region.

CHAPTER 1: THE MARINER'S CRAFT

1. Richard Walter, *A Voyage Round the World In the Years MDCCXL, I, II, III, IV. By George Anson, Esq.* (London: John and Paul Knapton, 1748).

2. Samuel Sturmy, *The Mariner's Magazine* (London: E Cotes, 1669), np.

3. Luís Vaz de Camões, *The Lusíads*, trans. and notes by Landeg White (New York: Oxford University Press, 2001). Lines cited are from p. 115, or Canto V, stanzas 86 and 89.

4. Thomas Carlyle, *History of Friedrich II of Prussia called Frederick the Great* (New York: Scribner, Welford and Company, 1873), vol. 4, 285.

5. Ibid.

6. On Defoe as the likely author of *A General History of the Pirates*, see James Kelly, "Defoe's Library," *The Library* 3, no. 3 (2002): 284–301.

7. Herman Melville, *Moby-Dick*, in Herman Melville, *Redburn, White-Jacket, Moby-Dick*, ed. G. Thomas Tanselle (New York: Library of America, 1983), 782.

8. There is an afterlife of craft for seafarers even today. Though technologies have radically routinized the practice, basic strategies remain the same, due to the unchanging environment of the violent, powerful, and uncontrollable ocean. Robert Foulke's description of seamanship in general corresponds in many points to the portrait of craft emerging in the following pages. Foulke writes that it is "a learned body of knowledge derived from past experience, applied physics, naval architecture, and marine engineering," encompassing "many specific skills in operating and maintaining machinery, handling boats, anchors, booms, winches," and state-of-the-art navigational equipment, and entailing also "a working knowledge of tides, currents, wave formations, weather patterns, aids to navigation, and rules of the road." Foulke distills the masterful practical demeanor required of this "art demanding foresight, initiative, the ability to improvise, a sense of proportion, and finely tuned judgment as seafarers deal with an unpredictable ocean." Foulke continues, "The practice of seamanship requires precision in the use of an extensive technical vocabulary, scrupulosity in the maintenance of hulls, spars, sails, engines, and equipment, reliability in following established routines, alertness to changing conditions at sea, and readiness

to cope with emergencies quickly and decisively. And because the sea is neither totally predictable nor tolerant of human mistakes, the practice of seamanship is often complex, demanding imagination and discrimination more than adherence to fixed rules of procedure." Robert Foulke, *The Sea Voyage Narrative* (New York: Routledge, 1997), 22.

9. *Cunning Intelligence in Greek Culture and Society*, by the philosophers Marcel Détienne and Jean-Pierre Vernant, offers a model for how to extract an ethos from texts where it plays a formative but unconceptualized role. In this study, Détienne and Vernant theorize a kind of excellence in action, *metis* (cunning), that, they argue, Plato and Aristotle refused to dignify because of its instrumental and potentially unethical application. Largely absent from the pages of philosophy, the traits of *metis* are instead presented through figures of speech and thought, as well as anecdotes found in books written in genres ranging from literature and history to how-to manuals. Attentive to motifs and figures that recur, and to the semantic fields shaping their formulations, Détienne and Vernant synthesize such patterns to give a nuanced conceptualization of *metis*. See Marcel Détienne and Jean-Pierre Vernant, *Cunning Intelligence in Greek Culture and Society*, trans. Janet Lloyd (Chicago: University of Chicago Press, 1991). I return to craft and *metis* in the notes to this chapter's closing section, "Practical Reason (Seventh Century BC–AD 2010)."

10. J. C. Beaglehole, "Textual Introduction," in *The Journals of Captain James Cook on his Voyages of Discovery*, ed. J. C. Beaglehole (Woodbridge, UK: The Boydell Press, 1999), vol. 1, ccliii. Hawkesworth's naration of Cook's voyage is found in volumess 2 and 3 of Hawkesworth's *An Account of the Voyages Undertaken by the Order of his Present Majesty for Making Discoveries in the Southern Hemisphere, And successively performed by Commodore Byron, Captain Wallis, Captain Carteret, and Captain Cook, in the Dolphin, the Swallow, and the Endeavour*. London: W. Strahan and T. Cadell, 1773, 3 volumes.

11. For a comparison of how each account narrates the same events, see the pages on Cook's voyage on the South Seas website of the Australian government: *http://southseas.nla.gov.au/index.html*; consulted June 2009.

12. Beaglehole notes Hawkesworth's embroideries indicating the professional writer. To use Beaglehole's words, "In a narrative which professed to be his own . . . he [Cook] may well have been astonished to encounter so many 'sentiments' upon Death, and the Nature of Fire, and the Romish Religion—though perhaps even more astonished at the references to Fénélon's Telemachus, and to the chaste Diana, with her nymphs, at Tolaga Bay." Beaglehole goes on to compare a passage from Cook's journals with one where "the studious imitator of Johnson succumbed." Here is Hawkesworth's rendition of how Cook perceives the attitude of the *Endeavour*'s crew amidst the terrible peril of shipwreck on 13 June 1770: "Upon this occasion I must observe, both in justice and gratitude to the ships company, and the Gentlemen on board, that although in the midst of our distress every one seemed to have a just sense of his danger, yet no passionate exclamations, or frantic gestures, were to be heard or seen; every one appeared to have the perfect possession of his mind, and every one exerted himself to the utmost, with a quiet and patient perseverance, equally distant from the tumultuous violence of terror, and the gloomy inactivity of despair." Compare

this to Cook's own version: "In justice to the Ships Company I must say that no men ever behaved better than they have done on this occasion animated by the beheavour of every gentleman on board every man seem'd to have a just sense of the danger we were in and exerted himself to the very utmost." J. C. Beaglehole, "Textual Introduction," in *The Journals of Captain James Cook*, vol. 1, ccxlvi–ccxlvii.

13. Beaglehole, ccii. Beaglehole discusses Cook's different manuscripts and their variants in his editorial comments on *The Journals of Captain James Cook*. For a summary of this discussion, see also Philip Edwards's introduction to the abridged Penguin edition of *The Journals of Captain Cook* (New York: Penguin Books, 2003), which he selected and edited.

14. James Cook, *The Journals of Captain Cook*, prepared from the original manuscripts by J. C. Beaglehole, 1955–1967, and selected and edited by Philip Edwards (New York: Penguin Books, 2003). This quote is from pages 138–139 and the "low, woody, islands" quote above from page 138. I use the Penguin edition because it selects key passages and is easily available. All misspellings, syntax, and absence of punctuation are a textual transcription of the original. Citations will be referenced by page number in the remainder of this chapter.

15. Samuel de Champlain, *Treatise on Seamanship and the Duty of a Good Seaman*, in *Works*, ed. H. P. Biggar (Toronto: The Champlain Society, 1936), vol. 6 (writings from 1629–1632; trans. W. D. LeSueur and H. H. Langton), 267.

16. Ibid., 267–8.

17. Ibid., 263.

18. Ibid., 260.

19. Dampier got his start as a pirate, and then became a privateer who pursued Spanish booty in the New World in the name of the English crown. He also circumnavigated the globe three times, writing *A New Voyage Round the World*, which was avidly read by armchair travelers and scientists alike. His *Discourse of the Trade-Winds* continued to be used for its hydrography into the nineteenth century. On Dampier's career, see Percy Adams, introduction to William Dampier, *A New Voyage Round the World* (New York: Dover Publications, 1968), vi–xv.

20. Champlain, 263.

21. Ibid., 261–62.

22. Ibid, 259.

23. J. Atkinson, *Epitome of the Art of Navigation; or a Short, Easy and Methodical Way to become a Compleat Navigator*, rev. and corrected by William Mountaine (London: William Mount and Thomas Page, 1744), 266.

24. Sanson Le Cordier, *Journal de Navigation, dans lequel est pleinement enseigné, & clairement démontré l'Art & la Science des Navigateurs* (Au Havre de Grace: Jacques Cruchet, 1683).

25. Ibid., 2.

26. Ibid., 2–3.

27. Antonio Pigafetta, *Magellan's Voyage, A Narrative Account of the First Circumnavigation*, trans. and ed. R. A. Skelton (New York: Dover, 1994), 41.

28. John Hattendorf, "*The Boundless Deep* . . ." (Providence, RI: John Carter Brown Library, 2003), 51. Hattendorf is citing Henry Manwayring's *Sea-man's Dictionary* (1644).

29. This account first appeared in a pamphlet. It was recently published as *Account of the very remarkable loss of the Great Galleon S. João*, in *The Tragic History of the Sea*, ed. and trans. C. R. Boxer, foreword by Josiah Blackmore, who was also its translator; other accounts in the collection are translated by Boxer (Minneapolis: University of Minnesota Press, 2001).

30. Le Cordier, 2.

31. See, for example, Lorraine Daston and Katherine Parks, *Wonders and the Order of Nature, 1150–1750* (New York: Zone Books, 1998). See also Stephen Greenblatt's discussion of the remarkable in New World contexts in *Marvelous Possessions: The Wonder of the New World* (Chicago: University of Chicago Press, 1992).

32. See Pigafetta, 41, for "strange" and "uncommon."

33. Champlain, 259.

34. Captain Thomas James, *The Strange and Dangerous Voyage of Captaine Thomas James, in his intended Discovery of the Northwest Passage into the South Sea* (London: John Legatt, 1633), 7.

35. Ibid., 15.

36. Champlain, 268.

37. Joseph Banks, *Endeavour Journal*, entry from June 11, 1770. Derived from the State Library of New South Wales 1998 Transcription of Banks's *Endeavour Journal*, vol. 2, 288. Published by South Seas, using the Web Academic Resource Publisher, 2004. Available at *http://nla.gov.au/nla.cs-ss-jrnl-banks-17700611*; consulted December 2009.

38. Champlain, 268.

39. James, 3. This tactic was used by captains as far back as Odysseus. In order to encourage his men to make it through the shoals of Scylla and Charybdis, Odysseus hid his knowledge of the danger, and the fact that some of his crew would be killed:

> . . . . I conceal'd
> The heavy wounds, that never would be heal'd,
> To be by *Scylla* open'd; for their feare
> Would then have robd all, of all care to stere;
> Or stirre an oare, and made them hide beneath:
> When they, and all, had died an idle death.

Cited from the translation by George Chapman of Homer, *The Odyssey*. (London: imprinted by Rich. Field for Nathaniell Butter, 1614), 186.

40. Daniel Defoe, *An Essay upon Projects* (London: Tho. Cockerill, 1697), 17.

41. Adams, introduction to Dampier, vii.

42. *The Oxford Companion to Ships and the Sea*, ed. Peter Kemp (New York: Oxford University Press, 1988), 438.

43. These narratives include Captain John Dean's *A Narrative of the Sufferings, Preservation, and Deliverance, of Capt. John Dean and Company; in the Nottingham-Gally of London* (London: S. Popping, 1711); a refutation of this account in a narrative published by seamen on board, Christopher Langman, Nicholas Mellon, and George White, *A True Account of the Voyage of the Nottingham-Galley of London* (London: S. Popping, 1711); as well as two other sensationalized versions of the events.

44. Dampier, 33. In a reverse transfer of knowledge, Dampier describes how a Moskito Indian marooned on the Juan Fernando island that was to be the abode of Alexander Selkirk some years later borrows from European know-how. Armed with a gun but no bullets, the Indian manufactured "Harpoons, Lances, Hook, and a long Knife, heating the pieces first in the Fire, which he struck with his Gunflint, and a piece of the Barrel of his Gun, which he hardned; having learnt to do that among the *English*," 66.

45. Joseph Conrad, *Lord Jim* (New York: Penguin, 1986), 47.

46. Joseph Conrad, *Typhoon*, in *Typhoon and Other Stories*, ed J. H. Stape (NY: Penguin, 2007), 32–33.

47. Banks June 12, 1770. Available at http://nla.gov.au/nla.cs-ss-jrnl-banks -17700612: consulted December 2009.

48. See George Vancouver, *A Voyage of Discovery to the North Pacific Ocean and Around the World*, first published in 1798.

49. Champlain, 262.

50. Ibid., 262.

51. Thomas R. Adams, *The Non-Cartographical Maritime Works published by Mount and Page* (London: The Bibliographical Society, 1985), 7–10, 16–17. Figures are based on Adams.

52. Charles Saltonstall, *The Navigator* (London: George Herlock, 1636), 7.

53. Sturmy, 17.

54. Captain Daniel Newhouse, *The Whole Art of Navigation* (London, 1708), Book III, 111.

55. James Love, *The Mariner's Jewel: Or, A Pocket Companion for the Ingenious* (London: Alexander Sims, 1703), 92.

56. Cited in Beaglehole, "Textual Introduction" to Cook's *Journals*, vol. 1, ccxlvi.

57. Ibid., cxciv.

58. Richard Mount, introduction to Daniel Newhouse, *The Whole Art of Navigation*, 3rd ed. (London: Richard Mount, 1708), n.p.

59. Cited in J. C. Beaglehole, "Cook the Navigator," *Proceedings of the Royal Society of London. Series A, Mathematical and Physical Sciences* 314, no. 1516 (December 16, 1969): 33.

60. Ibid., 28.

61. Saltsonstall, 1–2.

62. Champlain, 266.

63. Nathaniel Colson, *The Mariner's New Kalendar* (London: J. Darby 1677), 154–155.

64. Thomas Crosby, *Mariner's Guide* (London: James Hodges, 1751).

65. These ordinances were dealing with provisions. The "steward and cook of every ship" were charged "to render to the captain weekly (or oftener) a just and plain account of expenses of the victuals, as well flesh, fish, biscuit, meat, or bread, as also of beer, wine, oil or vinegar, and all other kind of victualling under their charge, that no waste be made." Richard Hakluyt, *Voyages and Discoveries*, a recent edition of Hakluyt's *Principal Navigations, Voyages, Traffiques and Discoveries of the English Nation*, ed., abridged, and intro. by Jack Beeching (New York: Penguin, 1972), 56.

66. Le Cordier, 3.

67. John Smith, *A Sea Grammar, with the Plaine Exposition of Smiths Accidence for young Sea-men, enlarged* (London: John Haviland, 1627), n.p.

68. R. A. Skelton's introduction to Pigafetta, 27.

69. Robert Marteau, *Fleuve sans fin. Journal de Saint-Laurent*, cited in Christophe Hardy, *Les Mots de la Mer* (Paris: Belin, 2002), 91.

70. Ilse Vickers links Daniel Defoe's method of narration to the way in which "the compilers of Baconian natural histories insisted upon the value and necessity of a simple, plain style," an insistence that the Royal Society underscores from its founding in the 1640s (44). Ilse Vickers, *Defoe and the New Sciences* (New York: Cambridge University Press, 1997), 44. Vickers quotes John Wilkins, a scientist formative in shaping the Royal Society: "'Obscurity in the discourse', Wilkins was convinced, was an 'argument of ignorance in the minde', while 'the greatest learning is to be seen in the greatest plainnesse'" (Wilkins 1646: 72). The new style "must persuade by its simplicity and integrity: it 'must be plain and natu-rall.'" Both these quotes citing Wilkins are found in Vickers, 44. In "the Baconian reform of science and education," Vickers emphasizes "the relation between science and language. . . . The distrust of language and the concomitant demand for plain prose which can be detected in the middle years of the seventeenth century, had three main sources: first, there was a general stylistic reaction against the extravagance of Elizabethan and Jacobean language; second, the influence of Bacon's experimental philosophy; and finally, the parallel movement in the church which advised that imaginative flights and stylistic embellishments be replaced with a new, pure style. These three movements overlapped to the extent that all three contrasted honest plainness with deceitful rhetoric" (42–43).

71. Sprat, 113. Cited in Vickers, 46.

72. Dampier, 4.

73. Ibid., 2.

74. Cited in Beaglehole, "Textual Introduction" to Cook's *Journals*, vol. 1, cxciii.

75. Captain François Leguat, *The Voyage of François Leguat of Bresse*, ed. and annot. Captain Pasfield Oliver (London: Hakluyt Society, 1891), lxxvii.

76. Dampier, 4.

77. Beaglehole comments that in a first draft of this occurrence, Cook explicitly named God's agency: "It pleased GOD at this very juncture to send us a light air of wind," a sentence Cook then revised to "At this critical juncture when all our endeavours seem'd too little a small air of wind sprung up . . ." (ccxiii).

78. *Loss of the Great Galleon S. João* in *Tragic History of the Sea*, 3.

79. Ibid., 5.

80. Ibid., 6–7.

81. Ibid., 21.

82. Champlain, 298.

83. Richard Norwood, *The Sea-man's Practice* (London: W. Godbid and J. Playford, 1680), 111–112. Fourteenth edition; first published in 1637.

84. James, 38–39.

85. Ibid., 55.

86. As late as Shackleton's navigation, a shadow of salvation hovers over survival. After months of drifting on an iceberg, Shackleton, relying on his superb pilot Worsley, navigated a twenty-foot open boat eight hundred miles through the

winter waters of the worst seas of the world in sixteen days, eventually to succeed in finding help at the whaling station on South Georgia Island. In concluding his description of this great feat of craft in *South*, Shackleton wrote, "When I look back at those days, I have no doubt that Providence guided us, not only across those snowfields, but across the storm-white sea that separated Elephant Island from our landing-place on South Georgia. I know that during that long and racking march of thirty-six hours over the unnamed mountains and glaciers of South Georgia, it seemed to me often that we were four, not three. I said nothing to my companions on the point, but afterwards Worsley said to me, 'Boss, I had a curious feeling on the march that there was another person with us.'" Sir Ernest Shackleton, *South: The Story of Shackleton's Last Expedition* (Santa Barbara, CA: The Narrative Press, 2001), 230.

87. James Janeway, *Legacy to his Friends: Containing Twenty Seven Famous Instances of Gods Providences in and about Sea Dangers and Deliverances* (London: Dorman Newman, 1683), 34. First printed in 1674.

88. Ibid., 30.

89. Ibid., 50.

90. Charles Baudelaire, "Le Voyage," from *Les Fleurs du mal*, in *Oeuvres complètes* (Paris: Bibliothèque de la Pléiade, 1975), vol. 1, 134.

91. James, 38.

92. Dava Sobel and William H. Andrews, *The Illustrated Longitude* (New York: Walker and Co., 1998), 5–7.

93. I am quoting here from the 1639 French edition of Champlain's voyages, and give my translation. Samuel de Champlain, treatise bound in *Les Voyages de la nouvelle France Occidentale, dicte Canada* [words omitted] *Avec un traitté des qualitez & conditions resquises à un bon & parfaict Navigateur pour cognoistre la diversité des Estimes qui se font en la Navigation. Les Marques & enseignements que la providence de Dieu à mises dans les Mers pour redresser les Mariniers en leur route, sans lesquelles ils tomberoient en de grands dangers* [words omitted] (Paris: Claude Collet, 1639), title page.

94. Champlain (English edition), 295.

95. "*To resolve a Traverse*, is to reduce or bring several Courses into one," writes Atkinson in an *Epitome of the Art of Navigation; or a Short, Easy, and Methodical Way to become a Compleat Navigator*, 64.

96. Champlain, 299.

97. Edwin Hutchins, *Cognition in the Wild* (Cambridge, MA: MIT Press, 1995), 28–29.

98. Ibid., 113–114.

99. Nathaniel Bowditch, *The American Practical Navigator; An Epitome of Navigation*, bicentennial edition (Bethesda, MD: National Imagery and Mapping Agency, 2002), 1.

100. Conrad, *The Mirror of the Sea*, 25.

101. Ibid., 64.

102. Theodor Adorno and Max Horkheimer, *Dialectic of Enlightenment*, trans. John Cumming (New York: Continuum Books, 1972), 4.

103. Jonathan Raban, "Introduction," *The Oxford Book of the Sea*, ed. Jonathan Raban (New York: Oxford University Press, 1993), 6.

104. Cited from Chapman's translation of Homer, 185.

105. Adorno and Horkheimer, 61.

106. In *Cunning Intelligence in Greek Culture and Society*, Marcel Détienne and Jean-Pierre Vernant correct this tendentious portrait of Odysseus as harbinger of bourgeois *ratio*. Instead, they explain the embodied reason at issue when Homer calls Odysseus *polymetis*: endowed with different kinds of cunning. *Metis*, they suggest, is the term given to those who master the arts of practice; for them, *metis* is the classical term for practical reason. Odysseus exhibits these capacities in navigating, and, according to Détienne and Vernant, the cunning of the pilot was a commonplace of classical Greek culture, which held up the navigator as a paragon of practical reason *(metis)*. See their discussion of this, notably in their chapter 8, titled "The Sea Crow," 215–58. Aristotle, too, framed the ship's pilot as a paragon of *phronesis*, his version of practical reason articulated in the *Nicomachean Ethics*. Détienne and Vernant prefer the term *metis* to *phronesis* for practical reason in antiquity because Aristotle wants to encompass ethical action as well as effective action with his notion of *phronesis*, a juncture that is difficult to effect for Aristotle, as it is for philosophers across Western thought.

When Détienne and Vernant detail the *metis* of the classical pilot, they include a number of human traits that will be carried forward to the craft of the modern mariner. The *metis* of the pilot in the Mediterranean, like that of the global mariner, thrives in high-risk situations of uncertainty, and the classical pilot, too, was skilled in seizing *chairos*, opportunity, finding the path, what was called in Greek *poros*, out of the impasse, designated in Greek as *aporia*, a term that also signifies an impasse in thought. At the same time, both the pilot and Odysseus in Détienne and Vernant's account partake of qualities that set the *metis* of Greek antiquity apart from the modern mariner's craft. *Metis* imitates the wiles of the gods, rather than distinguishing human agency, as in modernity. In addition, *metis* is pervaded by the classical respect for the limits of the human condition and human knowledge. The classical Odysseus is the navigator who turns back when he reaches the straits of Gibraltar, the pillars of Hercules, that mark the end of the flat classical world, in contrast to craft's interest in working at the edges of knowledge in quest of their supercession.

107. Indeed, Adorno and Horkheimer themselves remark that Homer's epic was disliked by "cultural fascists," because they sense that it is perfumed with a "democratic spirit . . . redolent of seafarer and traders." Adorno and Horkheimer, 44.

108. Champlain, 259.

109. Adorno and Horkheimer, 113. Adorno and Horkheimer do recognize this aspect of Odysseus, "ever physically weak against the powers of nature" (46). They also compare him to a picaresque hero.

110. See Sekula, 48.

CHAPTER 2: REMARKABLE OCCURRENCES AT SEA AND IN THE NOVEL

1. G.W.F. Hegel, *Lectures on the History of Philosophy* (Sterling, VA: Thoemmes Press, 1999), vol. 3, 158–59. Reprint of edition printed London: K. Paul, Trench, Trübner, 1892–1896; trans. E. S. Haldane and Frances Simson.

2. These figures are from Martin Green, *Dreams of Adventure, Deeds of Empire* (New York: Basic Books, 1979), 71. On Defoe's interest in maritime literature, see also Arthur W. Secord's *Studies in the Narrative Method of Defoe* (1963), David Fausett's *The Strange Surprizing Sources of Robinson Crusoe* (1994), and Anna Neill's *British Discovery Literature and the Rise of Global Commerce* (2002).

3. Janeway's title continued, "*Containing Twenty Seven Famous Instances of Gods Providences in and about Sea Dangers and Deliverances.*"

4. Daniel Defoe, *The Life and Strange Surprising Adventures of Robinson Crusoe of York, Mariner*, edition cited titled *Robinson Crusoe*, ed. Michael Shinagel (New York: W.W. Norton, 1994), 4, 13. The novel was originally published in 1719. Subsequent citations will be given by page in the text of the chapter.

5. Ian Watt, *The Rise of the Novel* (Berkeley: University of California Press, 1957), 66.

6. Ibid., 5.

7. Ibid., 72.

8. Thus, Watt: "the basis for Robinson Crusoe's prosperity, of course, is the original stock of tools which he loots from the shipwreck . . . [s]o Defoe's hero is not really a primitive nor a proletarian but a capitalist" (87).

9. Virginia Woolf views Crusoe as *homo faber*, humanity defined in the work of making, which she contrasts with the Romantic approach to nature. However, Woolf disregards the oceangoing frame for his improvisations. In Defoe's novel, Woolf writes, "[t]here are no sunsets and no sunrises; there is no solitude and no soul. There is, on the contrary, staring us full in the face nothing but a large earthenware pot." Virginia Woolf, "Robinson Crusoe," from *The Second Common Reader* (1932), excerpted in Shinagel's *Robinson Crusoe*, 285.

10. Michael Nerlich, *Ideology of Adventure*, trans. Ruth Crowley (Minneapolis: University of Minnesota Press, 1987), vol. 2, 274.

11. Ibid., 267.

12. Anthony Ashley Cooper, Earl of Shaftesbury, "Soliloquy: or Advice to an Author," in *Characteristicks of Men, Manners, Opinions, Times* (London: John Darby, 1711), 1, 344.

13. Of this time, Defoe writes, "Necessity, which is allow'd to be the Mother of Invention, has so violently agitated the Wits of men this time, that it seems not at all improper, by way of distinction, to call it *The Projecting Age*." Daniel Defoe, *An Essay Upon Projects* (London: Tho. Cockerill, 1697), 1.

14. Ibid., 4.

15. Citations in this paragraph from ibid., 14, 4, 33–34.

16. Citations in this paragraph from ibid., 17, 17–18, 16.

17. These details are from Emerson W. Baker and John G. Reid, *The New England Knight: Sir William Phips, 1651–1695* (Toronto: University of Toronto Press, 1998), 27; see also details on 28–29. They cite "a Spanish narrative of 1687," recalling "that Phips had 'for some years followed the art of discovering shipwrecked vessels, not without considerable success'" (27).

18. Fans of Hergé's *Tintin* may be interested to know that this information may have come through the intermediary of the London-based naval officer, Sir Richard Haddock, a real-life ancestor of Hergé's fictional Captain Haddock. Hergé's pattern of adventure as problem-solving in the *Tintin* series owes much to Defoe's

adventure poetics, down to the supplementary relation of text and image, a technique I discuss in the section on the cunning reader.

19. *An Essay upon Projects* terms the ability of craft to overcome great dangers to the point of defying common sense "the Magick of their Art." Sailors, Defoe observes, "are Fellows that bid Defiance to Terror, and maintain a constant War with the Elements; who by the Magick of their Art, Trade in the very confines of Death" (124). Defoe singles out the mariner's compass when he mentions the beginning of successful projecting, along with the invention of gunpowder. He also authorizes the projecting spirit by giving it maritime antecedents in the Bible, dating its exercise back to Noah's ark. In connecting Noah with modern projecting, Defoe evinces the early modern interest in finding antecedents for modernity, including modern technology, in religious history. In the *Arte de Navegar*, which was the state-of-the-art practical manual on seamanship in the mid-sixteenth century, Pedro de Medina devotes a chapter to navigation in antiquity, crediting its inspiration to God, when God ordered Noah to make an ark. In describing this foundation, Medina gives practical detail on how the ship was built. When he speculates on the details, he conveys a practical approach to religious texts, concerned with human agency, rather than Providence. See Book 2, Chapter VI: "De l'Excellence de la Navigation & de son antiquité," in Pierre de Médine, *L'Art de Naviguer*, preface by Michel Serres (Paris: Les Belles Lettres, 2000). Medina's work was originally published in Spanish in 1545 and first published in French in 1554.

20. Daniel Defoe, *The Complete English Tradesman, in Familiar Letters* (London: Charles Rivington, 1726), quotes from 92, v.

21. Richard Hakluyt, *Voyages and Discoveries,* a recent edition of Hakluyt's *Principal Navigations, Voyages, Traffiques and Discoveries of the English Nation,* ed., abridged, and intro. by Jack Beeching (New York: Penguin, 1972), 36.

22. G.W.F. Hegel, *Hegel's Philosophy of Right*, trans. and with notes by T. M. Knox (New York: Oxford University Press, 1967), 151.

23. Indeed, Crusoe tells us that in his account, he has left only the "Adventures," and not the "Sea-Journals" themselves, for fear of boring his readers: "As I have troubled you with none of my Sea-Journals, so I shall trouble you now with none of my Land-Journal: But some Adventures that happen'd to us in this tedious and difficult Journey, I must not omit" (208).

24. Daniel Defoe, *A New Voyage Round the World, By a Course never sailed before* (London: A. Bettesworth, 1725), 2–3.

25. Scholarship on this novel generally explains the notions of "strange" and "surprising" as qualifying events that violate probability, in line with the "strange, therefore true claims" of what Michael McKeon has called naive empiricism in *The Origins of the English Novel, 1600–1740* (Baltimore: Johns Hopkins University Press, 1987), 47ff. Fausett too discusses problems around the distinction between fact and fiction shaping Defoe's practice. See David Fausett, *The Strange Surprizing Sources of Robinson Crusoe* (Amsterdam: Rodopi, 1994), 185ff.

26. "Strange" was a synonym for what we would today call "extreme"—in particular, extremely dangerous, as in the title of *The Strange and Dangerous Voyage of Captaine Thomas James.* "Surprising," too, can indicate unusual danger, as in the following passage from Dampier's *A New Voyage Round the World*:

"Our People were a little surprized at this sudden Adventure, yet fired their Guns, and rowed farther into the Lagune, for they durst not adventure to come out again thro' the narrow Entrance." William Dampier, *A New Voyage Round the World* (New York: Dover Publications, 1968), 168.

27. Defoe, *A New Voyage Round the World*, 2–3.

28. Dampier, *A New Voyage Round the World*, 3. Subsequent citations will be referenced by page number within the chapter. Dampier coined the term "mixt relation" to apologize for the disorganization on the grounds that what mattered was the information conveyed and its chronological sequence.

29. Defoe, *A New Voyage Round the World*, 3, 4.

30. Ibid., 3.

31. See the selections from these authors in Shinagel's *Robinson Crusoe* for a summary of their points.

32. McKeon, 317.

33. Critics dispute the extent to which Crusoe is a psychological character. Some critics lay great emphasis on his psychological individuality; some, coming from the perspective of adventure fiction, emphasize the relatively flat, "everyman" quality of his personality. Jean-Yves Tadié and Martin Green both stress that adventure novels commonly use simplified, straightforward protagonists, who are easy to identify with and help involve the reader in the action. See, for example, Jean-Yves Tadié, *Le Roman d'aventures* (Paris: Presses Universitaires de France, 1982), 9.

34. Ibid., 8.

35. Thus, the usage of "performance" in Charles Saltonstall's *Navigator*, which aimed to teach the "way of working, ruling, guiding, governing, and constraining ["a gallant Ship"] to performe the expert Navigators pleasure in the Sea." Saltonstall, *The Navigator* (London: George Herlock, 1636), 2.

36. My discussion in the preceding paragraph uses the notions of plausible, authentic, and probable set out by McKeon in *The Origins of the English Novel*. See also Catherine Gallagher's discussion of normative modern fictionality in *Nobody's Story*.

37. Jacques Rivière, *Le Roman d'aventure* (Paris: Editions des Syrtes, 2000), 54, 68. Originally published in *La Nouvelle Revue Française*, 1913.

38. Defoe himself wrote two sequels for *Robinson Crusoe*. Before *The Count of Monte Cristo*, Alexandre Dumas wrote a sequel for James Fenimore Cooper's *The Pilot*, titled *Captain Paul*. *The Mysterious Island* is Verne's sequel to *Twenty Thousand Leagues under the Sea*. Defoe's adventure pattern still helps organize Hergé's graphic serial novels about Tintin and Captain Haddock. Forester and O'Brian wrote not just sequels but series in their twentieth-centuy maritime adventure fiction.

39. Jonathan Swift, *Travels into Several Remote Nations of the World. In Four Parts. By Lemuel Guillver*, republished as *Gulliver's Travels*, ed. Albert J. Rivero (New York: W.W. Norton, 2002), 94.

40. Thus, compare the passage in *Gulliver's Travels* with the version of these directions cited in chapter 1. While Sturmy's *The Mariner's Magazine* is excerpted in the Norton *Gulliver's Travels*, it should be remembered that Sturmy is not a unique source for Swift, but rather one expression of directions shared and recorded within the collectivity of craft.

41. Philippe Hamon, "Rhetorical Status of the Descriptive," trans. Patricia Baudoin, *Yale French Studies* 61, *Towards a Theory of Description* (1981), 17. Hamon takes this notion from Gotthold Lessing in Lessing's *Laokoön,* where it was called "dramatized" description.

42. Rivière, 54.

43. Ibid., 54.

44. Frank Lestringant identifies the thought process shared by Crusoe and any reader competent in overseas travel narratives on seeing the footprint: "[c]anni-bals, without a doubt; man-eaters . . . Robinson reinvents the Cannibals, step by step, just as Columbus [did]." Frank Lestringant, *Cannibals: The Discovery and Representation of the Cannibal from Columbus to Jules Verne,* trans. Rosemary Morris (Berkeley: University of California Press, 1997), 137–38.

45. Herbert Simon, *The Sciences of the Artificial,* quoted in Edwin Hutchins, *Cognition in the Wild* (Cambridge, MA: MIT Press, 1995), 117. Hutchins is discussing here the translation of information across different kinds of representational media and techniques characterizing the work of navigation in the era before GPS—a process I return to in this chapter, as well as in my discussion of Conrad in chapter 5.

46. The question of salvation will be susceptible to such practical problem-solving in Defoe's *Captain Singleton* as well, culminating in Captain Bob's opportunistic version of Pascal's wager, when he prudently "repents" for the past evil deeds that have enriched him, following the advice of the Quaker William.

47. The problem is intimated, but not posed as such, when Crusoe first runs away to sea. He is scared out of his wits by rough weather, and promises God that he will repent for his rebellion if he can only arrive safe on shore, which he in fact then does. But even as he then gives thanks to Providence, the plot justifies Crusoe's survival in another equally plausible way. A dialogue between Crusoe and a season'd sailor raises the possibility that the inexperienced Crusoe overestimated the dangers: "*I warrant you were frighted, wa'n't you, last Night, when it blew but a Cap full of Wind? A Cap full d'you call it?* said I, *'twas a terrible Storm: A Storm, you Fool you,* replies he, *do you call that a Storm, why it was nothing at all; give us but a good Ship and Sea Room, and we think nothing of such a Squall of Wind as that*" (8). Was Crusoe's survival due to Providence or to craft? This question will be implied repeatedly throughout Crusoe's brushes with danger, until he asks it outright apropos of the ears of corn.

48. In his *Strange and Dangerous Voyage,* Thomas James recounts how he cured his crew of scurvy by some tender greens that he grows from European seed when spring finally comes, after their hellish winter in the Artic circle, in James Bay.

49. Wolfgang Iser, *The Implied Reader: Patterns of Communication in Prose Fiction from Bunyan to Beckett* (Baltimore: Johns Hopkins University Press, 1978), 40.

50. See Denis Diderot, "In Praise of Richardson" (1762), in *Denis Diderot: Selected Writings on Art and Literature,* trans. Geofrey Bremner (New York: Penguin 1994).

51. Wolfgang Iser, *The Act of Reading: A Theory of Aesthetic Response* (Baltimore: Johns Hopkins University Press, 1980), 67.

52. Ibid., 67.

53. Indeed, it would be interesting to reconstruct the maritime genealogy of the phenomenological rhetoric of the horizon so important to Iser.

54. Defoe, *A New Voyage Round the World*, 4.

55. Cited in Richard Phillips, *Mapping Men and Empire: A Geography of Adventure* (New York: Routledge, 1997), 5.

56. In Crusoe's words: "we had several spare Yards, and two or three large sparrs of Wood, and a spare Top-mast or two in the Ship; I resolv'd to fall to work with these, and I flung as many of them over board as I could manage for their Weight, tying every one with a Rope that they might not drive away; when this was done I went down the Ship's Side, and pulling them to me, I ty'd four of them fast together at both Ends as well as I could, in the Form of a Raft, and laying two or three short Pieces of Plank upon them crossways, I found I could walk upon it very well" (37).

57. Defoe's use of narrative problems to teach technical information resembles the genre of the story problem in the early modern era, aimed at teaching practical mathematics. In these problems, found in manuals of seamanship, as in other kinds of practical manuals for trades using computation, short stories gave the contexts for computations and framed them in dramatic situations. Indeed, the most vivid word problems in the treatises of seamanship sound like episodes waiting to be turned into an adventure narrative: "Suppose a Merchant-ship in 45d. 30m. North Latitude, falls into the Hands of Pyrates, who take away his Sea-Compass; after which, he saileth as directly as he can 67 Leagues between the South and West, and at the end of two Days meets a Ship of War, who also had been the Day before in 45d. 30m. North Latitude, and had sailed thence SE. by S. 39 Leagues; now the Merchant-ship left those Pyrates lying to and fro where they robbed him, and the Man of War being desirous to find them; I demand what Course he must shape to speak to them?" James Atkinson, *Epitome of the Art of Navigation; or a Short, Easy and Methodical Way to become a Compleat Navigator*, rev. and corrected by William Mountaine (London: William Mount and Thomas Page, 1744), 73. The identical problem was already printed on the same page in the 1714 edition (8th ed.) that I consulted at the John Carter Brown Library. In *Gulliver's Travels*, Swift parodies this use of the word problem as an aid to teaching applied mathematics when he explains how to track the mobile location of the Island of Laputa, subject to magnetic attraction. "To explain the manner of its Progress, let *AB* represent a Line drawn cross the Dominions of *Balnibarbi*, let the line *cd* represent the Load-stone, of which let *d* be the repelling end, and *c* the attracting end, the Island being over C," and so on. Swift, *Gulliver's Travels*, 143.

58. On the history of *Robinson Crusoe*'s illustrations, see David Blewett, *The Illustration of Robinson Crusoe, 1719–1920* (Gerrards Cross, Buckinghamshire, UK: Colin Smythe, 1995). On Defoe's interest in contemporary mapping, see for example, the images and overview by J. Kenneth Van Dover, *Defoe's World Mapped: English Horizons in 1720* (Chicago: Newberry Library, 1988). Available at *http://www.newberry.org/smith/slidesets/ss10.html*; consulted December 2009.

59. Hutchins, 126.

60. Daniel Defoe, *The History and Remarkable Life of the truly honourable Colonel Jacque Commonly called Colonel Jack* (Whitefish, MT: Kessinger

Publishing Company, 2006), 67. Reprint of edition printed New York: University Press, 1904, ed. G. H. Maynadier.

61. See Giancarlo Maiorino's *At the Margins of the Renaissance: Lazarillo de Tormes and the Picaresque Art of Survival* (University Park, PA: Penn State University Press, 2003). Cesare Casarino offers the frame of the "the exotic picaresque" for sea fiction before the nineteenth century, including it within other novels of travel to remote or exotic lands. See Cesare Casarino, *Modernity at Sea: Melville, Marx, Conrad in Crisis* (Minneapolis: University of Minnesota Press, 2002), 8–9.

62. Jody Greene, "Captain Singleton and *The Rise of the Novel*," in *The Eighteenth Century: Theory and Interpretation* (forthcoming).

63. Daniel Defoe, *The Life, Adventures & Piracies of the Famous Captain Singleton*, intro. Edward Garnett (Charleston, SC: BiblioBazaar, 2007). The phrases quoted in this paragraph are found on pages 27, 39, and 40.

64. William Rufus Chetwood, *The Voyages and Adventures of Captain Robert Boyle* (New York: Garland, 1972), 2.

65. Ibid., 22.

66. Ibid., 28.

67. Ibid., 167.

68. Ibid., 70.

69. L'Abbé Prévost, *Voyages du Capitaine Robert Lade* (Paris: Didot, 1744).

70. "But the most useful and remarkable thing I took from the Journal of Mr. Ritwood was a table of the latitude & longitude of the principal Ports, Islands, Rivers, Bays, & other remarkable places on the West Coast of America in the South Sea from Northern California to the Straits of Magellan in the South . . . ." A table then follows, from which I reproduce a selection in the original French:

	Latit.		Longit.	
	D.	M.	D.	M.
La Californie,	24	40	255	15
Sa Pointe Orientale,	24	4	258	15
Cap Saint-Luc,	25	30	259	50
Derniere Pointe du Continent,	24	40	260	55 . . . .

And so on down for several pages down to

Cap Corzo,	46.	35.	312.	22

Prévost, *Robert Lade*, vol. 1, 297, table on 298–303.

71. The quotes from the novel in this paragraph are found in Prévost, *Robert Lade*, vol. 1, 35–36.

72. This storm gives a good example of how Defoe transforms his mariner sources. Compare Defoe's storms from a lengthy description of Dampier on how he handles a monsoon: "At Twelve a-Clock at Night it blew a very fierce Storm. We were then riding with our best Bower a Head; and though our Yards and Top-mast were down, yet we drove. This obliged us to let go our Sheet-anchor, veering out a good Scope of Cable, which stopt us till Ten or Eleven a-Clock the next Day" and so on. Dampier, 295. Defoe's technical details, in contrast, do not burden the reader with too much professional information, but rather address the

location of the island that will be one of the problems confronting Crusoe, but also his reader, across the narrative.

73. Alain René Le Sage, *The Adventures of Robert Chevalier, call'd de Beauchene. Captain of a Privateer in New-France* (London: T. Gardner, 1745), vol. 1, "*The* Bookseller *to the* Reader" (n.p.).

74. Carl Schmitt, *The Nomos of the Earth*, trans. G. L. Ulmen (New York: Telos Press, 2003), 93–94.

75. Daniel Defoe [under the pen name of Captain Johnson], *A General History of the Pyrates* [1724], ed. Manuel Schonhorn (Mineola, NY: Dover Publications, 1999), 6.

76. Ibid., 153.

77. Ibid., 71, 85, 84.

78. Ibid., 85.

79. Ibid., 384.

80. Ibid., 384.

81. Ibid., 388.

82. Ibid., 417.

83. Female protagonists also manipulate their bodies as a technology to procure survival in Defoe's adventure novels set back on land. Moll's first use of her body is on the marriage market; as her charms fade, she adds "dexterity" as a thief. Buffeted around the margins of society, these characters evince the picaro's art of survival. At the same time, with Moll and Roxana, the picaro's cunning starts to mutate into a knowledge of worldliness, as they put a feminine practical reason in the service of social climbing, using it to profit from the edge zones between classes, and not simply survive them.

84. A good example of how Random fuses the healing art of the ship's surgeon with the picaro's cunning occurs when Random contracts a contagious fever that rages on board ship. As an experienced surgeon, Random knows that "I stood no chance for my life, if I should be obliged to lie in the cockpit. . . . I wrote a petition to the captain representing my case, and humbly imploring his permission to lie among the soldiers in the middle-deck, for the benefit of the air." When the Captain turns him down, he cannot "brook the thought of perishing so pitifully," and "prevailed upon the soldiers (whose good-will I had acquired) to admit my hammock among them." Eventually, he is lent the "well-aired" berth of a sergeant "the bones of whose nose I had . . . set to rights, after they had been demolished." Tobias Smollett, *The Adventures of Roderick Random*, ed. Paul–Gabriel Boucé (New York: Oxford University Press, 1999), quotes come from page 190.

85. In the *Nicomachean Ethics*, Aristotle uses the example of both the doctor and the pilot, and prefers the doctor, because he heals, and thus exercises a profession clearly in the service of the good, in contrast to the more ambiguous possibilities for a voyage safely navigated by a skillful pilot.

86. Smollett, 342.

CHAPTER 3: SEA ADVENTURE FICTION, 1748–1824?

1. Philip Edwards, *The Story of the Voyage: Sea-Narratives in Eighteenth-Century England* (New York: Cambridge University Press, 1994), 8.

2. The Robinsonade, imagining a new society following marooning on a desert island, will not be concerned with the work of seafaring until after Cooper renews sea adventure fiction in the 1820s.

3. For an overview of the sailor as a character in novels of this time, and indeed, across the history of the novel, see James Peck, *Maritime Fiction: Sailors and the Sea in British and American Novels, 1719–1917* (New York: Palgrave, 2001).

4. Jane Austen, *Mansfield Park*, ed. James Kinsley (New York: Oxford University Press, 2008), 48.

5. Fanny Burney's brother, James Burney accompanied Captain Cook and rose through the ranks to become a rear admiral. He also wrote narratives of the history of discovery and exploration that span from the buccaneers to his own experience sailing with Cook. Austen had two brothers who had professions in the navy, Charles and Francis. Both started as midshipmen and eventually became rear admirals.

6. James Fenimore Cooper, preface to *The Red Rover* (1850), in *Sea Tales, The Pilot, Red Rover*, eds. Kay Seymour House and Thomas Philbrick (New York: Library of America, 1990), 429.

7. Jane Austen, *Northanger Abbey*, ed. Marilyn Butler (New York: Penguin, 2003), 102.

8. See John Ruskin, *Modern Painters*, in Elibron Classics (Adamant Media, 2005). Reprinted from edition published London: George Allen, 1906. The phrases are used throughout Ruskin's discussion of Turner in vol. 4.

9. One reason for the poets' preference for narrative inheres in the nature of the sea voyage, which unfolds through time, the medium of narrative as well. A voyage is inherently chronological, or better chronotopical, to take up Bakhtin's terms for the imbrication of time and space in narrative. For time on a voyage is also a coordinate of space: this is quite literally the case in the measure of longitude. Only when sublimation of the sea is so achieved that the sea becomes a distanced, static landscape can it be delineated in lyric, rather than narrative, poetry.

INTERLUDE: THE SUBLIMATION OF THE SEA

1. T. S. Eliot, *The Wasteland, A Facsimile and Transcription*, ed. and intro. Valerie Eliot (New York: Harvest Books, 1971), 136.

2. See John Ruskin, *Modern Painters*, in Elibron Classics, vol. 4 (Adamant Media, 2005). Reprinted from edition published London: George Allen, 1906, the phrases are used throughout.

3. Longinus, *On Great Writing (On the Sublime)*, trans. G.M.A. Grube (New York: The Liberal Arts Press, 1957), 13.

4. Ibid., 18.

5. Ibid., 19. Longinus's instances of transgressive rhetoric include what he calls hyperboles, which "under the stress of strong emotion . . . help to express a certain grandeur in the situation" (50). He also cites disordered syntax: "words" [that] "burst forth without connectives" and are "hurried" (31), and more generally "[h]yperbaton," "an arrangement of words or ideas which departs from the normal sequence" (33). The boundary between rhetoric and reality dissolves when extravagant, fabulous details intrude in a discourse composed in accordance with

criteria of probability and reason: "our attention is drawn away from the argument's proof and we are startled by an imaginative picture which conceals the actual argument by its own brilliance" (27).

6. Nicolas Boileau, *Réflexions sur Longin* (Réflexion 10), in *Oeuvres de Nicolas Boileau Despréaux* (Amsterdam: D. Mortier, 1718), vol. 1, 136. The following quotes in the next two paragraphs are from the same passage.

7. This transformation was first noted by Samuel H. Monk when he renewed critical interest in the sublime in the twentieth century. See Samuel H. Monk, *The Sublime: A Study of Critical Theories in Eighteenth-Century England* (New York: Modern Language Association, 1935).

8. Ian MacLaren, "Arctic Exploration and Milton's 'Frozen Continent.'" *Notes and Queries* new ser. 31 (1984): 325–26. See also Anne-Julia Zwierlein's article, "Satan's Ocean Voyage and 18th-Century Seafaring Trade," in *Fictions of the Sea. Critical Perspectives on the Ocean in British Literature and Culture*, ed. Bernhard Klein (Farnham, Surrey, UK: Ashgate, 2002), 49–76.

9. John Milton, *Paradise Lost*, ed. Gordon Teskey (New York: W.W. Norton, 2005), book 2, 588–95.

10. Ibid., book 2, 571.

11. In *Epic and Empire*, David Quint notes that John Milton's figure of Satan revises heroic narratives of epic mariners from Odysseus to Camões's da Gama. For Quint, the significance of this revision is to make Satan and his devils "Merchant Adventurers," and thereby to indict "European expansion and colonialism." From my argument, it should now be clear that though mariners and merchants partner together—thus, the search for the Northwest Passage was the search for a profitable trade route to the East—they are not substitutable for one another, neither in the realm of literary figuration, nor in the nature of their work. Modeling Satan on the mariner, Milton also interrogates the empowered agency of craft, and its potential to subvert a religious world view. See David Quint, *Epic and Empire* (Princeton, NJ: Princeton University Press, 1993), 265.

12. Milton, book I, 194–95.

13. Ibid., book I, 76–78.

14. Ibid., book I, 180, 184, 190–91.

15. Ibid., book I, quotes from lines 257, 296–300.

16. Ibid., book I, 292–94.

17. Ibid., book I, 239–41.

18. Ibid., book I, 242–45.

19. Ibid., book, I, 13–16. Milton's *Paradise Lost* was called "[b]old, and sublime," inspiring "Terrour and Delight," in a poem by Joseph Addison, "An Account of the Greatest English Poets," published in *The Annual Miscellany for The Year 1694* (London: Jacob Tonson, 1694), 322. For a discussion of Milton's status as sublime in the first decades of the eighteenth century, see Leslie E. Moore, *Beautiful Sublime: The Making of Paradise Lost, 1701–1734* (Stanford, CA: Stanford University Press, 1990).

20. On Milton's familiarity with *The Lusíads*, which had appeared in 1655 in English translation by Richard Fanshawe, see John T. Shawcross, "John Milton and His Spanish and Portuguese Presence," *Milton Quarterly* 32, no. 2 (1998), 41–52, p. 42 in particular.

21. Luís Vaz de Camões, *The Lusíads*, trans. Landeg White (New York: Oxford University Press, 2001), Canto V, stanza 26, lines 5–8.

22. This romance of practice, however, only involves the portrayal of da Gama's navigation. Camões's language becomes more ornamental when it comes to his portrayal of the Muslim world and the battle between different orders of gods.

23. Milton, book I, 286–91.

24. On Milton's relation to Galileo, textual and actual, see, for example, George F. Butler, "Milton's Meeting with Galileo: A Reconsideration," *Milton Quarterly*, 39, no. 3 (2005): 132–39.

25. I am indebted to Nikolai Slivka for this reading. In an e-mail of December 1, 2009, he reflects on possible interpretations generated by the ambiguity. He notes, "[p]erhaps Milton is mortifying a certain complacency with regards to such technologies of inspection and imperial rule as the telescope; a complacent reader smugly would have Galileo looking at the moon/orb/shield/Satan's armor from a position of (unmerited) equipoise. Another reader by contrast might have Satan looking at Galileo through a telescope—a trope therefore for the way in which modern man becomes *subjected* to his own technology (something along the lines of a simplified Frankfurt-School critique). Still another reader might see this as an instance where Milton is intentionally encoding at the level of ambivalent syntax a central crux of technological advance (a more nuanced Frankfurt-School-inflected notion)."

26. Milton, book I, 26.

27. Jonathan Richardson, *An Essay on the theory of painting* (1725), cited in Andrew Ashfield and Peter de Bolla, eds., *The Sublime: A Reader in British Eighteenth-Century Aesthetic Theory* (New York: Cambridge University Press, 1996). This and the subsequent quote are found on pages 48 and 47.

28. Joseph Trapp similarly compared the sublime's impulse to go beyond pre-existing limits with the modern conquest of space: "nature has formed man of an inquisitive genius, and placed him in the world to behold and admire the wonders of it, not as an idle spectator, but as one concerned in its busiest scenes . . . The vast expanse of the universe cannot bound his imagination; he extends his thoughts into other worlds, and is lost only in infinity." Trapp then quotes a line from Thomas Creech's translation of Lucretius: "'His vigorous and active Mind is hurl'd / Beyond the seeming limits of the World.'" Joseph Trapp, *Lectures on Poetry* (1742), cited in Ashfield and de Bolla, 56.

29. Alexander O. Exquemelin, *The Buccaneers of America*, trans. Alexis Brown, intro. Jack Beeching (New York: Dover Publications, 2000), 89.

30. Ibid., 107.

31. Daniel Defoe [under the pen name of Captain Johnson], *A General History of the Pyrates* [1724], ed. Manuel Schonhorn (Mineola, NY: Dover Publications, 1999), 85.

32. John Dennis, *The Grounds of Criticism in Poetry* (1704), cited in Ashfield and de Bolla, 38.

33. Joseph Addison, *The Spectator*, no. 489, Saturday, September 20, 1712, cited in Ashfield and de Bolla, 69.

34. Catherine Gallagher also notes the relation of this vicarious activity to work, citing Burke's passage: "as common labor, which is a mode of pain, is the

exercise of the grosser, a mode of terror is the exercise of the finer parts of the system." Gallagher suggests that this passage links "the agony of the poet to the unhappiness of the laborer"; Catherine Gallagher, *The Body Economic* (Princeton, NJ: Princeton University Press, 2006), 28.

35. In *Preserving the Self in the South Seas 1680–1840*, Jonathan Lamb suggests that the passion of "self-preservation" so important for Burke, as for other seventeenth- and eighteenth-century philosophers, in fact was shaped by early modern accounts by mariners of their struggles for self-preservation on the Edge zones of the maritime frontier, though he does not suggest the sublime as an experience of such self-preservation for armchair travelers. Rather, Lamb's primary interest is how narratives of frontier navigation contribute to modern subjectivity, and he focuses on the relation of self-preservation to the "je ne sais quoi," a category from seventeenth-century French neoclassical aesthetic theory to describe a kind of ineffable experience that cannot be put into words. The "je ne sais quoi" contributed to Boileau's articulation of the sublime, along with creating the opaque modern subject of interest to Lamb. Sara Suleri makes a related link between the obscurity of the sublime and the European experience of confronting unknown regions of the globe apropos of Burke's speech on Fox's East India Bill, twenty-five years after his *Philosophical Inquiry*. In Suleri's words, "The 'false and cloudy medium' upon which the speech insists allows Burke to illustrate painstakingly how British colonial discourse must come to terms with the central representational unavailability that Indian cultures and histories, even its sheer geography, must pose to the colonizing eye." Sara Suleri, *The Rhetoric of English India* (Chicago: University of Chicago Press, 1992), 27.

36. James Cook, *The Journals of Captain Cook*, selected and edited by Philip Edwards (New York: Penguin, 2003), 168.

37. Ibid., 166.

38. Charles Baudelaire, "Le Voyage," from *Les Fleurs du mal*, in *Oeuvres Complètes* (Paris: Bibliothèque de la Pléiade, 1975), vol. 1, 134.

39. Indeed, Addison cites as an example of the sublime a well-known prayer for the sailor: "*They that go down to the sea in ships, that do business in great waters: these see the works of the Lord, and his wonders in the deep. For he commandeth and raiseth the stormy wind, which lifteth up the waters thereof. They mount up to the heaven, they go down again to the depths, their soul is melted because of trouble. They reel too and fro, and stagger like a drunken Man, and are at their wits end. Then they cry unto the Lord in their trouble, and he bringeth them out of their distresses. He maketh the storm a calm, so that the waves thereof are still. Then they are glad, because they be quiet; so he bringeth them unto their desired haven.*" Addison observed that ocean travel makes him think of the sublime as described by Longinus: "As I have made several voyages upon the sea I have often been tossed in storms, and on that occasion have frequently reflected on the descriptions of them in ancient poets. I remember Longinus highly recommends one in Homer [quoted in the section on Longinus above] . . . because he has gathered together those circumstances which are the most apt to terrify the imagination, and which really happen in the raging of a tempest." Joseph Addison, *The Spectator*, no. 489, Saturday, September 20, 1712. Cited in Ashfield and de Bolla, 69.

40. Ibid., 69.

41. From John Baillie, *An Essay on the Sublime* (1747), cited in Ashfield and de Bolla, 90, 96–97.

42. Edmund Burke, *A Philosophical Enquiry into the Origin of our Ideas of the Sublime and Beautiful*, ed. Adam Phillips (New York: Oxford University Press, 1998), 36–37 (Part I, 7).

43. Anthony Ashley Cooper, Third Earl of Shaftesbury, from *Characteristicks*, cited in Ashfield and de Bolla, 72.

44. Ibid., 76–77.

45. Shaftesbury's invective is worth citing at length, not only for its vehemence, but because his criticism gets all the details of overseas travel narrative right even as he dismisses the form: "Yet so enchanted we are with the *travelling Memoirs* of any casual Adventurer; that be his Character, or Genius, what it will, we have no sooner turn'd over a Page or two, but we begin to interest our-selves highly in his Affairs. No sooner has he taken Shipping at the Mouth of the *Thames*, or sent his Baggage before him to *Gravesend*, or *Buoy in the Nore*, but strait our Attention is earnestly taken up. If in order to his more distant Travels, he takes some Part of EUROPE in his way; we can with patience hear of Inns and Ordinarys, Passage-Boats and Ferrys, foul and fair Weather; with all the Particulars of the Author's Diet, Habit of Body, his personal Dangers and Mischances, on Land, and Sea. And thus, full of Desire and Hope, we accompany him, till he enters on his great Scene of Action, and beings by the Description of some *enormous Fish*, or *Beast*. From monstrous *Brutes* he proceeds to yet more *monstrous Men*. For in this Race of Authors, *he* is ever compleatest, and of the first Rank, who is able to speak of Things the most *unnatural* and *monstrous*." Anthony Ashley Cooper, Earl of Shaftesbury, "Soliloquy: or Advice to an Author," in *Characteristicks of Men, Manners, Opinions, Times* (London: John Darby, 1711), 1, 346–47.

46. Immanuel Kant, *Critique of Judgment*, trans. and intro. J. H. Bernard (New York: Hafner Press, 1951), 110–11, "Analytic of the Sublime" §29.

47. Raban makes an exception for Addison's "troubled ocean," which he calls "the immediate ancestor of the modern romantic sea. Suddenly, the water itself is in focus and in the foreground of the picture." Jonathan Raban, "Introduction," *The Oxford Book of the Sea*, ed. Jonathan Raban (New York: Oxford University Press, 1993), 8.

48. See Alain Corbin, *The Lure of the Sea: The Discovery of the Seaside in the Western World 1750–1840*, trans. Jocelyn Phelps (New York: Penguin, 1995), 53. Corbin notes the depiction of the sea as a source of peril and danger in Dutch maritime paintings of the seventeenth century, as well as their function to transmit information.

49. George Gordon, Lord Byron, *Childe Harold's Pilgrimage*, in *The Complete Poetical Works of Lord Byron* (Boston: Houghton Mifflin, 1905), 82.

50. George Gordon, Lord Byron, *The Corsair*, in *The Complete Poetical Works of Lord Byron* (Boston: Houghton Mifflin, 1905), 338.

51. Defoe, *A General History of the Pyrates*, 85.

52. Hakim Bey's alter ego is Peter Wilson, who has written about pirates and other outlaws.

53. Addison, *The Spectator*, 1712, cited in Raban, 81.

54. Marie von Kügelgen, letter to Friederike Volkmann, June 22, 1809. English translation from the Web Gallery of Art: *http://www.wga.hu/frames-e.html?/html/f/ friedric/1/105fried.html*; consulted January 2008. The original German passage can be found in Hilmar Frank, *Aussichten in Unermessliche: Perspektivität und Sinnof- fenheit bei Caspar David Friedrich* (Berlin: Akademie Verlag, 2004), 85.

55. Raban, 9.

56. Ibid., 9.

57. William Falconer, *The Shipwreck*, 3rd ed. (London: T. Cadell, 1769), Canto I, 17–20. Citations will subsequently be referenced by canto and line within the text of the chapter.

58. This information is from a biography of Turner on the National Gallery's website. Available at *http://www.nga.gov/press/exh/242/chrono.shtm*; consulted December 2009.

59. On Turner's relation to Dutch and other maritime art, see the essays in *Turner and the Masters*, ed. David Solkin (London: Tate, 2009), such as Sarah Monks's essay "Turner Goes Dutch," 73–85, and Ian Warrell's essay, "Turner Paints Himself into History," 207–23.

60. According to a display caption of the picture on the Tate's website, "[w]e don't know whether this painting was inspired by an actual shipwreck, or the re- issue in 1804 of a famous poem on the theme by William Falconer. Turner defines the essence of such an experience through overwhelming impressions of realism and horror. The dark tonality, characteristic of Turner's early paintings, provides a foil to the white crests and swirls of the waves." Available at *http://www.tate. org.uk/servlet/ViewWork?workid=14737*; consulted December 2009.

61. James Hamilton, *Turner and the Scientists* (London: Tate, 1998), 74ff.

CHAPTER 4: SEA FICTION IN THE NINETEENTH CENTURY: PATRIOTS, PIRATES, AND SUPERMEN

1. Friedrich Nietzsche, *Thus Spoke Zarathustra*, trans. Walter Kaufmann (New York: Viking Press, 1966), 155–56.

2. Thomas Philbrick describes several antecedents in the early American novel, notably Royal Tyller's *The Algerine Captive, or, The Life and Adventures of Doc- tor Updike Underhill* (1797). None of these works were sufficiently compelling to catch on as a genre, which is to say as a socially recognized poetics, appeal- ing to many readers and writers. Thomas Philbrick, *James Fenimore Cooper and the Development of American Sea Fiction* (Cambridge, MA: Harvard University Press, 1961), 31 ff. My understanding of Cooper's sea fiction is indebted to Phil- brick's study throughout this chapter.

3. The novel had already been well reviewed in a number of English newspapers within six weeks of its publication (February 5, 1824). American reviewers were initially more hesitant than their British counterparts about the interest of the book. Details on Cooper's international reception and chronology are from Kay Seymour House's edition of Cooper's *The Pilot: A Tale of the Sea* (Albany: State University of New York Press, 1986).

4. I coined this notion in my article, "Traveling Genres," *New Literary History* 34, no. 3 (2003): 481–499, where I first published a description of nineteenth-century sea fiction, which this chapter reworks.

5. Philbrick, 84. Frederick Chamier and William Glascock are other noted British authors of maritime fiction at the time. For an extensive overview of American and British sea literature, see also Charles Lee Lewis, *Books of the Sea: An Introduction to Nautical Literature* (Annapolis, MD: U.S. Naval Institute, 1943).

6. Other maritime novels penned by French writers include *Le Négrier* (1832) by Edouard Corbière (father of the French symbolist poet, Tristan Corbière), and Auguste Jal's *Scènes de la vie maritime* (1832). Willard Thorp gives further details in "Cooper Beyond America," in *New York History* 35, no. 4 (October 1954): 522–39 (Special Issue—James Fenimore Cooper: A Re-Appraisal). Available at *http://external.oneonta.edu/cooper/articles/nyhistory/1954nyhistory-thorp.html*; consulted December 2009. See also Eric Partridge's "Fenimore Cooper's Influence on the French Romantics," *Modern Language Review* 20, no. 2 (April 1925), 174–78. On Cooper's reception in France, see also G. C. Bosset, *Fenimore Cooper et le roman d'aventure en France vers 1830* (Paris: Vrin, 1928).

7. Popular American sea novelists of the 1840s and 1850s included Ned Buntline, pen name of Edward Zane Carroll Judson (E.Z.C. Judson), who, like Cooper, wrote novels about both the sea and the Western frontier. Maturin Murray Ballou penned *The Sea-Witch or the African Quadroon: A Story of the Slave Coast* and *The Adventurer; or, The Wreck on the Indian Ocean,* among many others novels. Charles Averill, Harry Halyard, and Joseph Holt Ingraham are other popular American sea novelists mentioned in *Virgin Land: The American West as Symbol and Myth*, by Henry Nash Smith, a bibliography of dime novels on the University of Virginia website. Available at *http://xroads.virginia.edu/~Hyper/HNS/Carson/resource.htm*; consulted December 2009.

8. *Library Journal*, quoted on the back cover of Captain Frederick Marryat, *The Phantom Ship* (Ithaca, NY: McBook Press, 2000).

9. Gesa Mackenthun, *Fictions of the Black Atlantic in American Foundational Literature* (New York: Routledge, 2004), 84. Admiral Mahan was registering the shift of American interest away from the maritime frontier by the end of the nineteenth century when he observed, "How changed the present condition is, all know. The center of power is no longer on the seaboard. Books and newspapers vie with one another in describing the wonderful growth and the still undeveloped riches, of the interior." Cited from Alfred T. Mahan, *The Influence of Sea Power upon the French Revolution and Empire, 1793–1812,* quoted by Christopher Connery, "Ideologies of Land and Sea: Alfred Thayer Mahan, Carl Schmitt, and the Shaping of Global Myth Elements," *boundary 2* 28, no. 2 (2001): 184.

10. Honoré de Balzac, "Lettres sur la littérature, le théâtre et les arts," no. 1, *Revue Parisienne*, July 25, 1840, vol. 1, no. 1, p. 69.

11. Authors of urban mystery novels, starting with Balzac and Dumas, invoked Cooper's native Americans to frame their work as investigating "the Mohicans and Apaches of Paris." But there is a qualitative difference between Cooper as a source of inspiration, and Cooper's patterns taken up as such.

12. Philbrick, vii.

13. See, notably, the essays in *The Global Eighteenth Century*, ed. Felicity Nussbaum (Baltimore: Johns Hopkins University Press, 2005).

14. Srinivas Aravamudan, for example, shows the use made of the oriental tale by Eliza Haywood for finding "some ingenious ways of reinvigorating national allegory" as well as trumping "novelistic realism by resisting the imposition of national-realist boundaries." Srinivas Aravamudan, "In the Wake of the Novel: The Oriental Tale as National Allegory," *NOVEL: A Forum for Fiction* 33, no. 1 (1999): 26.

15. I take the terms *core* and *periphery* applied to literary production from Franco Moretti, who fuses world systems theory with Bourdieu's model of the literary field to invent a model for literary relations at the supranational scale. Moretti contrasts the cultural geographies at the hub of literary markets, institutions and innovations with those that look to the center from the "periphery," either of national or international culture. See Moretti's *Atlas of the European Novel 1800–1900* (London: Verso, 1998).

16. Anonymous review, "The Novels of James Fenimore Cooper," *Atlantic Monthly* 4, no. 23 (September 1859): 395. Alexandre Dumas, preface to *Le Capitaine Paul*, first published in 1838 (Paris: Michel Levy, 1858), 1. The view that *The Pilot* was preeminent among Cooper's novels or the subgenre of nautical novels recurs throughout nineteenth-century reception, even in the grudging opinion of critics who did not rank maritime adventure fiction highly, such as William Hazlitt: *The Pilot* "is the best of his works; and truth to say, we think it a masterpiece in its kind. It has great unity of purpose and feeling. Every thing in it may be said—'To suffer a *sea-change*/Into something new and strange.'" "American Literature—Dr. Channing," *Edinburgh Review* (October 1829): 125–31, cited in George Dekker and John P. McWilliams, *Fenimore Cooper: The Critical Heritage* (Boston: Routledge and Kegan Paul, 1973), 159.

17. James Fenimore Cooper, *The Pilot*, in *Sea Tales, The Pilot, The Red Rover*, eds. Kay Seymour House and Thomas Philbrick (New York: Library of America, 1990), 3. Subsequent citations will be referenced with page numbers in the body of the chapter.

18. Walter Scott, *Waverley, or 'tis sixty years since* (London: Penguin Classics, 1985), 36.

19. Cooper, Preface to *The Red Rover* in *Sea Tales, The Pilot, The Red Rover*, 429. Subsequent citations will be referenced by page number in the body of the chapter.

20. John Davis, *The Seamans Secrets* (London: John Dawson, 1633), n.p.

21. Casarino notes nineteenth-century sea fiction's continuity with previous picaresque genres, as I discuss in a note in chapter 2.

22. Robert Foulke, *The Sea Voyage Narrative* (New York: Routledge, 1997), 23.

23. William Gilmore Simms, "The Writings of Cooper," first published in *Magnolia* (1842), cited in Dekker and McWilliams, 223.

24. Jane Austen, *Emma*, ed. Fiona Stafford (New York: Penguin, 2003), 7.

25. Unsigned review from the *New-York Mirror* (1824) in Dekker and McWilliams, 75.

26. See Robert Louis Stevenson, *Treasure Island* (New York: Viking, 1996).

27. Herman Melville, preface to *Typee: A Peep at Polynesian Life*, ed. John Bryant (New York: Penguin Books, 1996), 1.

28. Joseph Conrad, "Legends," in *Last Essays, The Collected Works of Joseph Conrad* (New York: Routledge, 1995), 46.

29. Simms, in Dekker and McWilliams, 223.

30. Karl Marx, *Capital*, trans. Samuel Moore and Edward Aveling, ed. Frederick Engels (New York: The Modern Library, 1906), 197–198.

31. See, for example, Peter Linebaugh and Marcus Rediker's *The Many-Headed Hydra*, Jameson's analysis of Conrad in *The Political Unconscious*, or Moretti on Melville in *Modern Epic*. See, too, Casarino's *Modernity at Sea*.

32. At times, authors of sea fiction give a sentimental frame to their portrayal as well, suggesting that they paint the rigors of sea life to encourage "interest," and hence social improvement in the condition of sailors. Thus, Cooper's 1849 preface to *The Pilot* used the language of sentimental socialism, soliciting sympathy for the "most numerous" "suffering class"—i.e., the working class. Cooper writes, "Perhaps, in some small degree, an interest has been awakened in behalf of a very numerous, and what has hitherto been a sort of proscribed class of men, that may directly tend to a melioration of their condition" (7).

33. Charles Kingsely, *Alton Locke* (London: Chapman and Hall, 1850), vol. 1, 122.

34. Charles Kingsley, *Westward Ho!* (Leipzig: Bernhard Tauchnitz, 1855), vol. 2, 18–19.

35. Ibid., 19.

36. Joseph Conrad, *The Mirror of the Sea* (Marlboro, VT: The Marlboro Press, 1988), 20.

37. Extract from Leigh Hunt's review of *The Pilot*, *Tatler*, ii (April 7, 1831), 737, cited in Dekker and McWilliams, 162.

38. Francis Parkman, "The Works of James Fenimore Cooper," *North American Review*, lxxiv (January 1852), in Dekker and McWilliams, 249.

39. Anonymous review, "The Novels of James Fenimore Cooper," 395.

40. See Lukács's analysis of Scott in *The Historical Novel*. I thus diverge from Mackenthun and other critics in understanding Cooper's plot rewards of marriage and career for his young men as unsatisfying or even beside the point at the level of the novel's dramatic energy. The dissatisfaction of contemporaries with Cooper's love plots would support this reading, as would the observations of Conrad as well as Bakhtin, that the reassertion of biographical events like marriage represents the death of adventuring. In Conrad's words on Cooper's novels, "the stress of adventure and endeavour must end fatally in inheritance and marriage." Joseph Conrad, "Tales of the Sea" (1898) in *Notes on Life and Letters*, eds. J. H. Stape and Andrew Busza (New York: Cambridge University Press), 47.

41. Walter Scott, *The Pirate* (New York: Thomas Nelson and Sons, 1905), 504. Reprinted Whitefish, MT: Kessinger Publishing, 2004.

42. Ibid., 564.

43. Ibid., 564.

44. George Sand, "Extract from 'Fenimore Cooper,'" *Autour de la Table* (Paris, 1856), in Dekker and McWilliams, trans. D. B. Wood, 265.

45. Ibid., 265.

46. Ibid., 262. A number of reviews anthologized by Dekker and McWilliams view Cooper's extraordinary frontiersmen as sailors of the plains. In the words of Simms, "Hawkeye, the land sailor of Mr. Cooper, is, with certain suitable modifications," the Pilot, "breasting the storm, tried by, and finally baffling all its powers, as the Prometheus in action." Simms, in Dekker and McWilliams, 224.

47. George Gordon, Lord Byron, *The Corsair* (1814), in *The Complete Poetical Works of Lord Byron* (Boston: Houghton Mifflin, 1905), 338. Philbrick notes the debt of *The Red Rover's* pirates to *The Corsair's* exaltation of the ocean as "an avenue to self-realization" (64).

48. Sand, "Extract from 'Fenimore Cooper,'" 265.

49. Daniel Defoe, *Robinson Crusoe*, ed. Michael Shinagel (New York: W.W. Norton, 1994), 4.

50. Jeanne-Marie Santraud writes, "The American revolt is that of a people calling for free access to the ocean." Jeanne-Marie Santraud, *La Mer et le roman américain dans la première moitié du dix-neuvième siècle* (Paris: Didier, 1972), 18.

51. James Fenimore Cooper, *The Travelling Bachelor; or, Notions of the Americans* (New York: Stringer and Townsend, 1852), vol. 1, 9.

52. Review of *The Prairie*, *Colburn's New Monthly Magazine* (1827), in Dekker and McWilliams, 121.

53. Alexis de Tocqueville, *Democracy in America*, ed. Isaac Kramnick, trans. Gerald Bevan (New York: Penguin, 2003), 478.

54. Ibid., quotes from 473, 470, 474.

55. Cited in Dekker and McWilliams, 6.

56. In Philbrick's view, "[t]he sea novel . . . owes its inception to the meeting of maritime nationalism and romanticism in the imagination of James Fenimore Cooper" (42). Philbrick accords a role to the sublime sea of Romanticism in particular. Thomas Philbrick, "Cooper and the Literary Discovery of the Sea," presented at the 7th Cooper Seminar, "James Fenimore Cooper: His Country and His Art," SUNY Oneonta, July 1989. Available at *http://external.oneonta .edu/cooper/articles/suny/1989suny-philbrick.html*; consulted March 30, 2007. My difference from Philbrick turns on the image of the ocean as a dreary waste before Romanticism, whereas I understand it as the theater of craft. This leads me to understand Cooper as picking up Romantic figures to be sure, but also taking a position against the sublime seas when he moors craft to patriotism.

57. Carl Schmitt, *The Nomos of the Eart*, trans. G. L. Ulmen (New York: Telos Press, 2003), 289, 290.

58. "The United States: American Literature, Novels of Mr. Cooper,'" in *Le Globe*, June 19, 1827, signed F.A.S. (Sainte-Beuve). Translation by J. P. McWilliams, in Dekker and McWilliams, 128.

59. Cited in Dekker and McWilliams, 137. The place of women poses a problem to this idealization of the new republic as a community of shipboard labor. Lieutenant Maturin Murray Ballou's *Fanny Campbell or, The Female Pirate Captain. A Tale of the Revolution* (New York: Samuel French, 1844) solves the problem by allowing women into the community of craft when they cross-dress and show themselves the equals of men as regards their mastery of maritime knowledge. This was the case of the pirates Anne Bonny and Mary Read in *A General*

History of the Pyrates. Fanny is their descendant, with clean morals and a dedication to patriotism, in keeping with nineteenth-century sea fiction's more general transvaluation of the eighteenth-century maritime picaresque.

60. See Thomas Bender, *A Nation Among Nations: America's Place in World History* (New York: Hill and Wang, 2006).

61. Georges Bataille, "The Notion of Expenditure," in *Visions of Excess: Selected Writings, 1927–1939,* ed. and trans. Allan Stoekl with Carl R. Lovitt and Donald M. Leslie Jr. (Minneapolis: University of Minnesota Press, 1985), 119.

62. Herman Melville, *White-Jacket,* in *Redburn, White-Jacket, Moby-Dick,* ed. G. Thomas Tanselle (New York: Library of America, 1983), 498.

63. Philbrick, 51.

64. Dumas, preface to *Le Capitaine Paul,* cited earlier.

65. The review continued, "He confers reality on all his descriptions. We hear the roar of the waves—the splash of the oars—the hoarse language of the seamen. . . . Yet nothing is overwrought." 1824 review in *New-York Mirror,* cited in Dekker and McWilliams, 74–75. Edgar Allen Poe, too, noted Cooper's continuity with Defoe in a snidely dismissive review, taking *The Pilot* to task for its lack of character development or plot. Nonetheless, Poe owned that the novels did have an "interest" for readers that "depends, first upon the nature of the theme; secondly, upon a Robinson-Crusoe-like detail in its management." Edgar Allan Poe, review, *Graham's Magazine* xxiv (November 1843), cited in Dekker and McWilliams, 207.

66. On Cooper's familiarity with Gothic conventions, see a number of articles on SUNY's informative James Fenimore Cooper website, including Donald Ringe's "*The Last of the Mohicans* as a Gothic Novel" [1986 SUNY seminar] and "*The Bravo*: Social Criticism in the Gothic Mode" [1991 SUNY seminar], as well as Kerry Dean Carso's "The Old Dwelling Transmogrified: James Fenimore Cooper's Otsego Hall" [2001 SUNY seminar]. Available at *http://external.oneonta.edu/cooper/articles/suny.html*; consulted December 2009.

67. When Roland Barthes describes how Balzac advances his narratives by luring his readers into a gripping dance of information, he is unwittingly registering how much Balzac has learned from Cooper's adventure fiction, both from Cooper himself and from Eugène Sue, whose importance to Balzac is detailed in this chapter's closing section.

68. Anne Radcliffe, *The Mysteries of Udolpho* (New York: Oxford University Press, 1998), 360.

69. "To make anything very terrible, obscurity is necessary," wrote Edmund Burke in his treatise on the sublime. Edmund Burke, *A Philosophical Enquiry into the Origin of Our Ideas of the Sublime and Beautiful,* ed. Adam Philips (New York: Oxford University Press, 1998), 54.

70. Radcliffe highlights the terrors of Emily Saint-Aubert, heroine of *The Mysteries of Udolpho,* with chiaroscuro: "the man, shaking the torch, passed on . . . the light shewed the high black walls around them, fringed with long grass and dank weeds, that found a scanty soil among the mouldering stones," etc. Radcliffe, *The Mysteries of Udolpho,* 345.

71. George Sand's previously cited enthusiasm is indicative. Charlotte Brontë was less favorable in her letters. See Charlotte Brontë, *Selected Letters of Charlotte Brontë,* ed. Margaret Smith (New York: Oxford University Press, 2007), 27.

72. Richard Henry Dana Jr., *Two Years Before the Mast*, in *Two Years Before the Mast and Other Voyages*, ed. Thomas Philbrick (New York: Library of America, 2005), 4.

73. Cited in House's introduction to The State University of New York Press edition of *The Pilot*, xxxviii.

74. Critics recognized Cooper's debt to plain style when they cited his "air of rough freedom, sometimes approaching, but never we think, amounting to coarseness— . . . thrown over the whole," *New-York Mirror* ii (December 1824), cited in Dekker and McWilliams, 75.

75. Jules Verne, *Les Grands Navigateurs du XVIIIe siècle* (Paris: Ramsay, 1977), 140.

76. Anne-Gaëlle Weber observes that Verne will in fact elaborate on just these scenarios in one of his own science fiction sea novels, *Les Enfants du capitaine Grant*. See Anne-Gaëlle Weber, *A beau mentir qui vient de loin: Savants, voyageurs et romanciers au XIXe siècle* (Paris: Honoré Champion, 2004), 69.

77. See Louis J. Parascandola's introduction to Frederick Marryat, *Mr. Midshipman Easy* (New York: Henry Holt, 1998), xii. Subsequent quotes will be referenced by page number within the text of the chapter. There are, notably, strong Bildungsroman elements to *The Naval Officer or Scenes and Adventures in the Life of Frank Mildmay*. Frank Mildmay is not at the start a superior being like the Pilot or the Rover, but rather makes his apprenticeship in craft as he rises through the ranks. At the same time, as the novel progresses, elements of the Bildungsroman start to undergo the influence of adventure fiction, as is evident in Marryat's treatment of the courtship plot. Though Mildmay does return home to marry the virtuous genteel lady he has been "courting" through his absence, he only does so after multiple affairs with beauties around the globe, as contemporary critics noted with some discomfort. For informative details on Marryat's career as mariner and novelist, as well as an overview of his novels, their reception, and themes, see Maurice-Paul Gautier, *Captain Frederick Marryat 1792–1848* (Paris: Didier, 1973).

78. Conrad, was, I think picking up on the absence of Bildung in Marryat's novels when he praised Marryat's ability to depict adventures at sea, in contrast to his treatment of social relations on land. In Conrad's opinion, Marryat's "novels, like amphibious creatures, live on the sea and frequent the shore, where they flounder deplorably. The loves and the hates of his boys are as primitive as their virtues and their vices. His women, from the beautiful Agnes" of *Mr. Midshipman Easy* are "with the exception of the sailors' wives, like the shadows of what has never been." In Conrad, "Tales of the Sea," 46.

79. See the chapter "Du Midship au Lieutenant," 27 ff., for details on this service in Gautier, *Captain Frederick Marryat*.

80. Thus, when Jack poaches as a teenager, he invokes the arguments about equality to serve his own gentleman's sense of entitlement. "'But, Mr Easy, allowing the trespass on the property to be venial, surely you do not mean to say that you are justified in taking my fish . . . you cannot deny but that they are private property.'" To which Jack responds, "'that will admit of much ratiocination . . . but,—I beg your pardon, I have a fish.' Jack pulled up a large carp . . . unhooked it, placed it in his basket, renewed his bait with the greatest sang froid, and then throwing in his line, resumed his discourse. 'As I was observing, my dear sir . . .

that will admit of much ratiocination. All the creatures of the earth were given to man for his use—man means mankind—they were never intended to be made a monopoly of. Water is also the gift of heaven, and meant for the use of all,'" etc. (26–27).

81. For the details of Jack's maritime adventuring, Marryat drew on his own experience as midshipman to Lord Cochrane, cruising the Atlantic and Mediterranean around the Straits of Gibraltar, in the Napoleonic Wars.

82. Gautier suggests that most abuses for Marryat go back to "the Admiralty, whose anachronistic power exerts its noxious and paralyzing influence even on board ship." Gautier, 291. Gautier details how Marryat had already penned a pamphlet critical of the Navy in 1822.

83. Marryat, *The Phantom Ship*, 14.

84. Ibid., 60.

85. Catherine Gallagher, "Floating Signifiers of Britishness in the Novels of the Anti-Slave-Trade Squadron," in *Dickens and the Children of Empire*, ed. Wendy S. Jacobson (New York: Palgrave Macmillan, 2000), 78–79. Conrad concurred about Marryat's ability to put his characters' picaresque itinerary in the service of British imperialism. In Conrad's formulation, Marryat's pen "serves his country as well as did his professional skill and his renowned courage" in the Royal Navy. Marryat was "the enslaver of youth not by the literary artifices of presentation, but by the natural glamour of his own temperament," echoed in "young heroes" for whom "the beginning of life is a splendid and warlike lark." And again, "It is by his irresistible power to reach the adventurous side in the character, not only of his own, but of all nations, that Marryat is largely human." Conrad, "Tales of the Sea," 46.

86. See Gayatri Spivak's "Three Women's Texts and a Critique of Imperialism," originally published in *Critical Inquiry* 12, no. 1 (autumn 1985): 243–61. See also Edward Said's chapter on Jane Austen in *Culture and Imperialism* (New York: Vintage Books, 1994), 80–97.

87. Bourdieu specifies that in the domain of poetics, for position-taking to become a position—i.e., an established and imitated literary practice—it will generally resolve impasses at the level of the literary field as well as provide imaginary solutions to broader intractable social questions.

88. These features also characterize sentimental fiction, catapulted to international celebrity in the middle of the eighteenth century, with the novels of Richardson and then Rousseau. I discuss sentimental fiction as a traveling genre in my chapter, "Sentimental Communities," in *The Literary Channel*, eds. Margaret Cohen and Carolyn Dever (Princeton, NJ: Princeton University Press, 2002).

89. Charles Augustin de Sainte-Beuve, *La Revue des Deux-Mondes*, cited in preface by Guy Schoeller to Eugène Sue, *Romans de Mort et d'Aventure* (Paris: Robert Laffont, 1993), ii.

90. Sue, preface to *Kernok le pirate* and *El Gitano*, cited in Bosset, 122. Sue pursued this project in his *Histoire de la Marine Française*, a four-volume work first published in 1835.

91. James Fenimore Cooper to Eugène Sue, March 1831, in *The Letters and Journals of James Fenimore Cooper*, ed. James Franklin Beard (Cambridge, MA: Harvard University Press, 1960), II, 56.

92. Ibid. Sue was to cite Cooper as model throughout his career, from the preface of his first full-length roman maritime, *Atar-Gull*, dedicated to Fenimore Cooper, to his view that urban mystery novels investigated "the Mohicans of Paris."

93. Sue, preface to *La Salamandre*, in *Romans de Mort et d'Aventure*, 1325. Subsequent citations from the preface and novel referenced by page number in the text of the chapter.

94. Honoré de Balzac, "La Salamandre," March 1832 in *La Revue des Deux Mondes*, cited in the dossier to Sue, *Romans de Mort et d'Aventure*, 1335.

95. Théophile Gautier, "Histoire de la Marine," part 1, in *La Chronique de Paris*, a periodical directed by Balzac, February–March 1832, included in the dossier for *Romans de Mort et d'Aventure*, 1338. Gautier worked up to his praise by objecting that to understand Sue, one would have to "learn the seaman's dictionary by heart." Gautier's objection underscores a difference in national literary traditions. While Anglophone critics enjoyed plain style, it violated the linguistic purity of French neoclassical aesthetics. Gautier, 1337.

96. Sara James, "Sue, Marie-Joseph Eugène," in *Encyclopedia of the Romantic Era*, ed. Christopher John Murray (New York: Taylor and Francis, 2004), vol. 2, 1104.

97. Sue, *Atar-Gull*, in *Romans de Mort et d'Aventure*, 206. This novel contains innocent characters, but no virtuous embodiments of craft. Rather, craft is possessed by the slave ship captain Brulart and Atar-Gull, who organizes a diabolical vengeance on his master.

98. Sue, *La Vigie de Koat-Vën*, in *Romans de Mort et d'Aventure*, G. C. Bosset commented that Sue did not realize the project of naval celebration that he imagined and that from his first novella, "the nautical element takes up less space than in Cooper. Kernok is a bold and happy mariner, but he is not an enthusiastic mariner" (Bosset, 125). Rather, Bosset observes that Sue's emphasis in his maritime portraits is on morality and psychology. The shift from the craft of the mariner to Szaffie's psychological skills at social manipulation is the endpoint of this process.

99. Balzac, "La Salamandre," in *Romans de Mort et d'Aventure*, 1335.

100. Peter Brooks's *Melodramatic Imagination: Balzac, Henry James, Melodrama, and the Mode of Excess* (New Haven, CT: Yale University Press, 1975) remains a defining archaeology of popular melodrama and emphasizes the form's importance for Balzac.

101. Balzac, "La Salamandre," in *Romans de Mort et d'Aventure*, 1335.

102. See Jonathan Crary's "Gericault, the Panorama, and Sites of Reality in the Early Nineteenth Century," *Grey Room 9* (fall 2002): 5–25, for a discussion of Géricault's dialogue with the contemporary popular spectacle of the panorama.

103. In Gramsci's words, "In any case it seems that one can claim that much of the would-be Nietzschean 'supermanism' has its source and doctrinal model not in *Zarathustra* but merely in Alexandre Dumas's *The Count of Monte-Cristo* . . . In Balzac, too, there is much of the serial novel. Even Vautrin is a superman in his way." Antonio Gramsci, *Selections from Cultural Writings*, ed. David Forgacs and Geoffrey Nowell-Smith, trans. William Boelhower (London: ElecBook, 1999), 596.

104. In comparison to the brutal, lawless freedom of post-Revolutionary society, Balzac would paint the freedom of the seas as an escape. One of the only

portrayals of happiness in his novels concerns Julie's daughter, in *La Femme de trente ans*. Hélène runs off with a pirate, and enjoys a lyrical idyll, until the law of the land returns to squash out such romanticism.

105. See Karsten Harries, "The Philosopher at Sea," in *Nietzsche's New Seas. Explorations in Philosophy, Aesthetics, and Politics*, eds. Michael Allen Gillespie and Tracy B. Strong (Chicago: University of Chicago Press, 1988), 21–44. Luce Irigaray offers another approach to Nietzsche's interest in the ocean from the perspective of archetypes in *Marine Lover of Friedrich Nietzsche*, trans. Gillian C. Gill (New York: Columbia University Press, 1991).

106. Nietzsche, *Thus Spoke Zarathustra*, 155–56.

107. Ibid., 230.

CHAPTER 5: SEA FICTION BEYOND THE SEAS

1. Edgar Allan Poe, *The Narrative of Arthur Gordon Pym of Nantucket*, in *The Narrative of Arthur Gordon Pym of Nantucket and Related Tales*, ed. J. Gerald Kennedy (New York: Oxford University Press, 2008), 175.

2. Routinization is relative. The sea remained a dangerous profession. "10,827 seamen on the sailing ships of just one nation, Britain, were lost at sea in the seven years of 1873–1880." Cited in Jerry Allen, *The Sea Years of Joseph Conrad* (New York: Doubleday, 1965), 3. In 1880, a year of record storms, "1209 seamen were lost at sea in British ships alone" (113).

3. Foulke describes the uneven nature of the shift from sail to steam: "No year served as a decisive turning point, and no single development was the prime cause of the sailing ship's demise; the technological perfection of sailing ships and the development of steamships occurred more or less simultaneously." Robert Foulke, *The Sea Voyage Narrative* (New York: Routledge, 1997), 139. Nonetheless, as Foulke goes on to point out, by the 1880s, steamships were well on the way to "depress sailing-ship freights permanently," due to technological improvements, from "the development of strong iron hulls, screw propellers, and high–pressure steam engines," to the "opening of the Suez canal in 1869" that, "by decreasing the gap between coaling stations, made the long-distance trades to India and the Far East practicable for steamers."

4. Casarino observes, "The world of the sea . . . had occupied the central position in the functioning of mercantile capitalism . . . The world of the sea under industrial capitalism . . . became, if anything, more important than ever for the functioning of an international political economy that was now for the first time coming into being as a tendentially global capitalist system." Cesare Casarino, *Modernity at Sea: Melville, Marx, Conrad in Crisis* (Minneapolis: University of Minnesota Press, 2002), 4.

5. Casarino notes the contradiction between the forms of labor represented in sea fiction and nineteenth-century modernity as a productive tension generating modernist works of sea fiction in the nineteenth century, although his focus is on industrial modernity and the novel more generally, rather than on the specificity of sea adventure fiction and the history of maritime innovation. For Casarino, "the predicament of the nineteenth-century sea narrative: [is] what narrative

structures can one use when one has a new tale to tell, when one is announcing the invisible and powerful presence of something radically new that does not yet actually exist anywhere," and that tale is the tale of nineteenth-century imperialism and industrial capitalism. As a result, sea fiction became "the site where visions of the new . . . came to incubate within old forms of representation so as to then explode those forms from the interior" (Casarino, 5).

6. J. Doyne Farmer proposed the notion that in late modernity, adventure is increasingly taking place in "the mental domain" in a paper presented at Stanford's Center for the Study of the Novel Conference on "Adventure," November 11, 2005. The paper, "The Evolution of Adventure in Literature and Life," is available at *http://www.santafe.edu/~jdf/papers/adventure4.pdf*.

7. Joseph Conrad, *The Nigger of the "Narcissus,"* ed. Robert Kimbrough (New York: Norton, 1979), 146, 148.

8. Philbrick observes that "Melville's literary career itself owes its inception to Cooper and his contemporaries." Thomas Philbrick, *James Fenimore Cooper and the Development of American Sea Fiction*, (Cambridge, MA: Harvard University Press, 1961), 265–66. Andrew Delbanco provides details on Melville's readings throughout *Melville, His World and Work* (New York: Knopf, 2005).

9. Herman Melville, *Moby-Dick or The Whale*, in *Redburn, White-Jacket, Moby-Dick*, ed. G. Thomas Tanselle (New York: Library of America, 1983), 782. Subsequent citations will be referenced by page numbers in the text of the chapter.

10. Herman Melville, *Typee: A Peep at Polynesian Life*, ed. John Bryant (New York: Penguin Books, 1996),1. Similarly, at the preface's end, "there are some things related in the narrative, which will be sure to appear strange, or perhaps entirely incomprehensible, to the reader; but they cannot appear more so to him than they did to the author at the time" (2). Subsequent citations referenced by page in the text of the chapter.

11. Herman Melville, *Redburn*, in *Redburn, White-Jacket, Moby-Dick*, 12. Further citations will be referenced by page number in the text of the chapter.

12. Indeed, among the maritime practices of this decade, there would be only two other possible arenas for a tale of craft on the frontiers of expanding modernity: exploration of the polar regions, which were the subject of Cooper's *Sea Lions*, for example, or the practice of clipper ships, the last major technological innovation in the working age of sail. Clipper ships were built to show that sailing ships could compete with steam transport—and indeed, clipper ships under the right conditions did beat the Cunard steamships, notably on one transatlantic crossing that took only an incredible fourteen days. Like whaling, this subject matter would be suitable for an American author pursuing the nationalist component of nineteenth-century sea fiction. Clipper ships were invented by American engineers and associated with them ("Yankee Clipper"). But while clipper ships were in the vanguard of technology, they navigated oceans that were comparatively routine, in contrast to the extreme work of whaling.

13. J. N. Reynolds, *Mocha Dick: or the White Whale of the Pacific* (New York: Charles Scribner's Sons, 1932), 89.

14. Cited in Michael J. Davey, *A Routledge Literary Sourcebook on Herman Melville's Moby-Dick* (New York: Routledge, 2004), 72. The November 22, 1851, review in the *Albion* concurred: "Not only is there an immense amount of

reliable information before us; the *dramatis personae*, mates, harpooners, carpenters, and cooks, are all vivid sketches done in the author's best style. What they do, and how they look, is brought to one's perception with wondrous elaborateness of detail; and yet this minuteness does not spoil the broad outline of each" (71).

15. Wai Chee Dimock observes that Ahab's "antiquated feudal barbarism" substitutes for American democracy, a regression that tortures Starbuck. See Wai Chee Dimock, *Empire for Liberty: Melville and the Poetics of Individualism* (Princeton, NJ: Princeton University Press, 1991), 122. Melville will return to the failure of the ship's collectivity of craft in his later novellas, *Billy Budd*, and *Benito Cereno*. This latter novella rewrites Sue's *Atar-Gull*, which had been translated in the United States as *Atar Gull, a Nautical Tale* by William Henry Herbert (New York: Henry L. Williams, 1846).

16. Joseph Conrad, *Heart of Darkness*, ed. Robert Kimbrough (New York: W.W. Norton, 1988), 9.

17. Casarino, 135. These sentences, Casarino also observes, "reach further and further toward an unreachable limit . . . stretch[ing] the very linguistic unit to its furthest limits. This is not simply a question of length; more importantly, it is a question of structure."

18. Samuel Otter, *Melville's Anatomies* (Berkeley: University of California Press, 1999), 5. Foulke, too, notes the importance of the anatomy for Melville, emphasizing the novel's erudition on whaling as on a range of other subjects.

19. Richard Brodhead notes that these subjects are not the province of some other cultural system called "religion," or, I would add, philosophy. "They are instead literature's province, questions literature is empowered to address and explore." Richard Brodhead, ed., "Introduction," in *New Essays on Moby-Dick* (New York: Cambridge University Press, 1986), 5.

20. Richardson, cited in Andrew Ashfield and Peter de Bolla, eds. *The Sublime: A Reader in British Eighteenth-Century Aesthetic Theory* (New York: Cambridge University Press, 1996), 48, 47.

21. On the phenomenological figure of philosophy as an adventure in a lineage launched by Hegel, see Michael J. MacDonald, "Losing Spirit: Hegel, Lévinas, and the Limits of Narrative," *Narrative* 13, no. 2 (May 2005): 182–94.

22. According to Simon Leys, Hugo "also was concerned to soak up a huge literature on the sea, both classic and contemporary: he knew the writings of the great mariners and pirates of the past, he had even read the memoires of Marteilhe; just like Balzac, he was influenced by the sea novels of Fenimore Cooper, and above all by those of the younger brother of them both, Eugène Sue; *La Mer* by Michelet had been for him at once a powerful stimulant and a provocation. But above all, his curiosity was never purely confined to books: he took every opportunity to adventure out on the water, he spent time with the seamen of the Channel, he knew these men and he admired them, he initiated himself into their craft [métier] and their language." Simon Leys, *La Mer dans la Littérature Française: De Victor Hugo à Pierre Loti* (Paris: Plon, 2003), vol. 2, 8. For an introduction to Hugo's career from the vantage point of the ocean, see also the website on "Hugo l'homme océan," under the auspices of the French National Library: *http://expositions.bnf.fr/hugo/expo.htm*; consulted December 2009.

23. From "Océan," where Hugo also remarked, "I have had two matters [affaires] in my life, Paris and the ocean," cited in Leys, vol. 2, 7.

24. Allan Sekula makes this point in *Fish Story*, 42.

25. Victor Hugo, *Toilers of the Sea*, trans. Isabel F. Hapgood (New York: Signet, 2000), xiii. Subsequent citations will be referenced by page number within the text of the chapter.

26. Henry James, "Victor Hugo," *The Nation* 1866, anthologized in Henry James, *Literary Criticism: French Writers, Other European Writers, Prefaces to the New York Edition* (New York: Library of America, 1984), 447.

27. I cite here from notes for the preface by Hugo found in Victor Hugo, *Les Travailleurs de la mer*, ed. Yves Gohin (Paris: Gallimard, 1980), 593. As Victor Brombert observes, "Hugo's notes for the original preface make his intention clear. After dealing with 'Misery' in his previous novel, he was now attempting 'the glorification of Work.'" Victor Brombert, *Hugo and the Visionary Novel* (Cambridge, MA: Harvard University Press, 1984), 140–41.

28. David Charles notes Hugo's interest in embodied reason in *La Pensée technique dans l'oeuvre de Victor Hugo: le bricolage de l'infini* (Paris: Presses Universitaires de France, 1997), when he aligns Gilliatt's heroism in the novel with the classical concept of *metis*, elaborated by Marcel Détienne and Jean-Pierre Vernant. In Charles's view, Gilliatt's *metis* has an archaic significance. Gilliatt steps in with an older kind of knowledge to help the novel's pioneer of steamboat transportation Mess Lethierry, when Lethierry's vanguard technology fails. Charles thus reads Gilliatt's multifaceted, embodied skill as Hugo's longing for unalienated labor and his critique of progress, with its degradation in industrialization. My difference concerns the fact that Hugo's portrayal concerns the ethos of modernity, exploring the limits in quest of their supersession.

29. Henry James, "Victor Hugo," 447.

30. Brombert notes a "poetic process of substitution, transfer, conversion," which starts to dissolve the material world into language and literature. Victor Brombert, "*Les Travailleurs de la mer*: Hugo's Poem of Effacement," *New Literary History* 9, no. 3 (*Rhetoric I: Rhetorical Analyses*; spring 1978): 581–90, esp. 589, which I have cited.

31. Henry James, "Victor Hugo," 451.

32. Ibid., 447.

33. Hugo was also interested in the poetic dimension that reverberated from the maritime language of work. In *Les Misérables*, Hugo singled out "that admirable language of the sea" as a noble form of "argot," contrasting the heroic argot of skilled work with the disreputable argot of the underworld. In the language "so compleat and so picturesque spoken by Jean Bart, Duquesne, Suffren, and Duperré," Hugo could hear the "whistling of the rigging and furniture of the ship [agrès]," the "noise of the speaking-trumpet," the "shock of the boarding axes," "the violent swell," "the wind," and "bursts of canon fire." Victor Hugo, *Les Misérables* (Paris: Garnier Frères, 1963), vol. 2, 190.

34. Philippe Hamon, "Rhetorical Status of the Descriptive," trans. Patricia Baudoin, *Yale French Studies* 61 (1981): 1–26, 21.

35. "Hugo is a surrealist when he is not stupid," declared André Breton. André Breton, *Manifeste du surréalisme* in *Oeuvres complètes*, ed. Marguerite Bonnet (Paris: Bibliothèque de la Pléiade, 1988), 329.

36. Arthur Rimbaud, *Le Bateau ivre* in *Poésies complètes*, with preface by Paul Verlaine (Paris: L. Vanier, 1895), 18. The lines, in Samuel Beckett's translation, run: "Thenceforward, fused in the poem, milk of stars, / Of the sea, I coiled through deeps of cloudless green, / Where, dimly, they come swaying down, / Rapt and sad, singly, the drowned;" in Samuel Beckett, *Collected Poems in English and in French* (New York: Grove Press, 1977), 95.

37. Pierre Loti is another late-nineteenth-century author who starts from the poetics of sea fiction to explore the frontiers of the psyche. See, for example, his exoticist sea novel, *Aziyadé* (Paris: Gallimard Folio, 1991). (Full subtitle: *Extrait des notes et lettres d'un lieutenant de la marine anglaise entré au service de la Turquie le 10 mai 1876 tué dans les murs de Kars, le 27 octobre 1877* [excerpted from the notes and letters of a lieutenant in the English navy, who enlisted in the service of Turkey, March 10, 1876, killed on the walls of Kars, the 27 October, 1877].) For Loti, another name for the frontier is transgression, and he moves it from the sea to the domain of morality. *Aziyadé* opens with an English naval officer AWOL from his corvette in Salonica. His flight from duty will plunge him into an exploration of bisexuality, as well as the betrayal of his office and national responsibility.

38. Joseph Conrad, *A Personal Record*, eds. Zdzislaw Najder and J. H. Stape (New York: Cambridge University Press, 2008), 105.

39. Conrad, *Heart of Darkness*, citations in last two sentences on 38.

40. Peter Villiers, *Joseph Conrad Master Mariner* (Dobbs Ferry, NY: Sheridan House, 2006), 96.

41. John Galsworthy, *Castles in Spain*, 74–76, cited in Villiers, 96.

42. Conrad, *A Personal Record*, 72.

43. Joseph Conrad, *Lord Jim* (New York: Penguin, 1986), 47. Subsequent citations will be referenced by page numbers in the body of the chapter. For Jameson in *The Political Unconscious*, this passage indicates Conrad's engagement and discomfort with mass literature. Jameson writes, "the non-place of the sea is . . . the space of the degraded language of romance and daydream, of narrative commodity and the sheer distraction of 'light literature.'" Fredric Jameson, *The Political Unconscious: Narrative as a Socially Symbolic Act* (Ithaca, NY: Cornell University Press, 1981), 213. However, as Jameson observes, the sea is also a place of work, and this work finds its expression in sea novels, as well. It should now be clear that sea fiction is more influential and complex than its caricature in *Lord Jim*, for no one more than Conrad.

44. Joseph Conrad, "Tales of the Sea" (1898), in *Notes on Life and Letters*, eds. J. H. Stape and Andrew Busza (New York: Cambridge University Press, 2004), 48.

45. Joseph Conrad, "Geography and Some Explorers," in *Last Essays, The Collected Works of Joseph Conrad* (New York: Routledge, 1995), 21.

46. Ibid., 18.

47. Ibid., 21.

48. *Lord Jim: A Tale*, takes up a generic tag that dates back to Cooper as well: *The Red Rover. A Tale* (1828), *The Two Admirals. A Tale* (1842), and *The Wing-and-Wing; Or Le Feu-Follet. A Tale* (1842).

49. Joseph Conrad, *Typhoon*, in *Typhoon and Other Stories*, ed. J. H. Stape (New York: Penguin, 2007), vii, subsequent page references in the text.

50. From *The Daily Chronicle* (London), December 22, 1897, cited in Joseph Conrad, *The Nigger of the "Narcissus,"* 217.

51. Conrad, *The Nigger of the "Narcissus,"* 14. Subsequent citations will be referenced by page number in the text.

52. See Denis Murphy, "Seamanship in Chapter Three of *The Nigger of the 'Narcissus,'*" in critical dossier to Conrad, *The Nigger of the "Narcissus,"* 135–41.

53. Virginia Woolf, "Joseph Conrad," in *The Common Reader, First Series,* ed. and intro. Andrew McNeillie (New York: Harcourt, 1984), 226.

54. Joseph Conrad, *The Secret Sharer,* in *Heart of Darkness and The Secret Sharer,* ed. Albert Guerard (New York: Signet Classics, 1950), 19–61. I quote from the passage that plays out across pages 59–60.

55. Joseph Conrad, *The Mirror of the Sea* (Marlboro, VT: The Marlboro Press, 1988), 78.

56. Edwin Hutchins, *Cognition in the Wild* (Cambridge, MA: MIT Press, 1995), 126, 117.

57. See Ian Watt's chapter on *Lord Jim* in *Conrad and the Nineteenth Century* (Berkeley: University of California Press, 1979), notably 270 ff. The maritime framework reveals that these different techniques are all part of the same work of information processing, and that the goal is clarity, rather than obscurity.

58. To bolster his denial that he called Jim a cur, that is to say, Marlow not only describes his own intent but points Jim toward the dog, the physical referent.

59. Erskine Childers' *The Riddle of the Sands* (1903) is another early work of spy fiction, where spy fiction emerges from the adventure of the sea. In the navigation of the misty, convoluted marshes of the North Sea, a crafty seaman and his friend, who at first thinks he is off on a sea holiday of light literature, uncover information that leads them to a German plot to invade Britain.

60. Conrad, *A Personal Record,* 103–104. Conrad narrates the final problem at length, and it demonstrates the role given to imaginative problem-solving in the mariner's training:

> Finally he shoved me into the North Sea (I suppose), and provided me with a lee–shore with outlying sandbanks—the Dutch coast, presumably. Distance, eight miles. The evidence of such implacable animosity deprived me of speech for quite half a minute.
>
> "Well," he said—for our pace had been very smart indeed till then.
>
> "I will have to think a little, sir."
>
> "Doesn't look as if there were much time to think," he muttered, sardonically from under his hand.
>
> "No, sir," I said, with some warmth. "Not on board a ship I could see. But so many accidents have happened that I really can't remember what there's left for me to work with."
>
> Still half averted, and with his eyes concealed, he made unexpectedly a grunting remark.
>
> "You've done very well."
>
> "Have I the two anchors at the bow, sir?" I asked.
>
> "Yes."
>
> I prepared myself then, as a last hope for the ship, to let them both go in the most effectual manner, when his infernal system of testing resourcefulness came into play again.

"But there's only one cable. You've lost the other."

It was exasperating.

"Then I would back them, if I could, and tail the heaviest hawser on board on the end of the chain before letting go, and if she parted from that, which is quite likely, I would just do nothing. She would have to go."

"Nothing more to do, eh?"

"No, sir. I could do no more."

He gave a bitter half-laugh.

"You could always say your prayers."

He got up, stretched himself, and yawned slightly. . . . He put me in a surly, bored fashion through the usual questions as to lights and signals, and I escaped from the room thankfully—passed!

Conrad, *A Personal Record*, 104–5.

61. Note to Jules Verne, *The Invasion of the Sea*, trans. Edward Baxter, notes by Arthur B. Evans (Middletown, CT: Wesleyan University Press, 2001), 208 n.5.

62. Whether Verne's invention of technologies on the verge of being realized is praiseworthy has been disputed by critics of science fiction. In the view of H. G. Wells, Verne was limited by the fact that he "'dealt almost always with actual possibilities of invention and discovery,'" while the innovation of Wells was to "'hold the reader to the end by art and illusion.'" Cited in Timothy Unwin, *Jules Verne, Journeys in Writing* (Liverpool, UK: University of Liverpool Press, 2005), 10.

63. In *A Thousand Plateaus*, Deleuze and Guattari reference maritime modernity in describing how what they call "smooth space," an untheorized, nomadic space known in local practice, is increasingly organized into the abstracted grids of "striated space." Though Deleuze and Guattari do not specifically discuss the notion of the freedom of the seas, their argument for smooth spaces does invoke the Annales historian of the early modern Atlantic, Pierre Chaunu. "[W]e will follow Pierre Chaunu when he speaks of an extended confrontation at sea between the smooth and the striated during the course of which the striated progressively took hold." Gilles Deleuze and Félix Guattari, *A Thousand Plateaus: Capitalism and Schizophrenia*, trans. Brian Massumi (Minneapolis: University of Minnesota Press, 1987), 479.

64. Ibid., 480. Verne is a notable absence for these authors so fond of science fiction, perhaps because Verne overlays his prescient vision with the discourse of nineteenth-century positivism. It is thought-provoking that Verne attributed the quality of neonomadism to his *Nautilus* in the service of guerrilla warfare against imperial power, rather than world domination. In *L'Ile mystérieuse,* the reader will learn that Nemo, creator and captain of the *Nautilus*, is an Indian prince who has declared war on Britain for crushing the 1857 Rebellion, destroying his hopes for independence, along with his family and friends.

65. Carl Schmitt, *The Nomos of the Earth*, trans. G. L. Ulmen (New York: Telos Press, 2003), 178. Christopher Connery underscores Schmitt's prescience as regards a "current globalist discourse," at the "threshold of a wholly new conceptual framework, perhaps a postspatial one." Christopher Connery, "Ideologies of Land and Sea: Alfred Thayer Mahan, Carl Schmitt, and the Shaping of Global Myth Elements," *boundary 2* 28, no. 2 (2001), 193.

66. Jules Verne, *Twenty Thousand Leagues under the Sea*, trans. and intro. William Butcher (New York: Oxford University Press, 1998), 5. Subsequent citations are by page number within the text.

67. On Verne's fidelity to science of his time, see Michel Serres, *Jouvences sur Jules Verne* (Paris: Editions de Minuit, 1974), 83. Timothy Unwin concurs in *Jules Verne, Journeys in Writing*, 10.

68. Diana Knight is describing an aspect of Verne's poetics of performability when she writes that "since the materials at hand are diverted from their natural purpose into some entirely unforeseen destiny (wrecked balloon canvas into underwear and windmill sails), Barthes likens this process to 'the very principle of *bricolage*': 'We sense the proximity of this code—which is a perpetual introduction of new, unexpected classifications—to linguistic operations: the Engineer's transformational power is a verbal power, for both consist in combining elements (words, materials) in order to produce new systems (sentences, objects).'" Diana Knight "Where to Begin?" *The Yale Journal of Criticism*, vol. 14, no. 2 (2001): 493–501, 497.

69. In Hetzel's "Avertissement de l'éditeur," in *Voyages et aventures du capitaine Hatteras*, Hetzel ascribes to Verne the project to "summarize all the knowledge of geography, geology, physics, and astronomy that modern science has amassed, and to retell, in the attractive and picturesque way that is his hallmark, the history of the universe" (cited by Unwin, 26, his translation). Hetzel underplays Verne's interest in extending the frontier zones of modernity, one aspect of Verne's enterprise so clearly visible from the vantage point of the sea.

70. The South Pole would first be reached only in December 1911, then January 1912, by Amundsen and Scott. On reaching it, Scott, who would perish there, recorded his feelings in his log. They evince the bitter yield of an unknown navigation reminiscent of Cook's comments on being the first discoverer of sands and shoals: "The Pole. Yes, but under very different circumstances than we expected . . . Great God! this is an awful place and terrible enough for us to have laboured to it without the reward of priority." Quoted on NASA webpage "Live from Antarctica 2," *http://quest.arc.nasa.gov/antarctica2/main/t_guide/side_ajournal.html*; consulted December 2009. The ice threatening Nemo was a terrible challenge across the history of exploring the Arctic and Antarctica.

71. Théophile Gautier, "Les Voyages imaginaires de M. Jules Verne," first appeared in *Le Moniteur Universel*, July 16, 1866. Cited by Arthur B. Evans, "Jules Verne and the French Literary Canon," in *Jules Verne: Narratives of Modernity*, ed. Edmund J. Smyth (Liverpool, UK: Liverpool University Press, 2000), 12.

72. Roland Barthes describes the delight of Verne's readers in "The Nautilus and the Drunken Boat," in *Mythologies*. For Barthes, this delight is "the bliss of their closure, the perfection of their inner humanity. The *Nautilus*, in this regard, is the most desirable of all caves: the enjoyment of being enclosed reaches its paroxysm when, from the bosom of this unbroken inwardness, it is possible to watch, through a large window-pane, the outside vagueness of the waters, and thus define, in a single act, the inside by means of its opposite." Roland Barthes, *Mythologies*, selected and trans. Annette Lavers (New York: Hill and Wang, 1972), 66–67. From the perspective of maritime modernity, the delight comes, however, as much from Verne's fanciful jury-rigging, opening an oasis of pleasure in the stringent practice of modernity's frontier.

73. George Basalla, *The Evolution of Technology* (New York: Cambridge University Press, 2001), 76.

74. Ibid., 67.

AFTERWORD: JACK AUBREY, JACK SPARROW, AND THE WHOLE SICK CREW

1. See Foulke's postcript in *The Sea-Voyage Narrative* on the afterlife of sea adventure fiction in the twentieth century. Robert Foulke, *The Sea Voyage Narrative* (New York: Routledge, 1997), 159ff.

2. Richard Henry Dana Jr., preface to *Two Years Before the Mast* in *Two Years Before the Mast and other Voyages*, ed. Thomas Philbrick (New York: Library of America, 2005), 4.

3. Patrick O'Brian, *The Thirteen-Gun Salute* (New York: W.W. Norton, 1992), quotes in this paragraph from pages 296–99. O'Brian wrote a popular biography of Cook's chief scientist, Sir Joseph Banks.

Bibliography

The following bibliography includes works cited as well as some additional works consulted that are directly involved in the book's argument.

I. Primary Materials Pertaining to the Maritime Print Corpus

Some of these materials were published in repeated editions modified over the years. As editions were republished, their text might change significantly, and attribution of authorship might shift. A number of these works are also published in translations. My goal is to offer the reader a bibliography that is informative but also manageable. In our era of the Internet, it is my sense that a reference to one edition of a book should open a path to its publication history. Hence, I have in general cited only one edition of each book I consulted, unless I quote from two different editions. I have generally cited an English translation unless it was not easily available. Where possible, I have tried to cite accessible editions of works available today, such as selections from the journals of James Cook published by Penguin and the journals of Joseph Banks available online. When works are not in current circulation, I have tried to cite editions available through scholarly electronic databases, such as Early English Books online.

Anonymous. *Account of the very remarkable loss of the Great Galleon S. João.* In *The Tragic History of the Sea*, ed. C. R. Boxer, trans. C. R. Boxer and Josiah Blackmore, 3–26. Minneapolis: University of Minnesota Press, 2001. The other shipwreck narratives in the volume are part of the maritime print corpus as well.

Atkinson, James. *Epitome of the Art of Navigation; or a Short, Easy and Methodical Way to become a Compleat Navigator*, revised and corrected by William Mountaine. London: William Mount and Thomas Page, 1744.

Banks, Joseph. *Endeavour Journal*. From the State Library of New South Wales, 1998 Transcription of Banks's *Endeavour Journal*. Published by South Seas, using the Web Academic Resource Publisher, 2004. Available at *http://southseas .nla.gov.au/journals/banks/about.html*; consulted December 2009.

Barrow, Jean. *Abrégé chronologique, ou, Histoire des découvertes faites par les Européens dans les différentes parties du monde: extrait des relations les plus exactes & des voyageurs les plus véridiques par M. Jean Barrow*, trans. M. Targe. Paris: Chez Saillant, 1766. 12 vols.

Bernardin de Saint-Pierre, Jacques-Henri. *Voyage à l'Isle de France*. [Rose Hill], Ile Maurice: Editions de l'Océan Indien, 1986.

Blaue, Willem Janszoon. *The Light of Navigation* [English translation, printed by William Johnson in Amsterdam, 1612], intro. R. A. Skelton. Reprinted Amsterdam: N. Israel Publisher—Meridian Publishing Co, 1964.

Boswell, James. *The Life of Samuel Johnson*, ed. David Womersley. New York: Penguin, 2008.

Bowditch, Nathaniel. *The American Practical Navigator, An Epitome of Navigation*. Bethesda, MD: National Imagery and Mapping Agency, 2002.

Bougainville, Louis-Antoine de. *Voyage autour du monde par la frégate La Boudeuse et la flute L'Etoile*. Paris: La Découverte, 1997.

Bulkeley, John, and John Cummins. *A Voyage To the South Seas, In the Years 1740–1*. Philadelphia: James Chattin, 1757.

Byron, John. *The Narrative of the Honourable John Byron*. London, 1780.

Champlain, Samuel de. *Treatise on Seamanship and the Duty of a Good Seaman*. In *Works*, ed. H. P. Biggard, trans. W. D. LeSueur and H. H. Langton, vol. 6, 253–346. Toronto: The Champlain Society, 1936.

Champlain, Samuel de. *Les Voyages de la Nouvelle France occidentale, dicte Canada* [words omitted] *Avec un traitté des qualitez & conditions resquises à un bon & parfaict Navigateur pour cognoistre la diversité des Estimes qui se font en la Navigation. Les Marques & enseignements que la providence de Dieu à mises dans les Mers pour redresser les Mariniers en leur route, sans lesquelles ils tomberoient en de grands dangers,* [words omitted]. Paris: Claude Collet, 1639.

Chase, Owen. *The Wreck of the Whaleship Essex*. San Diego: Harcourt Brace, 1999.

Colson, Nathaniel. *The Mariner's New Kalendar*. London: J. Darby, 1677.

Cook, James. *The Journals of Captain Cook*. From manuscripts prepared by J. C. Beaglehole, selected and edited by Philip Edwards. New York: Penguin Books, 2003.

———. *The Journals of Captain James Cook*, ed. J. C. Beaglehole. Woodbridge, UK: The Boydell Press, 1999. 4 vols.

Cooke, Edward. *A Voyage to the South Seas and Round the World Perform'd in the Years 1708, 1709, 1710, and 1711 by the Ships* Duke *and* Dutchess *of Bristol*. London: Linton and Gosling, 1712.

Cortès, Martin. *The Art of Navigation. First, written in the Spanish Tongue by that Excellent Marriner and Mathematician of these times, Martine Curtis*, trans. Richard Eden. London: printed by B. A[lsop]. and T. Fawcet for J. Tap, 1630.

Crosby, Thomas. *Mariner's Guide*. London: James Hodges, 1751.

Cutler, Nathaniel. *A General Coasting Pilot*. London: James and John Knapton, William and John Innys et al., 1728.

Dampier, William. *A New Voyage Round the World* [1697], ed. Percy Adams. New York: Dover Publications, 1968.

Dana, Richard Henry Jr. *Two Years Before the Mast and Other Voyages*, ed. Thomas Philbrick. New York: Library of America, 2005.

Darwin, Charles. *Journal of Researches into the Natural History and Geology visited during the Voyage of H.M.S. Beagle*. Republished as *The Voyage of the Beagle*, ed. E. J. Browne and Michael Neve. New York: Penguin Classics, 1989. Abridged.

Davis, John. *The Seamans Secrets*. London: John Dawson, 1633.

Dean, Captain John. *A Narrative of the Sufferings, Preservation, and Deliverance, of Capt. John Dean and Company; in the Nottingham-Gally of London*. London: S. Popping, 1711.

Defoe, Daniel. *Atlas Maritimus & Commercialis*. London: James and John Knapton, William and John Innys et al., 1728.

———. *The Complete English Tradesman, in Familiar Letters*. London: Charles Rivington, 1726.

———. *An Essay upon Projects*. London: Tho. Cockerill, 1697.

———. [Under the pen name of Captain Johnson]. *A General History of the Pyrates* [1724], ed. Manuel Schonhorn. Mineola, NY: Dover Publications, 1999.

———. *A New Voyage Round the World, By a Course never sailed before*. London: A. Bettesworth, 1725.

———. *The Storm: Or, A Collection Of the most Remarkable Casualities and Disasters Which happen'd in the Late Dreadful Tempest Both by Sea and Land* (1704). Republished as *The Storm*. New York: Penguin, 2005.

Desperthes, Jean Louis Hubert Simon. *Histoire des naufrages*. Paris: Née de la Rochelle, 1788–1789.

Doncker, Hendrick. *The Sea-Atlas or The Watter-World, Showing all the Sea-Coasts of y Known parts of y Earth*. Amsterdam: Henry Doncker, 1660.

Exquemelin, Alexandre O. *The Buccaneers of America*, trans. Alexis Brown, intro. Jack Beeching. New York: Dover Publications, 2000.

Fielding, Henry. "The Journal of a Voyage to Lisbon." In *The Journal of a Voyage to Lisbon, Shamela, and Occasional Writings*, ed. Martin C. Battestin, with Sheridan W. Baker and Hugh Amory. New York: Oxford University Press, 2008.

Garcie, Pierre. *The Rutter of the Sea*. London: William Copeland, 1567.

Gellibrand, H. *An Epitome of Navigation*. London: Richard Mount, 1695.

Hakluyt, Richard. *Voyages and Discoveries*, a recent edition of Hakluyt's *Principal Navigations, Voyages, Traffiques and Discoveries of the English Nation*, ed. abridged, and intro. by Jack Beeching. New York: Penguin, 1972.

Haselden, Thomas. *The Seaman's Daily Assistant, being a short, easy, and plain Method of Keeping a Journal at Sea*. London: J. Mount and T. Page on Tower-Hill, 1757.

Hawkesworth, John. *An Account of the Voyages Undertaken by the Order of his Present Majesty for Making Discoveries in the Southern Hemisphere, And successively performed by Commodore Byron, Captain Wallis, Captain Carteret, and Captain Cook, in the Dolphin, the Swallow, and the Endeavour*. London: W. Strahan and T. Cadell, 1773. 3 vols.

James, Captain Thomas. *The Strange and Dangerous Voyage of Captaine Thomas James, in his intended Discovery of the Northwest Passage into the South Sea*. London: John Legatt, 1633.

Janeway, James. *Legacy to his Friends: Containing Twenty Seven Famous Instances of God's Providences in and about Sea Dangers and Deliverances*. London: Dorman Newman, 1683.

Langman, Christopher, Nicholas Mellon, and George White. *A True Account of the Voyage of the Nottingham-Galley of London*. London: S. Popping, 1711.

La Pérouse, Jean-François de Galaup. *Le Voyage de Lapérouse*, 1785–1788, eds. John Dunmore and Maurice de Brossard. Paris: Imprimerie nationale, 1985.

Le Cordier, Sanson. *Journal de Navigation, dans lequel est pleinement enseigné, & clairement démontré l'Art & la Science des Navigateurs*. Au Havre de Grace: Jacques Cruchet, 1683.

Leguat, Captain François. *The Voyage of François Leguat of Bresse*, ed. and annotated by Captain Pasfield Oliver. London: Hakluyt Society, 1891.

Love, James. *The Mariner's Jewel: Or, a Pocket-Companion for the Ingenious.* London: Alexander Sims, 1703.

Manwayring, Henry. *The Sea-mans Dictionary.* Facsimile edition of 1644. Menston, UK: Scolar Press Ltd., 1972.

Médine, Pierre de. *L'Art de Naviguer*, preface by Michel Serres. Paris: Les Belles Lettres, 2000.

Newhouse, Captain Daniel. *The Whole Art of Navigation*, 3rd ed. London: Richard Mount, 1708.

Norwood, Richard. *The Sea-man's Practice.* London: W. Godbid and J. Playford, 1680.

Pigafetta, Antonio. *Magellan's Voyage, A Narrative Account of the First Circumnavigation*, trans. and ed. R. A. Skelton. New York: Dover, 1994.

Prévost, Abbé. *Histoire générale des voyages.* Paris: Didot, 1746–1759. 15 vols.

Quirós, Pedro Fernández de. *Histoire de la découverte des régions australes.* Paris: L'Harmattan, 2001.

Rogers, Woodes. *A Cruising Voyage Round the World.* London: printed for A. Bell and B. Lintot, 1712.

Saltonstall, Charles. *The Navigator.* London: George Herlock, 1636.

Seller, John. *Atlas Maritimus.* London: John Seller, 1672.

———. *The Coasting Pilot.* London: John Seller, 1673.

———. *Practical Navigation: or, An introduction to that whole art.* London: printed by J. Darby, 1669.

Shackleton, Ernest Henry. *South: The Story of Shackleton's Last Expedition, 1914–17.* Santa Barbara, CA: The Narrative Press, 2001.

Smith, John. *A Sea Grammar, with the Plaine Exposition of Smiths Accidence for young Sea-men, enlarged.* London: John Haviland, 1627.

Smollett, Tobias. *Compendium of Authentic and Entertaining Voyages: digested in a chronological series.* London: R. and J. Dodsley [etc.], 1756.

Stevin, Simon. *The Haven-finding Art.* London: G.B.R. Newberry and R. Barker, 1599.

Sturmy, Samuel. *The Mariner's Magazine.* London: E Cotes, 1669.

Sue, Eugene. *Histoire de la Marine Française.* Paris: Béthune et Plon, 1845. 4 vols.

Vancouver, George and John Vancouver. *A Voyage of Discovery to the North Pacific Ocean, and Round the World.* London: G. G. and J. Robinson, 1798.

Wakely, Andrew. *Mariners Compass Rectified Carefully corrected and . . . enlarged . . . By J. Atkinson.* London: Richard Mount, 1716.

Waghenaer, Lucas. *The Mariners Mirrour*, trans. Anthony Ashley. London: John Charlewood, 1588.

Walter, Richard. *A Voyage Round the World In the Years MDCCXL, I, II, III, IV. By George Anson, Esq.* London: John and Paul Knapton, 1748.

II. Literature

To keep this bibliography concise, I have generally referenced only one or two representative works of each author, although in some cases, s/he wrote other—even many other—novels relevant to my analysis. In the cases of a few seminal writers, such as Defoe and Conrad, I have included more works, although I did not try to be exhaustive here either.

Anonymous. *The Life of Lazarillo de Tormes, Parts One and Two*, trans. Robert Rudder. New York: Frederick Ungar Publishing Co., 1973.

Austen, Jane. *Emma*, ed. Fiona Stafford. New York: Penguin, 2003.

———. *Mansfield Park*, ed. James Kinsley. New York: Oxford University Press, 2008.

———. *Northanger Abbey*, ed. Marilyn Butler. New York: Penguin, 2003.

———. *Persuasion*. New York: Penguin Books, 1998.

Ballou, Lieutenant Maturin Murray. *The Adventurer; or, The Wreck on the Indian Ocean*, Boston: F. Gleason, 1848.

———. *Fanny Campbell or, The Female Pirate Captain. A Tale of the Revolution*. New York: Samuel French, 1844.

———. *The Sea-Witch or the African Quadroon: A Story of the Slave Coast*. New York: Samuel French, 1855.

Balzac, Honoré de. *La Femme de trente ans*. Paris: Gallimard, 2001.

———. *Illusions Perdues*. Paris: Gallimard Folio, 1972.

———. *Le Père Goriot*. Paris: Gallimard Folio, 1999.

Baudelaire, Charles. *Les Fleurs du mal*. In *Oeuvres complètes*, vol. 1, 1–196. Paris: Bibliothèque de la Pléiade, 1975.

Beckett, Samuel. *Collected Poems in English and in French*. New York: Grove Press, 1977.

Bernardin de Saint-Pierre, Jacques-Henri. *Paul et Virginie*. Paris: Gallimard, 1984.

Breton, André. *Manifeste du surréalisme*. In *Oeuvres complètes*, ed. Marguerite Bonnet, 311–46. Paris: Bibliothèque de la Pléiade, 1988.

Brooke, Frances. *History of Emily Montague*. London: J. Dodsley, 1769.

Buntline, Ned. [Pen name of Edward Zane Carroll Judson.] *King of the Sea. A Tale of the Fearless and the Free*. Boston: Flag of Our Union Office, 1847.

Burney, Francis. *Evelina: Or, The History of a Young Lady's Entrance into the World*. New York: Oxford University Press, 1982.

Burroughs, William. *Cities of the Red Night*. New York: Henry Holt and Co., 1995.

Camões, Luís Vaz de. *The Lusíads*, trans. Landeg White. New York: Oxford University Press, 2001.

Chamier, Frederick. *The Arethusa: A Naval Story*. Philadelphia: E.L. Carey, 1837.

Chetwood, William Rufus. *The Voyages and Adventures of Captain Robert Boyle*. New York: Garland, 1972.

Childers, Erskine. *The Riddle of the Sands: A Record of Secret Service*. New York: Oxford University Press, 1995.

Clancy, Tom. *The Hunt for Red October*. New York: Mass Market Paperback, 1992.

Clarke, Arthur C. *2001: A Space Odyssey*. New York: Orbit, 1990.

Coleridge, Samuel Taylor. "The Rime of the Ancyent Marinere." In Samuel Taylor Coleridge and William Wordsworth, *The Lyrical Ballads*, 7–32. New York: Oxford University Press, 1996.

Conan Doyle, Arthur. *The Complete Adventures and Memoirs of Sherlock Holmes*. New York: Bantam Classics, 1986.

Conrad, Joseph. *Heart of Darkness*, ed. Robert Kimbrough. New York: W.W. Norton, 1998.

———. *Heart of Darkness and The Secret Sharer*, ed. Albert Guerard. New York: Signet Classics, 1950.

———. *Lord Jim*. New York: Penguin, 1986.

———. *The Nigger of the "Narcissus,"* ed. Robert Kimbrough. New York: W.W. Norton, 1979.

———. *Nostromo: A Tale of the Seabord*, eds. Véronique Pauly and J. H. Stape. New York: Penguin Classics, 2007.

———. *The Secret Agent*, ed. Michael Newton. New York: Penguin Classics, 2007.

———. *Typhoon*. In *Typhoon and Other Stories*, ed. J. H. Stape, 3–102. New York: Penguin, 2007.

Cooper, James Fenimore. *The Letters and Journals of James Fenimore Cooper*, ed. James Franklin Beard. Cambridge, MA: Harvard University Press, 1960. 6 vols.

———. *The Pilot: A Tale of the Sea*, ed. Kay Seymour House. Albany: State University of New York Press, 1986.

———. *The Sea Lions; or, The Lost Sealers*. New York: Stringer & Townsend, 1849.

———. *Sea Tales, The Pilot, The Red Rover*, eds. Kay Seymour House and Thomas Philbrick. New York: Library of America, 1990.

Corbière, Edouard. *Le Négrier*. Paris: La Découvrance Editions, 2007.

Defoe, Daniel. *The Fortunes and Misfortunes of the Famous Moll Flanders*. New York: The Modern Library, 1926.

———. *The Farther Adventures of Robinson Crusoe*. London: W. Taylor, 1719.

———. *The History and Remarkable Life of the Truly Honourable Colonel Jacque Commonly called Colonel Jack*. Whitefish, MT: Kessinger Publishing, 2006. Reprint of edition printed New York: University Press, 1904, ed. G. H. Maynadier.

———. *The Life, Adventures & Piracies of the Famous Captain Singleton*, intro. Edward Garnett. Charleston, SC: BiblioBazaar, 2007.

———. *The Life and Strange Surprising Adventures of Robinson Crusoe of York, Mariner*, republished as *Robinson Crusoe*, ed. Michael Shinagel. New York: W.W. Norton, 1994.

Dumas, Alexandre. *Le Capitaine Paul*. Paris: La Découvrance Editions, 2008.

———. *Le Comte de Monte Cristo*. Paris: Gallimard Folio, 1998. 2 vols.

Eliot, T. S. *The Wasteland, A Facsimile and Transcription*, ed. and intro. Valerie Eliot. New York: Harvest Books, 1974.

Falconer, William. *The Shipwreck*, 3rd ed. London: T. Cadell, 1769.

Galdós, Benito Pérez. *Trafalgar: La Corte de Carlos IV*, ed. Dolores Troncoso. Barcelona: Critica, 1995.

Genet, Jean. *Querelle de Brest*. Paris: L'Imaginaire, 1981.

Gibson, William. *Neuromancer*. New York: Ace Books, 1984.

Glascock, William. *Tales of a Tar with characteristic anecdotes*. London: H. Colburn and R. Bentley, 1830.

Gordon, George, Lord Byron. *The Complete Poetical Works of Lord Byron*. Boston: Houghton Mifflin, 1905.

Graffigny, Françoise de. *Lettres d'une péruvienne*, eds. Joan DeJean and Nancy K. Miller. New York: Modern Language Association, 1993.

Heliodorus, *The Ethiopian Romance*, trans. Moses Hadas. Philadelphia: University of Pennsylvania Press, 1999.

Hergé. [Georges Remi.] *The Secret of the Unicorn*. London: Little Brown Young Readers, 1974.

Hillerman, Tony. *The Dark Wind*. New York: Harper Torch, 2004.

Hölderlin, Friedrich. "Patmos." In *Friedrich Hölderlin, Selected Poems and Fragments*, trans. and ed. Michael Hamburger, 231–43. New York: Penguin, 1998.

Homer. *The Odyssey*, trans. George Chapman. London: imprinted by Rich. Field for Nathaniell Butter, 1614.

Hugo, Victor. *Les Misérables*. Paris: Garnier Frères, 1963. 2 vols.

———. *Toilers of the Sea*, trans. Isabel F. Hapgood. New York: Signet Classics, 2000.

———. *Les Travailleurs de la mer*, ed. Yves Gohin. Paris: Gallimard, 1980.

Jal, Auguste. *Scènes de la vie maritime*. Paris: Gosselin, 1832.

Kingsley, Charles. *Alton Locke*. London: Chapman and Hall, 1850. 2 vols.

———. *Westward Ho!* Leipzig: Bernhard Tauchnitz, 1855. 2 vols.

Kipling, Rudyard. *Captain Courageous*. New York: Signet Classics, 1964.

Lem, Stanislaw. *Solaris*, trans. Joanna Kilmartin and Steve Cox. New York: Harvest Books, 1987.

Le Sage, Alain René. *The Adventures of Robert Chevalier, call'd de Beauchene. Captain of a Privateer in New-France*. London: T. Gardner, 1745. 2 vols.

London, Jack. *The Sea Wolf and Other Stories*. New York: Signet Classics, 2004.

Loti, Pierre. *Aziyadé. Extrait des notes et lettres d'un lieutenant de la marine anglaise entré au service de la Turquie le 10 mai 1876 tué dans les murs de Kars, le 27 octobre 1877*. Paris: Gallimard Folio, 1991.

Marryat, Captain Frederick. *Mr. Midshipman Easy*, intro. Louis J. Parascandarola. New York: Henry Holt, 1998.

———. *The Naval Officer, or Scenes and Adventures in the Life of Frank Mildmay*. New York: Derby & Jackson, 1857.

———. *The Phantom Ship*. Ithaca, NY: McBook Press, 2000.

Melville, Herman. *Benito Cereno*. New York: Bedford, Saint Martin's, 2006.

———. *Billy Budd and Other Tales*, intro. Joyce Carol Oates. New York: Signet Classics, 1998.

———. *Typee: A Peep at Polynesian Life*, ed. John Bryant. New York: Penguin, 1996.

———. *Redburn, White-Jacket, Moby-Dick*, ed. G. Thomas Tanselle. New York: Library of America, 1983.

Milton, John. *Paradise Lost*, ed. Gordon Teskey. New York: W.W. Norton, 2005.

O'Brian, Patrick. *The Thirteen-Gun Salute*. New York: W.W. Norton, 1992.

Poe, Edgar Allan. *The Narrative of Arthur Gordon Pym of Nantucket*. In *The Narrative of Arthur Gordon Pym of Nantucket and Related Tales*, ed. J. Gerald Kennedy, 1–178. New York: Oxford University Press, 2008.

Prévost, L'Abbé. *Histoire du Chevalier des Grieux et Manon Lescaut*, published as *Manon Lescaut*, ed. J. Sgard. Paris: Flammarion, 1995.

———. *La Jeunesse du Commandeur*. Paris: Flammarion, 2005.

———. *Voyages du Capitaine Robert Lade*. Paris: Didot, 1744.

Radcliffe, Anne. *The Mysteries of Udolpho*. New York: Oxford University Press, 1998.

Reynolds, J. N. *Mocha Dick: or the White Whale of the Pacific*. New York: Charles Scribner's Sons, 1932.

Rimbaud, Arthur. *Le Bateau ivre*. In *Poésies complètes*, pref. Paul Verlaine, 17–22. Paris: L. Vanier, 1895.

———. "The Drunken Boat," trans. Samuel Beckett. In Samuel Beckett, *Collected Poems in English and in French*. New York: Grove Press, 1977.

Sabatini, Rafael. *Captain Blood*. Washington, DC: Regnery Publishing, 1998.

Salgari, Emilio. *Sandokan: The Pirates of Malaysia*, trans. Nico Lorenzutti. ROH Press, 2007.

Scott, Michael. *Tom Cringle's Log*. New York: Henry Holt, 1999.

Scott, Walter. *The Pirate*. New York: Thomas Nelson and Sons, 1905. Reprinted Whitefish, MT: Kessinger Publishing, 2004.

———. *Waverley, or 'tis sixty years since*. London: Penguin Classics, 1985.

Smollett, Tobias. *The Adventures of Roderick Random*, ed. Paul-Gabriel Boucé. New York: Oxford University Press, 1999.

Staël, Germaine de. *Corinne ou l'Italie*. Paris: Champion, 2000.

Stephenson, Neal. *Snow Crash*. New York: Bantam Books, 1992.

Stevenson, Robert Louis. *Treasure Island*. New York: Viking, 1996.

Sue, Eugène, *Atar Gull, a nautical tale*, trans. William Henry Herbert. New York: Henry L. Williams, 1849.

———. *Romans de Mort et d'Aventure*, ed. Guy Schoeller. Paris: Robert Laffont, 1993.

Swift, Jonathan. *Travels into Several Remote Nations of the World. In Four Parts. By Lemuel Guillver*, republished as *Gulliver's Travels*, ed. Albert J. Rivero. New York: W.W. Norton, 2002.

Tyler, Royall. *The Algerine Captive, or, The Life and Adventures of Doctor Updike Underhill*. New York: Modern Library, 2002.

Verne, Jules. *Correspondance inédite de Jules Verne et de Pierre-Jules Hetzel 1863–1886*, eds. Olivier Dumas, Piero Gondolo della Riva, and Volker Debs. Geneva: Editions Slatkine, 2001. 3 vols.

———. *Les Enfants du capitaine Grant*. Paris: Livre de Poche, 2005.

———. *The Invasion of the Sea*, trans. Edward Baxter, notes by Arthur B. Evans. Middletown, CT: Wesleyan University Press, 2001.

———. *The Mysterious Island*. New York: Signet Classics, 2004.

———. *Twenty Thousand Leagues under the Sea*, trans. and intro. William Butcher. New York: Oxford University Press, 1998.

Woolf, Virginia. *To the Lighthouse*. New York: Harvest Books, 1989.

———. *The Waves*, ed. Gillian Beer. New York: Oxford University Press, 1998.

III. PHILOSOPHY, HISTORY, AND THEORY UP TO AND INCLUDING CONRAD

This section includes secondary material, notably philosophy and literary criticism from the era of global seafaring up to and including Conrad. I also include some classical authors important for early modern, Enlightenment, and Romantic theorists, such as Aristotle and Longinus, as well as for my own argument.

Addison, Joseph. "An Account of the Greatest English Poets." In *The Annual Miscellany for The Year 1694*, 317–27. London: Jacob Tonson, 1694.

Anonymous review. "The Novels of James Fenimore Cooper." *Atlantic Monthly* 4, no. 23 (1859): 394–95.

Aristotle. *Nicomachean Ethics*, eds. J. L. Ackrill and J. O. Urmson, trans. David Ross. New York: Oxford University Press, 1998.

Ashfield, Andrew, and Peter de Bolla, eds. *The Sublime: A Reader in British Eighteenth-Century Aesthetic Theory*. New York: Cambridge University Press, 1996. Quotations from Joseph Addison, John Baillie, John Dennis, Jonathan Richardson, and Joseph Trapp are cited in this anthology. So are quotations from Shaftesbury on the sublime, although not on sea voyage literature.

Bacon, Francis. "The New Organon." In *The New Organon and Related Writings*, ed. Fulton H. Anderson. Indianapolis: Bobbs-Merrill, 1984.

Balzac, Honoré de. "Lettres sur la littérature, le théâtre et les arts," no. 1. *Revue Parisienne*, July 25, 1840, vol. 1, no. 1, pp. 47–98.

Boileau, Nicolas. "Réflexions sur Longin." In *Oeuvres de Nicolas Boileau Despréaux*, vol. 1, 86–174. Amsterdam: D. Mortier, 1718.

Brontë, Charlotte. *Selected Letters of Charlotte Brontë*, ed. Margaret Smith. New York: Oxford University Press, 2007.

Burke, Edmund. *A Philosophical Enquiry into the Origin of our Ideas of the Sublime and Beautiful*, ed. Adam Phillips. New York: Oxford University Press, 1998.

Carlyle, Thomas. *History of Friedrich II of Prussia called Frederick The Great*, vol. 4. New York: Scribner, Welford and Company, 1873.

Conrad, Joseph. *Last Essays, The Collected Works of Joseph Conrad*. New York: Routledge, 1995.

———. *The Mirror of the Sea*. Marlboro, VT: The Marlboro Press, 1988.

———. *A Personal Record*, eds. Zdzislaw Najder and J. H. Stape. New York: Cambridge University Press, 2008.

———. "Tales of the Sea." (1898) In *Notes on Life and Letters*, eds. J. H. Stape and Andrew Busza, 46–49. New York: Cambridge University Press, 2004.

Cooper, James Fenimore. *The Travelling Bachelor; or, Notions of the Americans*. New York: Stringer and Townsend, 1852. 2 vols.

Dekker, George, and John McWilliams. *Fenimore Cooper: The Critical Heritage*. Boston: Routledge and Kegan Paul, 1973.

Diderot, Denis. "In Praise of Richardson." In *Denis Diderot: Selected Writings on Art and Literature*, trans. Geofrey Bremner. New York: Penguin, 1994.

Engels, Frederick. *The Condition of the Working Class in England*, ed. Victor Kiernan. New York: Oxford University Press, 1987.

Hegel, G.W.F. *Lectures on the History of Philosophy*, trans. E. S. Haldane and Frances Simson, vol. 3. Reprint of edition printed London: K. Paul, Trench, Trübner, 1892–1896. Sterling, Thoemmes Press, 1999.

———. *Hegel's Philosophy of Right*, trans. and with notes by T. M. Knox. New York: Oxford University Press, 1967.

James, Henry. "Victor Hugo." *The Nation* 1866. Anthologized in Henry James, *Literary Criticism: French Writers, Other European Writers, Prefaces to the New York Edition*. New York: Library of America, 1984.

Kant, Immanuel. *Critique of Judgment*, trans. and intro. J. H. Bernard. New York: Hafner Press, 1951.

Kügelgen, Marie von. Letter to Friederike Volkmann, June 22, 1809. English translation from the Web Gallery of Art: *http://www.wga.hu/frames-e.html?/html/f/friedric/1/105fried.html*; consulted January 2008. The original German passage can be found in Hilmar Frank, *Aussichten in Unermessliche: Perspektivität und Sinnoffenheit bei Caspar David Friedrich*, 85. Berlin: Akademie Verlag, 2004.

Longinus, *On Great Writing (On the Sublime)*, trans. G.M.A. Grube. New York: The Liberal Arts Press, 1957.

Marx, Karl. *Capital*, trans. Samuel Moore and Edward Aveling, ed. Frederick Engels. New York: The Modern Library, 1906.

Nietzsche, Friedrich. *Thus Spoke Zarathustra*, trans. Walter Kaufmann. New York: Viking Press, 1966.

Ruskin, John. *Modern Painters*. In Elibron Classics, Adamant Media, 2005. 4 vols. Reprint of edition published London: George Allen, 1906.

Shaftesbury, Anthony Ashley Cooper, Earl of. "Soliloquy: or Advice to an Author." In *Characteristicks of Men, Manners, Opinions, Times*, vol. 1, 153–364. London: John Darby, 1711.

Tocqueville, Alexis de. *Democracy in America*, ed. Isaac Kramnick, trans. Gerald Bevan. New York: Penguin, 2003.

Verne, Jules. *Les Grands Navigateurs du XVIIIe siècle. Histoire des grands voyages et des grands voyageur*. Paris: Ramsay, 1977.

IV. Critical Materials (History, Theory, and Criticism)

In this section, I include secondary works in the century following Conrad that I cite or that play an important role in shaping my argument. These works range from theory and history to literary criticism and aim to give a portrait of the diverse fields that intersect in maritime literary and cultural studies.

Adams, Percy G. *Travelers and Travel Liars, 1660–1800*. Berkeley: University of California Press, 1962.

Adams, Thomas R. *The Non-Cartographical Maritime Works published by Mount and Page*. London: The Bibliographical Society, 1985.

Adorno, Theodor, and Max Horkheimer. *Dialectic of Enlightenment*, trans. John Cumming. New York: Continuum Books, 1972.

Allen, Jerry. *The Sea Years of Joseph Conrad*. New York: Doubleday, 1965.

Aravamudan, Srinivas. "In the Wake of the Novel: The Oriental Tale as National Allegory." *NOVEL: A Forum on Fiction* 33, no. 1 (fall 1999): 5–31.

Arendt, Hannah. *The Human Condition*. Chicago: University of Chicago Press, 1998.

Armstrong, Nancy. *Desire and Domestic Fiction*. New York: Oxford University Press, 1987.

Armstrong, Nancy, and Leonard Tennenhouse. *The Imaginary Puritan: Literature, Intellectual Labor, and the Origins of Private Life*. Berkeley: University of California Press, 1994.

Aubenque, Pierre. *La Prudence chez Aristote*. Paris: Presses Universitaires de France, 1986.

Austin, J. L. *How to Do Things with Words*, 2nd ed. Cambridge, MA: Harvard University Press, 1975.

Bailyn, Bernard. *Atlantic History: Concept and Contours*. Cambridge, MA: Harvard University Press, 2005.

Baker, Emerson W., and John G. Reid. *The New England Knight: Sir William Phips, 1651–1695*. Toronto: University of Toronto Press, 1998.

Bakhtin, Mikhail, *The Dialogic Imagination: Four Essays*, ed. Michael Holquist, trans. Caryl Emerson and Michael Holquist. Austin: University of Texas Press, 1981.

———. *François Rabelais and His World*, trans. Helen Iswolsky. Bloomington: Indiana University Press, 1984.

Barthes, Roland. *Mythologies*, selected and trans. Annette Lavers. New York: Hill and Wang, 1972.

Basalla, George. *The Evolution of Technology*. New York: Cambridge University Press, 2001.

Bataille, Georges. *Visions of Excess: Selected Writings, 1927–1939*, ed. and trans. Allan Stoekl with Carl R. Lovitt and Donald M. Leslie Jr. Minneapolis: University of Minnesota Press, 1985.

Baucom, Ian. *Specters of the Atlantic: Finance Capital, Slavery, and the Philosophy of History*. Durham, NC: Duke University Press, 2005.

Beaglehole, J. C. "Cook the Navigator," *Proceedings of the Royal Society of London. Series A, Mathematical and Physical Sciences* 314, no. 1516 (December 16, 1969): 27–38.

Bender, Thomas. *A Nation Among Nations: America's Place in World History*. New York: Hill and Wang, 2006.

Bey, Hakim. *The Temporary Autonomous Zone, Ontological Anarchy, Poetic Terrorism*. New York: Autonomedia, 2003.

Blewett, David. *The Illustration of Robinson Crusoe, 1719–1920*. Gerrards Cross, Buckinghamshire, UK: Colin Smythe, 1995.

Blum, Hester. *The View from the Masthead*. Durham, NC: University of North Carolina Press, 2008.

Blumenberg, Hans. *Shipwreck with Spectator: Paradigm of a Metaphor for Existence*, trans. Steven Rendall. Cambridge, MA: MIT Press, 1997.

Bolster, W. Jeffrey. *Black Jacks: African-American Seamen in the Age of Sail*. Cambridge, MA: Harvard University Press, 1992.

Bonehill, John, and Geoffrey Quilley, eds. *William Hodges 1744–1797—The Art of Exploration*. New Haven: Yale University Press for the National Maritime Museum, 2004.

Bosset, G. C. *Fenimore Cooper et le roman d'aventure en France vers 1830*. Paris: Vrin, 1928.

Bourdieu, Pierre. *The Rules of Art: Genesis and Structure of the Literary Field*, trans. Susan Emanuel. Stanford, CA: Stanford University Press, 1996.

Braudel, Fernand. *The Mediterranean and the Mediterranean World in the Age of Philip II*, trans. Sian Reynolds. New York: Harper & Row, 1972.

Brodhead, Richard, ed. *New Essays on Moby-Dick*. New York: Cambridge University Press, 1986.

Brombert, Victor. *Victor Hugo and the Visionary Novel*. Cambridge, MA: Harvard University Press, 1984.

———. "*Les Travailleurs de la mer*: Hugo's Poem of Effacement." *New Literary History* 9, no. 3 (*Rhetoric I: Rhetorical Analyses*; spring 1978): 581–90.

Brosse, Monique. *La Littérature de la mer en France, en Grande-Bretagne et aux Etats-Unis*. Thesis, Université de Lille, 1983. 2 vols.

Burnett, John. *Dangerous Waters: Modern Piracy and Terror on the High Seas*. New York: Plume, 2003.

Butler, George F. "Milton's Meeting with Galileo: A Reconsideration." *Milton Quarterly* 39, no. 3 (2005): 132–39.

Casanova, Pascale. *The World Republic of Letters*, trans. M. B. DeBevoise. Cambridge, MA: Harvard University Press, 2004.

Casarino, Cesare. *Modernity at Sea: Melville, Marx, Conrad in Crisis*. Minneapolis: University of Minnesota Press, 2002.

Charles, David. *La Pensée technique dans l'oeuvre de Victor Hugo: le bricolage de l'infini*. Paris: Presses Universitaires de France, 1997.

Chaunu, Huguette, and Pierre Chaunu. *Séville et L'Atlantique, 1504–1650*. Paris: Armand, 1955–1959.

Cohen, Margaret. "Chronotopes of the Sea." In *The Novel*, ed. Franco Moretti, vol. 2, 647–66. Princeton, NJ: Princeton University Press, 2007.

———. "Fluid States." *Cabinet* 16 (2005): 75–82.

———. "Historical Fiction." In *Oxford Encyclopedia of Maritime History*, vol. 3, 2–7. New York: Oxford University Press, 2007.

———. "Modernity on the Waterfront: The Case of Haussmann's Paris." In *Urban Imaginaries: Locating the City*, eds. Thomas Bender and Alev Cinar. Minneapolis: University of Minnesota Press, 2007.

———. "Sentimental Communities." In *The Literary Channel*, eds. Margaret Cohen and Carolyn Dever, 106–132. Princeton, NJ: Princeton University Press, 2002.

———. *The Sentimental Education of the Novel*. Princeton, NJ: Princeton University Press, 1999.

———. "Traveling Genres." *New Literary History* 34, no. 3 (2003), 481–99.

Connery, Christopher. "Ideologies of Land and Sea: Alfred Thayer Mahan, Carl Schmitt, and the Shaping of Global Myth Elements." *boundary 2* 28, no. 2 (2001): 173–201.

Corbin, Alain. *The Lure of the Sea: The Discovery of the Seaside in the Western World 1750–1840*, trans. Jocelyn Phelps. New York: Penguin, 1995.

Crary, Jonathan. "Gericault, the Panorama, and Sites of Reality in the Early Nineteenth Century." *Grey Room* 9 (fall 2002): 5–25.

Daston, Lorraine, and Katherine Parks. *Wonders and the Order of Nature, 1150–1750*. New York: Zone Books, 1998.

Davey, Michael J. *A Routledge Literary Sourcebook on Herman Melville's Moby-Dick*. New York: Routledge, 2004.

De Certeau, Michel. *Arts de faire*. Paris: Union Générale d'Editions, 1980.

Delbanco, Andrew. *Melville, His World and Work*. New York: Knopf, 2005.

Deleuze, Gilles, and Félix Guattari. *A Thousand Plateaus: Capitalism and Schizophrenia*, trans. Brian Massumi. Minneapolis: University of Minnesota Press, 1987.

Détienne, Marcel, and Jean-Pierre Vernant. *Cunning Intelligence in Greek Culture and Society*, trans. Janet Lloyd. Chicago: University of Chicago Press, 1991.

Dimock, Wai Chee. *Empire for Liberty: Melville and the Poetics of Individualism*. Princeton, NJ: Princeton University Press, 1991.

Edwards, Philip. *The Story of the Voyage: Sea-Narratives in Eighteenth-Century England*. New York: Cambridge University Press, 1994.

Evans, Arthur B. "Jules Verne and the French Literary Canon." In *Jules Verne: Narratives of Modernity*, ed. Edmund J. Smyth, 11–39. Liverpool, UK: University of Liverpool Press, 2000.

Farmer, J. Doyne. "The Evolution of Adventure in Literature and Life," November 11, 2005. Available at *http://www.santafe.edu/~jdf/papers/adventure4.pdf*; consulted December 2009.

Fausett, David. *The Strange Surprizing Sources of Robinson Crusoe*. Amsterdam: Rodopi, 1994.

Foulke, Robert. *The Sea Voyage Narrative*. New York: Routledge, 1997.

Gallagher, Catherine. *The Body Economic*. Princeton, NJ: Princeton University Press, 2006.

———. "Floating Signifiers of Britishness in the Novels of the Anti-Slave-Trade Squadron." In *Dickens and the Children of Empire*, ed. Wendy S. Jacobson. New York: Palgrave Macmillan, 2000.

———. *The Industrial Reformation of English Fiction*. Chicago: University of Chicago Press, 1988.

———. *Nobody's Story: The Vanishing Acts of Women Writers in the Marketplace, 1670–1820*. Berkeley: University of California Press, 1994.

Gautier, Maurice-Paul. *Captain Frederick Marryat 1792–1848*. Paris: Didier, 1973.

Gerassi-Navarro, Nina. *Pirate Novels: Fictions of Nation Building in Spanish America*. Durham, NC: Duke University Press, 1999.

Gilroy, Paul. *The Black Atlantic*. London: Verso, 1993.

Gove, Philip. *The Imaginary Voyage in Prose Fiction*. New York: Columbia University Press, 1941.

Gramsci, Antonio. *Selections from Cultural Writings*, ed. David Forgacs and Geoffrey Nowell-Smith, trans. William Boelhower. London: ElecBook, 1999.

Green, Martin. *Dreams of Adventure, Deeds of Empire*. New York: Basic Books, 1979.

Greenblatt, Stephen. *Marvelous Possessions: The Wonder of the New World*. Chicago: University of Chicago Press, 1992.

Greene, Jody. "Captain Singleton and *The Rise of the Novel*." In *The Eighteenth Century: Theory and Interpretation*. [Forthcoming.]

Hamilton, James. *Turner and the Scientists*. London: Tate, 1998.

Hamon, Philippe. "Rhetorical Status of the Descriptive," trans. Patricia Baudoin. *Yale French Studies* 61, *Towards a Theory of Description* (1981): 1–26.

Hardy, Christophe. *Les Mots de la Mer*. Paris: Belin, 2002.

Harries, Karsten. "The Philosopher at Sea." In *Nietzsche's New Seas. Explorations in Philosophy, Aesthetics, and Politics*, eds. Michael Allen Gillespie and Tracy B. Strong, 21–44. Chicago: University of Chicago Press, 1988.

Hattendorf, John. *"The Boundless Deep . . . ": the European Conquest of the Oceans, 1450 to 1840*. Providence, RI: John Carter Brown Library, 2003.

"Hugo l'homme océan," [online dossier about Victor Hugo]. Hosted by the French National Library. Available at *http://expositions.bnf.fr/hugo/expo.htm*; consulted December 2009.

Hutchins, Edwin. *Cognition in the Wild*. Cambridge, MA: MIT Press, 1995.

Irigaray, Luce. *Marine Lover of Friedrich Nietzsche*, trans. Gillian C. Gill. New York: Columbia University Press, 1991.

Iser, Wolfgang. *The Act of Reading: A Theory of Aesthetic Response*. Baltimore: Johns Hopkins University Press, 1980.

———. *The Implied Reader: Patterns of Communication in Prose Fiction from Bunyan to Beckett*. Baltimore: Johns Hopkins University Press: 1978.

James, Sara. "Sue, Marie-Joseph Eugène." In *Encyclopedia of the Romantic Era*, ed. Christopher John Murray, vol. 2, 1104–1106. New York: Taylor and Francis, 2004.

Jameson, Fredric. *The Political Unconscious: Narrative as a Socially Symbolic Act*. Ithaca, NY: Cornell University Press, 1981.

Kahn, Victoria. *Machiavellian Rhetoric: From the Counter-Reformation to Milton*. Princeton, NJ: Princeton University Press, 1994.

Kemp, Peter, ed. *The Oxford Companion to Ships and the Sea*. New York: Oxford University Press, 1988.

Klein, Bernhard, ed. *Fictions of the Sea. Critical Perspectives on the Ocean in British Literature and Culture*. Farnham, Surrey, UK: Ashgate Press, 2002.

Klein, Bernhard, and Gesa MacKenthun, eds. *Das Meer als kulturelle Kontaktzone: Räume, Reisende, Repräsentationen*. Konstanz: University Press, 2003.

———. *Sea Changes. Historicizing the Ocean*. New York: Routledge, 2003.

Knight, Diana. "Where to Begin?" *The Yale Journal of Criticism*, 14, no. 2 (2001): 493–501.

Lamb, Jonathan. *Preserving the Self in the South Seas 1680–1840*. Chicago: University of Chicago Press, 2001.

Lestringant, Frank. *Cannibals: The Discovery and Representation of the Cannibal from Columbus to Jules Verne*, trans. Rosemary Morris. Berkeley: University of California Press, 1997.

Levine, Robert S., ed. *The Cambridge Companion to Melville*. New York: Cambridge University Press, 1998.

Lewis, Charles Lee. *Books of the Sea; An Introduction to Nautical Literature*. Annapolis, MD: U.S. Naval Institute, 1943.

Leys, Simon. *La Mer dans la Littérature Française: De Victor Hugo à Pierre Loti*, vol. 2. Paris: Plon, 2003.

Linebaugh, Peter. *The London Hanged: Crime and Civil Society in the Eighteenth Century*. New York: Cambridge University Press, 1992.

Linebaugh, Peter, and Marcus Rediker. *The Many Headed Hydra: Sailors, Slaves, Commoners, and the Hidden History of the Revolutionary Atlantic*. Boston: Beacon Press, 2002.

"Live from Antarctica 2," NASA webpage *http://quest.arc.nasa.gov/antarctica2/main/t_guide/side_ajournal.html*. Consulted Dec. 2009.

Lukács, Georg. *The Theory of the Novel*, trans. Anna Bostock. Cambridge, MA: MIT Press, 1974.

———. *The Historical Novel*, trans. Hannah and Stanley Mitchell. London. Merlin Press, 1962.

Macherey, Pierre. *For a Theory of Literary Production*, trans. Geoffrey Wall. Boston: Routledge and Kegan Paul, 1978.

Mackenthun, Gesa. *Fictions of the Black Atlantic in American Foundational Literature*. New York: Routledge, 2004.

MacLaren, Ian. "Arctic Exploration and Milton's 'Frozen Continent.'" *Notes and Queries* new ser. 31 (1984): 325–26.

———. "'Zealous Sayles' and Zealous Sales: Making Books out of Failures to sail the Northwest Passage, 1620–1850." *Princeton University Library Chronicle* 64 (winter 2003): 252–87.

Maiorino, Giancarlo. *At the Margins of the Renaissance: Lazarillo de Tormes and the Picaresque Art of Survival*. University Park, PA: Penn State University Press, 2003.

McKeon, Michael. *The Origins of the English Novel*. Baltimore: Johns Hopkins University Press, 1987.

Miller, Christopher. *The French Atlantic Triangle: Literature and Culture of the Slave Trade*. Durham, NC: Duke University Press, 2008.

Monk, Samuel H. *The Sublime: A Study of Critical Theories in Eighteenth-Century England*. New York: Modern Language Association, 1935.

Moore, Leslie E. *Beautiful Sublime: The Making of Paradise Lost, 1701–1734*. Stanford, CA: Stanford University Press, 1990.

Moretti, Franco. *Atlas of the European Novel 1800–1900*. London: Verso, 1998.

———. *Modern Epic: The World-System from Goethe to García-Marquez*. London: Verso, 1996.

Neill, Anna. *British Discovery Literature and the Rise of Global Commerce*. New York: Palgrave, 2002.

Nerlich, Michael. *Ideology of Adventure*, trans. Ruth Crowley. Minneapolis: University of Minnesota Press, 1987. 2 vols.

Nussbaum, Felicity, ed. *The Global Eighteenth Century*. Baltimore: Johns Hopkins University Press, 2005.

Otter, Samuel. *Melville's Anatomies*. Berkeley: University of California Press, 1999.

Partridge, Eric. "Fenimore Cooper's Influence on the French Romantics." *Modern Language Review* 20, no. 2 (April 1925): 174–78.

Philbrick, Thomas. "Cooper and the Literary Discovery of the Sea." Presented at the 7th Cooper Seminar, *James Fenimore Cooper: His Country and His Art*, SUNY Oneonta, July 1989. Available at *http://external.oneonta.edu/cooper/articles/suny/1989suny-philbrick.html;* consulted December 2009.

———. *James Fenimore Cooper and the Development of American Sea Fiction*. Cambridge, MA: Harvard University Press, 1961.

Phillips, Richard. *Mapping Men and Empire: A Geography of Adventure*. New York: Routledge, 1997.

Prendergast, Christopher. *Order of Mimesis: Balzac, Stendhal, Nerval, Flaubert.* New York: Cambridge University Press, 1986.

Quint, David. *Epic and Empire.* Princeton, NJ: Princeton University Press, 1993.

Raban, Jonathan, ed. *The Oxford Book of the Sea.* New York: Oxford University Press, 1993.

Roberts, Miquette. *The Unknown Turner.* With contributions from Catherine Cullinan, Colin Grig and Joyce Townsend, published online by Tate Britain (http://www.tate.org.uk/britain/turner/tp_unkownturner.pdf).

Robbins, Bruce. *The Servant's Hand.* Durham, NC: Duke University Press, 1993.

Rivière, Jacques. *Le Roman d'aventure.* Paris: Editions des Syrtes, 2000.

Ryle, Gilbert. *The Concept of Mind.* Chicago: University of Chicago Press, 1984.

Said, Edward. *Culture and Imperialism.* New York: Vintage Books, 1994.

Santraud, Jeanne-Marie. *La Mer et le roman américain dans la première moitié du dix-neuvième siècle.* Paris: Didier, 1972.

Scarry, Elaine. *Resisting Representation.* New York: Oxford University Press, 1994.

Schmitt, Carl. *Land und Meer.* Stuttgart: Klett-Cotta, 1954.

———. *The Nomos of the Earth,* trans. G. L. Ulmen. New York: Telos Press, 2003.

Secord, Arthur. *Studies in the Narrative Method of Defoe.* New York: Russell and Russell, 1963.

Sekula, Allan. *Fish Story.* Düsseldorf: Richter Verlag, 2002.

Serres, Michel. *Jouvences sur Jules Verne.* Paris: Editions de Minuit, 1974.

Shawcross, John T. "John Milton and His Spanish and Portuguese Presence." *Milton Quarterly* 32, no. 2 (1998): 41–52.

Siskind, Mariano. "Captain Cook and the Discovery of Antarctica's Modern Specificity: Towards a Critique of Globalism." *Comparative Literature Studies* 42, no. 1 (2005): 1–23.

Smith, Henry Nash. *Virgin Land: The American West as Symbol and Myth*, a bibliography of dime novels on the University of Virginia website. Available at *http:xroads.virginia.edu/~HYPER/HNS/Carson/resource.htm*; consulted December 2009.

Sobel, Dava, and William H. Andrews. *The Illustrated Longitude.* New York: Walker and Co., 1998.

Solkin, David, ed. *Turner and the Masters.* London: Tate, 2009.

Spate, O.H.K. *The Spanish Lake.* Minneapolis: University of Minnesota Press, 1979.

Spivak, Gayatri. "Three Women's Texts and a Critique of Imperialism." *Critical Inquiry* 12, no. 1 (autumn 1985): 243–61.

Steinberg, Philip. *The Social Construction of the Ocean.* New York: Cambridge University Press, 2001.

Suleri, Sara. *The Rhetoric of English India.* Chicago: University of Chicago Press, 1992.

Tadié, Jean-Yves. *Le Roman d'aventures.* Paris: Presses Universitaires de France, 1982.

Taylor, E.G.R. *The Haven Finding Art: A History of Navigation from Odysseus to Captain Cook.* London: Hollis & Carter, 1971.

Thorp, Willard. "Cooper Beyond America." *New York History* 35, no. 4 (October 1954): 522–39. Special Issue—James Fenimore Cooper: A Re-Appraisal. Available at *http://external.oneonta.edu/cooper/articles/nyhistory/1954nyhistory -thorp.html*; consulted December 2009.

Unwin, Timothy. *Jules Verne, Journeys in Writing*. Liverpool, UK: University of Liverpool Press, 2005.

Van Dover, J. Kenneth. *Defoe's World Mapped: English Horizons in 1720*. Chicago: Newberry Library, 1988. Available at *http://www.newberry.org/smith/ slidesets/ss10.html*; consulted December 2009.

Venayre, Sylvain. *Rêves d'aventure*. Paris: De la Martinière, 2006.

Vernant, Jean-Pierre. *Mythe et pensée chez les Grecs*. Paris: Maspero, 1965. 2 vols.

Vickers, Ilse. *Defoe and the New Sciences*. New York: Cambridge University Press, 1997.

Villiers, Peter. *Joseph Conrad Master Mariner*. Dobbs Ferry, NY: Sheridan House, 2006.

Wallerstein, Immanuel. *The Modern World System*. New York, Academic Press, 1974. 3 vols.

Watt, Ian. *Conrad in the Nineteenth Century*. Berkeley: University of California Press, 1979.

———. *The Rise of the Novel*. Berkeley: University of California Press, 1957.

Weber, Anne-Gaëlle. *A beau mentir qui vient de loin: Savants, voyageurs et romanciers au XIXe siècle*. Paris: Honoré Champion, 2004.

White, Andrea. *Joseph Conrad and the Adventure Tradition*. New York: Cambridge University Press, 1993.

Wigen, Kären. Introduction to *American Historical Review* Forum, "Oceans of History," *American Historical Review* 111, no. 3 (June 2006), 717–21.

Woolf, Virginia. "Joseph Conrad." In *The Common Reader, First Series,* ed. and intro. Andrew McNeillie, 223–30. New York: Harcourt, 1984.

Index